Conflict and Order

AN INTRODUCTION TO INTERNATIONAL RELATIONS

Conflict and Order

AN INTRODUCTION TO INTERNATIONAL RELATIONS

Forest L. Grieves

UNIVERSITY OF MONTANA

Houghton Mifflin Company

BOSTON   ATLANTA   DALLAS   GENEVA, ILLINOIS

HOPEWELL, NEW JERSEY   PALO ALTO   LONDON

Library of Congress Catalog Card Number: 76-10901
ISBN: 0-395-24332-7

To Irmgard, Kevin, and Emily.

Contents

Preface

This book is intended for university and college students encountering the formal study of international relations for the first time. It has been written with the knowledge that students enrolled in an introductory international relations course have varied kinds of academic backgrounds and preparation. Often beginning students will have little or no training in political science, or even in the social sciences. For that reason, I have avoided social science methodology and techniques and have tried to be modestly interdisciplinary and traditional.

My aim in writing this book was to convey some sense of the excitement, intricacy, and importance of international relations to as wide an audience as possible. I have tried to provide those introductory students, for whom this may be the only formal contact with the study of international relations, with a basic understanding of the structure and forces of the world in which they live. For those who will be going on to pursue more advanced studies in international relations, I have tried to introduce the analytical and methodological problems encountered by professional scholars and to survey international relations as a field of study.

This book has three goals. The first goal is to examine the framework of international relations and the nature of the primary participants—the nation-state system and the nation-states. Second, a basic analytical perspective on the flow of international relations is provided by tracing two general themes: the impetus toward international conflict and the search for international order. Although this book does not intend to offer a comprehensive theory of international relations, it undertakes a general survey of the major kinds of organizing theories of international relations that have been put forth in recent years. The third goal is to provide the reader with substantive information concerning the "stuff" of international relations from which the reader, with an instructor's guidance, can begin to form personal conclusions about the meaning of international events. In an effort to enhance the substantive coverage, in-depth studies of selected important issues (sometimes written into the flow of the text, sometimes appearing as individual case studies) are integrated into the book.

This volume is intended to be comprehensive enough to serve as the core text for a semester-length introductory course in international relations, yet compact enough for a quarter-length course. In either case, the use of supplementary materials would be appropriate. Students should be aware of the need to keep up with current events, for a textbook can offer only background and perspective on rapidly changing international affairs.

The author is grateful to A. Robert Thoeny, Memphis State University; Don C. Piper, University of Maryland; Naomi B. Lynn, Kansas State University; and Gerald Watson, University of Northern Colorado, for their useful comments during the preparation of this book. I am particularly indebted to Professor Clifton Wilson of the University of Arizona for many thoughtful recommendations. Any errors however remain solely my responsibility. Susan Guthrie and Rose Harrod assisted with the typing of the final manuscript. Three to whom I owe a very special acknowledgment are my wife, Irmgard, for her unwavering assistance and encouragement throughout, and my children, Kevin and Emily, for their understanding and patience with their father's work.

Missoula, Montana   Forest L. Grieves

Conflict and Order

AN INTRODUCTION TO INTERNATIONAL RELATIONS

Part I
The Problem of
World Politics

Provocative Issues
of Our Time

In ancient Rome there was a class of Etruscan priests and sooth-sayers called *haruspices*. These *haruspices* specialized in deducing the will of the gods and interpreting events by studying the entrails of animals killed in sacrifice. They were a class of lesser priests, but they nevertheless had a substantial amount of importance. While they never formed a state priesthood, there was in fact under the empire a collegium of some 60 *haruspices* who functioned as a body of salaried expert advisers.

Perhaps not too surprisingly, the art of entrail reading even-tually fell into disrepute, and with it the position of entrail inspector. However, beginning students of international relations, groping for some understanding of the apparent chaos they see in world politics, are apt to wonder if some modern-day *haruspices* might not be needed to conjure up an orderly picture of the confusing and fast-moving international events of the twentieth century. Or worse, and perhaps more significant in this age of alleged supersophistication and skepticism, beginning students might secretly supect that mod-ern governments are already relying heavily on the advice of such soothsayers for direction in their foreign policies.

The study of international relations is not easy. The complexity of world events, the secrecy with which many foreign policy deci-sions are made, the conflicting motives of governments, and the diversity of the world's cultures and ideologies make the untangling and understanding of "what's going on" appear hopeless. On the other hand, international relations are intriguing and interesting—not without a sense of dangerous adventure. We want to under-stand international relations, and we *need* to, because of such threats as nuclear holocaust, environmental disaster, overpopulation, and starvation.

Interest in international relations and a need to study them are not enough, however. We need the historical background, academic techniques, and theories to help us probe complex events so that we can better understand them. Unfortunately, our ability to interpret international events has been outdistanced by the questions we can pose concerning them.

PROBLEMS OF POLITICAL UNDERSTANDING

The student of international relations is confronted with certain dilemmas, the dimensions of which will become clearer in later chapters. The character of these difficulties is suggested by the following three interrelated considerations upon which this book is based: the *nature of human beings,* the *nature of the state,* and the *nature of a world of sovereign states.*

Of primary concern is the *nature of human beings.* One can hardly begin to understand social life without some idea of what people themselves "are really like." Unfortunately, the nature of humanity confounds us. The moral debate of "people are basically good" versus "people are basically bad" need not be opened here, although its relevance to political perception should not be underestimated. Of more immediate concern for political understanding, however, is the dilemma of "people as struggling animals" versus "people as rational creatures."

The essence of this dilemma was captured by two English political theorists writing in the seventeenth century—Thomas Hobbes and John Locke. Although both men were writing about contemporary political conditions, they were both trying to explain the bases for human society. Both were what are called social contract theorists. They suggested that at one time in human history, people lived in a State of Nature. For reasons that vary according to which theorist one reads, people came together at some hypothetical point in history to form a social contract, leaving the primitive State of Nature to enter organized society. How we perceive mankind is crucial to our picture of a State of Nature, and to an explanation of why people left the State of Nature and the kind of society that results.

Hobbes, in a political treatise appearing in 1651 entitled *Leviathan,* saw people as being very like the other animals—beasts caught up in the struggle for survival. The State of Nature was characterized by perpetual war, by "... continual fear and danger of violent death; and the life of man solitary, poor, nasty, brutish, and short." [1] To improve their condition, people formed society under the rule of an all-powerful sovereign who could maintain social

1 Thomas Hobbes, *Leviathan,* The Bobbs-Merrill Company, Inc., New York, 1958, p. 107.

order by force. The answer to the power struggle was superior power, a monopoly of power by the leader of the state. People were obliged to support their sovereign, Hobbes argued, because the only alternative was the uncontrolled violence of the State of Nature.

John Locke, writing his *Treatise of Civil Government* (1690) under more liberal conditions in England following the Glorious Revolution, saw people as rational beings, a cut above the other animals. The State of Nature was not the gloomy condition perceived by Hobbes. Rather, Locke felt that people were able to figure out ways of controlling, or avoiding, conflict. They did not have to fight. The State of Nature was perceived to be inadequate. Human reason suggested that institutionalized conflict-control mechanisms (that is, legislative, executive, judicial) made more sense. Hence, people formed the social contract not out of fear of certain death in a war-ridden State of Nature, but in the belief that rational solutions could be found to human conflict.

Even a cursory survey of human relations produces supporting evidence for either view. We can see people as self-serving creatures caught up in a perpetual and vicious power struggle, or we can see them just as convincingly as rational creatures able and willing to resolve their conflicts without resorting to violence. One ultimately has to accept one of these assumptions about human nature. A theme running through this book is that although the dilemma of true human nature is unresolved, we have an obligation to accept people as rational beings able to understand and order their relations with others. This acceptance gives meaning and purpose to human relations. This is not to say that meaning and purpose cannot be achieved in other ways, for example, from religious belief. The point, however, is that we must lead people away from the jungle, away from the Hobbesian portrayal of human nature. Then we can accept human relations, and ultimately international relations, as susceptible to rational control. This acceptance does not, however, require us to be unrealistic and forget that there is an irrational, baser side to human nature.

A second consideration upon which this book is based concerns the *nature of the state*. The basic political unit into which the modern world is divided is the sovereign state. States are much more than human beings "writ large," although what states represent depends on the assumptions about what people are and how they should be governed. States possess certain qualities that must be understood before we can make sense out of international relations. The complex questions concerning the nature of the state will be probed in detail in the remainder of Part I, The Problem of World Politics.

A third consideration is the *nature of a world of sovereign states.* A basic assumption of this book is that conflict is inevitable in a world in which more than 140 sovereign states must coexist and live out their futures as they perceive them. While the roots of that conflict are not entirely clear, it seems to be the natural result of living together in a social situation. Part II, A World in Conflict, examines the dimensions of conflict in modern international relations. But even though the presence of conflict may have to be accepted as a given, this book also assumes that rational solutions can be found to the problem of conflict. Part III, In Search of Order, is a study of the mechanisms and techniques for controlling conflict and maintaining international order. Part IV, The Future of International Relations, reviews the material covered in the book and gives some thoughts on the future direction of international relations.

THREE INTERNATIONAL EPISODES

The following three episodes suggest some of the excitement and frustration involved in studying international relations. These episodes cover a broad period of modern history and demonstrate some of the issues raised in the preceding section. In particular, the reader should look for the kinds of interaction that occur at the individual, national, and international levels, as well as attempt to distinguish the themes of conflict and order.

The Ordeal of Dr. Hácha

In the late 1930s, the international situation was rapidly deteriorating. During the first half of the decade, Japan had invaded Manchuria and Hitler had come to power in Germany. Both countries had withdrawn from the League of Nations, and their foreign policies had become increasingly strident. Italy, under the leadership of Mussolini, invaded Ethiopia in 1935. A "Rome-Berlin axis" was established by an accord between Hitler and Mussolini in 1936. The

Axis was solidified in May 1939 by a formal German-Italian alliance, and expanded the following year by the addition of Japan. Several other smaller states in Europe also later joined the Axis coalition.

The League of Nations, the hope of many of being an organized way to control international relations after World War I, seemed paralyzed in the face of the growing Axis threat to international peace. The paralysis extended beyond the League, however, to the leading Western nations that might have been expected to counter growing Axis strength. The United States was intensely isolationist, while both Great Britain and France appeared to have a genuine desire for peace and to be mesmerized by Hitler's power.

The height of Anglo-French attempts to keep the peace in Europe by appeasing Hitler was the Munich Pact of 1938. This pact allowed Germany to annex the Sudetenland, a section of Czechoslovakia bordering Germany whose population was largely Germanic. The West thought that the Munich Pact would bring peace, the Eastern Europeans lost confidence in Western resolve to protect them from German domination, and Hitler continued to pursue the policies that would ultimately lead to the invasion of Poland on September 1, 1939, and the start of World War II. Any initial check from the East on Hitler's power politics was averted by the August 1939 nonaggression pact between Germany and Russia, which had imperialist designs of its own.

Nearly lost in the flow of the grand international politics of this stormy period was one of the many human stories that are involved in international relations. One of the statesmen who had to face Hitler was Emil Hácha of Czechoslovakia.

A 1942 biographical account of Dr. Hácha concluded: "When a People's Tribunal in a restored, post-War democratic Czechoslovakia sits in judgment of Emil Hácha, it will probably find few redeeming features in his career." [2]

This harsh assessment was made of the man who had become the third president of Czechoslovakia. His status among his compatriots is something outsiders are in a poor position to judge, but he is nevertheless of some interest to students of international relations for his role in one of the more bizarre incidents of modern world politics.

2 *Current Biography*, The H. W. Wilson Company, New York, 1942, pp. 321–322.

Born on July 12, 1872, Emil Hácha was educated as a lawyer. He practiced law briefly and then entered the civil service of the Austro-Hungarian monarchy. Although he was never associated with the movement for Czech autonomy, under the new republic of Czechoslovakia Hácha was given a seat on the high court in 1918. By 1925, he had advanced to first president of the court, a post roughly equivalent to the position of chief justice of the United States Supreme Court—a post he held for thirteen years.

Following the fateful Munich Conference of 1938, the process of carving away Czech territory began. Finally, Eduard Beneš was forced to resign as the second president of the republic. Although Hácha had no previous experience in politics (and was in his late sixties), a special committee of Czechs and Slovaks asked him to assume the presidency. A man of law and letters (his varied experience included service on the League of Nations' Permanent Court of International Justice and the translation into the Czech language of Rudyard Kipling's *Jungle Books*), the aging Hácha was ill-equipped for the political turmoil into which he was being thrust.

It was believed that Dr. Hácha was the kind of conservative who would placate the Führer. In spite of naming fascists, pro-Germans, and others not associated with the Czech nationalism of Masaryk and Beneš (the founders of the Czechoslovakian republic) to his cabinet, he still could not satisfy the Nazi government in Berlin. Following Nazi-instigated agitation, Czechoslovakia was carved up further by the creation of an "independent" Slovakia on March 14, 1939. In an attempt to salvage what remained of Czechoslovakia, President Hácha (described by one author as "aging," "bewildered," and "senile" [3]) traveled to Berlin to meet with Hitler himself. He walked into a carefully prepared trap.

Arriving in Berlin late in the evening of March 14, Dr. Hácha and his daughter were received with all the formal, public protocol due a visiting head of state. Having learned that during his trip to Berlin German troops had already occupied some Czech territory and that German military units were poised all along the border ready to strike, the old man was finally ushered in to see Hitler after 1:00 A.M. on the morning of March 15, 1939.

The Führer bullied the old man, declaring that the Wehrmacht

3 William L. Shirer, *The Rise and Fall of the Third Reich,* Simon and Schuster, New York, 1960, chap. 13.

already had orders to invade at 6:00 A.M. and would smash all Czech resistance. Only an order from the Czech president for the Czech army to allow German troops to occupy the country peacefully would avoid a bloodbath. Such an order would pave the way for incorporation of Czech territory into Hitler's Reich.

Sometime after 2:00 A.M. that morning Dr. Hácha was reportedly dismissed from Hitler's presence and taken into an adjoining room, where Field Marshal Goering and Foreign Minister von Ribbentrop bullied him further, threatening to bomb the beautiful city of Prague. According to German records captured after the war, Dr. Hácha fainted under the pressure. Hitler's physician, who specialized in injections, revived the old man so that he could undergo further badgering.

Deserted by Czechoslovakia's "allies" at Munich, presiding over a country that was already dismembered, with the German Wehrmacht poised to attack his homeland, and reeling from the "persuasion" of Hitler and his lieutenants, Dr. Hácha caved in. Sometime around 4:00 A.M. on March 15, Dr. Hácha, after a further injection, returned to Hitler's presence to sign away his country with a document that the Führer had already prepared. This communiqué, dated Berlin, March 15, 1939, read:

The Führer and Reichs Chancellor, in the presence of Foreign Minister von Ribbentrop, today received at their request the Czechoslovak President, Dr. Hácha, and the Czechoslovak Foreign Minister, Dr. Chvalkovsky, in Berlin.

At the meeting the serious events of recent weeks on present Czech territory were examined with full frankness. Both sides agreed that the aim of all efforts must be to safeguard the calm, order and peace in this part of central Europe.

The Czechoslovak president declared that, in order to serve this goal and to achieve ultimate peace, he confidently put the fate of the Czech people and the country in the hands of the Führer of the German Reich. The Führer accepted this declaration and indicated his intention to take the Czech people under the protection of the German Reich and to guarantee the autonomous development of their characteristic ethnic life.[4]

This move sealed the fate (if it had not already been sealed) of what was left of Czechoslovakia. By 6:00 A.M. on the morning of

4 Document reprinted in Michael Freund, *Deutsche Geschichte*, C. Bertelsmann Verlag, Gütersloh, 1960, p. 629 (my translation).

March 15, Wehrmacht troops were pouring unopposed into Czech territory. By that evening, Adolf Hitler was able to make a triumphal entry into Prague and spend the night in Hradčany Castle, the ancient seat of Bohemian kings. The first democracy central Europe had ever known, built on the dreams of men like Masaryk and Beneš, had come to an end.

This remarkable episode in world politics was not without precedent. Hardly a year earlier the German Führer had bullied Kurt von Schuschnigg, the Austrian chancellor, into signing away his country at Berchtesgaden. The *Anschluss* between Germany and Austria, increasing the size of the Reich, had been the result. Unfortunately for Dr. Hácha, captured German documents reveal that he groveled before the arrogant Führer and his cohorts in a desperate, vain attempt to win favor for his country. Hácha's view afterward was: "Today they will curse me, in a few years they will understand me, and in fifty years they will recognize that it was a blessing for the country." [5]

Perhaps Dr. Hácha had saved his country for the moment, but casting the fate of the Czechs with Nazi Germany (even if there was no practical alternative at the time) was hardly an acceptable salvation. For his cooperation with Berlin, he was named president of Bohemia and Moravia, completely coming to terms with his Nazi overlords. Emil Hácha died on June 27, 1945, before his trial as a collaborator and war criminal.

As human beings we may imagine how we might have acted had we been in Dr. Hácha's position. As students of international relations we are faced with a host of provocative questions, in spite of the fact that the fall of the Third Reich gives us the rare opportunity of access to government archives and a chance to analyze usually intimate decision-making processes.

To what extent should states compromise in their relations with other states? The term "Munich" has become synonymous with appeasement. British Prime Minister Neville Chamberlain, upon returning from the conference that set in motion events that would lead to the invasion of Czechoslovakia and ultimately World War II, felt confident enough to promise "peace in our time." Chamberlain had been deceived by the Führer. Hácha had been intimidated by him. How can governments deal rationally with a willful, cunning, and

5 *Ibid.*, p. 630.

venturesome dictator? Neither our knowledge of history nor our present ability to interpret international affairs can provide solid answers.

The Cuban Missile Crisis

Another dimension to some of the issues involved in the machinations of the leaders of the Third Reich can be seen in the 1962 Cuban missile crisis. Leaders of states were again involved in the "poker game" of international politics, but this time they were playing for nuclear stakes.

The world of the 1960s was substantially different from the world of the 1930s. Fascism was no longer a major ideology, and the Cold War ideological struggle was between communism and democracy. The Soviet Union and the United States had emerged following World War II as superpowers, the titular leaders of large power blocs possessing not only vast resources but terrifying atomic arsenals as well. U.S. President John Kennedy and Soviet Premier Nikita Khrushchev faced each other as bargaining "equals," each having the means to alter substantially the fate of humanity.

The Cuban missile crisis was the first time in history that general world destruction was within the immediate grasp of two states locked in confrontation. The crisis itself developed over the U.S. discovery of Soviet-provided offensive missiles in Cuba—missiles capable of delivering atomic weapons quickly to the U.S. mainland. The mere presence of the missiles in Cuba threatened to upset the delicate Soviet-American nuclear balance of power.

As Robert Kennedy, the brother of the American president, was later to write in his memoir of the crisis, *Thirteen Days,*

On Tuesday morning, October 16, 1962, shortly after 9:00 o'clock, President Kennedy called and asked me to come to the White House. He said only that we were facing great trouble. Shortly afterward, in his office, he told me that a U-2 had just finished a photographic mission and that the Intelligence Community had become convinced that Russia was placing missiles and atomic weapons in Cuba.

That was the beginning of the Cuban missile crisis—a confrontation between the two giant atomic nations, the U.S. and the U.S.S.R., which brought the world to the abyss of nuclear destruction and the end of mankind. From that moment in President Kennedy's office until Sunday morning, October 28, that was my life—

and for Americans and Russians, for the whole world, it was their life as well.[6]

The context of the missile crisis was hardly propitious for either the United States or its young president. There were difficulties in Southeast Asia, particularly Laos. Relations with Latin America were not good. Cuba had "gone communist," the American naval base Guantanamo in Cuba had been under pressure, the Bay of Pigs fiasco was fresh in everyone's mind, the Cuban-Soviet axis seemed to be giving the Soviet Union a foothold in the Western Hemisphere, and *Fidelismo* was an ideological beacon for others in Latin America who saw in the Cuban revolution a model for their own countries. Berlin was under pressure. The Berlin Wall had recently been built, and Soviet Premier Khrushchev was threatening to sign a separate peace treaty with East Germany—with the understanding that Western access rights to Berlin could no longer be guaranteed by the Soviet Union. To top everything off, the United States was preparing for midterm national elections.

Three overlapping levels of analysis suggest themselves. First, one level concerns the decision-making process and interpersonal dynamics. Upon first learning of the offensive nature of the missiles placed in Cuba on October 15, the president and a group of his closest associates (calling themselves the "Executive Committee" of the National Security Council) met secretly to ponder strategy to counter the Soviet move. The national decision-making process is of substantial interest to students of international relations. *How* states formulate their foreign policy moves helps explain international politics. Some states have varying forms of dictatorship; others have relatively open forms of decision-making. An understanding of the dynamics of these processes will help states both understand and anticipate the actions of other states. The reports of those involved in advising President Kennedy reveal much about how people work together to hammer out policy. Advice ranged from the hawkish advocacy of unlimited force to dovish peace-at-any-price.[7] Most interesting from a decision-making perspective, however, was the subtle pressure advisers imposed upon themselves to recommend

6 Robert F. Kennedy, *Thirteen Days: A Memoir of the Cuban Missile Crisis,* W. W. Norton & Company, Inc., New York, 1969, p. 1.
7 *Ibid.,* pp. 26–28. See also Theodore C. Sorensen, *Kennedy,* Harper & Row, Publishers, Incorporated, New York, 1965, chap. 24.

what they thought the president wanted to hear. President Kennedy and others were aware of this problem, and Kennedy often stayed away from the meetings for this very reason.[8] Nevertheless, this is a frightening aspect of foreign policy decision-making, given the traditional assumption that democracies allow for the evolution of logical, broadly based decisions.

A second level of analysis, overlapping with the first, concerns American foreign policy. This includes the issues of the role of Congress vis-à-vis that of the president in foreign policy formulation, and the national interest and goals of the United States. The third level of analysis concerns the larger international issues of the effects of state decisions on the world in general and the roles of alliances and international organizations.

After the Kennedy Executive Committee had considered the photographic evidence of a Soviet offensive missile build-up in Cuba —evidence showing that surface-to-surface missiles capable of reaching and destroying U.S. cities were being emplaced—a response by the U.S. government could not be avoided. The Soviet Union had been saying both publicly and privately that the Soviet military interest in Cuba was purely defensive. The U-2 photographs revealed the Soviet Union's duplicity. At first the Executive Committee met in total secret—neither the U.S. public nor the Soviet Union was aware that the U.S. government was preparing to call the Soviet move. Had the United States failed to act, this would have fueled the belief that the American government was indecisive, bungling, and timid. After all, the U.S. response to Hungary, Suez, Sputnik, the Gary Powers U-2 incident, Castro's revolution, the Bay of Pigs, and the Berlin Wall had added to that myth. On the other hand, overreaction by the United States might have come off as either a pompous and empty bluff or a military provocation from which the Soviet Union could not back down.

President Kennedy's handling of the missile crisis is widely regarded as a diplomatic success, although it was not without attendant dangers. The Executive Committee considered various responses to the Soviet challenge ranging from a protest note to Moscow to a military attack on Cuba or the Soviet Union. The U.S. policy goal was to convince the Soviet Union that the United States "meant

8 See the discussion on this point offered by Irving L. Janis, *Victims of Groupthink: A Psychological Study of Foreign-Policy Decisions and Fiascoes*, Houghton Mifflin Company, Boston, 1972, especially chap. 6.

business" and that disruption of the world military status quo by introducing into the Western Hemisphere offensive missiles capable of hitting the United States would not be tolerated. At the same time, the Soviet Union could not be backed by an ultimatum into an embarrassing corner from which the only retreat would have been an unacceptable loss of international and domestic prestige.

Finally, on October 22, 1962, the American public and the world were informed of the U.S. response to the Soviet challenge. Secrecy had been maintained on the Executive Committee deliberations (a rather unusual feat in the modern American era of "news leaks," although President Kennedy had to intercede personally with the news media to delay the publication of the story) until a careful, coherent U.S. policy had been evolved. In a dramatic nation-wide address, President Kennedy announced:

This urgent transformation of Cuba into an important strategic base —by the presence of these large, long-range, and clearly offensive weapons of sudden mass destruction—constitutes an explicit threat to the peace and security of all the Americas, in flagrant and deliberate defiance of the Rio Pact of 1947, the traditions of this Nation and Hemisphere, the joint resolution of the 87th Congress, the Charter of the United Nations, and my own public warnings to the Soviets on September 4 and 13. This action also contradicts the repeated assurances of Soviet spokesmen, both publicly and privately delivered, that the arms build-up in Cuba would retain its original defensive character and that the Soviet Union had no need or desire to station strategic missiles on the territory of any other nation.[9]

The President went on to warn that "neither the United States of America nor the world community of nations can tolerate deliberate deception and offensive threats on the part of any nation, large or small." [10] He then outlined the U.S. response, the most dramatic element of which was a "quarantine" of Cuba. The quarantine was really a selective naval blockade (a blockade is normally considered an act of war) designed to prevent the further introduction of offensive weapons into Cuba. In addition, President Kennedy noted that U.S. forces were being alerted, that any nuclear missile launched from Cuba would lead to a "full retaliatory response upon the Soviet Union," and that the machinery of the Organization of American

9 *Public Papers of the Presidents of the United States,* U.S. Government Printing Office, Washington, D.C., 1963, p. 806.
10 *Ibid.,* p. 807.

States and the U.N. Security Council was being called upon. Finally, he called upon Chairman Khrushchev to halt and reverse Soviet missile efforts in Cuba.

U.S. diplomacy was very effective in solidifying at least general support for its position, even though those countries supporting Kennedy's stand knew they were going to the brink of nuclear war along with the United States. Not only did the OAS unanimously support Kennedy, but some Latin American countries even offered military assistance. America's European allies (especially England, France, and West Germany) supported the U.S. stand. U.S. diplomatic efforts even evoked commitments from some African states, considered unfriendly toward the United States, that they would not allow their airport facilities to provide necessary refueling aid to Soviet aircraft in case of war. All these efforts were capped with devastating effect by Adlai Stevenson, U.S. ambassador to the United Nations, in his televised confrontation with Soviet Ambassador V. A. Zorin at a meeting of the Security Council. Mr. Stevenson reminded the Soviet ambassador that he had previously denied the existence of Soviet offensive weapons in Cuba and asked if the Soviet Union still held to that position. Mr. Zorin refused to answer, saying that the official Soviet response would come "in due course." Mr. Stevenson then replied: "I am prepared to wait for my answer until hell freezes over, if that's your decision. And I am also prepared to present the evidence in this room." [11] He then revealed the U.S. photographs of the Soviet missile sites.

Moscow's reaction to America's throwing down the gauntlet reflected some uncertainty, as letters to Washington indicated. Most important, however, all sides seemed intent on gaining time, talking first and fighting only as a last resort. Most Soviet ships turned away from the blockade; the United States let pass through the blockade those ships that did approach it, as visual inspection revealed they were not likely to be transporting missiles; and U Thant, the U.N. secretary-general, was active in offering his "good offices" to help the superpowers talk over the confrontation. Finally, on October 27, President Kennedy accepted Premier Khrushchev's offer to remove the missiles in return for a no-invasion pledge on the part of the United States. Other differences were then quickly settled. Cuban Premier Fidel Castro refused to permit on-site inspection of

11 Kennedy, p. 54.

the missile-base dismantling by the United Nations, but the United States was content with its own aerial surveillance. Thus ended the world's first nuclear confrontation, and in the eyes of some observers, the Cold War ended as the realization of what nuclear war meant finally sank in.

Beyond the obvious macabre thrill of playing with nuclear fire, however, the lessons of the Cuban missile crisis as an exercise in international relations are not entirely clear. Kennedy admirers can see in his handling of the crisis a brilliant, skillfully handled foreign policy success. The United States "got tough," and the Soviet Union was forced to back down and remove the missiles. Any suggestion that the Soviets might have extracted a *quid pro quo* agreement from the United States for the removal of U.S. missiles in Turkey aimed at the Soviet Union is usually brushed aside because it is generally accepted that those missiles were obsolete anyway and scheduled to be dismantled. On the other hand, it can be argued, as Premier Khrushchev subsequently did, that the Cuban confrontation was really a Soviet diplomatic success because an American pledge was won not to invade Cuba—which was, after all, what the Soviet Union had wanted all along. One piece of supporting evidence for this position is that, surprisingly, no real effort had been made to camouflage the missile sites despite known U.S. air surveillance.

Another question concerns the proper role of deterrence strategy and nuclear bluff in modern diplomacy. Is nuclear "rocket rattling" a viable tool in modern international relations, or has the awesomeness of nuclear diplomacy in fact made it unusable? The context of the missile crisis may never be repeatable. All parties were cautious, the Soviet Union was at an obvious geographical disadvantage, the decision-making groups in Washington and Moscow were small, and the Western allies were surprisingly united (a factor that no doubt weighed heavily in Soviet decisions). What if one or more of the following factors had been present: a crisis over Berlin, an American public outraged and Congress in turmoil, the Soviet Union backed into a humiliating corner, venturesome leaders in either country, incomplete facts from the scene of confrontation, or a mistake by military commanders in the field? As it was, President Kennedy did not lack advice that could have driven the situation out of control (no doubt things were not much different in Moscow), an American U-2 was shot down over Cuba, an American bomber on a mission over Alaska temporarily lost its bearings and headed for the Soviet Union, and American military forces were hounding Soviet submarines in the Cuban area. A miscalculation, lack of a cool head, or even a simple accident at any point might have brought disaster. Clearly there is a further need for a careful evaluation of the nuclear implications of modern diplomacy.

The United Nations Conference on the Human Environment

The threat of nuclear destruction is not the only modern worry. From all sides we are hearing prophecies of impending, and perhaps inevitable, environmental doom. The outpouring of crisis literature is itself reaching crisis proportions. Whatever the scientific validity of the claims and counter-claims concerning environmental abuse, even a cursory glance around cannot fail to cause some concern for our future on this planet.

The Rhine River in Europe is reputedly so full of chemical effluent at points that photographic film can be developed in water taken directly from the river. In any case, the beautiful Rhine has long been grimly called "Europe's sewer." Italian beaches are said to be washed by dirty water from an increasingly polluted Mediterranean Sea. Similar charges are made concerning the Baltic Sea, the Soviet Union's famed Lake Baikal, and the American Great Lakes. The Eastern United States even has a river that has been declared a fire hazard because of the amount of flammable effluent dumped into it. Even where pollution has not been a major problem, one form or another of mismanagement has caused the depletion or outright disappearance of river life beneficial to humans.

Air pollution is no less of a problem. Police officers in downtown Tokyo are forced to wear oxygen masks, the air in most big cities is hardly fresh, and in areas as far apart as Los Angeles, California, and Warsaw, Poland, there is concern that urban air pollution is killing nearby forests.

There are persistent warning cries that the earth's resources are being overexploited. The recent energy crisis has focused attention on people's delicate dependence on fuel resources such as petroleum, coal, and natural gas. Dependence on the living resources of nature is hardly less significant. Whaling and fishing fleets range to the far corners of the globe. Charges of overexploitation (or, in the case of some species of whales, even of extinction) are heard more frequently as some states have defensively staked out "conservation zones" in areas of the ocean bordering their shores.

The list of environmental issues goes on indefinitely. One can easily accept the idea that the current generation has been raised in an era of supertanker disaster, pesticide danger, atomic radiation, chemical additives in foods, population explosion, the threat of insufficient food resources, and weather modification. In fact, *widespread* ecological concern is a relatively new phenomenon, having been until recently primarily the concern of only a few developed, industrialized states. Much of the world has been occupied with more immediate problems—disease, hunger, and development. Whatever national concerns may be important, however, the realization is growing that all people have a common fate on "spaceship earth." There is, after all, "only one earth"—a phrase that became the slogan of the United Nations Conference on the Human Environment.

Sverker Aström, the Swedish ambassador to the United Nations, formally focused the world's attention on ecological matters on December 3, 1968, when he proposed to the United Nations an international environmental conference to be hosted by the Swedish government in Stockholm during 1972. He concluded his remarks by saying: "There are many issues on which the members of the United Nations are divided. On the issue now before the General Assembly we are hopefully all united." [12]

The United Nations agreed to hold the conference under its auspices. The environmental problem deserved worldwide attention, and the United Nations was in a good position to coordinate a coherent, universal response to the challenge of a deteriorating environment. In late 1970, U.N. Secretary-General U Thant appointed Maurice Strong, who had headed the Office of Development in the Canadian Foreign Ministry, as secretary-general of the U.N. environmental conference. Mr. Strong organized a Secretariat that began to prepare for the Stockholm Conference. The process of soliciting reports and circulating documents achieved a substantial part of the purpose of a U.N. conference on the environment before the conference even met: world attention and interest had been captured. States found themselves (many for the first time) reviewing

12 Stanley Johnson, "Stockholm 1972," *New Statesman*, June 2, 1972, 742.

the status of their own national environments and asserting policy views on environmental management.

When the United Nations Conference on the Human Environment formally convened in June 1972, some twelve hundred delegates from 114 states were in attendance. The hope that the world would be united on such a common-interest issue as environmental abuse was quickly shattered, however. Political posturing threatened to dominate the conference, suggesting that politics might after all be the world's biggest pollutant.

Three political issues dominated. First, the Soviet Union and its European communist allies (with the exception of independently minded Rumania) boycotted the conference as a protest against the failure to invite East Germany. Invitations were based on the twenty-year-old "Vienna Formula," which specified that only members of the General Assembly or of one of the specialized agencies of the United Nations may participate and vote in U.N. conferences. West Germany qualified (as a member of a specialized agency); East Germany did not. This problem has of course since been solved by the admission of both Germanies as full members of the United Nations. Whatever the merits of the politics involved, the East Bloc boycott meant that a fifth of the world's industrial capacity (a major source of environmental abuse) was not at Stockholm.

Second, the People's Republic of China—a recent newcomer to the United Nations—found in the conference an opportunity to outmaneuver the Russians and seize leadership of the developing countries. They repeatedly denounced the "machinations of the colonialists, imperialists and neocolonialists." The American adventure in Vietnam was roundly criticized by China as an exercise in environmental degradation, although the People's Republic of China failed to support a resolution halting atomic testing.

A third, and potentially far-reaching and serious, political issue was the deep split between the industrialized states and the developing states. This split was not purely political, but was intertwined with economic and environmental issues. The crux of the split was that the industrialized, "have" states were the ones suffering the most from the effects of environmental abuse—belching smokestacks, automobile exhaust fumes, chemically polluted rivers, aircraft noise, and pesticide residues in food products. The developing, "have-not" countries found many of these problems irrelevant. They were concerned more with feeding the hungry and building up the economies of their countries. There was a tendency to see the environmental fuss being made by the developed countries as a device to deny the have-nots the fruits of twentieth century scientific progress and to keep them perpetually underdeveloped. To some it seemed to be a new form of colonialism. To the developed nations fell the frustration of crying "danger!" to those who would not listen.

Observers can read into the Stockholm Conference and its achievements largely what they want to. One observer noted at the conclusion:

We have during these last 12 days witnessed a gigantic ritual, a three-ring circus played out in three conference sites. The earphones, the microphones, the simultaneous translation, the closed circuit television, the empty seats and the sometimes empty speeches —all this has made it hard to gain any clear sense of where the conference was at or where it was headed.[13]

While the official conference was grinding along, there was a flurry of "unofficial" activity. People from all over the world had gathered (although there was strong suspicion that they represented largely the youth of middle-class Northern Hemisphere families) in Stockholm to gain attention for a variety of ecological causes. One of the more widely covered protests was a demonstration and parade calling attention to the allegedly imminent extinction of the blue whale—not only the largest mammal but also the largest animal ever to inhabit our planet. This magnificent creature has apparently been driven to the brink of extinction by unrestricted national whaling practices—perhaps a sad commentary on the ability of the international community to police itself.

The conference itself, in spite of the political ritual, managed to get down to a substantial amount of business. It met in three committees, each discussing two agenda items. The range of items under consideration included the environmental implications of the planning and management of human settlements, education and culture, natural resources management, development, pollutant control, and the international organization's role in action proposals. Many

13 Stanley Johnson, "Stockholm Roundup," *New Statesman*, June 16, 1972, 818.

nongovernmental organizations (NGOs), such as the Sierra Club, "lobbied" at the conference. While their influence cannot be determined, no doubt they had some impact on delegates' views.

The results of the conference represented, as might have been expected, the lowest common denominator of agreement among so many differing sovereign states. A Declaration on the Human Environment was passed that, although general in tone, did represent a crystallization of world attitudes on humanity and the environment. The first two points of the Declaration are instructive:

1 Man is both the creation and the designer of his environment, which provides him with the means of survival and the opportunity for intellectual, moral, social and spiritual development. The long and tangled path of humanity's development on this planet has now reached a stage where through the rapid progress of science and technology, man has now gained the power to alter the environment in the most different ways and to an unprecedented extent. Both aspects of human environment—the natural and that which he created—are important preconditions for his well-being and the exercise of basic human rights, even the right to life itself.
2 Protection and improvement of the human environment are important problems which affect prosperity and economic development throughout the world. They are the urgent concern of the peoples of the whole world and the responsibility of all governments.

The declaration was obviously a compromise between concern for the environment and concern for development.

The conference also resulted in concrete proposals that were passed on to the United Nations General Assembly. A permanent environmental organ, under an executive director (a position given to Maurice Strong) aided by an Environmental Secretariat of about 30, was approved unanimously by the General Assembly. This new United Nations Environmental Program (UNEP) would have its headquarters in Nairobi, Kenya. The reaction to locating the headquarters in a developing country was somewhat cynical in some quarters, as the major environmental problems seemed to be in the industrial countries. Maurice Strong countered with three observations. First, however it is perceived, the environment *is* a global issue. Second, the Nairobi headquarters will help ensure the continued interest of the developing countries in environmental affairs and demonstrate "how inextricably interwoven is the environmental future of rich and poor." Finally, in this modern era, communications with Nairobi are just as easy as with Geneva or New York.[14]

The policy-making body of UNEP is a governing council (operating under the U.N. Economic and Social Council) composed of representatives of 58 states. Other important "action" proposals to be approved were the Earthwatch program (an atmospheric monitoring network) and an International Referral Service (for the wide exchange of environmental information). The general budget for UNEP programs (the operating budget of UNEP itself will be provided from the regular United Nations budget) is placed at $100 million for a five-year period, with the United States providing 40 percent on a matching basis. This money is intended to be primarily "seed" money to encourage countries to start environmentally related programs of their own.

There is indeed only one earth. Democrats, communists, fascists, the rich, and the poor of all races need food, air, and clean water. Nature's revenge for humanity's neglect will humble us all equally. Concern for the environment may prove to be the factor that will finally unite countries as no other force in history has been able to do. On the other hand, the pressures of dwindling resources and competition for them may set the world to fighting as it never has before. The "spirit of Stockholm" is significant in that it represents an effort to follow the former course. The states of the world perceived a common problem and came together in an attempt to find sane, timely, and mutually acceptable solutions. The process was as important as the results. There will be other problems tomorrow, and the mechanisms evolved today for international problem-solving will play a major role in the direction the future takes.

CONFLICT AND ORDER

The three cases just discussed are basically clear to observers. One can follow the flow of events and grasp the main political issues. Yet each of these events raises more questions than it answers. Perhaps Hitler was unique; however, would a democratic Germany not also have tried to dominate Czechoslovakia, presumably using

14 Henry Pelham Burn, "Conversation with Maurice F. Strong," *Vista*, February 1973, 43.

different techniques? Are there unwritten laws that govern the conduct of nation-states, suggesting that large, dynamic states will "naturally" push around weaker neighbors? What about the technique? The Soviet Union's treatment in 1968 of Mr. Dubček, the Czechoslovak leader during the Prague Spring, suggests that some regard the bullying of foreign leaders as a means of conducting international relations. We are fortunate to have an inside look at the making of U.S. foreign policy during the Cuban missile crisis, yet we know little concerning Soviet and Cuban decision-making. There is even some doubt as to whether the missiles were in fact removed. Missile-shaped objects were seen leaving on ships. What if there are secret bases still in Cuba? Why can't the United Nations simply inspect Cuban territory? Why the fuss at Stockholm? The case for the environment is clear . . . the world must heed the warning. Delegates to the United Nations from the underdeveloped countries have been in New York and have seen the pollution of an industrial society. Why do they insist on pushing ahead with development in their own countries, knowing in advance the path they are following? Why doesn't the United Nations simply establish environmental controls and enforce them?

The list of questions is endless. The difficulty in answering them stems largely from the nature of the world in which we live, as well as from our ability to interpret that nature. We can gain some analytical insight into the preceding three episodes and provide a transition to the substantive material examined in Parts II and III of this book by reviewing those episodes in the context of the conflict and order topics in Parts II and III.

In the *conflict* area, the episodes illustrate the following situations:

A. The Bomb: Nuclear Power
   1. Episode 1 (Hitler's move against Czechoslovakia): Prenuclear age
   2. Episode 2 (Cuban missile crisis): Nuclear age—crisis situation
   3. Episode 3 (U.N. environmental conference): Nuclear age—accommodation situation
B. Ideology and Power Politics
   1. Ideological expansion; raw power politics; domination of a minor power by a major power within an eroding balance-of-power system

    2. Ideological conflict; major power politics; political interaction by matched major powers within a stabilized (by nuclear terror?) bipolar system

    3. Ideological interaction; multipower politics; political interaction by a majority of the world community within a rule-attempting context

C. Third World

    1. Pre-Third World era

    2. Third World countries are minor international actors

    3. Third World countries appear as relevant international participants

In the *order* area, the following observations concerning international accommodation emerge:

A. International Law

    1. Virtually nonapplicable

    2. Applicable as (a) a means of defining conflict issues, (b) a means of communication, and (c) a means of policy argument

    3. Applicable as an objective (that is, the search for a law-creating agreement)

B. International Organization

    1. Nonutilized

    2. Partially utilized

    3. Fully utilized

C. Diplomacy

    1. Bilateral

    2. Bilateral and multilateral

    3. Multilateral

Before a more detailed examination of the presence of conflict and the search for order in modern international relations is given, it is useful to look first at some of the major organizing theories and the historical background of international relations.

The Problem of Theory

Unfortunately, the substance of "international relations" is very poorly defined. The respected scholar Quincy Wright notes that "international relations refers both to the facts of international life and to the exposition of those facts." [1] There is some division, however, among international relations specialists over the dimensions of both facets.

Perhaps the best solution is a straightforward, simple conceptualization of international relations that can be modified later as the student's knowledge of the substance and methods of international relations grows.

WHAT IS "INTERNATIONAL RELATIONS"?

The concept of international relations as an area of study rests on two assumptions: (1) the nation-state (a term discussed in Chapter 3) is the basic political unit in the world today, and (2) there are interactions between and among these units that form the basis of international relations. These interactions must be assumed to be (1) intellectually identifiable, forming what might be called the "arena of world politics" (or the "international system," based on the assumption that there are recurrent and coherent patterns of interaction), (2) worthy of study, and (3) worthy of study under the separate academic heading of "international relations." Figure 2-1 portrays this view of international relations, but some refinement is clearly necessary. First, while nation-states are the most important participants (or "actors," as they are often called) in world politics, they are not monolithic entities. Individuals and groups are active in one form or another, and in most nation-states this activity will have some relevance to international relations. They may affect foreign policy decisions within their state, or they may in fact engage in relations with similar entities in other countries, or indeed, even with foreign governments themselves. Examples would include prominent scientists, labor unions, multinational corporations, and wildlife preservation groups, although obviously there is a very large spectrum of potential participants.

Second, international organizations (e.g., the United Nations,

1 Quincy Wright, *The Study of International Relations*, Appleton-Century-Crofts, Inc., New York, 1955, p. 9.

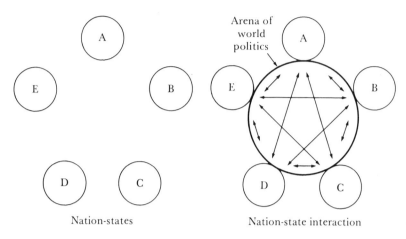

FIGURE 2-1. A View of International Relations

NATO, or the International Red Cross) participate in international relations. Although they consist of member states, or perhaps of national groups, such organizations tend to take on personalities of their own. For a full understanding of international relations, their role must be understood.

Finally, while the importance of what takes place in the world political arena can be perhaps readily granted, it is not so clear why international relations should be a separate area of study. Why cannot traditional academic areas such as economics or diplomatic history treat what goes on internationally? The answer is that they can, in part. The commitment to international relations is a commitment to a perspective, to stepping back from the world and trying to obtain a coherent picture of the totality of international activity. To return to Quincy Wright's view of international relations, there is a commitment to the importance and identifiability of the "facts of international life" and to the proposition that if the "exposition of those facts" is to be meaningful, some kind of coherent and unified approach must be developed. While the study of international relations has generally been linked closely with the study of politics, the intellectual tradition of that study has always been interdisciplinary, incorporating the views and findings of scholars from such diverse fields as anthropology, economics, history, law, philosophy, psychology, and sociology.

One noted observer of international relations, Stanley Hoffmann, offers a handy operational definition which suggests that "... international relations is concerned with the factors and the activities which affect the external policies and the power of the basic units into which the world is divided." [2] He goes on to note that a distinguishing feature of international relations is the decentralized nature of the milieu in which they take place.[3] There is no ready centralizing focal point for study like that for American national government, for example.

International relations is more than just the sum of national foreign policies, however, as Figure 2-1 might perhaps intimate. Professor Hoffmann's definition hints at the wide range of factors relevant to the world political arena. A further refinement is the concept of "linkage politics" developed by James Rosenau.[4] Linkage politics reflects the idea that events in the arena of world politics are linked with internal national events, and vice versa. If one accepts the view that events in one realm are a response to actions in the other (in fact, they will even overlap at points), then any meaningful boundary line between international and national is difficult to maintain. If one country has a national election, devalues its currency, or decides to cut the size of its army, these are as much international as internal national events. The idea of an identifiable arena of world politics is of value primarily for analytical convenience, as it aids observers in studying and interpreting the flow of events.

The "exposition of the facts" of international relations within universities varies somewhat in title. A review of American university catalogues reveals that international relations is normally a subfield of the discipline of political science, although some universities treat it as a separate area. Some scholars have argued that international relations should form a separate, identifiable, autonomous discipline.[5] In any case, international relations as an area of study has traditionally been broken down into three subareas: international politics, international organization, and international law.

International politics comprises what many use the broader title of international relations to refer to, and indeed, in many respects the titles appear synonymous. The former focuses primarily on the international *political* process, which is in fact broad enough to

---

2 Stanley Hoffmann (ed.), *Contemporary Theory in International Relations*, Prentice-Hall, Inc., Englewood Cliffs, N.J., 1960, p. 6.
3 *Ibid.*, p. 1.
4 James N. Rosenau (ed.), *Linkage Politics*, The Free Press, New York, 1969.
5 See, for example, Hoffmann, pp. 1–4.

encompass many aspects of organization and law. A good, broad definition of *politics* is the "is"/"ought" definition.[6] The underlying assumption of this definition is that everyone (or every group, or every nation-state) has some conception of what the state of affairs *ought* to be—excluding perhaps those few hermits who eschew all ties with social life. Given that assumption, politics is the process through which these entities (individuals, groups, nation-states) attempt to make what the state of affairs in fact *is* conform to their understanding of what the state of affairs *ought* to be. That is politics. One finds relevant courses appearing in university catalogues under such general areas as diplomacy, foreign policy, diplomatic history, military policy, communications, and theory. For the convenience of introductory students, however, this book employs the terms "international relations" and "international" or "world politics" interchangeably, both because scholars in the field often do and because any distinction in practice is becoming increasingly blurred.

International organization as an area of study focuses on the institutions (e.g., the United Nations, NATO) that can be superimposed on the nation-state system to regulate relations among independent nation-states (although other international "persons," such as individuals and public and private organizations, are increasingly becoming part of that study).

International law is concerned primarily with the legal regulation of the relationships among nation-states and other international persons; it includes a body of law and a court system. Law and organization are attempts to control the potential for chaos in the international arena. In the area of politics one finds both the greatest source of international turmoil and the most frequently used vehicle for controlling that turmoil.

ROLE AND PURPOSE OF THEORY

The relatively neat classifications above do not camouflage the nagging basic problem of *what to study* in international relations and *how to study it*. If the events in the arena of world politics are to be more than unrelated, apparently chaotic occurrences, then we

6 The author is indebted to Charles O. Jones, University of Pittsburgh, for passing on this view of politics.

need some theories to tie them together and give them meaning. For some reason, the mere mention of theory seems to terrify many students, who assume that they are about to be overwhelmed by technical social science jargon.

Unfortunately, because specialists in the field of international relations have a common professional problem, they have a natural tendency (as in all professions) to use a common frame of reference to communicate with one another—hence the development of jargon. Theory and a modest dose of jargon are the tools of the trade. To study international relations, one needs at least a moderate understanding of the problems and organizing concepts of the field as specialists perceive them. The term "theory" is used in this chapter in its broadest popular sense as a general explanation of selected phenomena, although some of the theories examined here would be more carefully categorized by advanced scholars as simply approaches or methods of analysis.

The question of *how* to study international relations involves the same methodological debate that is going on in all the social sciences. The debate has turned on the methods that should be used in studying social phenomena, producing a basic split between "traditionalists" and "behavioralists." This simple dichotomy does some violence to the facts, because there is a more refined spectrum of methodological positions. Nevertheless, these two terms capture the essence of the split, which has been purposely distorted in the following paragraphs to portray opposite poles so that beginning students will more readily grasp the bases for intellectual disagreement.

The traditional school (which includes the philosophical method of Plato and the historical-descriptive method so familiar from the vast majority of textbooks used in humanities, and even many social science, courses) uses basically a normative, qualitative, value-judgment approach. A traditional scholar studying the United Nations, for example, might do some library research, visit the United Nations in New York for several months, and maybe even interview in depth many individuals working within the United Nations. Ultimately the traditional scholar will present findings in the following spirit: "In *my* judgment, in *my* opinion, and based on the evidence *I* have examined, *I* believe the United Nations works in such and such a manner." The value of traditional findings is usually measured by the reputation of the scholar, the extent to which his or her judgment is trusted, the evidence of thorough research, the lucidity with which the discussion is presented, or the nerves touched with an eloquent or moving philosophical discourse. Most of the past scholarly activity in the humanities and social sciences has relied on the traditional method.

Within the last forty to fifty years, however, another method has captured a great deal of attention. It arose out of a growing dissatisfaction with the reliability, and ultimately the utility, of the traditional approach. It reflects as well an admiration of the scientific method used in the "hard" sciences. If twenty geologists were asked to study the same rock, they could probably all agree on what kind of rock it was. If twenty chemists were asked to predict what would happen if two chemicals, in specified proportions and under certain conditions, were to be mixed, agreement would be virtually certain. On the other hand, twenty observers sent off to the United Nations would probably return with a host of differing views. The behavioral school has been developed in the belief that it is possible to study society scientifically—perhaps not with the precision with which the chemists study a chemical substance, but at least in a more exacting, deliberate, and dependable way than that of the traditionalists.

The organizing concept became *behavior*, with a corresponding emphasis on the inductive method of science. It made little difference what grand theories and deduced principles said about social life, the behavioralists argued. What counted was the precise study and measurement of behavior, of what people and institutions were *really* doing. As hard data mounted on human activities, general conclusions could be inferred. Much attention has been devoted to breaking behavior into countable units that can be measured and manipulated by quantitative techniques—hence the emphasis on statistical methods, use of computers, and focus on such measurable behavior as voting (e.g., poll-taking and roll-call analysis). Behavioralists are also deeply concerned with the mechanics of study, putting great emphasis on the research design. They want to be sure that subsequent scholars, using the same methods, can come close to duplicating the study. Behavioralists believe that there are recurring patterns of behavior that are identifiable, capable of being studied, and ultimately predictable.

A bitter debate raged for a time between these two methodological schools. Traditionalists insisted that human behavior was unique and unpredictable, except within the vaguest of limits. Computers would never replace human judgment. Besides, grand theory suggested goals and gave life meaning. There was some fear that the behavioral focus on what *is* would divert attention from what *ought* to be, which had frightening implications. What if the behavioralists' studies led them from trying to predict human behavior to controlling it? Behavioralists, for their part, scoffed at the traditionalists. The computer age was upon us, not to mention the nuclear age. Old-fashioned "gut feelings" about what "the Russians might do" internationally were no longer adequate. We needed to refine our knowledge of social life to the level of a real science. Some behavioralists even took the extreme position that no generalization about social life was valid unless it was provable by hard scientific data. Fortunately for the social sciences, and to the credit of the scholars involved, the methodological dispute has subsided. No doubt the process of accommodation was aided by the realization that the methods of the traditionalists were neither as inexact nor as unsystematic as they had been portrayed, and the realization that the conclusions of the behavioralists were neither as precise nor as value-free as had been predicted. Rather than being regarded as mutually exclusive, these two methodological approaches are now generally regarded as complementary. In studying the provocative issues of our day, there is no reason to write off intellectual contributions from any source. How one weighs those contributions depends on one's own values regarding methods. Certainly all the theories of international relations reviewed below are failures in the sense that they do not explain international relations to everybody's satisfaction. The methodological difficulty of *how* to study international relations becomes intertwined with the even more basic issue of *what* to study. Even assuming that we have general agreement on the existence of a vaguely defined world political arena, how do we know what to look for in that arena? What is important? Perhaps the following survey will offer some perspectives.

SOME PROMINENT ATTEMPTS TO MAKE SENSE OUT OF WORLD POLITICS

Realism and Utopianism

World War I challenged utopian theories of international relations. Ideas of international morality, faith in international legalism, and

Wilsonian idealism were countered during the interwar period by a growing emphasis on realism. Realists exhibited a disdain for utopian principles and expressed faith in "fundamental concepts" such as self-interest and the use of power.

The noted scholar E. H. Carr offered an early analysis of these two views of international relations in his important book *The Twenty-Years' Crisis, 1919–1939*.[7] In that work he chastised both utopianism and realism. The utopians were guilty of moralizing, not understanding the lessons of history, and overestimating the ability of people of good will to control international events. At the same time he accused the realists of cynicism, of regarding people as helplessly caught up in a web of power, and of determinism. He advised that the soundest course would be a careful mixture of both positions. The utopians can give us meaningful goals and a moral standard against which to measure conduct, while the realists are able to remind us of both the historical record of international relations and the limitations of rational theories in directing the ways in which nation-states will act internationally. This is essentially the position advocated in Chapter 1 of this textbook, and it will become clearer once the nature of the sovereign nation-state is examined in detail in Chapter 3.

Disappointment with the League of Nations and with what George Kennan called the "legalistic-moralistic" approach to international relations strengthened the realist position.[8] Hitler, World War II, and the postwar activities of the Soviet Union in Eastern Europe impressed Western international relations scholars with the philosophy of political realism. The pessimistic realization of the potential of atomic weapons only enhanced that impression. The result was that realism came to dominate the study of international relations from the 1940s to the 1960s, when other theories, such as systems theory, began to attract interest.

Prominent realists include the classical theorists Thomas Hobbes and Niccolò Machiavelli, the noted Protestant theologian Reinhold Niebuhr, George Kennan (former U.S. ambassador to the Soviet Union), and U.S. Secretary of State Henry Kissinger. Perhaps the scholar most associated with the realist view of international

7 Edward Hallett Carr, *The Twenty-Years' Crisis, 1919–1939: An Introduction to the Study of International Relations*, Macmillan & Co., Ltd., London, 1939.
8 See George Kennan, *American Diplomacy, 1900–1950*, The University of Chicago Press, Chicago, 1951.

relations, however, is Hans J. Morgenthau. His theory is worth examining in some detail, and his approach is generally representative of the realist school.

Morgenthau proposes a "realistic" look at human nature and human politics, which he sees as understandable only in terms of a natural struggle for power. Looking at international relations, he says:

International politics, like all politics, is a struggle for power. Whatever the ultimate aims of international politics, power is always the immediate aim. Statesmen and peoples may ultimately seek freedom, security, prosperity, or power itself. They may define their goals in terms of a religious, philosophic, economic, or social ideal. They may hope that this ideal will materialize through its own inner force, through divine intervention, or through the natural development of human affairs. They may also try to further its realization through nonpolitical means, such as technical co-operation with other nations or international organizations. *But whenever they strive to realize their goal by means of international politics, they do so by striving for power.*[9] (Emphasis added)

Although individual people are part of the natural struggle for power, this struggle, Morgenthau argues, is controlled *within* the nation-state. Sovereign states represent a monopoly of power (whatever the theoretical underpinnings of the domestic political process or the form of government), enabling them to maintain domestic order. This monopoly is normally supported by cultural ties, such as a common language, religion, national pride, customs, and morals. These ties are lacking in the world political arena, Morgenthau claims. There is no world monopoly of power and no common cultural tie. Nation-states in world politics are much like people in the State of Nature, and it is "every man for himself." This does not mean that international relations must necessarily be immoral or irrational. The realist would simply regard questions of morality and rationality as irrelevant to the iron law of politics—the struggle for power.

The realist believes that states must follow their "national interest," which is defined in terms of power. Morgenthau asserts that once the realist position is understood, international relations begins to make sense. Fundamentally, he argues, there are only three

9 Hans J. Morgenthau, *Politics Among Nations: The Struggle for Power and Peace*, 5th ed., Alfred A. Knopf, Inc., New York, 1973, p. 27.

foreign policy courses open to states: struggle to maintain power, increase power, or demonstrate power.[10] This means that states will support the status quo in an attempt to retain the power they have, they will try to expand their power (that is, imperialism), or they will try to bluff for prestige or other purposes in an effort to wield influence.

One of the persistent criticisms of the realist school concerns the definition of power. Even if we accept the proposition that power is at the root of international relations, as scholars we have then to ask: "What *is* power? How do we study it?" Morgenthau answers in part, saying that power is a psychological relationship among states. A state is powerful because other states regard it as powerful. For example, at the time of the *Sitzkrieg*, France was considered powerful until the Germans attacked and outflanked the French defense. "Psychological relationships" are as vague as the term "power" and not easily susceptible to measurement and study. If a cute little three-year-old child with big, soft brown eyes asks an adult for an ice cream cone, the adult can employ power and refuse, or alternatively can be swayed by the irresistible power of the child's charm. The relationship between the two is simple, but it is difficult for the scholar to define in solid terms. The immensely complex psychological relationships among the more than 140 nation-states of the modern world defy easy analysis.

There have been many attempts to construct a list of more concrete elements of national power. Depending on which scholar one consults, such a list usually includes such elements as: (1) geography, (2) natural resources, (3) technology, (4) population, (5) ideology, (6) national character, (7) morale, and (8) leadership. In fact, governments base their assessments of other governments on such lists. National profile studies are attempts to measure national capabilities—to measure national power—by referring to characteristics considered significant. Lists of the elements of national power are deceptive, however, for the problem of measuring power is not solved. With respect to geography, for example, Germany was traditionally considered to be disadvantaged by the lack of natural boundaries. Through much of European history, Germany was the battleground for everyone else's armies. Yet with the rise of

10 *Ibid.*, chaps. 4, 5, and 6.

Brandenburg-Prussia and the eventual consolidation of a German Empire under Bismarck (and later under Hitler), the lack of natural boundaries aided a strong Germany to expand. Is Japan aided or hindered by its geographical situation? Would the answer be the same for the Philippines? For the British Isles? China feels its large population to be a strength, yet India's millions are regarded as a liability. Does ideology weaken or strengthen the Soviet Union... or is it irrelevant to an assessment of Soviet power? Does high morale compensate for bungling leadership, or conversely, can brilliant leaders make up for low citizen morale? The point is that even these relatively explicit aspects of power are bewildering because of the many variables involved.

There are further criticisms of the realist school. If power is linked with the national interest, how do we know what the national interest is in any given instance? How do we know if we are increasing our state's power? Was the Vietnam adventure in the national interest of the United States? The answer depends on whom one listens to. Much of the reason for the internal agony in which the United States found itself over U.S. policy toward Southeast Asia stemmed from the inability to define to everyone's continuing satisfaction exactly what Americans thought they were doing in that part of the world. Has the era of nonrecognition of Castro's Cuba increased or decreased the power of the United States? The answers are not so easy. Also, there is the problem of determinism, for the realist school seems to discourage efforts toward the rational control of international relations. Why bother with the United Nations, international law, and appeals to the world's conscience if we are governed by the immutable laws of the struggle for power? Finally, there are also philosophical questions relating to the purpose of power. Should power be sought for its own sake, or is it a means to a higher end?

In defense of the realist approach, three major points should be made. First, the theory is both persuasive and supported by much historical experience. Second, the bold realist challenge has jolted scholars into a sober re-evaluation of their own assumptions. Third, even though many observers of international relations feel an obligation to challenge the bases of realism, many implicitly (or explicitly) come around to relying on realist perspectives—no small compliment.

Philosophies of History and Geography

Arnold Toynbee and Oswald Spengler are known for their interpretations of history based on the rise and fall of civilizations.
Others, like G. W. F. Hegel, saw history as an inexorable process of
unfolding Truth. The dialectical clash of ideas (dialectical idealism)
moved history toward its goal, because out of each clash of ideas a
higher level of Truth would be achieved. Claiming he found Hegel's
approach "upside-down," Karl Marx asserted that the dialectical
process actually involved the clash of material forces (dialectical materialism). He then employed the theory of the dialectic
(thesis $\longleftrightarrow$ antithesis $\rightarrow$ synthesis) in an economic interpretation
of history, that pitted one economic class against another. Marxists
are similar to realists in that they perceive the struggle for power,
but they define it in terms of economics. The causes of struggle are
seen as rooted more in the forces of history than in human nature.
The communist interpretation of international relations is examined
in greater detail in Chapter 5.

One basic criticism of philosophies of history is that they tend to
be deterministic, recalling the old religious debate of "free will"
versus "predestination." Society is considered to be subject to historical forces, with claims to special status within society being advanced by those "high priests" and their followers who profess to
understand these forces. A second general criticism of historical
philosophies concerns their dogmatism. Once certain propositions
are accepted, everything else falls neatly into place. Then the givens
tend to become taboo issues, and the deductions from those givens
are protected from critical scrutiny. Critics start looking like heretics
because they are challenging not merely scholarly perspectives on
the meaning of social events, but a whole philosophy of life based
on the discovery of certain "laws." A third observation is that such
philosophies strike skeptics as being "too pat." History is ransacked
for confirmation of "laws," while contrary material is for one reason or another denied. There is much to suggest that the many complex variables that determine the flow of human events defy an easy
and final explanation based on certain historical forces.

A related organizing theory for human activities is philosophies
of geography, often called simply "geopolitics." The main element
of geopolitical theory is a belief in the significance of the geographical variable both as an element of national power and as a deter-

minant in international relations. The geopolitical school seems to have two main branches. (1) The branch generally regarded as more legitimate merely insists that geography be considered as a factor in the study of world politics. (2) The other branch, now somewhat in disrepute, appears as a pseudoscience of geographical determinism, widely associated with the German geopoliticians who attempted to justify German expansion on geographical grounds.

Early proponents of geopolitical ideas were the German geographer Friedrich Ratzel (1844–1904), a formulator of the *Lebensraum* concept, and a Swedish professor, Rudolf Kjellén (1864–1922), who coined the term "geopolitics." Kjellén's book *The Great Powers* became a basic source for German geopoliticians, the foremost of whom was the retired Major General Karl Haushofer (1869–1946). Hitler was impressed with Haushofer and supported his founding of an academy of geopolitics in Munich. Haushofer had considerable influence within high German political and military circles, where his "scientific" theories were seen as a basis for policy. He argued that geography was the dominant influence in such areas of social life as law, ethics, and art. He also believed that a particular race was best suited to rule a particular region. In areas where the current population was unsuited (e.g., the Slavs in Eastern Europe), the race destined to dominate that area (that is, the Germans) would have to move them out. When Haushofer finally advised Hitler that geographical considerations militated against a German invasion of the Soviet Union, Hitler rewarded him by sending him to a concentration camp.

Two other important geopolitical theorists were the American naval officer Alfred Thayer Mahan (1840–1914) and the British geographer Sir Halford J. Mackinder (1861–1947). Mahan is noted for his theory of sea power, which declared that control of the globe was linked with control of the seas.[11] His theory, set forth in 1890, was largely superseded by developments in land transportation (especially railroads) that permitted the rapid movement of large amounts of supplies—although the geopolitical role of the seas remains significant.

Mackinder captured attention with his "heartland" theory when he presented in 1904 his famous paper entitled "The Geographical

11 See Alfred Thayer Mahan, *The Influence of Seapower Upon History, 1660–1783*, Little, Brown and Company, Boston, 1897.

Pivot of History" to the Royal Geographical Society of London.[12] He speculated that European (and eventually world) history was linked with efforts to control the "heartland," which he saw as the core area (from the Volga to the Yangtze and from the Arctic Ocean to the Himalayas) of the great Eurasian land mass. That land mass, which makes up two-thirds of the world's land area, he called the "world island." A further aspect of the theory was the concept of "rimland," including the Near Eastern, Indian, and European peninsulas. Mackinder concluded finally that whoever controls the world island controls the world (a theory, incidently, not lost later on Germany's geopoliticians).

Critics of Mackinder's theory suggest that just as Mahan's views on sea power were modified by advances in technology, so the importance of the heartland (and of geography itself) has been limited by strategic bombers, ICBMs, hydrogen bombs, and satellites. The theory should not be dismissed lightly, however, for it does have persuasive and significant aspects. It *does* matter, for example, who controls the heartland. This area is currently divided between the Soviet Union and the People's Republic of China. The domination of the entire area by either one of those powers would have a significant impact on international relations. A U.S. State Department representative recently insisted to this writer that there were those in the Department who, believing in the validity of Mackinder's heartland theory, had predicted the Sino-Soviet split before others were aware of it. The split was "inevitable," given the "natural" struggle for dominance of the heartland. Mackinder himself revised his theory before his death and called attention to a possible Atlantic alliance counterweight to power lodged in the heartland.[13] Focus on the rimland provides an obvious theoretical link with the postwar notion of "containment," associated with George Kennan, and with the rationale for the Western alliance system (NATO, SEATO), which attempts to consolidate and strengthen the rimland.

Whatever the validity of the philosophies of history and geography, they have served to focus the attention of other scholars on the importance of historical and geographical studies.

12 See Halford J. Mackinder, "The Geographical Pivot of History," *Geographical Journal*, 23 (April 1904), 434.
13 See Halford J. Mackinder, "The Round World and the Winning of the Peace," *Foreign Affairs*, 21 (July 1943), 595–605. See also Mackinder, *Democratic Ideals and Reality*, W. W. Norton & Company, Inc., New York, 1962.

Systems Theory

The systems concept has become extremely popular in recent years in political science and international relations, as well as in the social sciences as a whole. During the 1960s, systems terminology came to dominate much of the scholarly discussion of human relations. Unfortunately, some of the most important contributions to systems theory have not been readily accessible to the average reader because of jargon-ridden, high-level abstractions. This situation is particularly unhappy because systems theory offers vital new perspectives on social phenomena and data organization.

The basic idea of systems theory was transferred from such sciences as physics and biology into the social sciences. Much of the development of early social science systems theory was done by such scholars as Talcott Parsons and David Easton.[14] Names linked with the application of systems theory to the study of international relations include Morton Kaplan, Charles A. McClelland, and Richard Rosecrance.[15] The idea of system is basically very simple (in fact, one of the persistent criticisms of this approach is that it is so simple and general that it really answers none of the basic questions about politics), although the following definition might be cited as an example of how complexity somehow gets interjected:

A system of action is a set of variables so related, in contradistinction to its environment, that describable behavioral regularities characterize the internal relationships of the variables to each other and the external relationships of the set of individual variables to combinations of external variables.[16]

To approach a definition of system somewhat differently, we should make it clear that systems theory is a behavioral theory. It is

14 See Talcott Parsons, *The Structure of Social Action*, The Free Press, New York, 1949; *The Social System*, The Free Press, New York, 1951; and *Structure and Process in Modern Societies*, The Free Press, New York, 1960. See also David Easton, *The Political System*, 2d ed., Alfred A. Knopf, Inc., New York, 1971, and *A Systems Analysis of Political Life*, John Wiley & Sons, Inc., New York, 1965.
15 See Morton A. Kaplan, *System and Process in International Politics*, John Wiley & Sons, Inc., New York, 1957; Charles A. McClelland, *Theory and the International System*, The Macmillan Company, New York, 1966; and Richard Rosecrance, *Action and Reaction in World Politics*, Little, Brown and Company, Boston, 1963.
16 Kaplan, p. 4.

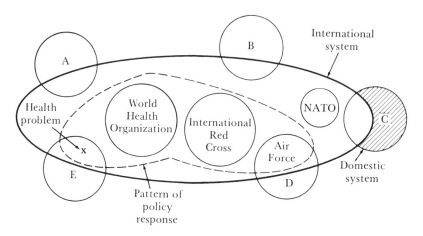

FIGURE 2-2. The International System

based on the assumption that over time human behavior appears to follow discernible patterns that can be identified and studied. These behavior patterns merge with other patterns to form what appear to be coherent systems of interaction. A system is nothing more than an intellectual device for viewing and describing these patterns. It is a means of drawing a circle in one's mind around a segment of human activity that appears highly interrelated, as opposed to events occurring elsewhere. Hence, we can (as Figure 2-2 suggests) draw circles to represent nation-states. The behavioral patterns (that is, culture, history, national goals) within nation-state *A* are identifiably different from those within *B*, *B* from *C*, and so forth. To press the system idea further (it comes, after all, from the natural and physical sciences), these states resemble one-celled animals, such as amoebae. When behavior patterns have been established (the historical process of creating a nation-state), the system seems to take on a life of its own, functioning like a living organism. The system acts and reacts to stimulae (as an amoeba would) and tries to maintain itself as a properly functioning system over time.

Once the idea of a system is accepted, one can visualize various levels of subsystems. For example, the human body has an identifiable digestive system, which in turn is made up of identifiable parts (stomach, intestines) that themselves perform a coherent group of functions. The specific boundaries and functions of social systems hinge on which systems theorist one is listening to. The basic idea, however, is to provide a way to organize mentally the apparent chaos of international relations. Assuming (see Figure 2-2) that we can picture an international system, with the nation-states and international organizations as identifiable subsystems (made up themselves of further subsystems), we can assume that the interactions among these subsystems themselves fall into identifiable patterns. One way of tracing such patterns is to focus on the policy patterns that develop in response to recurring public problems (called a policy subsystem). For example, we can assume that the international system will tend to respond to recurring health problem x in a similar way over time. If nation-state E gets health problem x, the World Health Organization, the International Red Cross, and nation-state D's air force can be counted on to respond because they have responded similarly in the past. The identification of other recurring problems will probably reveal other patterns of response.

This kind of conceptual picture helps us (1) get an overall view of the flow of international relations, (2) focus our attention on the specific issues we wish to study (e.g., health problem x) without becoming confused by all the other unrelated events happening simultaneously, and (3) achieve a certain predictive capability based on the theory of repeated patterns of behavior (which is the basis for identifying a system). The professional task of systems theorists is to spell out the exact rules and preconditions for identifying systems and studying the activities which they comprise so that subsequent scholars can duplicate the process.

In that context, Morton Kaplan proposed an intriguing aspect of using systems theory to study international relations. He spelled out some tentative rules for identifying the international system at any given point in time. He concluded that there were six different kinds of international systems and listed their characteristics (the six were balance-of-power system, loose bipolar system, tight bipolar system, universal system, hierarchical system, and unit veto system). In theory, he suggested, one should be able to predict future trends in international politics by observing the breakup of the characteristics necessary for one type of international order and the creation of those that would lead to a different type.[17]

Some of the difficulties of systems theory have already been mentioned. Two other criticisms of this approach also deserve mention.

17 *Ibid.*, especially chap. 2.

First, nonbehavioralists will assert, as part of their general criticism of behavioralism, that human actions are unique and that behavior patterns will be identifiable and predictable only within the broadest limits. Second, one can be properly skeptical about the ability of scholars to define systems precisely, and hence the problem of high-level abstractions.

Decision-making Theory

Decision-making theories are an attack on the common practice of reification, of regarding abstract concepts as concrete things and endowing these things with living personalities of their own. Examples abound: France made a deal with the Arabs, Germany precipitated a war, the foreign ministry was caught by surprise, Congress was unhappy with the executive, and the United Nations reacted with shock. Such expressions are used because they are convenient and seem to capture the essence of what we think we mean to say. The difficulty with the reification is that it does not have the intellectual precision necessary if scholars are to undertake the scientific (or at least the disciplined) study of politics.

Decision-making theorists may grant that the state is the basic unit in international relations, but they would maintain that "state action is the action taken by those acting in the name of the state. Hence, the state is its decision-makers." [18] Someone who speaks of Congress making a decision really means that a specific majority of the members of Congress agreed on a course of action. To say that Germany went to war really means that certain German decision-makers, acting in the name of the state, committed Germany to specific military and political actions that led to war. What the decision-making theorists are trying to do is threefold: (1) identify decision-makers, (2) set up a systematic means of studying how decisions are made (the decision-making process), and (3) offer a more meaningful and precise method of understanding international politics. The decision-making theorists are trying to explain what goes on within those circles in Figures 2-1 and 2-2 that represent nation-states. Figure 2-3 is a rough sketch of a sample decision-

18 Richard C. Snyder, H. W. Bruck, and Burton Sapin, *Decision-making as an Approach to the Study of International Politics,* Princeton University Press, Princeton, N.J., 1954. Monograph No. 3 of the Foreign Policy Analysis Project Series.

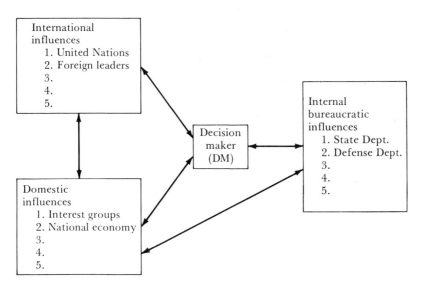

International
influences
   1. United Nations
   2. Foreign leaders
   3.
   4.
   5.

Decision
maker
(DM)

Internal
bureaucratic
influences
   1. State Dept.
   2. Defense Dept.
   3.
   4.
   5.

Domestic
influences
   1. Interest groups
   2. National economy
   3.
   4.
   5.

FIGURE 2-3. The Decision-making Process

making process.[19] The decision-maker (DM) is at the center of the
process. The decision-maker is influenced by, and has an influence
on, an international constituency, a domestic constituency, and the
bureaucratic constituency of the internal decision-making machinery. These constituencies also have some interaction with one another. The task of the decision-making theorist is to devise a list of
the relevant influences within each box so that they can be measured
and evaluated.

This presentation of the essence of decision-making theory is
really a very much simplified version of the impressive work that
has been going on in this area. To understand how and why decisions are made, however, the scholar must have some kind of model,
or at least a vague idea, of how the decision-making process works.
One student of decision-making, Graham Allison, has called our
attention to the importance of a model for the substantive conclusions we might draw concerning decisions. He notes that "professional analysts of foreign affairs (as well as ordinary laymen)
think about problems of foreign and military policy in terms of
largely implicit conceptual models that have significant consequences for the content of their thought." [20]

19 See the proposed diagram in *ibid.*, p. 34.
20 Graham T. Allison, *Essence of Decision: Explaining the Cuban Missile Crisis,*

Most analysts, he suggests, use what he calls the "rational actor" model or one of two alternatives—the "organizational process" model or the "governmental politics" model. The rational actor model judges the policy process on the basis of an ex post facto review of whether or not policy objectives were achieved (e.g., American policy during the Cuban missile crisis could be judged successful because the goal of having the Soviet missiles removed was apparently achieved).

The organizational process model attempts to link advanced theories of organizational and administrative behavior with an understanding of government decision-making.[21] The governmental politics model emphasizes the problems and importance of obtaining internal bureaucratic consensus as a means of evolving policy.[22]

In spite of the brevity of this survey of decision-making analysis, it would not be unfair to mention some of the more basic criticisms of this approach. A primary difficulty is the identification of the decision-maker. It may be that crucial decisions were actually made deep within the bureaucracy by minor officials who, by selecting materials to pass on to their superiors, really "made" the ultimate decision because the appearance of the facts structured the chief's final decision. Sometimes key decision-makers may not even realize they made a decision; they may only have a vague sense of having participated in the process. A second difficulty concerns measuring the relevant influences on a decision-maker. It may be true that the fact that a secretary of state had a fight with his wife, or a severe case of heartburn, on the eve of an important decision is of minimal significance for an understanding of the decision-making process. Nevertheless, the staggering number of potential influences, and their degrees of relevancy, make it doubtful that we are close to developing a science of decision-making. A third difficulty, of particular importance to the scholar, is access to the decision-making process for the purpose of study. Government decisions in the

Little, Brown and Company, Boston, 1971, p. 4. See also Allison, "Conceptual Models and the Cuban Missile Crisis," *American Political Science Review*, 62 (September 1969), 689–718.

21 See, for example, Herbert A. Simon, *Administrative Behavior*, The Macmillan Company, New York, 1959.

22 See, for example, Richard E. Neustadt, *Presidential Power*, John Wiley & Sons, Inc., New York, 1960, and Roger Hilsman, *To Move a Nation*, Doubleday & Company, Inc., Garden City, N.Y., 1967.

making are often kept secret, or at least out of easy public reach. The Cuban missile crisis is an example, although the after-the-fact coverage in that case was quite insightful. National security and the nature of diplomacy require a certain amount of secrecy. It could not be any other way. Even with past decisions, the continuing need for national security secrecy, inadequate records, and fallible human memories make reconstruction of events difficult. This is the situation in such relatively open societies as the United States, Canada, and the United Kingdom. In the closed societies of the Soviet Union and China, decision-making analysts have to rely mostly on speculation.

Other Theories

This chapter has offered a very modest survey of selected examples of prominent international relations theories. There are, of course, many other current attempts to figure out what is happening in the arena of world politics.

Content Analysis. Believing that real meanings are revealed whether the speaker is aware of it or not, some scholars are attempting to measure the "real" meaning by examining the choice of words in communications. Perhaps this is more of a technique than a formal theory, as one finds mathematical values being attached to parts of speech (nouns, adjectives, and so forth), word frequency being measured, and the wide use of computers in an attempt to evaluate more rigorously the substance of speeches by foreign diplomats, the content of the foreign press, and the like.

Game Theory. Game theory is based on two main considerations— the proposition that decisional situations in international relations are similar to those in games (e.g., chess, poker, bridge), and the hope that theories of gaming will offer a vehicle for laboratory testing of real-life situations. Closely linked with game theory is "simulation," the attempt to play out a real situation in mock surroundings as a test of game theories. A familiar example would be a model United Nations. More sophisticated examples would include the elaborate war games and strategy sessions conducted by the military and by various "think tank" institutes. Two prominent examples of the latter are the RAND Corporation in California and Hudson Institute in New York.

Conflict/Conflict Resolution. Much effort has been directed toward understanding human motivations, the sources of aggressive conduct, the dimensions of societal breakdown and upheaval, and the roles of different kinds of conflict management (e.g., mediation, deterrence, arms control, and disarmanent). Such studies overlap with psychology and sociology in searching for answers to such questions as "Why do people fight?" and "What causes revolutions?"

These questions are addressed in part in Chapter 4. It should perhaps be restated, however, that although this book accepts conflict as a part of social life and as a general organizing concept, no single conflict theory has been adopted here. As one leading study of international relations theories concludes: "At this time no single theory of conflict exists which is acceptable to social scientists in the several disciplines, much less to authorities in other scientific fields from which analogous concepts might be borrowed." [23]

Communications Theories. Scholars in this area probe the international flow of goods and services, the pattern of international political agreements, and other international contacts for clues explaining world politics. They are interested in such varied international transactions as student exchanges, treaties concluded, trade ratios, mail flow, reciprocal press coverage, and tourism in the belief that the level and kind of international contact is a significant index of the true nature of relations.

Integration Theories. This approach does not accept the nation-state as necessarily the ultimate and final stage of the world's political development. The world, after all, evolved into the nation-state system and may evolve beyond it. Scholars working in this area investigate the roots of the consensus-building that leads to the formation of political communities. They examine the nature of the integrative process in such areas as the creation of federal states and the formation of alliances.

There are still other theories, but this chapter has touched on the ones with which a beginning student should have at least a passing familiarity. A negative theory that has not been articulated (but one which might indeed become *the one* that is validated) is the

23 James E. Dougherty and Robert L. Pfaltzgraff, Jr., *Contending Theories of International Relations*, J. B. Lippincott Company, Philadelphia, 1971, p. 138.

assertion that international relations are not susceptible to theoretical organization. Perhaps human events are chaotic; they simply occur at random with neither rhyme nor reason. Theories don't have to promise the millenium in order to be posited. The goal of theory is to put forth propositions that can be proven or disproven. The nature of people and human history suggest that people are driven to come to terms with the universe—to understand it, to organize it, and to control it wherever possible. Sadly, that process has not always had commendable results, yet a failure even to try would be likely to bring an even worse result. The nature of the modern world, with its technological wizardry, awesome weaponry, environmental difficulties, and needy peoples, surely requires us to encourage attempts to understand ourselves. Finding an organizing theory for international relations is an exciting challenge. Part of the process of organizing our knowledge of modern international relations rests on an understanding of the historical context within which those relations developed—the subject of the following chapter.

BIBLIOGRAPHY

Allison, Graham T. *Essence of Decision: Explaining the Cuban Missile Crisis.* Little, Brown and Company, Boston, 1971.

Bobrow, Davis B. *International Relations: New Approaches.* The Free Press, New York, 1972.

Carr, Edward Hallett. *The Twenty-Years' Crisis, 1919–1939: An Introduction to the Study of International Relations.* Macmillan & Co., Ltd., London, 1939.

Coplin, William D. *Introduction to International Politics: A Theoretical Overview.* Markham Publishing Company, Chicago, 1971.

Deutsch, Karl, *The Analysis of International Relations.* Prentice-Hall, Inc., Englewood Cliffs, N.J., 1968.

Dougherty, James E., and Robert L. Pfaltzgraff, Jr. *Contending Theories of International Relations.* J. B. Lippincott Company, Philadelphia, 1971.

Farrell, R. Barry, ed. *Approaches to Comparative and International Politics.* Northwestern University Press, Evanston, Ill., 1966.

Garson, G. David. *Handbook of Political Science Methods.* Holbrook Press, Inc., Boston, 1971.

Graham, George J., and George W. Carey. *The Post-Behavioral Era: Perspectives on Political Science*. David McKay Company, Inc., New York, 1972.

Hoffmann, Stanley, ed. *Contemporary Theory in International Relations*. Prentice-Hall, Inc., Englewood Cliffs, N. J., 1960.

Jervis, Robert. *The Logic of Images in International Relations*. Princeton University Press, Princeton, N. J., 1970.

Kaplan, Morton A. *System and Process in International Politics*. John Wiley & Sons, Inc., New York, 1957.

————, ed. *New Approaches to International Relations*. St. Martin's Press, Inc., New York, 1968.

Knorr, Klaus, and James N. Rosenau, eds. *Contending Approaches to International Politics*. Princeton University Press, Princeton, N.J., 1969.

————, and Sidney Verba, eds. *International System: Theoretical Essays*. Princeton University Press, Princeton, N. J., 1961.

Lieber, Robert J. *Theory and World Politics*. Winthrop Publishers, Inc., Cambridge, Mass., 1972.

Mackinder, Halford J. *Democratic Ideals and Reality*. W. W. Norton & Company, Inc., New York, 1962.

Mahan, Alfred Thayer, *The Influence of Seapower Upon History, 1660–1783*. Little, Brown and Company, Boston, 1897.

McClelland, Charles A. *Theory and the International System*. The Macmillan Company, New York, 1966.

Morgan, Patrick M. *Theories and Approaches to International Politics: What Are We To Think?* Consensus Publishers, Inc., San Ramon, Calif., 1972.

Morgenthau, Hans J. *Politics Among Nations: The Struggle for Power and Peace*, 5th ed. Alfred A. Knopf, Inc., New York, 1973.

Mueller, John E., ed. *Approaches to Measurement in International Relations: A Non-Evangelical Survey*. Appleton-Century-Crofts, New York, 1969.

Rosecrance, Richard. *Action and Reaction in World Politics*. Little, Brown and Company, Boston, 1963.

Rosenau, James N., ed. *International Politics and Foreign Policy*, 2d ed. The Free Press, New York, 1969.

————, ed. *Linkage Politics*. The Free Press, New York, 1969.

Russell, Frank M. *Theories of International Relations*. Appleton-Century-Crofts, Inc., New York, 1936.

Simon, Julian L. *Basic Research Methods in Social Science: The Art of Empirical Investigation*. Random House, Inc., New York, 1969.

Singer, J. David, ed. *Quantitative International Politics*. The Free Press, New York, 1968.

Tanter, Raymond, and Richard H. Ullman. *Theory and Policy in International Relations*. Princeton University Press, Princeton, N.J., 1972.

Wolfers, Arnold. *Discord and Collaboration: Essays on International Politics*. The Johns Hopkins Press, Baltimore, 1965.

Wright, Quincy. *The Study of International Relations*. Appleton-Century-Crofts, Inc., New York, 1955.

Historical Context
of Present International
Relations

The study of modern international relations rests on the acceptance of the nation-state as the basic political unit in the world today. While much international intercourse occurs other than at the formal nation-state level (e.g., among individuals, corporations, and international organizations), the nation-state continues to dominate world politics as it has for over 300 years. Further, this situation is likely to continue indefinitely.

It is necessary, then, to consider the origins and emergence of the nation-state, what it represents, and the kind of international community that has developed because of it.

PREHISTORIC AND ANCIENT INTERNATIONAL RELATIONS

Prehistoric Times

The nation-state as we know it today did not exist until the Middle Ages, so in a technical sense "international" relations were impossible before that time. Realistically, however, we can well imagine that political activity involving international affairs was evident long ago—perhaps as early as among the first people on earth.

A landmark study of international relations, by Frank M. Russell, offers the following perspective:

International political thought in the strict sense may be regarded as including the reflections, speculations, ideas, and conclusions of men concerning the interrelations of the national states composing the modern international community. Broadly speaking, however, international political thought is as old as the existence of separate independent political communities, whether primitive tribes or ancient city-states and empires. Many of the institutions, practices, and ideas bearing on present-day international relations, commonly regarded as originating in the early modern period in Western Europe, were known to the ancients and were to be found in rudimentary form even among primitive peoples.[1]

Little is actually known about prehistoric people. There is no chronicle of their life. Scientists advance views on their nature based on fragmentary evidence left by their descendants and on observa-

1 Frank M. Russell, *Theories of International Relations*, Appleton-Century-Crofts, Inc., New York, 1936, p. 4.

tion of animal behavior. War seems to have been the primary form of alien contact, but there is no agreement about the causes of conflict—about whether early humans were naturally warlike or peaceful.

Political theorists and students of international relations are interested in this period for at least three reasons. First, we are constantly trying to uncover clues to the "true" nature of humanity, uninfluenced by civilization. Further, we are concerned with the reasons for and apparent impetus toward the formation of society —the very questions that such people as Hobbes and Locke were addressing. Third, there is a striking resemblance between the modern international situation and the primitive State of Nature. It is often suggested that modern nation-states coexist in a social system not unlike individuals in primitive society. If this comparison is valid, then at least two lines of inquiry suggest themselves. If we can figure out why and how primitive people were able to form a society, then we may find a way to integrate nation-states into a world community. Second, if we can identify patterns of interaction among primitive people, then we may simultaneously produce a theory to organize and explain international relations. Consequently, the modern anthropological study of primitive societies is of substantial interest to the study of international relations, at least from a theoretical standpoint.

China

A dominant fact in the history of ancient China was its virtual isolation from other states. Although the Chinese were aware of "barbarian" peoples around their borders, they regarded themselves as "the world," which the emperor ruled by the decree of Heaven. Foreign relations were simply not within their frame of reference. Consequently, as Frank M. Russell notes, "no systematic and comprehensive theory of interstate relations was developed in ancient China." [2] He writes further: "However, during the Golden Age of Chinese philosophy from about 530 B.C. to 23 B.C., when the various Chinese states within the empire flouted the central authority, assumed an attitude of virtual independence, and struggled with one another for mastery, certain fundamental precepts and many rules for interstate intercourse were laid down by the philosophers." [3]

2 *Ibid.*, p. 17.
3 *Ibid.*

Although Chinese sociopolitical philosophy was far from monolithic, the dominant tone was clearly set by the Chinese view of humanity and nature.[4] The Chinese saw nature as a grand, harmonious scheme in which people had a part. Nature was regarded as benevolent. Problems appeared only when people departed from the natural order of things. The phrase "being at one with the universe" epitomizes the Chinese view of the peaceful world. This view contrasts sharply with the Western Christian view, which has set the tone for modern international relations.

In the Western view, humanity, burdened with original sin, struggles constantly to master itself and the world. International relations, in the Western view, have reflected this struggle. The Chinese, on the other hand, started from the assumption of cosmic order and unity—an assumption based on both their philosophy and their geographical isolation. For the West, world order has not appeared as a given, but as a goal to be struggled toward by independent, warring political units. Even today, in spite of the passage of time and the turmoil of twentieth century ideology and politics, China and the West are still groping for a common understanding of world events, and their difficulty is due in no small measure to their different initial assumptions about humanity and nature.

India

Ancient India, particularly during the last few centuries before the birth of Christ, shows the first real sophistication in international relations with the development of techniques on how states should deal with one another. The Indian political situation was very different from that in China, which focused on unity. India was divided into many competing princely states, not unlike Italy during the 1400s and 1500s. This miniature world of independent states needed to develop accepted rules concerning aliens, ambassadors (including diplomatic privileges and immunities), and other forms of international conduct.

It should come as no surprise that a Machiavelli should appear in both the Indian and the Italian worlds, offering advice to rulers on the best way to further the interests of the state vis-à-vis other states.

---

4 See, for example, the Confucian, Taoist, Mo Ti, and Legalist schools of thought described in *ibid.*, chap. II.

The Indian adviser was a man named Kautilya, the prime minister of Emperor Chandragupta. Kautilya was the apparent author of the *Arthaśāstra* (*Treatise on Polity*), which appeared about 300 B.C.[5] The *Arthaśāstra*, although primarily concerned with internal state politics, offers what is probably the first comprehensive discussion of international relations.

Kautilya describes a "circle of states." These states are either attracted toward one another as friends or repelled as enemies, depending on their respective locations on the circle. Kautilya's "Doctrine of Mandala" teaches that adjacent states will be natural enemies because they have the largest potential area of disagreement. As an aside, this is an interesting proposition. The motto of the United Nations Educational, Scientific and Cultural Organization (UNESCO) is "War Begins in the Minds of Men." Presumably then, the road to peace is to learn more about one another, to bring ourselves closer together. Yet the Doctrine of Mandala appears to be saying that the farther apart we are, the likelier we are to have peace. History's most vicious wars have been fought between countries that were really quite close culturally and geographically.[6] The Doctrine of Mandala is also supported by crime statistics, which reveal that in most murders the murderer and victim know one another. Lest we think we have uncovered an iron law of politics, however, we should also consider the peaceful cases of the United States and Canada or of Switzerland and all its neighbors.

The *Arthaśāstra* goes on to outline the seven basic elements of the state, which, with due recognition of historical changes, sound very much like the elements of power the realists discussed in Chapter 2 were concerned with. These seven elements are: (1) the king, (2) ministers, (3) territory, (4) fortresses, (5) treasury, (6) army, and (7) allies. These seven elements were the basis of diplomacy, in which the role of the king was to use the other elements to improve the position of his state within the circle. His courses of action were (1) peace, (2) war, (3) equilibrium, (4) attack, (5) resignation to the protection of another, or (6) alliance-making. While this theory of international relations is very simplistic, it bears a striking resemblance to the things discussed in Chapter 2. This suggests either that the ancient Indians were ahead of their time or, alternatively, that

5 A. L. Basham, *The Wonder That Was India*, Grove Press, Inc., New York, 1954, pp. 50 and 79.
6 James Paul Wesley, "Frequency of Wars and Geographical Opportunity," *Journal of Conflict Resolution*, 6 (1962), 387–389.

we have not come very far in refining our knowledge of international relations.

Greece and Rome

From the standpoint of international relations, the world of the ancient Greeks almost represents a combination of the Chinese and Indian experiences. The Greeks tended to view the outside world as a barbaric no man's land much as the Chinese had, but the fragmented internal structure of the Hellenic world, divided up into city-states, greatly resembled India. As a matter of fact, the Greek world very much resembled a miniature version of the modern international community. As one observer notes,

[The] inability of Greek statesmen to develop a spirit of regional unity within the Hellenic circle was due to the strong sense of local patriotism developed within the city-states. The very forces of creative imagination which led to the development of the highest civilization that the world had yet known led to concentration upon the national interests of the separate states. The emphasis upon the character of the individual man, upon "humanity," which made possible the leadership of Greece in the civilized world, which produced works of literature and of art that became a standard for subsequent generations, tended to create rival communities, isolated from one another by the intenseness of their own small circle. To the Greek city-state independence played the same part it has played in our own times. If they had had the word *sovereignty* they would have used it.

Owing to the peculiar city-state organization of ancient Greece, the system of international law developed there bears a closer relation to that of modern times than does the international law of any subsequent period down to the year 1648.[7]

Unfortunately, however, the Greeks never produced any real theory on how relations among the city-states should be conducted. Writers like Plato and Aristotle were primarily concerned with people and the internal dimensions of the city-state. They addressed themselves to such problems as justice and harmony within the state, apparently considering the city-state complete in itself. While the Greeks were inward-looking, this should not obscure the fact that they made some contributions to the development of international

7 Charles Fenwick, *International Law*, 4th ed., Appleton-Century-Crofts, Inc., New York, 1965, pp. 6–7.

relations, such as arbitration (the practice of two disputing rulers going to a third for a binding decision) and asylum (although the practice of asylum was highly influenced by religion).

Ancient Rome, on the other hand, made an intriguing and mixed contribution to international relations thinking. Before Rome came to dominate the Mediterranean, its conduct of international relations was similar to that of the Greek city-states—as an equal among equals. During that period, rules of international conduct were evolved concerning treaties, diplomatic privileges and immunities, and rules of warfare. As the power of Rome grew, however, its treatment of others became increasingly arrogant. Finally an empire was built. The Roman Empire lasted from 27 B.C. to 476 A.D., when the rule of the last Roman emperor in the West ended.

The legacy of Rome for modern international relations is at least fourfold. First is *the concept of one world.* Roman legions marched off to conquer the known world, to give it a sense of unity it has not known since. That legacy is a mixed blessing. On the one hand it has fostered the almost romantic notion of "one world." This notion has virtually become an idea of a paradise lost—a notion that deserves further scrutiny. We accept almost as a given the view that the world should be one, yet we never seem to question whether world unity is necessarily good in and of itself. Will it, for example, ensure peace? Provide for the continuance of Danish cultural identity and language? Make the Russians more reasonable? On the other hand, the example of the Roman Empire has left us with the impression that the only way to unify the world is to go out and conquer everybody else. The actions of Napoleon and Hitler suggest that this impression is still common, as do the plots of the many books in which someone is always trying to take over the world.

A second legacy of the Roman Empire is *a view or theory of peace.* The great *Pax Romana,* the Peace of Rome, lasted from 27 B.C. to 180 A.D. It was a peace made possible largely by Rome's legions, but it was nonetheless peace. Imperial Rome dominated the "world," the empire was relatively free of troubles, and there was general prosperity. The period has been regarded as a Golden Age by those who see nationalism and the modern nation-state as the source of much of the turmoil in international relations. The key to peace is unity, even if that unity is rammed down our throats. There was speculation at the time of the American monopoly of the atomic bomb that here was a unique opportunity in history. For the first time since the Roman Empire, someone had the power to conquer everybody else. There was talk of a *Pax Atomica* or a *Pax Americana.* Some believed that because of the Rosenbergs,[8] pure historical blunder, or other reasons, the United States forfeited this unique opportunity, for the Soviet Union soon had the Bomb as well. A careful look at the post-World War II world indicates that there would have been very real limitations on any American attempt to overexploit its nuclear advantage, but the notion of a missed opportunity continues to find supporters. Those who believe in Marxist dynamics and the promise of a world-wide proletarian revolution have also suggested a possible *Pax Sovietica* as the ultimate hope for a unified world. Whatever the ideology, the pervading theme is that peace is possible only under a world government of some sort.

Governments and societies are based on myths. What counts is not so much reality as the perception of reality, which is colored by lack of communication and awareness, ideology, culture, or other belief structures. For this reason it is easy to see in the Roman experience the lessons one wants to see, to accept the myth of the *Pax Romana* while disregarding the huge military machine, bloodshed, and economic cost that made this peace possible. The vision of peace through conquest is undoubtedly an illusion. One scholar makes the following observation of ancient Rome:

If there was one primary factor which operated more than others to accomplish the downfall of Roman civilization it was imperialism. Nearly all of the troubles which beset the country were traceable in some measure to the conquest of a great empire.[9]

If there is an enduring political lesson in all the conquests, revolutions, and coups in history, it is that the mere seizure of control does not necessarily bring a concomitant ability to govern, or indeed make society more governable. Bringing the entire world under one political authority would not guarantee that the Golden Age of the *Pax Romana* could be reinstated, although this vision of peace continues to be tempting.

8 Julius and Ethel Rosenberg were found guilty in 1951 of betraying U.S. atomic secrets to the Soviet Union, thus ending the apparent American monopoly of the "ultimate" weapon. They were executed by the U.S. government on June 19, 1953.
9 Edward McNall Burns, *Western Civilizations: Their History and Culture,* 5th ed., W. W. Norton & Company, Inc., New York, 1958, p. 233.

A third legacy of ancient Rome is *the concept of the primacy of law.* Whatever assessment might be made of Rome's trampling of the aspirations of other peoples in the Mediterranean area, its pompous arrogance, or even its unbridled internal absolutism during the latter period of the Empire (284 A.D. to 476 A.D.), an undeniable Roman contribution was the idea that the best way to run things is through some form of legal system.

The Romans developed three great branches of law: *ius naturale* (natural law, based on philosophical assumptions about the rational order of nature), *ius civile* (the civil law, governing Rome and its citizens), and *ius gentium* (the law of peoples, which held that there are legal norms binding on all people regardless of nationality). The *ius gentium* is a forerunner of modern international law, which accepts the idea of the legal ordering of the relationships among nation-states. The value of this line of thinking is that it makes human affairs and conflicts susceptible to legal control. Reference to some standard of conduct (e.g., law) becomes at least an option for the nonviolent resolution of conflict.

A fourth Roman legacy concerns *terminology.* At first glance this might appear to be a heritage of minimum importance, yet the way in which a people label and refer to their world reveals much about their thought processes and perception of that world. Although this is often not recognized by the average citizen, Western civilization owes a tremendous debt in this context to the Romans. The most obvious and commonly known example is the legal terminology that the Western world inherited from the Romans. An important and currently relevant (especially in this age of ecological concern) international example of the terminology legacy is the concept of *res communis* (a common, or public, thing) and *res nullius* (a thing belonging to no one). These two terms relate to the Roman conception of property, in which every thing (*res*) was placed into some property classification.

The law was based on the proposition that all things initially belonged to no one (*res nullius*), but as human history progressed and people came to terms with their environment, virtually everything on the earth ended up being owned by someone. Exceptions were fish, fowl, and wild animals, which were things resistant to ownership, although they could be claimed by someone who could capture them. The thrust of the *res nullius* concept is that no one owns the item in question—it is there for the taking. This was a doctrine that perhaps made sense in an era of relative abundance and limited ability to exploit nature. Nowadays the *res nullius* idea has obvious difficulties for the international community as a hungry world sends massive whaling and fishing fleets to the far corners of the globe and seems unable to regulate its exploitation.

For those areas not apparently susceptible to occupation at all, the Roman jurists devised the concept of *res communis*, or community property, open to use by all. In this category were such things as air, running water, and the sea. To take just the example of the sea, it is easy to understand how the Romans could regard it as a common resource for all—no country had the national power or the technological base to lay a meaningful claim to it. Even the pretentious Spanish and Portuguese attempts to divide up the oceans in the fifteenth and sixteenth centuries were brushed aside. The twentieth century world, however, is technologically capable of making a major move to exploit the sea, and is urged on to do so by the pressure of dwindling resources. Many nations are insisting that the sea and the seabed are now *res nullius*, capable of occupation.

To prevent an "Oklahoma land-grab" mentality from taking over as nations race to beat others to new claims, a session of the United Nations Conference on the Law of the Sea met in 1974 in Caracas, Venezuela, followed by another session in Geneva, Switzerland, in 1975. Those nations attempting to support the *res communis* idea spoke of the sea and its resources as the "common heritage of mankind" that should be used for the common benefit of all nations. In contrast, nations wanting to extend national jurisdiction into the ocean depths acted in the spirit of *res nullius*. While that conference was not particularly conclusive, it does provide a modern example of the persistent relevance of legal terms and concepts inherited from the Romans, for the discussions in Caracas and Geneva were based on concepts articulated by Roman jurists.

EMERGENCE OF THE NATION-SYSTEM

Holy Roman Empire

The Roman Empire, whose decline had begun at least two centuries earlier, finally collapsed in 476 A.D. when the rule of the last of the Western emperors, Romulus Augustus, ended and a barbarian chieftain assumed the title of King of Rome.

The tremendous impact of the Roman Empire on both the spirit and substance of subsequent international relations has already been acknowledged. Imitation is the ultimate form of flattery, however, and much of subsequent European history has involved attempts to duplicate the Roman achievement of unifying the known world under a single political authority.

The Eastern division of the Roman Empire (or the Byzantine Empire), with its capital at Constantinople, continued for a time as a successor state after the fall of the Western Empire. But Byzantine claims to universality were ended by the rise of Charlemagne's empire in the West. Charlemagne was seen by some as the new Caesar, and his coronation as a Roman emperor by Pope Leo III in 800 A.D. appeared to mark the rebirth of the Western Roman Empire. Charlemagne's empire, however, hardly survived him; it was carved up by the Treaty of Verdun in 843 A.D. The great universal empire of the Caesars seemed doomed to disintegrate into thousands of feudal units, but another major attempt to retrieve the lost empire was soon made by the Saxon king Otto the Great. His military and political activities resulted in his being crowned Roman emperor in 962 A.D. by Pope John XII, thus launching formally the political entity known as the Holy Roman Empire. Although the boundaries changed during its history, the Holy Roman Empire included roughly the German states, Austria, Switzerland, northern Italy, Bohemia, Moravia, Belgium, and the Netherlands.

A long succession of emperors tried to gain some semblance of control over this realm, but Voltaire's famous quip to the effect that it was neither holy, Roman, nor an empire was a fair assessment. Real political control was in the hands of feudal lords and kings, who were constantly intriguing against one another. The formal demise of the Holy Roman Empire, which had long since become a political fiction, was brought about by Napoleon when Francis II renounced the imperial title in 1806. In the meantime the Byzantine Empire had also ceased to exist with the fall of Constantinople to the Turks in 1453—giving rise, incidently to a claim by Ivan III of Russia to the imperial title and subsequent tzarist visions of Moscow as the "Third Rome." The imperial dream is not dead, as the relatively recent actions of Hitler and Mussolini make clear, yet there are strong countervailing forces to efforts at empire building—in particular, nationalism, sovereignty, and the idea of the nation-state. The appearance or at least a crystallization of these forces in the West can be seen very clearly in the events surrounding the Thirty Years' War.

Thirty Years' War and the Peace of Westphalia

One has to use a certain amount of caution with "watershed" dates in history. Often these dates serve the analytical convenience of the historian as much as they represent a real change in world events. The Peace of Westphalia (1648) is a convenient starting point for the nation-state, but in fact it simply recognized forces that had been in the making for some time.

The incident that sparked the Thirty Years' War (1618–1648) was a dispute between the Holy Roman Emperor, Matthias, and the Czechs over the filling of a vacancy on the Bohemian throne. Protestantism and Czech nationalist sentiment were strong, and there was substantial resentment of the Catholic Austrian Habsburg domination of Bohemia in the name of the empire, which had gone on for a century. Imperial pressure to place one of Matthias' kinsmen on the Bohemian throne infuriated Czech leaders, who, in an act of defiance, inflicted the famous 1618 Prague "defenestration" on two of the emperor's representatives and a secretary at Hradčany Castle. Defenestration was a Czech method of expressing anger; the word means throwing out the window. All the victims survived their fall from the castle window unhurt by landing in a pile of manure, but the incident provoked the long series of wars known as the Thirty Years' War, fought mainly on German territory. Catholic Habsburg success in putting down the Czechs drew Protestant rulers in northern Europe into the war, and soon "anybody who was anybody" in Europe at the time became involved in what still remains one of Europe's more destructive wars.

Untangling the true motivating factors behind wars is always a tricky business, but there seem to be at least three forces involved in the Thirty Years' War, all of some significance to the study of international relations. One cause of the conflict was growing Czech nationalism. Nationalism, which was still a relatively new phenomenon, would subsequently come into full bloom in Napoleon's France. A second element in the conflict was religion. During the war, at one time or another, the Catholic Habsburgs and Bavaria were against Protestant Bohemia, the north German states, Denmark, Sweden, and (Catholic) France. England aided the Protestants on the side. Whether religion was indeed a motivating factor or simply a cover for political machinations is a question that need not be discussed here. In any case, the wars were a test of the influence of religion (and in particular of the unifying force of the Papacy) on international politics. Gustavus Adolphus, the brilliant Swedish king and military tactician, spoke of Sweden's role in the war as one of "freeing our oppressed religious brethren from the claws of the Pope." [10] A third issue in the conflict, one that explains why Catholic France aided the Protestants, was simple realpolitik (or power politics) and the maneuvering for political advantage. The Bourbons of France had long vied with the Habsburgs for dominance in Europe. The French, under the guidance of Cardinal Richelieu, perceived the war as a chance to break Habsburg power and advance Bourbon interests.

Whatever the causes of the Thirty Years' War, its ultimate significance is perhaps more important, even if nobody really won and even if the war was not really a crucial turning point in history. Of peripheral interest was the fact that Sweden's hopes of becoming a major power reached their zenith. Further, although the war cost the Swedish king Gustavus Adolphus his life, his contributions to military science were historic. On a more basic level, the real influence of the Pope on European (world) politics was ended. The rebellion of Protestant princes against the alleged unity of the Christian Commonwealth was resolved in favor of the doctrine of *cuius regio eius religio*. This principle, established earlier in the Religious Peace of Augsburg (1555), was reconfirmed. It provided that each lord could determine the religion of his or her subjects (dissidents had the right to emigrate, forfeiting their possessions). This settlement both explains the patchwork of religious communities in modern Germany and represents the breaking of papal power in classical European politics.

The Peace of Westphalia, which ended the Thirty Years' War, was in fact two treaties signed in the cities of Osnabrück and Münster after lengthy, tortuous negotiations (which should give a worthwhile perspective on the long negotiations in Paris over the winding down of the American involvement in the Vietnam conflict, which spent so much time on such things as the shape of the conference table). It was a landmark in international organization diplomacy— a subject for later chapters.

Finally, perhaps the most significant effect of the Peace of Westphalia was the splintering of the Holy Roman Empire (and of

10 Gerhard Geissler, *Europäische Dokumente aus fünf Jahrhunderten*, Esche Verlag G.m.b.H., Leipzig, 1939, p. 146.

Europe) into political entities that would develop into modern nation-states. The peace was a legal recognition of states (indeed, two states—Switzerland and the Netherlands—were created by it) and of the state system, both of which have been major factors in subsequent international relations for over three hundred years. One noted authority on international law, Leo Gross, makes this assessment of the Westphalian settlement:

The Peace of Westphalia, for better or worse, marks the end of an epoch and the opening of another. It represents the majestic portal which leads from the old into the new world. The old world, we are told, lived in the idea of a Christian commonwealth, of a world harmoniously ordered and governed in the spiritual and temporal realms by the Pope and Emperor.

.   .   .

In the spiritual field the Treaty of Westphalia was said to be "a public act of disregard of the international authority of the Papacy." In the political field it marked man's abandonment of the idea of a hierarchial structure of society and his option for a new system characterized by the coexistence of a multiplicity of states, each sovereign within its territory, equal to one another, and free from any external earthly authority. The idea of an authority or organization above the sovereign states is no longer. What takes its place is the notion that all states form a world-wide political system or that, at any rate, the states of Western Europe form a single political system. This new system rests on international law and the balance of power, a law operating between rather than above states and a power operating between rather than above states.[11]

Professor Gross goes on to cite Lord Bryce's observation that the Peace of Westphalia "did no more than legalize a condition of things already in existence, but which, by being legalized, acquired new importance."[12] The legal and political structure of the modern world was influenced by the Westphalian settlement. The givens on which we must base our understanding of current international relations stem from that settlement and its aftermath. Consequently, we need to understand the idea of the state and its role in world politics vis-à-vis other states.

11 Leo Gross, "The Peace of Westphalia, 1648–1948," *American Journal of International Law*, 42 (January 1948), 28–29.
12 *Ibid.*, p. 34, citing James Bryce, *The Holy Roman Empire*, rev. ed., 1866, p. 372.

ELEMENTS OF THE MODERN STATE

Three terms need clarification at the outset: "nation," "state," and "nation-state." Although the use of these terms in the literature of international relations, and especially in the popular media, is hardly consistent, their proper meaning is worth at least noting in passing. "Nation," although often used interchangeably with "state," is really a cultural term. It refers to a body of people united by a common sense of identity and shared values against "outsiders." This unity is usually based on such cultural factors as shared group history, language, religion, ethnic homogeneity, and common customs.

The term "state," on the other hand, refers to both a political idea and a composite legal entity that exists under international law. Presumably the term "nation-state" refers to a cultural unit, a "nation," whose boundaries are the same as the politico-legal boundaries of a "state"—a condition not often found in modern politics. The state of Yugoslavia, for example, is made up of several identifiable national groups (e.g., Serbs, Croats, Macedonians), while Germanic culture extends beyond the political boundaries of either West or East Germany to Austria, Switzerland, Luxembourg, and elsewhere. Nationalism—a strong sense of cultural identity and group membership—is often apt to take the form of actively trying to make national and state boundaries the same where they currently are not. Two examples are Hitler's efforts to bring Austria, the Sudetenland, and other "German" areas into the Reich, and the Ibos' unsuccessful attempt in 1968 to break away from Nigeria and form their own new state of Biafra.

One other term that deserves mention in passing is "inter*national*" relations. Purists might wish to argue that the term is used to refer to what are really inter*state* relations. The term "inter*national*" stems from the period when relations were primarily between nations, before the evolution of the state. Too much fussiness with definitional detail serves no real purpose here, however, as modern popular usage of all the terms just discussed is inconsistent and interchangeable. The primary purpose in calling attention to the more technical meanings of each term is simply to help the beginning student to understand them better.

To return to a closer look at the political and legal dimensions of the state, probably the first political theorist to describe the political essence of the modern state was Niccolò Machiavelli (1469–1527) in his celebrated treatise *The Prince*. He wrote in the context of independent and equal city-states in northern Italy, all engaged in intrigue against one another. The state (a term which Machiavelli apparently coined—*stato*) became both the organizing vehicle for survival in a hostile world and the instrument for aggrandizement vis-à-vis other states. In fact, *The Prince* is primarily advice to Italian rulers on how to establish and maintain a state. Interpretations of the true meaning of *The Prince* vary, but "Machiavellian" has become a synonym for amoral politics in the search for power for its own sake. Unfortunately, the Machiavellian image of power politics in interstate relations has become so lodged in people's minds that it often dominates the way in which we view the world.

The legal basis of the modern state under international law rests on the following four elements.

More or Less Permanent Population. Nomadic tribes are not sufficient; there must be a stable population base to support the existence of a state. However, there appears to be no minimum population needed to create a new state, as many modern microstates readily demonstrate. For example, the population of São Tomé and Príncipe, admitted to the United Nations as a new member in 1975, is around 70,000—slightly less than that of Great Falls, Montana.

Defined Territory. Many scholars see the real genesis of the state in the growth of the concept of territoriality. John Herz, for example, links the notion of the "territorial state" with the so-called gunpowder revolution of the Middle Ages.[13] A basic human and social consideration has always been security. This need could be provided for in the Middle Ages by nobility and their armies protected within castle walls, usually on a hilltop. Small villages surrounded these castles, and farmers headed out each day to tend their fields. Land was not militarily important; its only virtue was to provide crops, which farmers would gather up hastily as they rushed to the safety of the castle when danger threatened. Invading armies could burn and pillage whatever was left behind, but laying siege to the castle fortress was usually their major offensive weapon. With the

13 John Herz, "Rise and Demise of the Territorial State," *World Politics,* 9 (July 1957), 473–493.

introduction of gunpowder, however, John Herz argues, the "hard outer shell" of security had to be shifted from the castle wall to broader state boundaries. Now that it was possible to get blasted off the hilltop, territory became important as the first line of defense—and consequently a basic element of the state.

The territorial view of the genesis of the state is, of course, only one explanation. The origin of the state is lost in history, but it was probably the result of a variety of factors. These factors probably included the emergence of dynamic leadership, favorable agricultural or other geographical (and climatical) factors fostering the growth of a societal base, military dynamics of defense and conquest, specialization of labor, religious unity and the emergence of shamans as rulers, family growth and natural cohesion, and the simple administrative exigencies of controlling expanding group interaction when a number of people start congregating somewhere.

Organized Government. Some agency must have the ability to represent the people and the territory, both internally and abroad. From the standpoint of the international community, this government does not necessarily have to have a claim to moral legitimacy (although new states invariably assert such claims) or a democratic mandate to rule. The major legal prerequisite is that the government can claim organized control. In this regard, there is an element of some relevance to statehood that is really a fifth basic element—*recognition.*

An entity claiming to be a state must, in addition to the four basic legal requirements, be recognized as a state by the established states. Experts disagree on whether the act of recognition brings the new state into legal existence or whether it merely recognizes the new state as an accomplished legal fact. Nevertheless, recognition extended by an established state to a claimant entity is an individual matter between those two and does not hinge on what other states, or the United Nations, might do. For example, as of this writing the United States government does not recognize North Vietnam's claim to statehood, although North Vietnam is recognized by other states (primarily the communist bloc). Admission of North Vietnam to the United Nations as a new state would have no effect on U.S. recognition policy (although the United States, as a permanent member of the U.N. Security Council, would have the option of casting a veto against U.N. membership for North Vietnam). One state's failure to recognize another's claim to statehood (for whatever political reasons) is simply a refusal to enter into the normal range of international relations (e.g., exchange of diplomats or economic agreements) made possible through formal recognition.

Sovereignty. This fourth basic element of statehood is probably one of the more controversial and sensitive terms in international relations.[14] It is a myth-shrouded and emotionally charged political term that remains at the heart of what the state *is*. We are told that all states are sovereign and equal, yet even a casual observer can see that some states are clearly "more sovereign and equal" than others in their international relations. Some states insist that their sovereignty is being violated through economic imperialism, while in other states there are cries that national sovereignty is being undermined by joining the United Nations or by the lack of proper attention to defense expenditures. Unfortunately, as John Stoessinger so aptly notes in this regard, "it is very difficult, if not impossible, to discover where and in whom this sovereignty is actually vested." [15] The reason for this, of course, is that sovereignty is basically an abstraction that defies precise definition. Because it is so basic to an understanding of modern international relations, a brief survey is necessary of what sovereignty has generally meant, both in the past and today.

NATURE OF SOVEREIGNTY

Sovereignty as a social fact existed long before a legal concept of sovereignty was formulated. Sovereignty really stems from that period in ancient history when more than one state existed (defining "state" loosely). The rulers of such early states as Egypt, Greece, Persia, and Carthage possessed supreme power over a given territory and populace and were independent of any external power.

14 Material for this discussion on sovereignty is taken from Forest Grieves, *Supranationalism and International Adjudication,* University of Illinois Press, Urbana, 1969, chap. 1, and is used with the kind permission of the University of Illinois Press.
15 John G. Stoessinger, *The Might of Nations: World Politics in Our Time,* rev. ed., Random House, Inc., New York, 1965, p. 250.

Romans

The term "sovereignty" did not really develop until the Middle Ages; however, a rather precise legal concept of sovereignty was apparently used by the Romans. Marek Korowicz cites as an example the Roman legal concept of independence as stated by Proculus: "that nation is free which is not subject to any government of any other nation." [16] He notes the terms *liber* and *libertas*, which, although they mean "independent" and "independence," correspond exactly in meaning to "sovereign" and "sovereignty."

Middle Ages

The idea of sovereignty as the supreme power of the state arose during the Middle Ages. Bertrand de Jouvenel sees the growth of the concept of sovereignty as an answer to the "primordial character of the problem of who decides." [17] In the medieval period, it was the church that first solved this problem by its concentration of power in the spiritual realm. This plenitude of authority in a single office, de Jouvenel suggests, served as a model for the growth of sovereignty in the temporal realm.

The doctrine of sovereignty developed in the temporal realm as a principle of national unity. Kings sought to develop, during and after the decline of the church, strong national states and to bring under their centralized control the various elements of local authority.

Credit for the first systematic formulation of the doctrine of sovereignty belongs to Jean Bodin, who outlined the concept of the supreme power (*summa potestas, majestas,* or *suprema potestas*) of the state in his *Les Six Livres de la République* (1576). As France at this time was torn by a civil war, Bodin concluded that only a strong central authority could preserve order. This strong central authority was the "principal foundation of every State"; there could be no state without sovereignty, which is "the absolute and perpetual power of a State." [18]

16 Marek Korowicz, "Some Present Aspects of Sovereignty in International Law," *Recueil des Cours,* 102 (1961), 7.
17 Bertrand de Jouvenel, *Sovereignty: An Enquiry into the Political Good,* University of Chicago Press, Chicago, 1957, p. 4.
18 *De Republica,* L. I, IX, p. 125. Cited by Korowicz, p. 8.

Bodin was really concerned only with the concept of sovereignty *within* a state; however, since the sovereign is the single source from which all laws originate, a logical extrapolation is that the sovereign is not only above the law but independent of restrictions, internal or external. The Roman conception of sovereignty contained no limitations on the state's independence (*libertas*). Bodin's seemingly absolute sovereign, however, was subject to very substantial limitations. Bodin's doctrine of sovereignty can be summarized by the following points:

1 Sovereignty is the essence of the state.

2 The sovereign possesses supreme power over the territory and its inhabitants, unrestrained by any earthly law or power.

3 This supreme power is limited only by:

a Divine law.

b A sovereign's own obligations toward other sovereigns or toward individuals.

4 A sovereign should observe agreements made with other states.[19]

Later Views

The foregoing summary shows that Bodin linked his idea of sovereignty with a broader idea of a world community ruled by natural law. He made sovereignty essentially a principle of internal political order. Some subsequent writers, however, saw sovereignty instead as a principle of international disorder. The classic example is found in Hobbes' *Leviathan*, in which interstate relationships are similar to those of people in the State of Nature, characterized by war of every person against every person. Another classic example is Emerich de Vattel's *The Law of Nations*. He notes:

Nations being composed of men naturally free and independent, and who, before the establishment of civil society, lived together in the state of nature,—Nations, or sovereign states, are to be considered as so many free persons living together in the state of nature. But the body of the Nation, the State, remains absolutely free and independent with respect to all other men, and all "other" Nations, as long as it has not voluntarily submitted to them.[20]

19 See Korowicz, pp. 8–9.
20 Emerich de Vattel, *The Law of Nations*, new edition by Joseph Chitty, London, 1834, pp. I and V.

In modern terms, it must be noted that there are divergent views on the juridical meaning of sovereignty as well as on its location and consequences. It is, however, true that in many respects Bodin's formulation of sovereignty is probably the predominant concept held today, although there have been and still are many divergent concepts. For the purposes of our study, sovereignty can be defined (following Bodin) simply as the supreme power of the state over its populace and territory, independent of any external authority.

The object here is not to establish a strict juridical definition of sovereignty or to explore its many shades of meaning in legal and political theory. Rather, a simple working definition of sovereignty (naturally with due acknowledgment of the problems surrounding the use of the term) should be sufficient to give the perspective needed to understand what the concept has meant to the nation-state in the past and what it is likely to mean to international relations in the future.

Sovereignty, then, symbolizes one of the most basic assumptions of international relations—the authority of the state to act independently. This does not mean, however, that the sovereign state is free from obligations to its own citizens or to other states, or that the exercise of this sovereignty cannot be restricted. Korowicz uses the terms "qualitative" and "quantitative" to describe restrictions on sovereignty.[21] Unless a state is a dependent entity (such as occupied Germany), its sovereignty remains "qualitatively" unchanged. Yet every state is subject to certain "quantitative" limitations on its sovereignty that do not destroy the basic sovereign character of that state. The nature of these restrictions is outlined below.

LIMITATIONS OF SOVEREIGNTY

Quantitative restrictions come from two different but interrelated sources: the nature of world politics and voluntary submission to restrictions.

Nature of World Politics

A very significant limitation of state sovereignty has been effected by developments (perhaps inevitable and often quite unrelated to

21 Korowicz, pp. 8–9.

politics) in the past three hundred years of world history. Some of these developments are the following.

Decline of the State. The real basis of sovereignty is the territorial state, which became the basic sovereign unit (that is, the basic political unit) in international relations for a very practical reason. Sovereigns could hold only as much land as they could control and defend; conversely, people are only willing to recognize, in the long run, the authority that can protect them. After the breakdown of the feudal system, only the compact territorial state could provide such protection. There is much to suggest, however, that the concept of the territorial state is no longer meaningful. John Herz, for example, links the decline of the territorial state with the beginning of the nineteenth century.[22] This has come about because the hard outer shell of the state (that is, its territorial limits) is no longer impenetrable, mostly because of technology, communications, industrialization, and weapons.

Proliferation of Sovereign Nations. The number of nations has increased so rapidly (particularly in recent years) that an increasingly large number of sovereign states are forced to coexist. The existence of so many sovereign states has imposed many practical limitations on sovereign prerogatives. As far as the actual practice of states is concerned, Clyde Eagleton holds the following view:

No state since ... [the Peace of Westphalia] has ever been wholly independent. Sovereignty presumed omnipotence, but there can only be one highest, and such a situation has not been found since the fall of the ancient universal empires.... States are only relatively independent [and] domestic law is constantly subordinated to international law.... Sovereignty has now been replaced by responsibility, and the word now means, in its external sense, nothing more than the sphere of relative independence and exclusive jurisdiction reserved to it with the assent of the community, and limited by that community.[23]

Figure 3-1 shows this modified view of sovereignty in the modern state, in which the proliferation of states and their mutual expressions of sovereignty in fact limit sovereign prerogatives.

22 Herz, pp. 473–493.
23 Clyde Eagleton, *International Government*, rev. ed., The Ronald Press Company, New York, 1948, pp. 25–26.

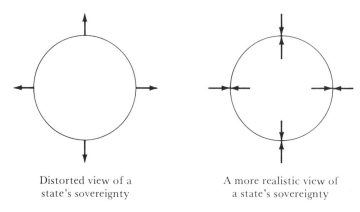

Distorted view of a
state's sovereignty

A more realistic view of
a state's sovereignty

FIGURE 3-1. The Modern Sovereign State

Rising Human Demands. Not only does the fact that nation-states are stumbling over one another when they attempt various courses of action indicate some limitations on sovereignty, but the mere closeness of quarters creates common problems, problems that do not stop at territorial boundaries. Increases in population and advances in technology are forcing nations to be interdependent. There are rising human demands for solutions to such common problems as disease, economic depression, pollution, or mere ease of communications—demands which one state alone cannot meet. This has increased the importance of international organizations as well as of individual persons in international relations.

Cooperation versus Intervention. The interdependence of states has also brought with it many problems never envisaged by the seventeenth century impenetrable sovereign states. Interdependence has made possible the economic blockade and ideological-political penetration. But even where friendly interstate cooperation has been the goal, dependence (e.g., economic vassalage) and outright intervention have developed. Many economic cooperation programs, even of the most general sort, result in a greater degree of intervention in the affairs of the recipient state than even a loose interpretation of full sovereignty would allow. As a brief example, in the well-known Point IV Program (Title IV of the Act for International Development, June 5, 1960, 64 *Stat.* 204 as amended), the granting of American funds was made conditional on American supervision and the observance, in the use of these funds, of certain American basic principles of fair labor standards, wages and working conditions, and management-labor relations.

New Concept of War. The *ius ad bellum*, the right to make war, has always been a sovereign prerogative and an instrument of national policy. The main objective of war has always been the attainment of greater security, power, glory, or wealth. It still made sense for Prussia to make war on France in 1870, or for Japan to make war on Russia in 1904. General destructiveness aside, one might even argue that war still had some vestige of meaning as late as 1945, but the advent of atomic weapons has wrought a profound change. Total war, though not impossible, is for all purposes of *rational* national policy prohibited.

B. V. A. Rölling sees two major functions of war as being affected by its "prohibition": (1) the function of war according to von Clausewitz (war as the continuation of politics by other means, that is, war in order to promote national interests and to change the existing legal position) and (2) the function of war according to Hugo Grotius (that is, war as the means of maintaining law).[24] Rölling may be overstating his case, but one fact stands out clearly: although states can and do use their atomic arsenals as "persuaders" in international politics, or use "limited wars" (with all the implications of possible escalation) as instruments of policy, the deadly seriousness of such action has a limiting effect on sovereignty that did not exist prior to 1945. Because of this, the smaller nations, because of their lack of atomic responsibility, are often more sovereign than the larger nations.

New International Actors. Partly because of many of the foregoing factors, new international actors, possessing some of the rights previously held exclusively by states, have appeared. In classic international law states have been the only true international actors (and they still are the only *full* members of the international community), yet today a more important role for individuals, multinational corporations, and international organizations is emerging in international relations. For example, there are two different ways to interpret the role of the sovereign state vis-à-vis the individual. In the words of Quincy Wright, one can

---

24 B. V. A. Rölling, *International Law in an Expanded World*, Djambatan, Amsterdam, 1960, pp. xix-xx.

interpret the state as sovereign, protecting or punishing individuals in its own interest under such guidance as it chooses to accept from international law, but it is also possible to interpret the individual as a jural personality with rights under international law which he can only pursue through the agency of his state and with duties under international law which the society of nations can enforce only through the agency of the state with jurisdiction over him.

The state, in other words, may be construed not as a sovereign entity valuable in itself, but as an agent on the one hand of the individuals that compose it, and on the other of the universal society embracing all humanity.[25]

Wright further points out that the first interpretation was generally accepted during the nineteenth century, while the second interpretation reflects state principles adopted during the past generation. He attributes the transition to the many general treaties specifying the rights of aborigines, minorities, workers, women, children, and other potentially oppressed classes.[26] The point is that individuals are slowly becoming more important in international affairs in comparison to states.

Further, the international relations of modern states have become extremely interdependent as a result of economic ties. Large multinational corporations have emerged as active forces, often able to defy the attempts of national governments to gain effective control over them. The major international oil companies, for example, have had an impressive amount of influence in international relations.

Similarly, the ever-increasing role of international organizations in regulating international relations has meant that many of them, in order to perform this role successfully, have assumed a juridical personality. For example, the International Court of Justice ruled in 1949, in the famous Bernadotte case, that the United Nations had the right to ask damages from the state of Israel for its negligence in protecting the life of the Swedish Count Folke Bernadotte, who was assassinated by a Jewish terrorist group while he was in Palestine on a U.N. peacekeeping mission. The government of Israel honored the U.N. claim. Although they are clearly not on an equal footing with states, the status of international organizations compared with states has been enhanced. This is substantially different

25 Quincy Wright, *Contemporary International Law: A Balance Sheet*, Doubleday & Company, Inc., Garden City, N.Y., 1955, p. 21.
26 *Ibid.*

from the situation in classic international law, in which states were the sole legal subjects, unchallenged by "lesser" entities. This, combined with the factors noted on the preceding pages, means that state sovereignty is subject to very real limitations stemming from the nature of the world itself.

Voluntary Submission to Restrictions

Although not always starkly delineated, the above restrictions on sovereignty have been largely the byproduct of world developments. Closely linked (and perhaps inseparable) are those international agreements through which states have agreed to limit their sovereign prerogatives—partly because events have forced them to, partly because such agreements were convenient, and partly because outright foresight prevailed. Beyond simple treaties, one finds the most sophisticated restrictions on sovereignty in international integrative movements, ranging from the loosely confederative international organization on the one hand to the fully integrated federal state on the other. These issues will be discussed in more detail in Part III.

THE EMERGING MODERN CONTEXT

OF INTERNATIONAL RELATIONS

Classical International Politics

The state traditionally handled international relations with other states on the basis of what is called balance-of-power politics. The great era of balance-of-power politics lasted historically roughly from the Congress of Vienna (1815) to World War I (1914). This period is often called the classical period in international relations. Like so many other political terms, however, "balance of power" has traditionally been rather vaguely defined. Recall the difficulties of trying to clarify the meaning of just the term "power." A noted American scholar, Inis Claude, writes that the term "balance of power" has been used much as cooks use the term "a pinch of salt." [27]

27 Inis Claude, *Power and International Relations*, Random House, Inc., New York, 1962, p. 12.

After studying the term, Inis Claude claims to have isolated four major uses of it: as a *situation*, a *policy*, a *symbol*, and a *system*.[28] Balance of power as a *situation* he finds to be purely descriptive, referring to a "situation in which power is literally 'balanced' by equivalent power." [29] That is, at a given point in time, two states apparently counterbalance one another in terms of power. Balance of power as a *policy* refers to a state reacting against any static power situation, especially if the power situation is unfavorable or "unbalanced," by actively undertaking to redress the balance of power. In classical European politics, England traditionally acted as "balancer," since its geographical position aloof from the continent enabled it to support any side and thus to balance the flow of European politics. A third use of the term is as a *symbol*. In this use the term does not necessarily have any substantive content. It is rather a way of expressing concern over the problem of power politics in international relations. Claude offers the example of President Woodrow Wilson blaming balance-of-power politics as the cause of World War I in Europe.

A fourth, and more complex, use of the term "balance of power" is to refer to a *system* for the ordering and regulation of international politics. Different writers have looked at the "system" idea differently, but a common feature is the idea that all states understand certain unwritten rules of international politics—rules that provide for the coherent ordering of relations (that is, a "system") within the arena of world politics.

Many observers perceive in the period from 1815 to 1914 a system, a set of understood rules that would enable states to conduct their relations peacefully. It was the apparent failure of this system that incurred the reproach of President Wilson. Views of the rules vary, but the classical balance-of-power system is usually perceived as having had several elements. First, and perhaps foremost, in the classical system, participation in international relations was restricted to a small circle of primarily European states of roughly equal size and strength, all governed by an elite group of rulers. The rulers were nobility, or at least the "upper crust," which not only meant that they "ran the show" in their own country largely free of the problems of public opinion, but also meant that they were part of

28 *Ibid.*, chap. 2.
29 *Ibid.*, p. 13.

an international "club" based on aristocratic intermarriage, sons of the "upper crust" dominating the foreign services, and family connections with diplomats in the service of other countries.

A second basic element in the maintenance of the system was a broadly based understanding and acceptance of an international status quo. Critical observers of classical European politics will immediately suggest that the status quo tended to be an understanding among the crowned heads of Europe that they would work to keep one another in power and fight creeping republicanism and democracy. Be that as it may, international order, whether it is based on a balance-of-power scheme or some other organizing concept, has to begin with substantial agreement on the particular desired state of affairs to be achieved or maintained. "Peace" is in fact a status quo—a "condition X" that is perceived as being desirable. Therein lies the major problem of achieving peace; it is easy to agree that we all want peace, but we agree very poorly on what is the substance of peace. The classical European rulers had at least an implicit understanding of "condition X," of "balanced power," and were thus able to regulate European politics for a century.

A third basic element of the system was the rather simple and straightforward nature of military science and weaponry. The resort to force in international politics, to war as an instrument of diplomacy, in the continuing adjustment of the power balance was an imaginable and usable option. The military capability of an opponent could be reasonably accurately assessed, and that capability was likely to be rather stable. There were no teams of research and development engineers cranking out new "ultimate" weapons. We are all so used to technological sophistication that even the wildest developments hardly impress us any more. In this era of hydrogen bombs, space satellites, and laser beams it is easy to lose perspective on the once dramatic implications of repeating rifles, steamships, the screw propeller, the machine gun, the tank, and the airplane—none of which ever enabled war as a policy vehicle to get out of hand.

Finally, another necessary element for the balance-of-power system was flexibility in alliances. States needed maneuverability in lining up friends and enemies on a continuing basis or there would be nothing to balance. England's historical role as balancer vis-à-vis continental European power alliances helped keep the system flexible. England's balancing role was perhaps summarized by the statement of Lord Palmerston, British prime minister from 1855 to 1865, that England had "no permanent friends and no permanent enemies, just permanent interests."

The idea of balance-of-power politics as a system governing the flow of international relations presents obvious problems to the scholar. The system worked because a limited circle of rulers understood and accepted the elements discussed above. For the international relations scholar, however, there is no clear definition of "power," "balanced power," the means by which it was determined when power became "unbalanced," or "national interest." Political philosophers will probably be concerned with the amorality and lack of normative goals reflected in Palmerston's comment. Finally, if we are determined in our search for a workable and peaceful means of regulating international relations, we have to ask whether the system indeed worked—it did not, after all, prevent World War I—and whether the elements making up the system (or new or modified elements) would be acceptable in the context of modern political philosophies.

Bipolarity, Multipolarity, or Something Else?

Not only did World War I apparently prove that the balance-of-power system was unable to keep the peace, but the system was widely blamed for causing the war. President Woodrow Wilson was a leading critic of balance-of-power politics, attacking the secret diplomacy, the overlapping alliances, and the philosophy of power politics. He advocated the League of Nations as a means of institutionalizing the balance-of-power system by bringing it out into the open and legitimizing it. This new system, known as "collective security," was to enable the world to police itself on the basis of public control of the use of force and universal respect for the rule of law. The League and collective security will be analyzed in Part III. The primary goal here is to portray the emerging context of international politics.

The League of Nations, in turn, failed to prevent World War II. Perhaps a significant reason was that states tried to retain the old balance-of-power habits without really using the League. By the end of World War II a new commitment was made to collective security, and by this time the classical European balance-of-power system was really dead—if for no other reason than that the world that had served as a base for the old rules had changed. For example:

1 The old-style elitism was diminishing as a result of the growing impact of public opinion and the "common person" on foreign policy, the rise of democratic institutions, and the development of professional diplomatic corps based on merit. Further, the world has expanded dramatically beyond Europe, in large part because of the breakup of the old colonial empires. It is worthwhile to look at a political map of the world for 1914, 1945, and the current year. Using United Nations membership as a yardstick of world growth, the original membership in 1945 was 51, and there are now over 140 members.

2 There is no longer an easy acceptance of the rules of the game, of a broadly based international status quo. This is in part due to the emerging nations. While they do not necessarily reject out of hand the old European rules of international diplomacy and law, they are at least saying, "We were not around when the old guidelines for international conduct were evolved, and we want to have some input too." As a matter of fact, whether because of their cultural inheritance from colonialism or simply because many of the traditional rules made sense given the nature of the nation-state system, the newer states have adopted a surprising number of the traditional rules of international law and diplomacy. The difficulty of getting agreement on a desirable international status quo is further exacerbated by ideology. Utopian dreams, despair over the human condition, and fearful reactions to the unknowns of change—reflected in revolutions, coups, wars of national liberation, and purges, all motivated by theories and would-be theories of the millenium—make the kind of compromise that produces agreement on a "Condition X" very difficult.

3 A third change is in the nature of war and the concomitant technology. People have been overwhelmed by science. This issue has been referred to above. Very simply, modern technology has raised some very serious questions about the usability of war as a policy option.

4 Finally, the free-wheeling image of classical international balance-of-power politics was destroyed by the rise of Cold War alliances. This image was on the way out after the formation of the Entente Cordiale (England/France) in 1904 [expanded to the Triple Entente (adding Russia) in 1907], aimed at stopping German expansion, especially through the Triple Alliance (Germany, Austria-Hungary, and Italy). Modern international relations have involved

a solidification of alliance systems, in particular within the rival blocs of East versus West.

The new world that emerged after World War II was dominated by two superpowers, the United States and the Soviet Union. These two countries, as a result of geography, national resources, fortunes of war, and the persuasiveness of atomic weaponry, came to dominate postwar international relations. The term describing this new state of affairs was "bipolarity." Bipolarity was characterized by the existence of two superpowers, each with its own political ideology, bloc of supporters, and client states. People came to speak of East versus West, communism versus democracy, and dictatorship versus the free world. These two poles of power so dominated international relations thinking during the immediate postwar period that deviance was hardly tolerated. There was no longer a balancer to ensure flexibility in world politics. There were, it is true, the so-called neutralist states (primarily, but not exclusively, Afro-Asian countries), with such spokesmen as Nehru of India and Nasser of Egypt, who claimed to have no stake in the Cold War. These countries claimed to have no interest in the ideological split between East and West; they wanted only to develop their own countries, and perhaps offer moral leadership on the side to cool off the increasingly belligerent superpowers. At best, however, the neutralist states could offer only moral advice. They did not have the military power to command the continuing and serious attention of the Big Two. Besides, the neutralists were hardly a unified bloc anyway.

Time passed, and there was no atomic holocaust. The bipolar world of "us" and "them" and "a few others" started breaking apart. Political observers started talking of "multipolarity" (or "polycentrism"). What was once thought to be a monolithic communist bloc started fragmenting. Out of the communist world that had formerly seemed totally dominated by Moscow appeared what is often called "national communism." Despite the vaunted "internationalism" of the communist movement, countries appeared to care about themselves first and the movement second. In addition to the expressions of national feeling in East Germany, Hungary, and Czechoslovakia, the fragmentation of the communist world has been apparent in Yugoslavia, Poland, Rumania, and, perhaps most dramatically, the People's Republic of China (the famous "Sino-Soviet split").

Perhaps, as part of the fragmentation process, one should note as well the pulling back from the communist orbit of such countries as Indonesia.

Not only was the "monolithic" communist world breaking up during this time, but the presumed unity of the Western noncommunist world was suffering as well. Much of the unity of the West had resulted from a common perception of a communist (that is, Soviet) threat. As Western views of that threat changed and the memory of World War II and its immediate aftermath receded, it became increasingly difficult to hold the Western alliance (as typified especially by the North Atlantic Treaty Organization, NATO) together. The continuing confrontation between two NATO allies, Greece and Turkey, is a prominent example of NATO's difficulties. A further divisive factor in the West was the recovery of Western Europe from its postwar disorder. The Europe that had been exhausted by the war and had desperately looked to the United States for strength was by the mid-1950s already a dynamic economic force in its own right. There was even talk of, if not a United States of Europe, at least a Europe united economically and politically as a new force in world politics. Also, "Third World" countries (Latin America is a prime example) no longer gave Western policies the automatic support they once did.

So the flow of world politics seems to have shifted in modern times from a classical balance-of-power system to bipolarity to multipolarity. The new centers of power would appear to be the United States, the Soviet Union, mainland China, Western Europe, and some sort of vague Third World bloc. Depending on how fussy one wanted to be, it might also be possible to consider Eastern Europe, India (a new proud possessor of the atomic bomb), economically vibrant Japan, and perhaps a few others as new centers of power.

What, then, is the real tenor of current international relations? There are at least three possible conclusions to be drawn from the currently dominant multipolar image. First, one can view the multipolar world in a new, emerging balance-of-power framework. Instead of a few dominant European countries maneuvering against one another, as was the case under the classical balance-of-power system, we now see a few dominant world blocs maneuvering. If there is a new balance-of-power system (that is, a package of understood rules that govern the progress of world politics), it is still in enough of a state of flux for few rules to have yet solidified. Some tentative elements, however, might be the following:

1 The resort to nuclear war is taboo, yet we are still groping for alternatives.

2 The Big Powers (the United States, the Soviet Union, and mainland China) seem to have worked out generally understood spheres of influence within which they assert dominance and will not tolerate outside interference beyond certain minimal levels. United States actions vis-à-vis perceived threats to the security of the Western Hemisphere (e.g., against leftist politics in Guatemala, the Dominican Republic, and Chile), Soviet actions in Eastern Europe, and China's attitude toward Southeast Asia support this thesis.

3 Having apparently accepted these spheres of influence, the Big Powers seem interested in wooing the noncommitted Third World states, but not in ways that would force other Big Powers to intervene.

4 The influence of the lesser powers on world politics hinges primarily on their moral suasion (in such arenas as the United Nations General Assembly), their economic power (such as the economic muscle of the European Economic Community or the new-found clout of the Organization of Petroleum Exporting Countries, OPEC), their strength through membership in an alliance system, or their ability to play off the larger powers against one another to their own benefit.

A second conclusion to be drawn from the multipolar image is that it is not a multipolar world at all. One can argue very persuasively that, in spite of all the recent fuss over the rebirth of Europe and Japan, the emergence of mainland China, and even the proliferation of nuclear weapons, the world is still essentially bipolar. In the last resort, only the two superpowers (the United States and the Soviet Union) *really* have the convincing ability to destroy each other and everybody else. How significant that ability is to the daily course of world events is still not clear, but this "true" bipolar locus of world power is a factor that other states cannot in the long run disregard.

A third conclusion regarding the multipolar image is that it is a valid image but also a fluid one. The multipolar structure of world power depends on what the issue is at any given moment. States coalesce around issues, making power alignments that depend on such issues as colonialism, economics, ideology, national pride, historical antagonisms, national security, and so forth. Is this simply another version of balance-of-power politics?

We are not likely to come to any satisfactory conclusions about the "true" nature of the current world structure. The complexities of social life defy easy analysis, even from the vantage point of history. Beginning students of international relations would be well advised to be suspicious of pat analyses of "what it's all about" and look instead for provocative themes and lines of thought that offer perspective and stimulate further thought. The most vital element is continuing re-evaluation. In that spirit, the task at hand is to begin a probe of the more important problems of modern world politics—the problems of a world in conflict.

BIBLIOGRAPHY

Claude, Inis. *Power and International Relations*. Random House, Inc., New York, 1962.

Cox, Richard H., ed. *The State in International Relations*. Chandler Publishing Company, San Francisco, 1965.

de Jouvenel, Bertrand. *Sovereignty: An Enquiry into the Political Good*. University of Chicago Press, Chicago, 1957.

Deutsch, Karl. *Nationalism and Its Alternatives*. Alfred A. Knopf, Inc., New York, 1969.

Dickinson, Edwin D. *The Equality of States in International Law*. Harvard University Press, Cambridge, Mass., 1920.

Duchacek, Ivo D. *Comparative Federalism: The Territorial Dimension of Politics*. Holt, Rinehart and Winston, Inc., New York, 1970.

Ganshof, François. *The Middle Ages: A History of International Relations*. Harper & Row, Publishers, Incorporated, New York, 1970.

Gulick, Edward Vose. *Europe's Classical Balance of Power*. Cornell University Press, Ithaca, N.Y., 1955.

Kissinger, Henry A. *A World Restored*. Houghton Mifflin Company, Boston, 1973.

Kohn, Hans. *The Idea of Nationalism*. The Macmillan Company, New York, 1961.

Krabbe, Hugo. *The Modern Idea of the State*. D. Appleton & Company, Inc., New York, 1922.

Langer, William L. *European Alliances & Alignments: 1871–1890*. Vintage Books, New York, 1964.

Laski, Harold J. *The Foundations of Sovereignty and Other Essays*. George Allen and Unwin, Ltd., London, 1921.

Machiavelli, Niccolò. *The Prince and The Discourses*. Modern Library, Inc., New York, 1950.

Merriam, Charles E. *History of the Theory of Sovereignty since Rousseau*. Columbia University Press, New York, 1900.

Nicolson, Harold. *The Congress of Vienna*. The Viking Press, Inc., New York, 1961.

Romani, Romano, ed. *The International Political System: Introduction & Readings*. John Wiley & Sons, Inc., New York, 1972.

Russell, Frank M. *Theories of International Relations*. Appleton-Century-Crofts, Inc. New York, 1936.

Singer, Marshall R. *Weak States in a World of Powers: The Dynamics of International Relationships*. The Free Press, New York, 1972.

Stankiewicz, W. J., ed. *In Defense of Sovereignty*. Oxford University Press, New York, 1969.

Vernon, Raymond, *Sovereignty at Bay*. Basic Books, Inc., New York, 1971.

Vital, David. *The Survival of Small States: Studies in Small Power/Great Power Conflict*. Oxford University Press, New York, 1971.

Part II
A World in Conflict

The Bomb:
Military Power and the
Nuclear Revolution

The background survey undertaken in Part I provides a basis for clearer understanding of the presence of conflict in modern international relations. The chapters in Part II focus on three prominent areas of conflict, examined under the general headings of the Bomb, ideology and political power, and the Third World.

While advanced students of international relations might wish to study specific conflict issues in more detail, these general headings are more useful for an introductory survey. They provide a convenient and efficient overview of important modern conflict areas and highlight continuing problems of an international society in which states must coexist.

Chapter 4 probes the basic questions concerning conflict in human society and examines the dimensions of the extreme form of conflict—war. Of particular importance in this regard is the nuclear revolution, which has had such a profound influence on modern international relations, often turning issues of traditional diplomacy into questions of nuclear strategy. The remaining chapters of Part II review modern perspectives on ideology and political power (the Cold War) in the shadow of nuclear technology (the Bomb), and the emerging challenge of the Third World.

THE MYTH OF SECURITY

Damocles was a courtier at the court of Dionysius I of Syracuse, a tyrant who impressed Damocles as being a ruler guaranteed a permanently happy and secure future by virtue of his great power. Damocles so persistently flattered the tyrant and praised his power that Dionysius resolved to teach him a lesson. He gave a banquet and had a sword suspended by a single hair over the head of Damocles in order to demonstrate to him the precarious nature of power and happiness. The expression "the sword of Damocles" has come to be a synonym for "an ever-present peril."

Human history has largely been dominated by the search for security from the perils of nature and the conflicts of social life. After such basic necessities as food and shelter, defense has always been a primary consideration, one requiring weapons. It was logical to accept the idea that the bigger and better the weapons, the more secure the defense. Guaranteed peace and happiness lay in having more power than one's potential enemies—even though increasing one's own strength might make neighbors nervous, lead them to review their own strength, and ultimately make them potential enemies.

Modern times have been labeled the "atomic age." This new age began in 1945 when the United States successfully tested an atomic bomb at Alamogordo, New Mexico. This new and awesome "ultimate" weapon was the result of a crash U.S. program begun in 1940 shortly after the discovery of fission in uranium by two German scientists in 1939. On August 6, 1945, the world's first atomic bomb was dropped on Hiroshima. Since that time, states have seemed to believe that the Bomb (the term is used here to refer to the whole spectrum of military thermonuclear technology) promised ultimate security and power. Not unlike the sword of Damocles, the Bomb and the security we think it represents hang suspended over our heads, threatening the human race and perhaps even the continued physical existence of the planet. The traditional dilemma of international relations takes on new and significant dimensions. The traditional concept of national sovereignty, whereby independent states possess ultimate control over their relations, as opposed to the need to regulate somehow states' actions that directly affect other states, thus ensuring international order, suddenly is affected by the nuclear shadow.

Three issues need our attention at this point: the role of conflict and the use of force in international relations, the nuclear revolution, and the military strategies of the major powers.

THE ROLE OF CONFLICT AND THE USE OF FORCE

A discussion of conflict in human affairs can very easily become abstract because we are often forced to pass judgment with no more than inadequate or unsatisfactory data about conflict or forced to ask unpleasant questions about ourselves. Counterpoint to the discussion is provided by moralists, on the one hand, who decry the whole issue of force, and the scientific bureaucrats and strategists, on the other hand, who speak blandly of overkill and total destruction.

To be sure, much of the debate about human conflict assumes certain givens. The acceptance of normative assumptions is largely a personal matter (one either believes or does not believe), not always subject to logical scrutiny. For example, how can one answer definitively the question about whether humans are basically rational creatures or depraved animals? One can marshal evidence to support either side, so ultimately one really has to accept what one wants to believe. There are, however, certain propositions on which this chapter is based that the reader should be aware of from the outset. One is, of course, free to accept or reject them as a personal frame of reference dictates.

1 *Human conflict is a fact of modern social life and is likely to remain so for the indefinite future.* Wherever people, groups, societies, and states find themselves together, some friction is likely. This view remains persuasive in spite of the reports of anthropologists who claim to have found conflict-free primitive societies in far-flung corners of the modern world. Further, this apparent fact is independent of the debate between those who feel that conflict is in fact healthy (both as an emotional outlet and as a way of keeping human interaction vigorous) and those who insist we need to follow some course designed to eliminate conflict. There is also no presumption that conflict necessarily must expand into violent conflict, although it must be admitted that willingness to resort to force also seems to be a fact of life. The theme of this chapter, and more broadly, of this book, is that while conflict may be unavoidable, human rationality must intervene to keep that conflict within acceptable bounds. Or to be more precise, the mechanisms of international relations must be designed to prevent a resort to the Bomb and a thermonuclear catastrophe, and at the same time to curb the use of force short of nuclear war.

2 *The abolition of war is a dream.* While the hidden terrors of a nuclear war are a just cause for our concern and demand our continuing serious attention, this is hardly a rational basis for insisting that the atomic age has abolished war. For example, a very readable and provocative book by Walter Millis and James Real entitled *The Abolition of War* analyzes the war system as it has been used throughout history as a political instrument.[1] Their conclusion is the real thesis underlying their entire discussion: war as a means

1 Walter Millis and James Real, *The Abolition of War*, The Macmillan Company, New York, 1963.

of dealing with the world's problems is completely outmoded, and more than this, the world has reached a level of military capability (probably for the first time in history) at which the *abolition of organized war* is a serious possibility. The Bomb (with its promise of instant destruction) has eliminated war as a rational instrument of foreign policy. Since history shows, they argue, that war can be controlled neither by military nor by political means, the obvious solution is that the war system itself must be abolished if it is not to abolish us.

While one may sympathize very deeply with the normative goal of this kind of argument, the honest scholar has to retain professional skepticism. At least two points have to be raised immediately. First, not only is there little cause for optimism about the reduction of violence in the world (after all, thermonuclear war is simply the most destructive of a whole range of options involving the use of force), there is substantial doubt that the Bomb is the *source* of the problem. Is the world in a sorry state because of the Bomb, or did someone come along and invent the Bomb because the world is in a sorry state? This author is convinced that the initial problem is not the Bomb. If we were to abolish the Bomb (hardly possible since we can neither trust current possessors to destroy *all* their nuclear weapons nor erase the knowledge of the Bomb from the minds of the makers) or had not invented the Bomb in the first place, we would have found something equally as bad or worse—which we may yet do anyway.

A second cause for skepticism about abolition-of-war thinking is that no one with a sense of history can help feeling a sense of déjà vu. There is no intention here of belittling such dreams, for after all, if we cease to hope, we lose our sense of human direction and purpose. The intention here is rather to show that the dream is not novel. A very important book appeared on the eve of World War I arguing that war had been abolished. Norman Angell, in *The Great Illusion*, tried to prove that war had become impossible.[2] His case was based on the growing economic interdependence of states, which he felt made war equally costly for victor and vanquished. While World War I bore out his view in this regard, it did not support his conclusion that war had become impossible because it no

2 Norman Angell, *The Great Illusion: A Study of the Relation of Military Power to National Advantage*, 4th ed., G. P. Putnam's Sons, New York, 1913.

longer made sense from a profit-and-loss standpoint. History is full of examples of why war is impossible, from social fatigue following the "all-destructive fury" of the Thirty Years' War (a war which allegedly retarded Germany's development for a century) to the development of such ultimate weapons as the crossbow. So, amid the dreams, the scholar must push on and try to find out why the human race (scattered into nation-states) can't seem to rise above itself.

3 *Theories of Armageddon are likely to be not only empty but even dangerous.* Armageddon is a Biblical place (Rev. 16:16) where the final battle between the forces of Good and Evil will be fought. In modern terms it is often used to characterize the inevitability of war, especially thermonuclear war. "There is going to be another world war one of these days, it's just a question of time." Human greed, malice, stupidity, or accident will trigger a world-wide show-down. It's *bound* to happen. Given the *inevitability* of this, the inexorable march of technological progress becomes critical. It takes only elementary logic to perceive that since we are going to have this war someday anyway, the sooner the better. At this point the corollary theory of pre-emptive war, or attacking a potential enemy before they can attack, becomes involved. Pre-emptive war has both the advantage of surprise (no small factor in modern military considerations) and seductive humanitarian overtones ("Why not have the Big War *now* rather than in 10 years? Casualties and human suffering will be less now than if we wait for technology to produce even crueler weapons. Let's get on with it!").

The problems with this line of thought should be obvious. Armageddon thinking has to be based on belief—there is no logical reason why this war should occur. Even if war *is* inevitable, the arguments for hastening it seem shallow. Biological factors condemn us all to ultimate death, but that is hardly reason to commit suicide as a teenager, or reason for seriously ill patients to give up hope when indeed a cure may be found. The danger lies in the fact that someone (or some government) may be tempted to provoke what they consider an inevitable conclusion. There was a popular political novel in the United States that portrayed a situation in which American nuclear bombers, through accident, were sent off to attack the Soviet Union. In the midst of frantic efforts to call back the bomber force, the American government contacted the Soviet government and explained the situation, which the Soviet leaders understood and accepted, holding off their own counterattack. Then in the story, an American adviser suggested to the U.S. government that, given the tremendous importance of surprise and split-second advantage in the nuclear age, one of those unique opportunities in history had presented itself. The Soviet guard was temporarily down, and the United States had an errant bomber force on the way. Not only should that force not be called back, but additional U.S. planes should be dispatched to complete the pre-emptive strike—thus somehow bringing the world closer to real peace.

4 *Wars may be inevitable but nuclear war is unthinkable.* There are two different views of this position. One, which is rejected in this chapter, is that thermonuclear holocaust is so horrible to contemplate that it should be blocked out of our minds. To focus our thoughts on thermonuclear war is to admit that it *is* thinkable, and therefore also possible. Psychologists speak of the psychological defense mechanism of denial. When something is too horrible to face, we keep our sanity by denying that the thing exists, by pretending that it is not there. Even for many of those who might face the atomic problem, the sense that this is forbidden dissuades them. As Nietzsche cautioned, "If you look too deeply into the abyss, the abyss will look into you." Raising questions about nuclear war is perhaps something better left alone.

The second view, which forms the basis for the survey we are about to undertake, is that while nuclear war may indeed be unthinkable as an international policy option, students of international relations have no choice but to "think about the unthinkable," to borrow a phrase from Herman Kahn, one of those who has considered this subject.[3] Only by having some understanding of the dimensions of war—especially nuclear war—can we hope to control the Bomb and perhaps ultimately even war itself.

On War

The first problem is to discover what war is and what causes it— a discouraging task, as it turns out.

One of the most surprising facts about war—that institution that has dominated so much of human history—is that there is still no

3 Herman Kahn, *Thinking About the Unthinkable,* Horizon Press, New York, 1962.

widely accepted definition of a war. Perhaps equally surprising to the beginning student of international relations will be the fact that the widespread serious study of war (and peace) is a relatively recent phenomenon as well as a newly respectable undertaking. Although the literature on war is considerable, it was largely the preserve of such observers as professional military writers (e.g., strategists, tacticians, memoirists), rational philosophers, moralists, and historians. The systematic application of social science techniques —merging with, complementing, and building upon the work of the groups just mentioned—has only come into its own within the last decade or so.

The tone for the modern empirical study of war was set by the classic two-volume work by Quincy Wright, *A Study of War*, which appeared in 1942.[4] This massive study investigated war by using quantitative techniques, looking at trends, offering interdisciplinary perspectives, and raising systematically the kinds of questions that needed the attention of scholars. After a slow beginning, one now finds university centers devoted to the study of international conflict, university classes studying the growing body of literature on conflict, war and peace institutes, and new academic journals looking at the problem of conflict and world order.

Quincy Wright summarized the definitional problem when he referred to "the specialized definitions which have been elaborated for professional purposes by lawyers, diplomats, and soldiers and for scientific discussion by sociologists and psychologists."[5] Even the recent interdisciplinary efforts to study the broad field of conflict and conflict resolution have failed to produce a definition that can satisfy every observer. Compounding the problem is the extensive popular use of many terms to express nuances of politics and emotion. Consider the following list of terms, compiled after a few moment's reflection on recent usage and undoubtedly overlooking much.

cold war	limited war
hot war	total war
world war	uncontrolled war

4 Quincy Wright, *A Study of War*, 2 vols., University of Chicago Press, Chicago, 1942.
5 *Ibid.*, vol. I, p. 9.

accidental war	guerrilla war
conventional war	preventive war
unconventional war	political war
undeclared war	propaganda war
economic war	psychological war
security action	insurgency
defensive war	police action
belligerency	imperialist war
war of national liberation	pre-emptive war
general war	preventive diplomacy
international war	proxy war
revolutionary war	local war
civil war	protracted war

Much of the complexity stems from the fact that the terms refer to different perspectives on war: e.g., war as a condition, techniques of war, or assumptions about belligerent behavior and the causes of war. Diplomats and lawyers are more likely to be concerned with identifying war as a condition. For example, an international relations dictionary defines "war" as:

hostilities between states or within a state or territory undertaken by means of armed force. A state of war exists in the legal sense when two or more states declare officially that a condition of hostilities exists between them. Beyond this, international jurists disagree as to the kinds of conditions, intentions, or actions that constitute war by legal definition. *De facto* war exists, however, whenever one organized group undertakes the use of force against another group.[6]

As the recent American military involvement in Vietnam showed, however, pinning down "war" as a precise condition is difficult. Not only was that particular conflict clouded by questions of guerrilla tactics and outside assistance, but many states had strong political reasons for avoiding calling the conflict a formal war (the Vietnam conflict is discussed in depth in the following chapter). Formal ideas of war have been popular in the past, in the Middle Ages, for example, but as the "Vietnams" (not to mention the

6 Jack C. Plano and Roy Olton, *The International Relations Dictionary*, Holt, Rinehart and Winston, Inc., New York, 1969, p. 77.

potential of thermonuclear war) make clear, formalistic definitions of war will perhaps have to be rethought. This is a domestic as well as an international problem. For example, the United States is faced (most notably because of the controversial American involvement in Korea and Vietnam) with a reappraisal of the respective roles of Congress and the president in "declaring war" and/or committing U.S. forces to battle.

Perhaps, looking at the techniques of war, we might wish to review the oft-quoted, and unfairly maligned, view of Karl von Clausewitz (1780–1831), the famous German military philosopher. He wrote in his treatise *On War* that war was not a special thing in itself, but simply one of the political options available for the conduct of foreign policy. He saw war as simply "an act of violence intended to compel our opponents to fulfill our will." However, he noted, "war is nothing but a continuation of political intercourse, with a mixture of other means." [7]

If we are to take this view that war is simply one form of political intercourse, how do we know when the line dividing nonviolent conflict from violence has been meaningfully crossed? We probably won't know because of the subtle shades of progression, but following the Clausewitz line of thinking, perhaps the dividing line is immaterial, as war is ultimately a question of political attitude and subject to all the vagaries of time and place. One interesting attempt to fix the threshold quantitatively was made by a scholar who tried to arrange all "deadly quarrels" on a continuum of violent conflict, ranging from one killed (murder) to ten million killed (World War II). The threshold of war was crossed when deaths went over 1,000.[8] While quantification is helpful in standardization, the cut-off points for various categories are likely to remain highly arbitrary. Besides, the basis for quantification (in this case deaths) may not take into account other equally significant dimensions of the use of force. As the above list of terms relating to war suggests, war is more than a condition. It is also the employment of forceful (and often subtle) techniques. Economic war or psychological war may, for example, produce drastic and far-reaching political and military consequences not measurable by battlefield casualties.

7 Karl von Clausewitz, *On War*, London, 1911, I, 2; III, 121.
8 See Lewis F. Richardson, *Statistics of Deadly Quarrels*, The Boxwood Press, Pittsburgh, Pa., 1960.

Finally, some of the listed war terms reflect concern for attitudes and behavior, linked with assumptions about the cause of war. The term "imperialist war" reflects both an attitude about the root causes of the war and an assumption about which states are guilty of having caused it. Also, much of the "nature of war" is found not on the battlefield, but in the hostile behavior and attitudes that characterize a state's foreign policy. Quincy Wright calls attention to the discussion of this psychological aspect of war in Hobbes' *Leviathan,* where the oscillations of war and peace are compared to the weather. Hobbes writes:

As the nature of foul weather lieth not in a shower or two of rain, but in an inclination thereto of many days together; so the nature of war consisteth not in actual fighting, but in the known disposition thereto during all the time there is no assurance to the contrary.[9]

Hobbes' view raises an interesting question for modern students. Can peace be defined simply as the absence of war (using "war" in the sense of actual military combat)? Perhaps so, but it is likely to be an unhappy peace, as the experiences of the leaders Schuschnigg, Hácha, and Chamberlain revealed on the eve of World War II.

The organized international community has had no better success in producing a useful definition of war. Article XI (1) of the League of Nations Covenant stated:

Any war or threat of war, whether immediately affecting any of the Members of the League or not, is hereby declared a matter of concern to the whole League, and the League shall take any action that may be deemed wise and effectual to safeguard the peace of nations.

The drafters of the covenant nevertheless eschewed a definition of war. It is true that Article X of the covenant spoke of members' obligations "to respect and preserve as against external aggression the territorial integrity and existing political independence of all Members of the League." In spite of that guidance, the League stumbled around in the mid-1930s trying to decide what Mussolini's invasion of Ethiopia in 1935—an action that Mussolini denied was

9 Thomas Hobbes, *Leviathan*, Part I, chap. 13. Cited in Wright, vol. I, p. 11.

a war—represented and what to do about it. Finally, the League decided that the Soviet Union's attack on Finland in 1939 was too much and expelled it from the League in December of that year. While this was an important act by the League, it was in part an empty gesture. World War II had begun on September 1, 1939, with the German invasion of Poland. The League hardly gets good marks for its definitional performance, however, for by December even the most casual observer was beginning to suspect that something very much like a war was going on.

The drafters of the United Nations Charter attempted to surmount the problems of the League. There is a reference in the Preamble to saving "succeeding generations from the scourge of war," but the operative paragraphs (that is, the meat of a document) of the charter avoid the term "war" and refer instead to "threats to the peace, breaches of the peace, and acts of aggression." (See Chapter VII of the charter.) Like its predecessor the League, unfortunately, the United Nations has also failed to come to grips with war.

The resort to force is presumably illegal under the U.N. Charter (except under the auspices of the Security Council in its peacekeeping role), as members are pledged to "refrain in their international relations from the threat or use of force..." (Art. 2, Sec. 4). Yet this prohibition is undercut by Article 51 of the charter, which recognizes the "right of individual or collective self-defense...." An interesting example of the result was the Israeli action in 1967. Harassed by her Arab neighbors and believing Arab offensive action was imminent, Israel took the position essentially that the charter did not require a state to be stupid and wait until it was attacked, and engaged in a little "active self-defense" by unleashing the Six-Day War.

Further, the United Nations has moved toward considering whether or not South Africa's policy of apartheid (racial separation) constitutes a "threat to the peace," yet it has seemed helpless in such situations as the Soviet invasions of Hungary (1956) and Czechoslovakia (1968) or the American struggle in Vietnam. For reasons that will be examined in subsequent chapters, the United Nations has been most successful militarily in "preventive diplomacy," a term used to mean the introduction of United Nations troops into a conflict situation, with the agreement of the disputing parties, to help keep belligerents apart and "cool off" local situations.

If the League and the United Nations have been vague in defining war, they have hardly been any more precise in telling us what peace is, although both organizations posited it as a primary goal. The United Nations Charter is the more precise in referring to economic, social, cultural, and humanitarian goals and offering a general framework for dealing with such problems, although the groundwork was provided by League experience.

On Conflict

Perhaps the time has come to step back from the definition of war and face the even more basic problem of "why?" Why do states, why do people, fight? Sadly, scholars aren't sure what the causes of conflict, and ultimately of war, are. Human life is so complex, and the social sciences so young, that definitive answers escape us—as indeed they may forever.

In 1925 the Conference on the Cause and Cure of War concluded that there were more than 250 causes of war, listed under the four general categories of political, economic, social, and psychological. After his study of these conclusions and his own monumental analysis of the causes of war, Quincy Wright's conclusion (which nowadays appears almost tongue-in-cheek) was that: "War has politico-technological, juro-ideological, socio-religious, and psycho-economic causes." [10] We must assume surely that the causes of war are complex enough to defy easy analysis.

Without getting hopelessly bogged down in material that is really the province of more advanced scholars, we might focus here on three general theories of the cause of war to illustrate the range of scholarship.

War Is Inherent in the Nation-State System. This view suggests that war is a basic part of the Westphalian structure that the modern world inherited. We will not have peace until we change the basic structure of international relations—in particular, until we abolish the nation-state. The line of thinking here runs roughly as follows: the nation-state exists because of separate, selfish communities of interest. *We* are separate from *you* because *you* speak a funny language, have odd beliefs, eat bizarre foods, and have a different history. *You* don't understand *our* problems and needs. Things were

10 Wright, vol. II, p. 739.

different for *you* over there in X. Do *you* know how it was here when Y invaded five years ago? By the way, weren't *you* friendly with Y eighty years ago when Z invaded X? *I'm* not sure *I* trust *you!* Our interests are different. The national-interest argument, the basic principle of the "realists" discussed in Chapter 2, makes conflict inevitable simply because states represent *different* interests. After all, states were created precisely because groups of people had different interests and wanted to protect them. International agreements are seen as viable only as long as they are in everybody's interest. If this line of reasoning is valid, one may wish to consider a related line of thought. If self-interest is what makes the world tick, what is the significance of the apparent emerging *world* interest? There are claims of a developing world culture based on the tremendous interaction made possible by the mass media, easy travel, and common problems (the Bomb, war, pollution, overpopulation, dwindling resources, perceived social injustices, and the like).

War Is Caused by the People and Beliefs Dominant in Given Nation-States. The modern world has two easy examples of this view: communism and democracy and/or capitalism. The outstanding example of the communist position was provided by V. I. Lenin in his classic work *Imperialism: The Highest Form of Capitalism,* first published in 1917. This treatise, which leaned heavily on the earlier work of J. A. Hobson, argued that the profit struggle within capitalist nation-states over limited resources could be ameliorated and temporarily postponed by expanding into overseas markets and resources. They could expand this way, Lenin wrote, only into underdeveloped countries that could be dominated and exploited by the more advanced capitalist states. This expansion could be seen in capitalist states' quest for colonies (imperialism), which would soon turn into competition for colonies as the underdeveloped areas of the world diminished. Lenin believed that the roots of war lay in the capitalist system and the resultant international imperialist competition. No doubt he would be puzzled if he could see the breakup of the old colonial empires and the international economic structure of the modern world.

On the other side of the ledger, the democratic states (such states tend to focus on their democratic *political* structure, as opposed to the communist emphasis on *economic* structure) see communism as the primary threat to peace. Marxism/Leninism is seen as the intellectual core of an international revolutionary movement dedicated to the violent overthrow of existing governmental systems, many of which have a commendable record of public participation in self-government. Communist intellectual theory strikes cynics not as the promise of the millenium, but simply as a new way to rationalize the domination of human beings by other human beings. This view is enhanced by the avowed communist goals of deliberate revolution and ultimate victory. Communist governments and their subversive ideology thus become a cause of war. These views of causal factors of war provide fertile ground for modern scholars who seek the roots of war not so much in the threat itself as in the threat-perception.[11] Beyond the conflict of communism and democracy, which has had such a prominent role in the East-West "Cold War" (examined in detail in the following chapter), other clashing belief systems also cause strife. Important examples include religion, economic creeds, and nationalism.

The Ultimate Causes of War Lie within People Themselves. The line of thinking here is that states do not make war, people do. We need, then, to take a closer look at people. The question that has dominated such study has been: is war part of human nature, *or* are people simply caught up in the social environment within which they find themselves? Not surprisingly, two major schools of thought have developed, one arguing the merits of each view—along with a third school which incorporates elements of both.

A prominent example of the "human nature" school is Sigmund Freud (1856–1939), the Austrian psychiatrist who is regarded as the founder of psychoanalysis. In essence, his view of human motivation involved the concepts of *id, superego,* and *ego.* The id represented the basic animal drive (urges for power, self-preservation, and sex) governed by the pleasure principle. A human body is an example of the id in action. The baby follows selfish instincts; it "wants." As the child grows, it is taught to control its desires through development of the superego, or conscience. Family, friends, and school convey

11 See, for example, L. F. Richardson, "Threats and Security," in *Psychological Factors of Peace and War,* ed. T. H. Pear, Philosophical Library, Inc., New York, 1950; J. David Singer, "Threat Perception and the Armament-Tension Dilemma," *Journal of Conflict Resolution,* 2 (1958), 90–105; and W. I. Thomas and F. Znaniecki, "The Definition of the Situation," in *Readings in Social Psychology,* ed. T. M. Newcomb and E. L. Hartley, Henry Holt and Company, Inc., New York, 1947.

to the child a sense of the restraints on selfish animal drives that society expects. The result of the tension between id drives and superego restraint is the ego, the conscious self, what a person *is*. It is not necessarily a perfect balance, however. Id-dominated people are aggressive, while superego-dominated people may be passive and cautious.

Freud felt that id drives were much too strong to be overcome. Superego development simply forces them into the subconscious, where they linger as suppressed desires, often coming to the surface in dreams, fears, or obsessions, or in (sometimes violent) abnormal behavior. War becomes a socially acceptable outlet for pent-up id energy. People can follow the id without arousing guilt feelings in the superego. The German philosopher Friedrich Nietzsche (1844–1900) captures the essence of this view of war in his well-known statements: "Say not that a good cause justifies any war. Say rather that a good war justifies any cause," and "War affords the joys of cold-blooded murder with a good conscience."

One hardly need look to psychology to find the roots of war in human nature. Many observers have seen social life as just an extension of the primordial struggle for survival. Freud notes in his famous open letter in 1932 to Albert Einstein that "[c]onflicts of interest between man and man are resolved, in principle, by the recourse to violence. It is the same in the animal kingdom, from which man cannot claim exclusion . . . ." [12] Thomas Hobbes' *Leviathan*, referred to in Chapter 1, is a good example of this view. Various "realists" and "Social Darwinists" are also examples. Conflict and violence appear to be inherent in human nature. Freud concluded, after reviewing the menace of war in his letter to Einstein, the following:

The upshot of these observations, as bearing on the subject in hand, is that there is no likelihood of our being able to suppress humanity's aggressive tendencies. In some happy corners of the earth, they say, where nature brings forth abundantly whatever man desires, there flourish races whose lives go gently by, unknowing of aggression or constraint. This I can hardly credit; I would like further details about these happy folk. The Bolshevists, too, aspire to do away with human aggressiveness by ensuring the satisfaction of material needs

12 Sigmund Freud, "On War," reprinted in *War: Studies from Psychology, Sociology, Anthropology*, ed. Leon Bramson and George W. Goethals, Basic Books, Inc., New York, 1964, p. 72.

and enforcing equality between man and man. To me this hope
seems vain. Meanwhile they busily perfect their armaments, and
their hatred of outsiders is not the least of the factors of cohesion
amongst themselves.[13]

The "human nature" school, which portrays human aggression
as held in check only by a thin social veneer (society's institutions
themselves often being subverted into an instrument for individual
or collective human aggression), is challenged by the "learned behavior" (or "environmental") school, which sees the social veneer
as the perverter of human nature. The idea of war does not lie
within people, it is learned from the environment. A classic statement of the learned behavior view was offered by Mark A. May in
A Social Psychology of War and Peace (1943). He argued:

Man's biological nature is neither good nor bad, aggressive nor sub-
missive, warlike nor peaceful, but neutral in these respects. He is
capable of developing in either direction depending upon what he
is compelled to learn by his environment and by his culture. It is a
mistake to assume that he can learn war more easily than peace. His
learning machinery is not prejudiced, as is sometimes thought, toward the acquirement of bad habits. The bias is in his social environment.[14]

He goes on to suggest that if people encounter friendly, rather than
hostile, relations with others, they will be "... far more strongly
predisposed to settle disputes, both domestic and foreign, by peaceful means." But, he continues, "if, on the other hand, man's environment and his culture are organized so that fighting is more reward-
ing than peaceful pursuits, he will acquire habits of aggression and
attitudes of hostility." [15]

A third, vaguely defined, "school" seems to incorporate elements
of the foregoing two (although there are certain common threads
and overlap in all three schools).

Erich Fromm, in his thoughtful book *Escape from Freedom*,
argues that on the one hand, human nature requires security, a sense
of belonging, and a vision of a personal future.[16] Yet, on the other

13 *Ibid.*, p. 77.
14 Mark A. May, *A Social Psychology of War and Peace*, Yale University
Press, New Haven, Conn., 1943, p. 20.
15 *Ibid.*
16 Erich Fromm, *Escape from Freedom*, Rinehart & Company, Inc., New
York, 1941.

hand, the evolving social environment has produced the very things people had hoped to avoid, in particular a new personal freedom made possible by the development of capitalism and Protestantism. People now find themselves cut loose from the security of the Church and a job in a small village where everyone knows everybody else. They find themselves instead caught up in modern, urban, industrial, mass society. They cannot face this freedom that has made them alone, insignificant, and powerless. Frantic to escape, they are likely to turn to membership in groups and movements. They need to "belong," and their "being somebody" is reflected in what the group is. Unfortunately, to compensate for their former insignificance, they may seek out extremist groups characterized by authoritarianism, destructiveness, and conformity. Hence conflict flourishes in modern society's cold, impersonal response to human need. Fromm explains Germany's embracing of Nazism on this basis. If Fromm's thesis is valid, we might well consider looking for the basis for future international conflict in the lack of humanity of modern social structures.

Another provocative view on conflict is offered by Konrad Lorenz, the noted student of animal behavior. He writes in his popular book *On Aggression* that people, like all animals, have an aggressive instinct. Looking at aggressive behavior in animals, he concludes that it serves three very important natural functions: (1) balanced distribution of animals of the same species over the available environment (e.g., too many tigers in one corner of the jungle would exhaust resources, and the tigers would all starve; aggression is a natural safety device forcing all to keep their distance); (2) selection of the strongest; and (3) protection of the young. Aggression has an undeserved bad reputation. Lorenz demonstrates that it is a natural vehicle for keeping order in nature and for preserving and improving a species. Lorenz further concludes that animals (with a few exceptions) have built-in control mechanisms for managing aggression. For example, stags fighting in the forest do not try to kill one another, for that would defeat the purpose of preserving the species. Although there are occasional accidents, the fighting is really a test of strength, with the participating animals sensing certain ground rules. Unfortunately, people, who also have the natural aggressive instinct, have had their control instincts dulled (and perhaps even bred out) by the advance of technology and the security of soft, modern living. So, contrary to the usual argument that human nature is the problem, Lorenz suggests that we have problems because we can't follow human nature. Intervening environmental factors short-circuit what would otherwise be a natural, self-regulating system.

The foregoing discussion of all these views on the roots of conflict was simply a broad survey of the kinds of thinking and lines of investigation that have been undertaken. Clearly, however, we are still a long way from understanding ourselves and why we fight. It might be well at this point to reflect on the more concrete impact of the presence of conflict on international relations.

On War . . . Again

However much we might wish to believe that war is an aberration that occasionally clouds international relations, the record unfortunately reveals otherwise. Modern attempts to add up the world's wars, even given all the qualifiers on what constitutes a "war" (a debate we will not reopen here), provide a devastating indictment of our ability to control aggression, although this does not prove we cannot do so in the future.

Quincy Wright's landmark study of war showed that up until World War II practically all states had been engaged in fighting internationally, domestically, or both. His conclusions seem reaffirmed by the widely quoted results of the Norwegian statistician in the 1960s who, using a computer, concluded that during 5,560 years of recorded human history there had been 14,531 wars, or 2.6135 a year, with only about 10 generations enjoying relatively undisturbed peace.[17]

Counting wars is only part of what interests us, however. In addition, we might also reflect on the subsurface violence observable in the modern world. Although perhaps not "war," the Cuban missile crisis, the Soviet invasion of Czechoslovakia, and the continuing turmoil in such areas as Northern Ireland are all of concern to the study of international relations.

Quincy Wright also calls attention to trends, such as (1) magnitude—the size of modern armies has tended to increase both absolutely and in proportion to the population; (2) discontinuity—there seems to be a trend toward a decrease in the length of wars and in

17 *Time*, Sept. 24, 1965, p. 30.

the proportion of war years to peace years; (3) intensity—the length and number of battles per war year have increased; (4) extent—the number of belligerents in a war, the speed with which war spreads, and the area involved have all increased; and (5) cost—both absolutely and in proportion to the populations, the human and economic costs of war have increased.[18] Wright's conclusions are instructive, yet even though his study covers only the period up to World War II, the most interesting conclusion of all concerns military and civilian casualties from war. He writes, "Probably at least 10 per cent of deaths in modern civilization can be attributed directly or indirectly to war." [19]

Enter the nuclear revolution. Suddenly Wright's figure is surprising not because so many have died, but because the figure seems almost insignificant in view of the Bomb's capabilities. As a matter of fact, the tremendous increases in world population and the lack of a major war since World War II should cause Wright's estimate of 10 percent to be revised downward. How are we to comprehend the fact that a modern nuclear war could surpass that figure in seconds? That the Chinese regime in Peking speaks (almost brags) of losing two or three hundred million people in the "next war"? That entire civilizations could disappear? Let us examine some of the specifics of the Bomb.

THE NUCLEAR REVOLUTION

The nuclear revolution has had at least six aspects: (1) suddenness, (2) proliferation, (3) research and development, (4) destructive potential, (5) delivery capability, and (6) military strategy.

Suddenness

The prospect of annihilation through military onslaught is hardly new. The tales of military battles "fought to the last man" and opponents swearing to "fight to the death" are legion. The wiping out

18 Wright, vol. I, chap. 9.
19 *Ibid.*, p. 246.

of civilians and the obliteration of their cities and fields are not new either. What *is* new is the suddenness with which annihilation can occur. A persistent theory cropping up throughout military history is that wars have always ground to a halt through their own inner forces (e.g., the vision of total destruction, incomprehensible suffering, exhaustion of the participants, and a growing desire to end it all and salvage something) before casualties reached a certain percentage (say 5 percent) of the total populations involved. What used to take years to destroy now takes seconds. If the military efficiency of destroying the enemy is to be the goal, then World Wars I and II were sorry wars indeed by modern standards. It took the world four years (1914–1918) in World War I to kill a mere 10,000,000, six years (1939–1945) in World War II to kill 25,000,000. These figures are conservative estimates, do not include the wounded and many of the war-related casualties, and do not make it clear that World War II had more participants and the dropping of two puny atomic bombs to help increase the death toll. We might do well to recall President Kennedy's estimate back in the tranquil years of the early 1960s: "... a full-scale nuclear exchange lasting less than 60 minutes, with weapons now in existence, could wipe out more than 300,000,000 Americans, Europeans, and Russians." Present weapons capabilities stagger the imagination. We might likewise ponder Herman Kahn's question in *On Thermonuclear War*, "Will the survivors envy the dead?" [20] Facing up to the prospect of sudden annihilation is something we will do because we must. After all, we triumphed over the dire prediction made at the time of the laying of the Atlantic Cable that the human race would be driven insane because people could not cope with receiving bad news so quickly.

Proliferation

As the new "ultimate" weapon (an honor now challenged by chemical/biological warfare and "death ray" laser beams), the Bomb was a revolutionary advance in and of itself, but the possibilities of the Bomb have been compounded by its coming into the possession of more and more states (this is often called the *n*th-nation problem). The U.S. monopoly on the Bomb ended when the Soviet

20 Herman Kahn, *On Thermonuclear War*, Princeton University Press, Princeton, N.J., 1961, p. 34.

Union developed one in 1949, followed by Great Britain in 1952, France in 1960, communist China in 1964, and India in 1974.

In 1967, the United States and the Soviet Union finally agreed to cooperate in preventing the spread of nuclear weapons. They presented a draft treaty intended to keep the number of nuclear nations at five (the United States, the Soviet Union, Great Britain, France, and communist China) to the seventeen-member Disarmament Conference in Geneva in 1968. France and China refused to sign. Certain other nonnuclear countries that were technologically capable of making their own Bomb and that had neighbors that caused them security concern (such as Israel and India) either did not sign or signed but subsequently failed to ratify the agreement. When India finally became a nuclear power in 1974, she was talking of using the Bomb for "river diversion and mining"—an explanation skeptics find suspect, especially in view of India's continuing tense relations with Pakistan and mainland China. There was also resistance to the United States–Soviet nonproliferation effort on the grounds that the treaty was "unequal," permanently solidifying the power of the Big Powers vis-à-vis weaker states.

The Nuclear Nonproliferation Treaty finally went into effect in 1970, with only three members of the "club"—the United States, the Soviet Union, and Great Britain—signing. The treaty may be an empty gesture, however, since a number of countries are in a position to get the Bomb very quickly. A 1974 estimate suggested that ten countries (Argentina, Brazil, Iran, Israel, Italy, Japan, Pakistan, South Africa, South Korea, and West Germany) could develop the Bomb before the end of the decade, and fourteen more (Algeria, Bangla Desh, Belgium, Chile, Colombia, Indonesia, Libya, North Korea, Portugal, Saudi Arabia, Spain, Switzerland, Turkey, and Venezuela) could develop it by the end of the century.[21] Any of these countries that undertook a real crash program could get the Bomb much more quickly.

Equally ominous is the spread of fissionable materials (uranium-235 and plutonium-239) for use in nuclear reactors or other peaceful uses of atomic energy. Such materials might be diverted into the building of an atomic weapon. Although there are strict controls over fissionable materials, they are apparently not strict enough to squelch persistent speculation in the mass media about the possibility

21 *Time*, Sept. 9, 1974, p. 28.

of domestic terrorist groups or irresponsible governments from small countries siphoning off enough fissionable material to build a "hostage" bomb. Such bombs would have primarily nuisance value. They would not be the "great equalizer" some observers have predicted. As will become clear, being a nuclear power is much more than being able to detonate one bomb. The United States and the Soviet Union are *still* the Big Two, although the proliferation of nuclear capability hardly seems likely to lead to stability in the world.

Research and Development

In part intrinsic to the nuclear revolution, the tremendous growth of national research establishments has had a profound influence on the development and utilization of the weaponry of the nuclear nation-state. The atomic age itself owes much to the gathering together of leading U.S. scientists in the famed Manhattan Project. Among the accouterments of a nuclear power are advanced computer technology, teams of scholars (e.g., a 1974 estimate of research scientists and engineers gave the United State 550,000 and the Soviet Union 625,000), research centers, "think tanks" for planning strategy, weapons proving grounds, government links with industry and universities, plentiful resources, and a strong economy.

Destructive Potential

In point of fact, the average citizen hasn't the foggiest notion of what "an explosion" really is like firsthand. There are many exceptions, of course, but generally our understanding of explosions comes from television and movies.

Vicarious realism is never entirely satisfactory, but perhaps a starting point for understanding explosive power is to understand how it is measured. A basic way is yield-to-weight ratio, or how much explosion is produced for each given pound of explosive material. The base explosive material used is TNT. We might focus first on the popular image of a stick of dynamite.* Modern ranchers will often buy a few pounds (30 to 40 sticks) of dynamite to blast

---

* Dynamite is in fact made from volatile nitroglycerin and some inert substance such as sawdust. Trinitrotoluene, or TNT, is a more stable high explosive, suitable for such uses as filling metal shells. This substitution should not spoil the example, however.

quickly an irrigation or drainage ditch. These sticks are commonly broken (carefully) in half and poked into holes in the ground made by a crowbar about 2 or 3 feet apart and stretching a half mile or so (depending upon terrain) across a field. A detonator attached to the first half-stick and wired to a car battery will explode it. The resultant shock will detonate the next half-stick, which will detonate the next, and so on. The chain reaction occurs so rapidly that an observer cannot tell at which end of the line of planted sticks the detonation took place. The explosion from "a few pounds of dynamite" will blacken the sky with mud, rocks, and other debris, sending everyone around scurrying for cover.

Nuclear power is measured in relation to the weight of TNT required to cause the same explosion, and it is measured not in pounds, but in tons. Nuclear yield is expressed in *kilotons*—the explosive equivalent of 1,000 tons of TNT—and *megatons*—the explosive equivalent of 1,000,000 tons of TNT. To put those facts in perspective, we can recall that the largest conventional bombs of World War II were the 5-ton "blockbusters." Imagine what 5 tons of the rancher's dynamite would do (compared with the "few pounds"), especially if it were dropped as a bomb in a heavily built-up urban area. The Hiroshima A-bomb was equivalent to 20,000 tons of TNT (or 20 kilotons). The current warhead of the American Minuteman ICBM (intercontinental ballistic missile) has a yield of 1,000,000 tons (or 1 megaton), with the largest Soviet missiles put at 5,000,000 tons (or 5 megatons). Modern bombers can deliver 20 megatons, and scientists talk of potential explosive devices of several hundred megatons. Scientists have speculated, moreover, that if a bomb of several hundred megatons could be exploded 150 miles above the earth, it could destroy everything on earth within the tangents drawn from the point of detonation. If that seems unreal, we might wish to consider that the United States and the Soviet Union have the ability to drop on each other from 10 to 20 tons of TNT per citizen. This obvious "overkill" ability serves only, as Winston Churchill once noted, to "make the rubble bounce." Yield-to-weight ratio is only one way of measuring destructive potential. Another is destructiveness per delivery unit, which should give us a different perspective. A single modern bomber can deliver more destruction than all the weapons in the history of war put together. Surely modern destructive potential has reached revolutionary levels.

Delivery Capability

An explosion is of no particular military value unless the weapon can be effectively employed on a prospective target—marking a difference between Class A and Class B nuclear powers. Two dimensions of delivery capability are speed and accuracy. The World War II bombers flew at speeds of 300 to 400 mph at altitudes of 30,000 to 40,000 feet; the modern (yet aging) American bomber, the B-52, has a speed of somewhere around 650 mph at altitudes of 50,000 feet and higher. The U.S. Air Force SR-71, which has replaced the U-2 "spy plane," set the Atlantic speed record (New York–London) on September 1, 1974, of 1 hour, 55 minutes, flying at speeds of 2,000 mph and altitudes of 80,000 feet. Prototype planes have flown even faster. Early rockets such as the 'buzz bombs" (V-1s) of World War II went about 400 mph. The Russian Sputnik, which launched the satellite age, had a speed of 17,000 mph. What this all means is that land-launched ICBMs (such as the U.S. Minuteman III, with a range of over 7,000 miles) can hit just about any target in the world within 30 to 40 minutes. The potential of satellite weapons makes delivery time virtually an academic question.

Delivery accuracy is also part of the equation. Accuracy is measured in terms of circular error probability (CEP), which represents the radius of a circle within which one-half of all weapons launched will land. For example, if two missiles with a CEP of 1 mile were to be fired at a target, at least one of the missiles should land within a mile of the target. Although governments jealously guard targeting figures of their missiles for obvious reasons, it is speculated that the CEP for Soviet and American missiles is measured in city blocks —not bad for weapons launched halfway around the globe.

Military Strategy

The aspects of the nuclear revolution reviewed so far should make it clear that a revolution in military thinking is also called for. The Bomb is more than a mere quantitative jump in destructive potential —it is also a qualitative jump, requiring a rethinking not only of military precepts but also of diplomatic methods. Hence, the evolving military strategies of the major powers are of no small interest to us.

Modern reviews of military strategy have tended to concentrate on the two superpowers. Such emphasis is not illogical for three reasons. The Bomb has so interested observers that nuclear strategy, and the countries with the technology to have a sophisticated nuclear strategy (that is, the Big Two), have dominated our studies. Second, the United States and the Soviet Union would be Big Powers in their own right, even without the Bomb. Finally, the allies of the Big Two have tended to mold their military thinking to conform with that of their dominant partners. The major exceptions, France and mainland China, while they are trying to make their own nuclear way, are still a long way from superpower status. Consequently, the major study below is of the Big Two.

The Weapons

It is always risky to write about weapons systems because government secrecy and the many conflicting estimates of who has what make definitive assessments difficult. Further, technological advances or politico-military developments quickly make everything out-of-date. The Strategic Arms Limitations Talks (SALT) between Washington and Moscow, begun during President Nixon's administration, resulted in a temporary limit on nuclear arms development and deployment. The SALT negotiations resulted in two agreements in May of 1972. One was an Interim Agreement on Offensive Missiles, to be in force until 1977 (unless it was replaced by a more comprehensive treaty, or unless one of the parties gave six months' notice and withdrew). The essence of that accord (see Table 4-1, Comparative U.S. and Soviet Strategic Nuclear Strength) was to limit intercontinental ballistic missiles (ICBMs) to the number deployed or under construction as of July 1, 1972. Submarine-launched ballistic missiles (SLBMs) were limited to those deployed or under construction as of May 26, 1972 (one exception was that the number of SLBMs could be increased if an equal number of ICBMs were dismantled).

The 1972 SALT agreement (often called SALT I, as further SALT II negotiations were undertaken in Geneva, Switzerland, in late 1972) was the result of a deliberate policy of allowing the So-

TABLE 4-1: Comparative U.S. and Soviet Strategic Nuclear Strength

Weapon	United States		Soviet Union	
	1974	1977	1974	1977
ICBM[a]	1,054	1,054	1,527	1,618
SLBM[a]	656	710	560	950
Nuclear missile- firing subs[b]	41	44	34	62
Warheads	7,100	9,690	2,300	3,950
Long-range bombers	440	448	140	130

[a] Regulated by the May 26, 1972, SALT agreement for the five-year interim period to 1977.

[b] U.S. Polaris/Poseidon; Soviet Yankee/Delta.

Source: Adapted from U.S. Department of State, Office of Media Services, Bureau of Public Affairs, *The Strategic Balance*, Publication 8751 (March 1974), pp. 1–3; and from *Time*, February 11, 1974, p. 18.

viet Union to achieve parity (or at least rough equality) in strategic weapons. Figure 4-1, United States and Soviet Strategic Offensive Delivery Vehicles, shows the leveling off of U.S. strategic capability as well as the Soviet effort to catch up during the 1960s and early

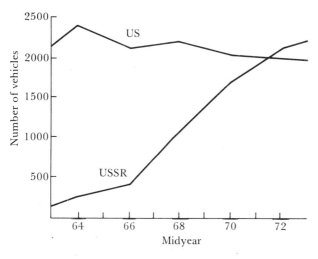

FIGURE 4-1. U.S. and Soviet Strategic Offensive Delivery Vehicles

1970s. The United States sees its offensive strength as being its ICBM force of 1,000 Minuteman (solid-fuel missiles with a payload of 1 megaton) and 54 older Titan II (liquid fuel but larger payload) missiles, all kept in well-protected underground silos; its Polaris/Poseidon SLBM system (SLBMs are generally comparable to ICBMs; they have a shorter range—3,000 to 4,000 miles—but the advantage of maneuverability, underwater invulnerability, and underwater launch capability); its superior long-range bomber force (B-52s); and its huge stockpile of nuclear warheads. Enhancing U.S. strategic missile capability, given the warhead stockpile, are MIRVs (multiple independently targeted re-entry vehicles), with which from three to ten separate warheads can be placed on a single ICBM/SLBM (e.g., the Minuteman III carries three warheads), thus multiplying targeting effectiveness. The multiple warheads separate from the parent missile in flight and are guided to independent targets miles apart, placing an extra burden on a defensive antiballistic missile (ABM) system. The United States is also presumed to have the advantage in missile accuracy and technological sophistication.

The Soviets' strategic offensive strength lies in their numerical superiority in ICBMs, larger ICBM payloads (e.g., the SS-9 has a range of more than 6,000 miles and carries a 25-megaton warhead), an SLBM/nuclear submarine force comparable with the U.S. force, and a newly evolved MIRV system in the SS-19 (comparable with the U.S. Minuteman III).

A second accord from SALT I concerned antiballistic missile (ABM) defense systems. Deployment was limited to 200 ABMs in each country, 100 around the capital city and 100 around an ICBM field. Although Soviet ABM capability is far greater than that of the United States, the modest controls of the SALT agreement were intended primarily to protect the Big Two from "minor" accidental ICBM firings, yet not create such a defensive threat that the Big Two would escalate their offensive capability. Also, such a modest ABM capability would protect the Big Two from countries with unsophisticated nuclear arsenals. As an example of how an ABM system works, the U.S. Safeguard system consists of four basic elements: (1) PAR (perimeter acquisition radar), which detects enemy ICBMs at long range shortly after they are launched, calculates attack paths, and passes the information to MSR; (2) MSR (missile site radar) directs two types of defensive missiles against incoming missiles: (3) Spartan, a long-range (400 miles) missile intended to intercept incoming missiles at ranges of 200 to 400 miles, and (4) Sprint, a smaller, faster, short-range (25 to 50 miles) missile designed to destroy any incoming missile that penetrated the Spartan defense.

A summit meeting was held in Moscow in July 1974 between the Soviets and the Americans. The two sides agreed to amend the SALT I ABM treaty to limit ABM deployment to one site instead of two. Since then a series of factors, not the least of which has been action by the U.S. Congress, have combined to eliminate the U.S. Safeguard ABM system.

In October 1974, a further summit meeting was held in Vladivostok at which the Big Two affirmed their intention of negotiating a new agreement that would last until 1985, incorporating the relevant provisions of the 1972 (SALT I) interim agreement. The SALT II negotiations, launched in late 1972, were resumed in Geneva in 1975 with a view toward implementing the Vladivostok agreement. The overall goal was to establish through 1985 firm ceilings on strategic delivery systems and MIRVs.

One item purposely not covered by SALT I was research and development (R&D); consequently, both superpowers are active in that area. In the face of some evidence that the Soviets are spending massively in this area, some American critics have talked of an "R&D gap." The United States is doing some research in the following areas, with the Soviet Union probably working along roughly similar lines: (1) development of the Trident missile-figuring submarine to replace the Polaris in the late 1970s, and of the B-1 bomber to replace the aging B-52 by 1980; (2) SCADs (subsonic cruise armed decoy) for B-52s and F-111s, which would resemble incoming aircraft on radar and would be decoys with nuclear warheads; (3) FOBS (fractional orbital bombardment system), with weapons that assume a trajectory like a satellite and can attack from more directions than missiles; (4) MaRVs (maneuverable re-entry vehicles), which would be more accurate than existing Minuteman warheads and would also be able to maneuver to evade defensive weapons on the way to targets; and (5) the Narwhal, a fast and maneuverable small submarine that would carry nuclear missiles.

This focus on strategic nuclear capability should not obscure the fact that both superpowers have an impressive tactical nuclear capability as well as the ability to fight a conventional World War II–type war. The United States apparently has a larger, more varied arsenal of tactical nuclear weapons (in the 1-kiloton range) to support battlefield troops in the face of Soviet numerical superiority. Both countries have roughly comparable navies, although American ships are on the average ten years older. Notable areas of difference are the U.S. dominance in attack carriers (14 carriers with 1,120 fighters and bombers; the Soviets have none) and Soviet dominance in conventional subs (200 to the United States' 14). While the two are about equal in nuclear-powered submarines (the United States has 101 to the Soviet Union's 115), the United States has an advantage in nuclear-powered surface ships, and the Soviets lead in guided-missile cruisers.

United States air strength lies in long-range bombers (see Table 4-1) and in the general technical superiority of its aircraft (although Soviet-built antiaircraft weapons in the hands of the Arabs were very effective against U.S.-built Israeli planes during the 1973 Middle East war), but the Soviets lead in numbers of tactical and fighter aircraft (4,500 to 3,900), strategic aircraft (815 to 347), and medium-range bombers (700 to 72). In terms of personnel, the United States has slightly over 2 million soldiers in uniform to the Soviet Union's 3.5 million. Both sides are also strong in the other essential resources (e.g., personnel, industry, allies) it takes to fight a major war.

Strategic Concepts

A basic discussion of nuclear strategy involves decisions about the types of wars that can occur. As in so many areas of international relations studies, the terminology in use is inconsistent. Such terms as "limited war" and "total war" were once common, but they were not flexible enough in describing participants, objectives, or weapons levels. Perhaps the following terms will be more useful for our purposes:

General war—involves the homelands of the Big Powers (especially the United States, the Soviet Union, and mainland China)

Local war—does not involve the homelands of the Big Powers

Total war—no restrictions on weapons used or objectives attacked

Limited war—limitations imposed on weapons used and objectives attacked

Based on these terms, the following options are possible:

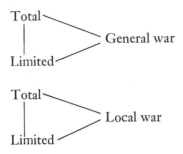

A *total general war* would be a "no-holds-barred" war between (or among) the Big Powers, probably also involving their allies. A *limited general war* might involve a brief nuclear exchange between Big Powers followed by quick negotiations for peace, or might simply be some type of conventional war between them. *Total local war* could involve either a Big Power using the Bomb on a small country or small countries fighting an all-out war against each other with no restrictions on the types of available weapons used. *Limited local war* might involve two smaller countries skirmishing over a border dispute. These terms are intended to be general, and consequently do not cover all the possible nuances of modern conflict. Clearly there are many levels of conflict between "total" and "limited" at the general and local war levels. The Korean and Vietnam conflicts would appear to be somewhere within the local war spectrum, although the United States, for example, would be likely to perceive those conflicts as more limited than would the participants immediately involved (that is, the Koreans and the Vietnamese).

Two conclusions relevant to strategic thinking are apparent from even these general terms. First, military policy options are increased, for now nuclear war becomes something more than an all-or-nothing possibility. Second, however, nuclear critics see in this very flexibility a new danger because it appears to make nuclear war more usable, more thinkable.

Perhaps the most pervasive concept in strategic thinking is the idea of deterrence. The essential rationale of deterrence is that military force is *not* to be used—military might is there to dissuade a potential enemy from attacking by convincing that enemy of the overwhelming superiority of one's own strength. The idea of deterrence is not new. Throughout history, kings and potentates have tried to impress one another with their military strength. A basic difference from the nuclear age, however, is that those kings could always *use* their armies and armadas if pushed far enough.

While the Bomb is also usable, we have already examined why it is hardly a comforting last resort. For that reason the most basic nuclear deterrent strategy is known by the singularly appropriate acronym (coined by Donald Brennan of the Hudson Institute) MAD —mutual assured destruction. Also known as the "balance of terror," MAD is a deterrent insofar as both sides know that no matter how total the use of nuclear weapons by one Big Power, the attacked state can always counterattack with a fatal blow. The image of two scorpions in a bottle captures the essence of MAD. Neither can back off or kill the other without being killed, so they are forced to maintain an uneasy truce. A major danger is misinterpreting an opponent's moves or making an accidental gesture that might provoke the opponent to attack. This was precisely the dilemma faced by the United States and the Soviet Union in the Cuban missile crisis, discussed in Chapter 1. To continue the scorpion analogy, a great deal of care had to be taken during the missile crisis to make all intentions and moves absolutely clear and credible while the bottle was being opened to let the scorpions back off cautiously.

On the assumption that ultimate confrontations like the Cuban missile crisis are both rare and potentially avoidable, the concept of "graduated deterrence" (also known as "flexible response") was developed. The idea here is to intimidate a potential opponent (most likely a weaker state) without an ultimate confrontation. In theory, the opponent should be dissuaded from action by the knowledge that whatever level of force is used, the stronger state can always use more.

There are two difficulties with the graduated deterrence theory, however. First, the real strength of deterrence lies in the *nonuse* of force, in the *threat*. Once hostilities start, the dynamics of battle are likely to take over and lead to escalation. Second, escalation will not necessarily be deterred by the weaker combatant's knowledge that the other has more power once actual combat has started. The "gambler's syndrome" may become involved—the losing player *has* to win back what has already been lost. The loser has "lost too much to quit now." If the larger power, for political or whatever reasons, does not take Clausewitz' advice on a quick and decisive war, a small war may grind on indefinitely as the weaker state becomes more determined and desperate. The longer such a conflict lasts, the more likely it is that outsiders will become involved, and pressure will mount on many sides for a "political" rather than a "military" solution to the conflict. The United States followed a graduated deterrence strategy in the Vietnam conflict, with the difficulties just discussed appearing.

Two further strategic concepts that beginning students are apt to encounter frequently are "counterforce" and "countercity" strategies. A counterforce strategy could only be followed by a very advanced nuclear power (probably only the United States and the Soviet Union at present) with accurate, sophisticated weapons capable of selectively wiping out the opponent's nuclear attack capability. A countercity strategy (sometimes called "minimum deterrence" because it poses a great psychological threat with a minimum of nuclear capability) is based on the ability to hit an opponent's cities—of tremendous emotional value, but not necessarily of real military value.

U.S. Military Strategy

Immediately after World War II American military strategy was dominated by the fear of a Soviet invasion of Western Europe. Soviet moves, particularly in Eastern Europe and Berlin, had convinced the United States that further Soviet aggression must be deterred. The creation of the North Atlantic Treaty Organization (NATO) in 1949 reflected Western determination to halt the perceived Soviet threat. The idea of strategic deterrence was not clearly articulated by American policy makers during those years, and evidence exists that they had not yet fully grasped the qualitative military implications of the Bomb, which was widely regarded as simply a more powerful weapon. The United States, like everybody else except perhaps the Russians, showed its exhaustion from World War II by dismantling its giant war machine and turning away from military matters. Some of the hesitancy in U.S. military policy formation reflected groping attempts to evaluate the rapidly changing world.

When the Korean War came in 1950, U.S. defense spending jumped from around $15 billion to about $40 billion. The Korean War was seen in some circles at that time as part of a worldwide aggressive effort by international communism directed from Moscow. The Truman administration justified high defense expenditures on the basis of a "crisis year" outlook. Large expenditures were temporarily necessary to turn back this new communist challenge, but as soon as the crisis was over things would get back to normal. This had been the American experience in sending aid under the Truman Doctrine in 1947 to meet the communist threat to Greece and Turkey. In spite of Korea, U.S. defense thinking still focused primarily on Europe and a strong NATO.

During the Eisenhower administration, U.S. strategic nuclear doctrine started to solidify as part of Eisenhower's promised "new look" at military strategy. The "crisis year" approach was discarded and replaced by the "long-haul" theory of a persistent threat that the United States could meet only if it spent its defense money frugally and wisely over a long period of time. Eisenhower's emphasis on a balanced budget (he believed that in the long run U.S. security was as dependent on a sound economy as on an expensive military establishment) resulted in arbitrary budget ceilings for the armed forces. Their missions were defined, as in fact U.S. defense strategy was defined, in terms of the budget allowance they received. The best way to stretch the defense dollar appeared to be to invest in nuclear devices, to the neglect of conventional forces. The nuclear strategy that naturally resulted from this budgetary policy was "massive retaliation." The formal articulation of that policy by Secretary of State John Foster Dulles in 1954 provoked a storm of protest from U.S. observers, including Henry Kissinger, Dean Acheson, Chester Bowles (a U.S. ambassador to India who later served President Kennedy in a variety of State Department functions), and General Maxwell Taylor.

General Taylor (who was subsequently special military adviser to President Kennedy and Chairman of the Joint Chiefs of Staff, and was finally appointed U.S. ambassador to South Vietnam by President Johnson in 1964) stated the essence of the protest in his widely read book *The Uncertain Trumpet*. He saw massive retaliation as a great fallacy, as a belief by American policy-makers ". . . that henceforth the use or the threatened use of atomic weapons of mass destruction would be sufficient to assure the security of the United States and its friends." [22]

22 Maxwell Taylor, *The Uncertain Trumpet,* Harper & Brothers, New York, 1960, p. 4.

He argued that massive retaliation was no longer useful as a military strategy. "In its heyday," he wrote, "Massive Retaliation could offer our leaders only two choices, the initiation of general nuclear war or compromise and retreat." [23] He cited among the examples of the failure of this doctrine Korea, the Chinese civil war, the guerrilla warfare in Greece and Malaya, Taiwan, Hungary, the Middle East, Laos, and Vietnam. Taylor's own proposal, which was used during the Kennedy administration, was called the "strategy of flexible response." He wrote:

This name suggests the need for a capability to react across the entire spectrum of possible challenge for coping with anything from general atomic war to infiltrations and aggressions such as threaten Laos and Berlin in 1959.

The new strategy would recognize that it is just as necessary to deter or win quickly a limited war as to deter general war. Otherwise, the limited war we cannot win quickly may result in our piecemeal attrition or involvement in an expanding conflict which may grow into general war which we all want to avoid.[24]

In January 1961, the Kennedy administration came into office. George Lowe, in his book *Age of Deterrence*, refers to 1961 as the "year of the big shift." [25] In his very first special message to Congress on the defense budget, President Kennedy called for defining expenditures in terms of commitments rather than defining commitments in terms of budget ceilings and for a "flexible response" strategy. He said:

Our defense posture must be both flexible and determined. Any potential aggressor contemplating an attack on any part of the free world with any kind of weapons, conventional or nuclear, must know that our response will be suitable, selective, swift and effective.[26]

The strategy of flexible response, or graduated deterrence, has remained at the heart of U.S. military thinking, with some modifications. The strategy was tested in Vietnam during the Kennedy and Johnson administrations, with highly unsatisfactory results. From

23 *Ibid.*, p. 5.
24 *Ibid.*, p. 6.
25 George Lowe, *The Age of Deterrence*, Little, Brown and Company, Boston, 1964, chap. 10.
26 Cited by John W. Gardner, ed., *To Turn the Tide*, Harper & Brothers, New York, 1962, p. 59.

a military standpoint the strategy surely had trouble because the United States could not "deter or win quickly a limited war." The worldwide political implications caused the Nixon administration to disengage and consider modifications in U.S. strategy.

The general outlines of that modified strategy, carried into the Ford administration, involve three items. First, under the growing burden (the U.S. defense budget was around $80 billion) of the nuclear arms race with the Soviet Union and the realization that it could not end as long as one side felt inferior, the Nixon administration articulated the concept of "nuclear sufficiency." The United States had sufficient nuclear strength for protection and would seek rough nuclear parity with the Soviet Union as a basis for what became the Strategic Arms Limitations Talks. Second, in the face of growing Chinese communist strength, since the presence of U.S. troops in Asia might lead to an unwanted confrontation (not to mention the problems of fighting a land war in Asia), the United States was to disengage from that continent. One dimension of that disengagement was the "saltwater strategy," involving a strong U.S. naval presence in the Pacific that would deter would-be aggressors from attacking the United States via the Pacific, serve as a ready forward arm of a U.S. attack force should that be necessary, and keep U.S. forces off the Asian continent in the relative safety of the fleet. A third item in the new U.S. strategy was the acceptance of the impossibility of an automatic U.S. response to all guerrilla warfare, "wars of national liberation," and other local disturbances around the globe. Further U.S. involvement in such conflicts would be likely to be limited to aid programs, and local governments would be expected to solve their own problems, with whatever diplomatic help the United States might be able to provide. Secretary of State Henry Kissinger's efforts to bring about a peace settlement among the Middle East combatants following the October War of 1973 is perhaps an example of an emerging U.S. strategy, although it must be admitted that the strategic importance of the Middle East makes *any* war there more than "just another local war."

Soviet Military Strategy

Soviet strategic policy can be covered much more briefly than U.S. strategy for at least two reasons. First, the fact of the Bomb's existence seems to contain its own internal, universal logic. Hence, much Soviet strategy is similar to that of the United States. As long as both the United States and the Soviet Union have fairly equal, highly sophisticated nuclear weapons systems, they are locked into the MAD deterrent strategy. The only likely way to break loose would be for one power to develop an effective counterforce capability that could destroy completely (or at least substantially) the opponent's counterattack capability, or to develop an impenetrable defense system. Such a development would have to come suddenly, however, or the other side would catch up and continue the arms race. A second reason for a quick survey of Soviet strategy is lack of data. Soviet secrecy and the cloistered nature of their policy process make study of their military strategy a matter of deduction and guesswork based on foreign policy statements and actions, apparent defense expenditures, and assorted publications (such as the widely studied book by General Vasily Sokolovsky, *Military Strategy*[27]).

Spurred on by the paranoia resulting from being a communist state surrounded by a hostile capitalist world, the Soviet Union has been primarily afraid of a capitalist attempt to destroy the system built out of the Bolshevik Revolution of 1917. Hitler's attack in 1941 and World War II did nothing to allay that fear, but by war's end the Red Army had proven itself strong enough to defend the Motherland—although not from the American Bomb. Deterring any potential U.S. nuclear attack immediately became a basic element of Soviet postwar military strategy.

Until the mid-1950s that deterrent strategy depended on using the presence of the Red Army in Eastern Europe to threaten U.S. allies in Western Europe. The Russians also concentrated on air defense measures and a program to get their own Bomb. By the late 1950s they had developed a modest bomber force capable of attacking the United States, so that both sides were now armed with nuclear weapons, if still quite unequally. The Russians have since concentrated on strategic missiles and their navy, resulting in the relationships discussed above and in Table 4-1.

The Soviet Union has ostensibly come to conclusions similar to those of the United States concerning the arms race and has appeared willing, even eager, to participate in the SALT negotiations.

27 Vasily D. Sokolovsky, ed., *Military Strategy: Soviet Doctrine and Concepts*, with an introduction by Raymond L. Garthoff, Frederick A. Praeger, Inc., New York, 1963.

Critics have suggested that the Soviet Union has been violating the spirit of SALT by spending massive amounts (estimates run as high as $20 billion) on the side to gain advantages. The overall Soviet defense budget is probably about $60 billion.

At the local war level, the Soviet Union has consistently perceived for itself a leadership role (and it has vied, often bitterly, with mainland China for dominance in this area) in aiding "wars of national liberation" around the world to help free "oppressed peoples" from "imperialist domination." Such a role is clearly consistent with the Soviet Union's revolutionary ideology and vision of "permanent operating factors" that will be generating worldwide revolution anyway. The Soviet Union has been generally careful to avoid any direct involvement of Soviet military forces, preferring instead to send economic and military aid (including technical advisers). This is essentially the strategy the United States has apparently come around to adopting, although the Soviet experiences in the Cuban missile crisis and during the Middle East wars of 1967 (Six-Day War) and 1973 (October War) show that even indirect involvement in local disputes can be risky.

One other important factor in current Soviet military strategy is the Sino-Soviet split. The military significance of that split between the two presumably allied communist powers can be seen in the unabated polemic conducted against each other in the press and public statements, the deployment of massive forces along their common border, and the persistent border clashes.

Military Strategies of the Lesser Nuclear Powers

Although mainland China has the Bomb, it does not yet have the advanced accompanying paraphernalia to mount a serious and sophisticated attack against either of the two superpowers. China's delivery capability is still linked with limited-range bombers and missiles. A 1975 estimate gave the Chinese a stockpile of 200 to 300 fission and fusion weapons and 20 to 30 medium-range and about 50 intermediate-range ballistic missiles. A multistage ICBM (with a potential range of 3,500 miles—capable of reaching Moscow and most Asian areas) had been produced but not yet operationally deployed.[28]

28 Drew Middleton, *New York Times,* Oct. 7, 1975, p. 13.

China's primary strategic consideration is defense of the homeland, the communist regime, and the fruits of the revolution. Possession of the Bomb enhances China's status in world councils, helps solidify China's Asian sphere of influence, and serves as an added deterrent (especially since relations between Washington and Peking have improved) to potential Soviet hegemony over China. One never quite knows how to evaluate the rhetoric of the communist press, but the Soviet Union has been speculating openly about the merits of a pre-emptive Soviet attack against Sinkiang province, the heart of China's nuclear complex.

Great Britain exploded an atomic bomb in 1952 and a hydrogen bomb in 1957, but by that time the increasing expense of a usable delivery capability began pricing Great Britain out of the market. Great Britain does not have the resources to be a full-fledged Big Power. Perhaps an independent British nuclear force made sense in the early 1950s, but Soviet counterforce advances made Great Britain more a potential Soviet target than a credible threat. To avoid being only a target, the British had to disperse their nuclear force, at great expense. The British nuclear force is now tied to a small nuclear Polaris fleet, which makes Great Britain highly dependent on the United States. The expense of converting to the more advanced Poseidon system will either force the British to abandon their nuclear power status or make them totally dependent on the United States.

Although in a somewhat stronger economic position than Great Britain, France finds it equally difficult to support a credible independent nuclear force. Depending on bombers for delivery, the French nuclear commitment seems increasingly anachronistic. General Charles de Gaulle saw France's independent nuclear strike force, or *force de frappe*, as a way to purchase status and guarantee French sovereignty. He did not trust the U.S. guarantee of an American nuclear shield for Europe and saw the *force de frappe* as a way to escape Yankee domination. He insisted France's nuclear force was credible, for although it might not deter a Soviet attack, it could at least exact a price for any such attack.

Advances in weapons technology are likewise outdistancing France's ability to keep up, and there are mounting domestic pressures within France for a reconsideration of the *force de frappe* and France's future European and world role as a nuclear power.

It remains to be seen what will become of the new Indian Bomb, although India's perennial difficulties in feeding the population make the policy decision to allocate meager resources to develop the Bomb highly questionable. There is no doubt that a certain amount of political status and deference accrues to those states that belong to the nuclear club. Whether the mere fact of owning the Bomb can be used to gain real long-term political or military advantage has yet to be demonstrated. In the meantime, however, the proliferation of nuclear weapons threatens to sever the hair supporting the sword of Damocles above the arena of world politics.

KOREA: THE UNITED STATES

IN A LIMITED LOCAL WAR

The Context of the Korean Conflict

The foregoing material gives us a better understanding of the effect of nuclear weapons on modern international relations and the background for interpreting in a modest way specific military confrontations. The Korean conflict illustrates many of the issues raised in this chapter: the use of force in international relations, the threat of the Bomb, and the concept of limited wars. More broadly, the Korean conflict lets us study such other areas of international interest as ideology and power politics, Big Power foreign policy and confrontation, and United Nations peace-keeping.

The Korean War occurred during the transitional period between World War II and the full blossoming of nuclear technology and strategy. The Soviet Union and the United States were able to keep their roles in the conflict limited. China felt more threatened by the proximity of the action and had to intervene, being careful not to provoke the United States into a nuclear attack. In the Cuban missile crisis, discussed in Chapter 1, the United States perceived the direct threat posed to the U.S. mainland by the Soviet offensive missiles in Cuba as grounds for immediate escalation into a serious nuclear confrontation. The implications of such diverse events as the Korean War and the Cuban missile crisis require us to step back and reflect on the broad concepts involved in the international use of military power, particularly nuclear power, that have been examined in this chapter.

Observers pondering World War II during the immediate aftermath of that conflict were invariably impressed by the awesome totality of it all, in terms of both objectives and means. Most of the world's states were touched in one way or another by the war, millions of soldiers were under arms, and economies had been geared up to support the war effort on an unprecedented scale. Common military points of reference included *Blitzkrieg*, unconditional surrender, unrestricted submarine warfare, strategic bombing, "blockbusters," V-2s, kamikaze warfare, prisoner-of-war torture, fifth-column movements, the Soviet technique of massing artillery to destroy an entire village with a single clap of thunder, and the "mushroom cloud."

Everyone immediately related to place names like London, Dresden, Berlin, Stalingrad, El Alamein, Leyte Gulf, Okinawa, Hiroshima, and Nagasaki. Perhaps equally significant, people also related to place names like Versailles, Munich, Ethiopia, Poland, Finland, and Pearl Harbor. Versailles became a Western synonym for armistice instead of victory, while the Germans, in particular, came to regard the Versailles settlement ending World War I as a "knife in the back" and an unsatisfactory conclusion to the war. Munich became a synonym for appeasement, for willingness to give potential troublemakers the benefit of the doubt in the hope of preserving peace. Ethiopia, Poland, Finland, and Pearl Harbor became examples of where trusting one's opponents could lead. On top of all this was the increasing postwar belligerency on the part of the Cold War opponents—the United States and the Soviet Union. One has to understand this atmosphere to understand the Korean conflict.

War Begins

Korea is a peninsula of some 85,000 square miles in East Asia jutting off the coast of China and separating the Yellow Sea from the Sea of Japan (see Figure 4-2, a sketch map of Korea). Chinese and Japanese influences have been strong throughout Korean history, but the Koreans are a distinct people with a distinct culture. Korea (or Chosen, as the Japanese called it) is important to modern world politics for two reasons: (1) its proximity to China, the Soviet Far East, and Japan, and (2) its formal annexation to the Japanese empire from 1910 to 1945. Although a provisional Korean national

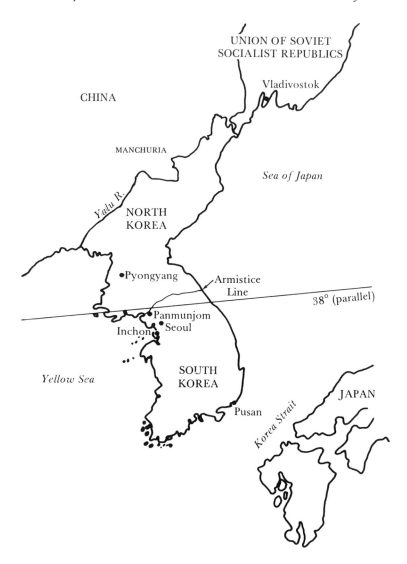

FIGURE 4-2. Korea

government under Syngman Rhee had been established in Shanghai after 1919, and although Korean independence had been promised by the United States, Great Britain, and China at the Cairo Conference (1943), the Korean peninsula became significant with the military defeat of Japan, which left a political vacuum in Korea.

In 1945, military units of the Soviet Union accepted the surrender of Japanese forces north of the 38th parallel in Korea, while the United States 24th Corps moved in and occupied Korea south of the 38th parallel. The 38th parallel was a purely arbitrary line intended for occupation convenience, but as the wartime alliance between the allies dissolved and the Cold War developed, a separate regime was set up in each sector. Under United Nations auspices popular elections were held in the south (they were not allowed in the north), leading to the formation of the Republic of Korea (ROK), with its capital at Seoul, in August 1948 under President Syngman Rhee. The following month the Democratic People's Republic of Korea (DPRK) was proclaimed in the north under the control of a Communist party with the capital in Pyongyang. By mid-1949, Soviet and American forces had withdrawn, leaving behind an artificially divided country with industry and trade concentrated in the north and agriculture in the south. Strained relations between the two Korean governments culminated in the surprise North Korean attack across the 38th parallel on June 25, 1950, starting the Korean War, which ground on until a cease-fire agreement was finally reached at Panmunjom on July 27, 1953.

The reasons for the North Korean attack are still disputed by Western observers. It has been considered (1) the result of a belief on the part of the North Koreans (and/or their Soviet backers) that they could quickly and easily reunify the country by force; (2) a Soviet gambit to dissuade Japan from entering the Western defense structure; (3) an attempt to eliminate a Western toehold and solidify a communist sphere of influence in Asia (an attempt perhaps inadvertently encouraged by U.S. Secretary of State Dean Acheson's statement several months earlier defining the American "defense perimeter" in the Pacific, which omitted Korea); (4) a maneuver involving Chinese and Soviet ambitions in which Korea was simply a pawn; or (5) Stalin's probing of the West's will to resist as a prelude to activity in the real target area—Europe.

The Western Response

Certainly most of these assessments capture parts of the truth. What was immediately important, however, was that the West—the United States in particular—viewed the invasion of South Korea as part of the communist world's plan for global domination and believed that Stalin was on the verge of launching World War III. Communist rhetoric; Soviet intransigence and belligerency in Berlin, Eastern Europe, and the Balkans (the United States and the Soviet Union had even fought each other "by proxy" in Greece and Turkey); and the recent "loss" of China to Mao's communist regime all bolstered this view. After the invasion by the North, only quick intervention in the Korean situation by the noncommunist world would head off further thrusts by the communists and escalation into a general war.

President Harry Truman, explaining the need for U.S. intervention in Korea, noted in his *Memoirs* that communist efforts there were similar to the earlier moves of Hitler, Mussolini, and the Japanese. Further, expressing a view characteristic of U.S. Cold War policy, he wrote:

I felt certain that if South Korea was allowed to fall Communist leaders would be emboldened to override nations closer to our own shores. If the Communists were permitted to force their way into the Republic of Korea without opposition from the free world, no small nation would have the courage to resist threats and aggression by stronger Communist neighbors. If this was allowed to go unchallenged it would mean a third world war, just as similar incidents had brought on the second world war.[29]

The Western response to the North Korean invasion was complicated by the fact that most citizens had never heard of Korea, United Nations machinery for keeping peace was untested, and Western military forces had been substantially dismantled following World War II. Much of the military force that was available was stationed in Western Europe to deter further Soviet moves there, and in fact, much of the military build-up during the Korean War occurred within NATO forces in Europe. West German Chancellor Konrad Adenauer's persistent concern for Berlin and the long, troubled "iron curtain" border with East Germany—along with the sense of urgency felt by the Allies over Korea—had hastened the re-creation of a German army.

Caught by surprise, the West was militarily unprepared for Korea and had no coherent strategy for the kind of conflict that erupted there. Both President Truman and Secretary of State Acheson were strongly committed to the spirit of the United Na-

29 Harry S. Truman, *Memoirs*, vol. II, *Years of Trial and Hope*, Doubleday & Company, Inc., Garden City, N.Y., 1956, p. 333.

tions and immediately called upon U.N. Secretary-General Trygve Lie and the Security Council for a response to the North Korean violation of the charter. The U.S. action in appealing to the United Nations was supported by the knowledge that it could expect generally favorable voting majorities in the United Nations as well as by the expectation of a United Nations endorsement of a policy move the United States knew it had to take anyway in response to the North Korean invasion. Because of the chance absence of the Soviet Union from the Security Council (the Soviet Union was boycotting the Council over the issue of representation of communist China instead of Nationalist China), the Security Council, unhampered by a Big Power veto, called upon North Korea to cease hostilities and withdraw to the 38th parallel. Member states of the United Nations were asked for support. Although the Soviet Union subsequently returned to deadlock the Security Council, the United Nations participated in the war through the support of the General Assembly and its "Uniting for Peace" resolution (see Chapter 8), which transferred peace-keeping initiative from the Security Council to the General Assembly. A unified command under the leadership of the United States united sixteen nations under the U.N. flag to repel the North Korean attack. U.S. General Douglas MacArthur was named supreme commander of the United Nations forces. The bulk of the U.N. commitment was provided by the United States and the Republic of Korea.

The Conduct and Conclusion of the War

The Korean War had at least five significant phases: (1) the North Korean advance, which ultimately pushed the defending U.N. forces into a defensive perimeter around the South Korean city of Pusan; (2) the initial counteroffensive by the United Nations command, capped by the brilliant surprise landing at Inchon, which re-established noncommunist control south of the 38th parallel; (3) the decision to cross the parallel into North Korea and ultimately to push on to the Yalu River separating Korea from China (General MacArthur was subsequently fired by President Truman largely because of disagreements over crossing the Yalu into China); (4) the North Korean counteroffensive, aided by large numbers of communist Chinese "volunteers," which pushed U.N. forces back toward the 38th parallel; and (5) military stalemate in the area of the 38th parallel, during which political negotiations to stop the fighting were held at Panmunjom.

The fact that the United States was militarily unprepared for Korea and had no solid strategic philosophy for that kind of conflict was initially masked by the need to do something immediately to salvage the deteriorating military situation in South Korea following North Korea's attack (the United States would surely have felt compelled to intervene even if the United Nations had not approved the operation) and by the U.N. success in regaining control up to the 38th parallel. The success of the Inchon landing goaded the U.N. command and U.S. decision-makers into rethinking their military goals in Korea. Instead of merely pushing the North Korean army back across the 38th parallel, they began to think of punishing North Korea for its mischief and even of forcibly reuniting the Koreas from the South (although not without misgivings, especially from U.N. members and U.S. allies). When China, refusing to respond to U.N. assurances of peaceful intent vis-à-vis itself, entered the war, there was a bitter debate in the United States over the merits of carrying the war to Chinese territory

In spite of American uncertainty about military objectives and ad hoc decisions on strategy, the Korean War remained a limited local war (although from the perspective of North and South Korea it might have appeared to be a total local war), fought for limited political objectives. It was a frustrating war, and the lessons concerning limited wars to come out of Korea (to be reaffirmed in the similar, yet strikingly different, Vietnam conflict, involving first France and then the United States) are worth noting by observers of international relations.

The case for escalating the war was asserted vigorously in the United States and was not unpersuasive. Yet while one could understand the urge to expand the conflict, such a policy would not have been without grave risk. To begin with, the United States was the major contributor to the war effort (except for South Korea, other U.N. allies generally made only token commitments). Americans came to feel a personal stake in the war, with a simultaneous growing disregard for the views of their allies. The American public was sympathetic to the image of tiny, beleaguered South Korea fighting bravely for its freedom against an outside invader. With memories of World War II still fresh, Americans had a sense of total war, invincible military might, unconditional surrender, and victory. These memories were reinforced by movie portrayals of allied military brilliance and the romantic side of war. A memory that died quickly was the fact that it had taken the combined military might of most of the world and several bitter years of war to defeat three powerful, but nevertheless relatively small, countries— Germany, Italy, and Japan.

Many Americans could not understand why victory did not come quickly in Korea, since the military forces under the U.N. command should have been superior in every respect to the North Korean army. A sense that the politicians were "meddling in the war" and forcing the superior U.N. forces to fight under wraps spread. Why was the war kept limited? Why didn't the United States use its superior technology to defeat North Korea? There was talk of impeaching President Truman, especially after the firing of General MacArthur. Limited war didn't make sense to many, especially when the stalemate at the 38th parallel and the Panmunjom negotiations dragged on and on.

Toward the end of 1951, heavy fighting wound down into small unit skirmishes that were bitterly fought, generally indecisive, and interrupted by political negotiations that often resulted in military withdrawals from areas won in hard combat the day before. Place names like "Heartbreak Ridge" and "Bloody Ridge" became landmarks of the war. General MacArthur expressed the frustration over this kind of war in his April 19, 1951, address to Congress: ". . . once war is forced upon us, there is no other alternative than to apply every available means to bring it to a swift end. War's very object is victory—not prolonged indecision. In war indeed, there can be no substitute for victory." A congressional minority report after the MacArthur hearings made a similar point:

We believe that a policy of victory must be announced to the American people in order to restore unity and confidence. It is too much to expect that our people will accept a limited war. Our policy must be to win. Our strategy must be devised to bring about decisive victory.[30]

An additional cause of U.S. frustration with the war was the

30 Hearings before the Committee on Armed Services and the Committee on Foreign Relations, *Military Situation in the Far East*, U.S. Senate, 82d Cong., 1st Sess., 1951, p. 3590.

philosophical, abstract nature of the reasons for fighting in Korea. Coming to the defense of a small country was one thing, but the long-range relevance of the effort to U.S. security was never clear to many critics. How could Americans be asked to give up their lives in a faraway land (especially when there were unparalleled opportunities for a happy, productive, good life at home) simply to send a political message to the communist world that the noncommunist world was "drawing the line" in Korea? The Cuban missile crisis, discussed in Chapter 1, even though it threatened general war and thermonuclear holocaust, probably received more support from the American public because the stakes appeared more immediately relevant and concrete. The American homeland was being threatened directly, and the villain was clear.

The identity of the "real troublemaker" was a problem in Korea, and this is likely to be the case in many local wars where small belligerent nations have large, powerful friends willing to aid them. The situation becomes particularly sticky from a diplomatic standpoint when that aid is covert or is offered in a way that frees the donor from formal, legal responsibility as a belligerent. It was no secret that Premier Kim Il Sung of North Korea had spent many years in Russia and had assumed power in Pyongyang with the approval of Stalin. Further, the Russians were sending aid to North Korea in the form of matériel and technical advisers. There were also reports that Russian pilots had been sighted at the controls of North Korean aircraft. Nevertheless, the Soviet Union avoided any direct confrontation with U.N. forces. Even the Chinese participated in the war as "volunteers," thus avoiding formal belligerency.

The United States also did not participate in the Korean effort as though it were a formal war. The United States regarded the campaign as a "police action," which was of great significance for U.S. domestic politics—in particular for the discussion of the relative war powers of the executive and the legislative branches of government. Fighting North Korea struck many Americans as equivalent to "being mean to a neighbor's dog that was digging up your lawn when one should actually be confronting the dog's master." If China and the Soviet Union were enabling North Korea to continue the war, then many felt that the war should have been taken *directly* to them—using atomic bombs if necessary.

On the other side of the ledger, there were persuasive reasons for not expanding the Korean conflict into either a total local war or some form of general war. The seriousness of Big Power confrontation was apparently understood by the Soviet Union, China, and the United States. While both China and the Soviet Union could have mounted serious offensives against U.S. allies in Western Europe and Asia, neither could have launched a substantial attack against the United States itself. That fact, combined with the U.S. ability to wreak unacceptable damage on their own countries, certainly dissuaded the two communist powers from any precipitous and uncalculated escalation. And in spite of congressional and public pressures, the Truman administration was likewise not disposed to unacceptable risks, since United States strength was already thinly deployed around the world, and Americans were faced with hard budgetary choices at home.

A special element in escalation considerations was the potential U.S. option of resorting to atomic warfare. One thoughtful student of military policy suggested four reasons why the United States did not use atomic weapons:

1 Many American policy advisors continued to feel that the Korean conflict was a Soviet feint and counseled conserving the then relatively limited supply of U.S. atomic weapons. The fear was that the United States might use all its nuclear weapons in Korea before the "real" Soviet offensive against Western Europe began.

2 There was also a feeling that there were no appropriate targets for nuclear weapons in Korea (although because of the novelty of atomic weapons, sophisticated strategic or tactical targeting doctrines had not yet been developed).

3 U.S. allies, in particular the British, expressed vigorous moral opposition to atomic warfare. A public comment by President Truman mentioning potential use of the atomic bomb, for example, led British Prime Minister Clement Attlee to fly to the United States for an immediate conference.

4 Finally, there was the chance that any U.S. initiation of atomic warfare might have provoked retaliation despite the very limited Soviet atomic capability—for example, against Pusan or Japan.[31]

The history of modern Korea is more than just a convenient example of a limited war, however. It is also the tragic story of a

31 See Morton H. Halperin, *Limited War in the Nuclear Age*, John Wiley & Sons, Inc., New York, 1963, pp. 39–58.

homogeneous people in a small country getting caught up in the politics and wars of powerful neighbors. Circumstances have divided this country into two ideologically opposed armed camps. Despite the dramatic joint communiqué issued on July 4, 1972, by the governments of Premier Kim Il Sung in the North and President Park Chung Hee in the South signifying their intention to discuss the problem of "unifying the divided Fatherland," it still remains to be seen whether much progress in that direction will materialize.[32] Public statements by several of the governments interested in the future of the Koreas, as well as by the Korean governments themselves, would seem to indicate a hardening of positions during the mid-1970s.

BIBLIOGRAPHY

Angell, Norman. *The Great Illusion: A Study of the Relation of Military Power to National Advantage*, 4th ed. G. P. Putnam's Sons, New York, 1913.

Aron, Raymond. *The Century of Total War*. Doubleday & Company, Inc., New York, 1954.

———. *On War*. Doubleday & Company, Inc., New York, 1959.

Art, Robert J., and Kenneth N. Waltz, eds. *The Use of Force: International Politics and Foreign Policy*. Little, Brown and Company, Boston, 1971.

Bramson, Leon, and George W. Goethals, eds. *War: Studies from Psychology, Sociology, Anthropology*. Basic Books, Inc., New York, 1964.

Brodie, Bernard. *War & Politics*. The Macmillan Company, New York, 1973

Buchan, Alastair. *War in Modern Society*. Harper & Row, Publishers, Incorporated, New York, 1968.

Clarke, Robin. *The Science of War and Peace*. McGraw-Hill Book Company, New York, 1972.

Clausewitz, Karl von. *On War*. Modern Library, Inc., New York, 1943.

Fromm, Erich. *Escape From Freedom*. Rinehart & Company, Inc., New York, 1941.

32 See L. K. Chopra, "Korea's Path of Unification," *Military Review*, 53 (February 1973), 19–29.

Garthoff, Raymond L. *Soviet Strategy in the Nuclear Age.* Frederick A. Praeger, Inc., New York, 1958.

Halperin, Morton H. *Defense Strategies for the Seventies.* Little, Brown and Company, Boston, 1971.

———. *Limited War in the Nuclear Age.* John Wiley & Sons, Inc., New York, 1963.

Herz, John. *International Politics in the Atomic Age.* Columbia University Press, New York, 1959.

Iklé, Fred Charles. *Every War Must End.* Columbia University Press, New York, 1971.

Janowitz, Morris. *The Professional Soldier.* The Free Press, Glencoe, Ill., 1960.

Kahn, Herman. *On Thermonuclear War.* Princeton University Press, Princeton, N.J., 1961.

———. *Thinking About the Unthinkable.* Horizon Press, New York, 1962.

Kissinger, Henry A. *Nuclear Weapons and Foreign Policy.* Harper & Brothers, New York, 1957.

———. *The Necessity for Choice.* Harper & Brothers, New York, 1961.

Knorr, Klaus. *On the Uses of Military Power in the Nuclear Age.* Princeton University Press, Princeton, N.J., 1966.

Lapp, Ralph. *The Weapons Culture.* Penguin Books, Inc., Baltimore, 1969.

Lawrence, Robert M. *Arms Control and Disarmament: Practice and Promise.* Burgess Publishing Company, Minneapolis, 1973.

Lorenz, Konrad. *On Aggression.* Bantam Books, Inc., New York, 1963.

Luard, Evan. *Conflict and Peace in the Modern International System.* Little, Brown and Company, Boston, 1968.

Luttwak, Edward. *A Dictionary of Modern War.* Harper and Row, Publishers, Incorporated, New York, 1971.

May, Mark A. *A Social Psychology of War and Peace.* Yale University Press, New Haven, Conn., 1943.

Millis, Walter. *Arms and Men.* G. P. Putnam's Sons, New York, 1956.

Millis, Walter, and James Real. *The Abolition of War.* The Macmillan Company, New York, 1963.

Osgood, Charles E. *An Alternative to War or Surrender.* University of Illinois Press, Urbana, 1962.

Pruitt, Dean G., and Richard C. Snyder. *Theory & Research on the Causes of War.* Prentice-Hall, Inc., Englewood Cliffs, N.J., 1969.

Rakove, Milton, L., ed. *Arms and Foreign Policy in the Nuclear Age.* Oxford University Press, New York, 1972.

Richardson, Lewis F. *Statistics of Deadly Quarrels.* The Boxwood Press, Pittsburgh, Pa., 1960.

Rosecrance, Richard, *International Relations: Peace or War?* McGraw-Hill Book Company, New York, 1973.

Russett, Bruce M. *Power and Community in World Politics.* W. H. Freeman and Company, San Francisco, 1974.

Schelling, Thomas C. *Arms and Influence.* Yale University Press, New Haven, Conn., 1966.

———. *The Strategy of Conflict.* Harvard University Press, Cambridge, Mass., 1960.

Snyder, Glenn H. *Deterrence and Defense.* Princeton University Press, Princeton, N.J., 1962.

Sokolovsky, Vasily D., ed. *Military Strategy: Soviet Doctrine and Concepts.* Frederick A. Praeger, Inc., New York, 1963.

Spiegel, Steven L., and Kenneth N. Waltz, eds. *Conflict in World Politics.* Winthrop Publishers, Inc., Cambridge, Mass., 1971

Taylor, Maxwell. *The Uncertain Trumpet.* Harper & Brothers, New York, 1960.

Tillema, Herbert K. *Appeal to Force: American Military Intervention in the Era of Containment.* Thomas Y. Crowell Company, New York, 1973.

Wolfe, Thomas W. *Soviet Strategy at the Crossroads.* Harvard University Press, Cambridge, Mass., 1964.

Wright, Quincy. *A Study of War.* University of Chicago Press, Chicago, 1942.

Ideology and
Political Power:
The Cold War and Beyond

Chapter 3 described the bipolar world, dominated by the United States and the Soviet Union, that emerged after World War II. The pronounced dominance of the two superpowers that characterized much of the postwar East/West jockeying for power has given way to multipolar international politics. One interesting dimension of shifting political alignments has been the emergence of North/South politics and the growing political voice of the Third World; these will be examined in the following chapter.

THE UNTANGLING OF IDEOLOGY AND POLITICS
EAST VERSUS WEST

In spite of the multipolar thrust of modern international relations, the East-versus-West confrontation demands our continuing attention for at least three reasons. First, the postwar jousting for power by the United States and the Soviet Union established political patterns that are still in existence. Second, the influence of the Big Two on the direction of modern world politics, although altered, continues to be significant. The preceding chapter examined the military dimension of that influence. Third, the East/West Cold War shows the interplay of ideology and politics in modern international relations. This chapter is primarily concerned with that interplay as it relates to Soviet and American foreign policies.

Few modern observers would contend that ideology of some kind is not closely intertwined with the foreign policies of most states. Defined in general terms, an ideology is a fundamental belief system involving basic assumptions about political, economic, religious, and other social values. It includes the acceptance of some concept of an ideal way of life, a commitment to defend it, and perhaps a desire to spread this "truth" to others.

It would be a mistake to view ideology, however, as the sole motivating force in human relations. Rather, ideology should more properly be regarded as only *one* of the dynamic elements of political life, both national and international. Ideology will be part of the perceptual prism through which national decision-makers will see the world. Further, these decision-makers will explain and justify their decisions by referring to the prevailing national ideology.

The scholar's task involves separating ideology as a decision-making factor from the often more immediate influences of forces affecting national political power. For the most part the task is never completed because ideology and political power are often so closely intertwined as to defy separate analysis. The following section examines briefly the theoretical tenets of democracy and communism. While the Cold War between the Soviet Union and the United States is often regarded as a purely ideological struggle, a closer look at the Cold War and the foreign policies of the Big Two reveals the simultaneous significant influence of power elites.

Democracy and Communism

Obviously, complex and highly varied political ideologies cannot be fully discussed in a few pages. Nevertheless, a working familiarity with the basic tenets of the ideologies associated with the foreign policies of the Soviet Union and the United States is necessary to understand modern international relations.

Basic Democratic Tenets. Democracy, although its origins can be traced back to ancient Greece, is hardly a nice, neat package of ideological precepts. Rather than a systematic ideology, democracy is primarily a commitment to a way of doing things, a commitment to a political *process* based on popular sovereignty (ultimate authority to rule is vested with the people), political equality (all adults are equal in their ability to consent or dissent within the political process), and majority rule (law and policy decisions are linked to what the majority of the people, or their representatives, want at a given time).

Democracy is more than a sterile commitment to a process, but there is wide disagreement among democratic thinkers concerning the normative goals of democratic society. There is a general sense of working toward some undefined "good life" and perhaps toward the development of a "democratic person." The reason for the vagueness lies mainly with the fundamental democratic belief in rational empiricism—a belief in people's innate rational ability to sort out experiences and attach meaning to them. True democrats eschew ultimate answers and are suspicious of prepackaged rational doctrines that would offer dogmatic and "easy" explanations for what they know to be complex social problems. True democrats are willing to admit their confusion in the face of humanity's complexity, but they are nonetheless confident in their rational ability to try to figure it out. Those committed to democracy cannot label others heretics or deviationists. Those with opposing views must be respected (if not necessarily liked) simply because their input may be valuable in explaining the human condition. Nobody has a monopoly on truth, and those who advance such a claim are distrusted. The emphasis is on means, not ends, for no one is truly sure of the end. As one's experiences change, so should one's assessment of where one is and where one is going in history. True democrats are people eternally in search of truth, not really expecting to find it, yet still optimistic.

Another basic tenet of democratic thought is a firm belief in the individual (and the related concept of political equality) as the basic element of value—not the state, economic class, or other entity. The relative value attached to the individual varies from the free-swinging individualism of the American frontier mentality to the highly socialized individualism within a group context found in Western Europe. Whatever the relative value, individualism is strongly supported by the two major currents of Western civilization—the philosophical (people are special because they have the gift of reason) and the religious (all people are the children of one God, or all people have that special spark within them called a soul).

Democratic thought also has been influenced by the idea of contract that developed out of feudal arrangements. Thinkers such as Jean Jacques Rousseau and John Locke portrayed democratic society as based on contractual obligations in which government is bound and limited by contract (a constitution) with society (the ultimate source of political authority). Government is seen as an instrument to be used to achieve higher human goals. The state is only a means, not an end in itself. There are also strong natural-law assumptions in democratic thought. Human purpose and human rights existed prior to the creation of political entities such as the state, and they can be defined independently of the state. The democrat reserves the right to question the law of the state (human law is fallible) by referring to a higher law based either on religious principles (e.g., the citizen challenges the law of the state because he or she believes it to be immoral) or on rational principles (e.g., the citizen challenges the law because it appears unreasonable or stupid, or just doesn't make sense).

The elements discussed above are the basic aspects of democracy, but there is a great deal of dispute over the specifics of democracy, and surely the commitment to the freedom to dissent represented by a belief in rational empiricism would not lead one to expect otherwise. Democracy as a political philosophy itself, however, has many internal dilemmas that defy easy resolution—e.g., majority rule versus minority rights (especially when minorities based on such factors as ethnic origin, religion, language, or regionalism often tend to become permanent) or the democratic prerequisite of an informed public versus apathetic voters and potential manipulation of the masses by emotional issues. Perhaps the ultimate rationalization, if not resolution, of such problems lies in their remaining open for continuing examination and discussion.

A basic communist criticism of Western liberal formulations of democracy concerns the economic underpinnings of society, which communist observers feel Western democrats inadequately acknowledge. They see political equality (and therefore *real* democracy) as hinging on economic equality (or at least on a redefined societal relationship to economic forces), which communist regimes not surprisingly claim to offer. While it is true that Western democratic thinkers often seem to discuss politics as a subject separate from economics, communist critics are largely producing a Western straw man (that is, a creature created solely to be knocked down) for at least two reasons: (1) unrestrained laissez faire economics in Western countries has by and large been replaced by a substantial government role in economic life—in fact, trade unionism, social democracy, Christian democracy, and the like have been geared precisely toward ameliorating the kinds of social evils that led to Marxism; and (2) while communist theorists are substantially correct in seeing political power gravitating to those with economic power, they err when they suggest that a transfer of power from those with money to a government bureaucracy will necessarily result in a better deal for the public.

The communist regimes tend to see themselves as "democratic" (indeed, the term "people's democracy" is common) and Western governments as "capitalistic." Western critics of communist regimes reject their claims to being democratic, for although universal suffrage and exceedingly high voting turnouts are normal in communist systems, ruling communist parties claim they have a sole mandate to guide society and allow only a single slate of party-approved nominees to be presented to the electorate. Intraparty democracy within communist parties themselves presumably rests on the concept of "democratic centralism"—the idea that there will be free and open input into the party decision-making process until a final decision is made, which will then be unequivocally supported by all. In practice, democratic centralism tends to put the decision to open party policy to questioning into the hands of the party bureaucracy rather than the rank and file, and favors a self-perpetuating elite and *their* policies. In fact, grass roots initiatives are regarded as serious heresy to be contained and even punished—a view that Western democrats unconditionally denounce.

Democratic philosophy has at least two important implications for international relations: (1) the foreign policies of democratic states are closely linked with public opinion (both its virtues and its evils) and the vagaries of domestic politics; and (2) democratic states seem to lack the determined sense of mission and long-term goals associated with states following more dogmatic ideologies, although democratic states seem highly susceptible to short-term crusades.

Communist Ideology. Communism is often said to offer a more complete and coherent theoretical package than democracy, although it too has internal dilemmas and contradictions. The roots of communism as a form of social system go far back into history, and communal social arrangements have appeared in one form or another at many points around the world. The fundamental theme of communism is a commitment to the common ownership (that is, by all members of society jointly, not by separate individuals) of property, particularly the means of production. The Greek philosopher Plato portrayed a communist form of society in his well-known political treatise *The Republic.* Many subsequent political thinkers have perceived evils in private ownership and advanced varying schemes for restructuring society. A most important contribution to communist thought appeared in the year 1848, when Friedrich Engels and Karl Marx produced the *Communist Manifesto,* linking revolutionary communism to the problems of their contemporary industrial society. Subsequent communist thought has been heavily influenced by Marx's writings (such as *Das Kapital*, which analyzed and criticized capitalism and the industrial revolution), although basic Marxism has been greatly amplified and altered by its followers.

Basic communist theory as articulated by Karl Marx (Marxism) has three primary elements: (1) a dialectical philosophy, (2) an economic philosophy, and (3) a view of the state and revolution linked with economics. Marx borrowed the notion of the dialectic from Hegel, as already noted in Chapter 2, as a vehicle for explaining history. While Hegel had focused on the clash of ideas (dialectical idealism), Marx saw the meaning of history revealed in the clash of material forces (dialectical materialism) based on economic considerations, specifically economic classes. The *Communist Manifesto* proclaims, for example, that "the history of all hitherto existing society is the history of class struggles." During the feudal period lords (thesis) clashed with serfs (antithesis) producing a new middle class, the bourgeoisie (synthesis). Under bourgeois dominance (capitalism), the bourgeoisie itself (the new thesis) is challenged by the proletariat (antithesis). Out of this inevitable clash is supposed to come a new society as the triumphant working class eradicates the bourgeoisie and all other "exploitive" elements. The workers then move through a period of "dictatorship of the proletariat" toward a classless society free from social conflict.

A primary element in Marxist economic thought is the "labor theory of value," which posits that all value is created by labor. Since the actual cost of items is greater than the labor required to produce them, somebody is clearly making a profit without doing any work. The economic relationship between the exploiting class (bourgeoisie) and the exploited class (proletariat) determines the nature of all other social relationships. This view (economic determinism) holds that as the economic foundations of a society change (as they *must*, according to the dialectical view of class warfare), so must the rest of the societal structure.

The Marxist conception of the state and revolution is, not surprisingly, linked with the acceptance of economic forces as basic. Politics and the state (as part of the superstructure) are mere tools in the hands of the dominant economic class (the bourgeoisie) for the organized oppression of the workers. Revolution is inevitable, for "capitalism contains the seeds of its own destruction." In the capitalist system of profit-seeking competition, not everyone can win. As capitalists compete with one another over the exploitation of the masses, those who lose out fall back into the proletariat. The bourgeoisie becomes richer yet fewer, while the proletariat becomes more numerous, increasingly more exploited, and alienated. The inevitable outcome is violent revolution, resulting in proletarian victory and the march toward a true communist society. The state will wither away, for as the tool of the dominant class, it will not be needed in a classless society. Communist thinkers, following Marx, claim to have discovered a scientific explanation for the course of human events and a predictive capability based on an understanding of historical forces.

Neither Marx nor Engels devoted much attention to the prospect of a communist political party. Vladimir Ilyich Lenin, the Russian revolutionary leader, filled this gap by adding to Marxism the idea of dedicated, professional revolutionaries acting through a communist party to hasten the revolution and seize power. Although he accepted the Marxist belief in the inevitability of the revolution, Lenin was skeptical of a spontaneous proletarian uprising. He believed the party should be the "vanguard of the revolution" and work to provoke it. A further important theoretical contribution of Lenin was his theory of imperialism (discussed in Chapter 4), which analyzed the foreign policies of capitalist countries in an attempt to explain why World War I occurred (it was seen by communists as a war among capitalist states in their death throes) and why the war did not result in worldwide revolution and capitalist destruction. A prolific writer, Lenin's main ideas were developed in such widely known works as *What Is to Be Done?* (1902), *Imperialism—The Highest Stage of Capitalism* (1917), and *State and Revolution* (1918).

To this day, Marxism-Leninism has remained the core of communist ideology, although it has had widely divergent interpretations and modifications. Prominent examples of doctrinal interpretations have come from Josef Stalin, Josip Tito, Nikita Khrushchev, Mao Tse-tung, and Leonid Brezhnev, although covering all the nuances of doctrinal divergence would require a much longer list. Because these men are closely associated with particular aspects of foreign policy and international relations, they will be discussed later.

Western critics of communism as an ideology point to a whole host of internal theoretical contradictions and not infrequently portray it as a clever, but nevertheless transparent, rationale for seizing power and manipulating people. Marx is said to have attached too much importance to economic factors to the exclusion of other variables and badly underestimated the nature and resilience of "democratic capitalism." However, one must remember that Marx was writing in the context of the horrible social conditions stemming from the Industrial Revolution. Further criticism challenges the idea of the primacy of materialistic forces in determining the course of human life, the atheism, the emphasis on struggle, and the class view of society as a distorted portrayal—offering Thomas Hobbes' beast instead of John Locke's rational person, or perhaps a "fabricated person" instead of a "real person." Other challenges involve such issues as dogmatic communist claims to scientific truth, the jealously guarded communist party role as exclusive interpreter of the "truth," and the vagueness of such visions as the classless society and the withering away of the state.

The Role of Ideology. This discussion has not been intended as a thorough critical analysis of democracy and communism, although serious students of international relations should undertake that independently. Rather, it has had two goals. First, since ideology is apt to be a significant frame of reference for nation-states as they participate in international relations, a basic familiarity with the operating assumptions of their respective ideologies is crucial. The second goal is a partial warning. Ideologies are abstractions that meet only in the minds of political philosophers, whose job it is to ponder the manipulation of ideas and forces at the metaphysical level. Besides, there are hardly any "pure" ideologies to be pitted against one another, as the ideological debates among communists or the widespread dissent among democrats attest. An ideology may range from a vague commitment to a way of life to creation of and belief in an *Ersatzreligion*, or substitute religion. Ideologies are relevant to political life to the extent that they spark people's imaginations, posit goals and offer explanations, and become interwoven with the policies of state decision-makers. Only *states* (or other political entities able to *use* ideology), however, will participate in international relations. Much of the misunderstanding concerning the phenomenon of modern world politics known as the Cold War stems from not carefully separating abstract ideology from concrete politics.

The Cold War

A respected student of the Cold War, surveying the efforts of scholars and journalists to examine and explain it, recently concluded: "Despite the ensuing flood of literature, much of it excellent by any standard, the Cold War remains the most enigmatic and elusive international conflict of modern times." [1]

While there may be little agreement on the answers, there are at

1 Norman A. Graebner, "Cold War Origins and the Continuing Debate: A Review of the Literature," *The Journal of Conflict Resolution*, 13 (March 1969), 123.

least three primary questions concerning the Cold War: (1) What is the Cold War? (2) When did it start and end (if indeed it has ended)? (3) Where does responsibility for starting the Cold War lie? The answer to any one of these questions is likely to be linked to the answers to the others.

The term "Cold War" is used to refer generally to the intense hostility and tension that developed in Soviet-American relations (and more broadly in the relations between the "communist bloc" and the "Western world") following World War II. Without ever really developing into a "hot war," the Cold War has involved ideological hatred, political distrust, diplomatic maneuvering, military competition, espionage, and psychological warfare, as well as generally less-than-cordial relations.

The beginning of the Cold War and responsibility for it are very closely related questions; neither can be easily answered. Observers see the origin of the Cold War in the 1917 Bolshevik takeover in Russia, the Western intervention in Russia in 1918, the Yalta Agreement, or the division of Germany following Hitler's defeat. Still others feel that no particular event sparked the Cold War; rather, it is linked with traditional Russian imperialism, the threatening nature of communist ideology and its advocacy of revolution, the personal paranoia of Stalin, the inability of the victors to divide up the spoils following World War II, Western insensitivity to legitimate Russian security needs, or an irrational Western overreaction to communism.

It is possible, of course, to step back from all these issues and suggest that the origin of the Cold War can be found in the nature of the nation-state system and in ground rules more basic than contemporary political alignments. There are two large countries, the United States and the Soviet Union, that naturally will play a major role in world politics. Whatever their internal politics and ideologies, they are bound to interfere with one another in their international relations. The French observer Alexis de Tocqueville wrote over a century ago in his *Democracy in America* that the United States and Russia would emerge as potential rivals:

There are at the present time two great nations in the world, which started from different points, but seem to tend towards the same end. I allude to the Russians and the Americans. Both of them have grown up unnoticed; and while the attention of mankind was directed elsewhere, they have suddenly placed themselves in the front rank among the nations. . . .

The Anglo-American relies upon personal interest to accomplish his ends and gives free scope to the unguided strength and common sense of the people; the Russian centers all the authority of society in a single arm. The principal instrument of the former is freedom; of the latter, servitude. Their starting-point is different and their courses are not the same; yet each of them seems marked out by the will of Heaven to sway the destinies of half of the globe.[2]

In determining responsibility for the Cold War, one is certainly on intellectually solid ground in withholding blame. Following the line of reasoning advanced by de Tocqueville, one can view the Cold War as simply an abrasive, and perhaps unfortunate, phase in the relations of two large, dynamic states that are naturally colliding. Or one might find persuasive the view expressed by Louis Halle in *The Cold War as History* (1967) that the Cold War was a tragic and unavoidable condition created by World War II itself, sweeping both powers along with it.

Generally, however, two schools of thought have dominated Western assessments of responsibility for the Cold War, the orthodox and the revisionist. Although neither school presents a unified front, the former generally feels that Soviet Russia is primarily to blame for the Cold War, while the latter is more critical of Western (particularly American) policies. The orthodox view has been well articulated by public officials and formal policies of Western governments—particularly of the United States and Great Britain. This view has also been supported in varying degrees by such critical scholars as Robert Strausz-Hupé et al., *Protracted Conflict* (1959); Herbert Feis, *Between War and Peace: The Potsdam Conference* (1960); Norman A. Graebner, *Cold War Diplomacy, 1945–1960* (1962); John Spanier, *American Foreign Policy since World War II* (1960); and Dexter Perkins, *The Diplomacy of a New Age* (1967).

While the orthodox observers see Western postwar policy as a response to a real or imagined Soviet challenge, the revisionists have argued that Western aggressiveness and counterrevolutionary policies were the real causes of Soviet distrust and consequent belligerency toward the West. The revisionist school includes such people as D. F. Fleming, *The Cold War and Its Origins, 1917–1950* (1961); David Horowitz, *The Free World Colossus* (1965); and Gar Alpero-

2 Alexis de Tocqueville, *Democracy in America*, vol. I, Vintage Books, New York, 1956, p. 452.

vitz, *Atomic Diplomacy: Hiroshima and Potsdam* (1965). Neither school seems yet to have been able to muster the conclusive evidence necessary to win the support of its critics.

Determining when the Cold War ended hardly inspires any more agreement than figuring out who started it. Some say the Cold War ended with the death of Stalin in 1953, with more cordial East-West relations developing after Premier Nikita Khrushchev articulated the policy of "peaceful coexistence" in 1956. Others see the end of the Cold War as the 1962 "eyeball-to-eyeball" confrontation of the Cuban missile crisis, for then the full realization of the consequences of nuclear destruction finally reached both East and West. A third view holds that the efforts at détente undertaken by President Richard Nixon and Soviet party leader Leonid Brezhnev produced the end of the Cold War. Finally, some observers firmly believe that the Cold War, far from being over, still continues unabated, although it may often exist below the surface while East-West relations appear normal. A survey of the more significant aspects of the foreign policies of the Big Two will help us understand both the Cold War and contemporary international relations.

AMERICA IN THE IDEOLOGICAL AGE

Perhaps it is a symptom of the democratic emphasis on process rather than goals, or perhaps it results from the uniqueness of the American experience, but the United States has had a mixed history with regard to long-range, determined, coherent, and positive foreign policy. A critical observer might suggest that while Americans have a genuine desire to promote good in the world and to do what's right, they tend to lose interest in one issue quickly and wander to the next. In fact, Alexis de Tocqueville concluded as much in his *Democracy in America*; he further noted:

As for myself, I do not hesitate to say that it is especially in the conduct of their foreign relations that democracies appear to me decidedly inferior to other governments.... Foreign politics demand scarcely any of those qualities which are peculiar to a democracy; they require, on the contrary, the perfect use of almost all those in which it is deficient.... [A] democracy can only with great difficulty regulate the details of an important undertaking, persevere in a fixed design, and work out its execution in spite of serious obstacles. It cannot combine its measures with secrecy or await their consequences with patience.[3]

The American preoccupation with the frontier and with internal development in a large and richly endowed country, combined with geographical isolation from the great powers of Europe and the lack of powerful (potentially aggressive) neighbors at home, has left Americans unimpressed with the *need* to develop a coherent foreign policy. Despite the lack of clear-cut long-range goals, a survey of modern American foreign policy reveals at least nine identifiable stages in the development of that policy. They are: (1) *isolationism*, (2) *internationalism*, (3) *Truman Doctrine*, (4) *containment*, (5) *Marshall Plan*, (6) *"entangling alliances,"* (7) *foreign aid*, (8) *intervention*, and (9) *neo-isolationism*. *Isolationism* and *internationalism* each represent a historical phase, followed by a third phase (landmarks 3 through 6) that marks the beginning of Soviet-American confrontation following World War II. A fourth phase involves the extension and modification of that conflict through *foreign aid* and *intervention*. *Neo-isolationism* appears to represent a fifth phase, although the legacy of America's Indochina involvement must have time to solidify before any conclusive judgment can be made.

Isolationism

Isolationism dominated American foreign policy from the earliest days of the Republic to World War II. It represented a commitment, asserted by American leaders since George Washington, to keep the United States out of European quarrels and other political entanglements. The Monroe Doctrine, presented as a message to Congress in 1823 by President James Monroe, was a unilateral declaration to European powers that the United States would oppose foreign intervention in the Western Hemisphere and would reciprocally refrain from any involvement in European affairs—a policy obviously altered by the events of World Wars I and II.

This American policy was reinforced by a U.S. focus on domestic affairs, geographical isolation from Europe of the United States, European preoccupation with political affairs within Europe, and the

3 *Ibid.*, p. 243.

strength of British sea power, which imposed a *Pax Britannica* on the oceans and indirectly served U.S. interests. While de Tocqueville could write confidently in the 1830s that the United States had, "properly speaking, no foreign interests to discuss," it would be a mistake to conclude that isolationism meant that the United States was not engaged in international relations. The United States was participating in a broad spectrum of international activities, ranging from quiet commercial relations to war, primarily with England, France, Spain, Russia, Mexico, and Canada.

It is true that much of this activity was concerned with expanding American control over the North American continent and fulfilling dreams of "manifest destiny," a shadowy term that was used to explain the "natural" pressures impelling American expansion to the Pacific Ocean. By 1900, however, the United States was becoming aware of its growing strength in world affairs, as well as of the relevance of events elsewhere to U.S. interests.

The Spanish-American War (1898) reflected increasing American interest in Latin American affairs. It was followed in 1904 by the "Roosevelt Corollary" to the Monroe Doctrine, in which President Theodore Roosevelt proclaimed the right to intervene in Latin American affairs when chronic instability might provoke European intervention. The Monroe Doctrine, he said, might force the United States ". . . to the exercise of an international police power." [4]

U.S. interests in Asia were also growing, since the United States had acquired the Philippines as a result of the Spanish-American War. Concerned over the European powers' apparent preparations to carve up China and Japan into spheres of influence and exclusive economic advantage, U.S. Secretary of State John Hay articulated, and received qualified support for, an "open door" policy. Its goal was to ensure China's territorial and administrative integrity while ensuring equal commercial rights for outsiders.

Internationalism

Internationalism did not come easily for the United States in the twentieth century. When it did come, with America's involvement in World War I, it came perhaps too rapidly, resulting in a retreat to a more extreme form of isolationism between the wars than had

4 *Congressional Record,* 58th Cong., 3d Sess., 1904, p. 19.

existed before the war. American attitudes toward involvement in foreign affairs have always been somewhat ambivalent, based on a desire to help, on a belief that superior American resources would straighten things out, and on the desire to go home and resume business as usual when it was all over.

At first neutral, America was forced into World War I by persistent German unrestricted warfare. When war did come, President Woodrow Wilson's war message to Congress (April 2, 1917) proclaimed a fight

for democracy, for the right of those who submit to authority to have a voice in their own governments, for the rights and liberties of small nations, for a universal dominion of right by such a concert of free peoples as shall bring peace and safety to all nations and make the world itself at last free. To such a task we can dedicate our lives and our fortunes, everything that we are and everything that we have, with the pride of those who know that the day has come when America is privileged to spend her blood and her might for the principles that gave her birth and happiness and the peace which she has treasured. God helping her, she can do no other.[5]

American doughboys marched off to Europe, but following the Armistice of November 11, 1918, those who returned found the American public tired of war and once again leaning toward isolationism. The last of President Wilson's famous "Fourteen Points" (a statement of war aims delivered at a joint session of Congress, January 8, 1918) had proclaimed: "A general association of nations must be formed under specific covenants for the purpose of affording mutual guarantees of political independence and territorial integrity to great and small states alike." [6] The League of Nations was the result of Wilson's fourteenth point, but the League represented a formal commitment to involvement in international relations that the United States (in particular the U.S. Senate, which refused to support U.S. entry into the League) was apparently not yet willing to make.

The approach of World War II could hardly shake the United States out of its isolationist mood. In the midst of lengthy debate and disagreement concerning America's role in the face of growing international tension, the country's reaction was guarded to the

5 For the full text, see Woodrow Wilson, *War Message*, 65th Cong., 1st Sess., Senate Document No. 5, 1917, pp. 3–8.
6 See United States Serial 7443, Document 765, Jan. 8, 1918.

plight of France and England, Churchill's pleas for American aid, and increasing Axis belligerency. It was the surprise Japanese attack on Pearl Harbor on December 7, 1941—the "date which will live in infamy"—that finally pushed the United States into the war. President Roosevelt's war message to Congress the following day ended on a note not unlike that struck by President Wilson nearly a quarter of a century earlier:

No matter how long it may take us to overcome this premeditated invasion, the American people in their righteous might will win through the absolute victory. . . .

With confidence in our armed forces—with the unbounding determination of our people—we will gain the inevitable triumph—so help us God.[7]

Chapter 4 has already called attention to the fact that a country entering a war with a sense of righteous indignation and a commitment to victory can perhaps more easily rationalize its situation than a country involved in limited wars for political goals incomprehensible to many citizens. For a country with America's traditional disinclination for long-term foreign involvements, World Wars I and II were poor training for the world that would emerge in 1945. Determined to "be prepared" for the peace that would follow World War II and to avoid the debacle surrounding U.S. nonparticipation in the League of Nations, the United States was an active participant in developing the United Nations, which it subsequently optimistically joined. Observers of U.S. foreign policy often refer to the "revolution in American foreign policy" that occurred during the 1940s, when a dramatic shift was made from determined noninvolvement (except on "special occasions") to exuberant overinvolvement.

The optimism surrounding the launching of the United Nations in 1945 soon faded. Not only were nations not so diligent in practice in adhering to promises they had made on paper, but strains that had developed during the war (particularly between the Soviet Union and its Western allies) were becoming more pronounced. Agreements and understandings reached at the Yalta and Potsdam conferences, particularly those concerning the occupation of Germany and the fate of Central Europe, were undermined by ideological differ-

7 Full text in *Congressional Record*, 77th Cong., 1st Sess., Dec. 8, 1941, pp. 9519–9520.

ences that had been muffled in the common fight against fascism and by the emergence of two superpowers, the United States and the Soviet Union, with the national interests and sense of world importance one would expect of large nation-states.

Truman Doctrine

A growing sense of frustration over developing international events and a belief that American power could—and should—control the course of events pulled the United States further and further into world politics. The general spirit of internationalism represented by the U.S. commitment to the United Nations was slowly modified into more specific commitments to meet specific challenges outside the United Nations framework. The first of these was the *Truman Doctrine*, a dramatic new departure in United States foreign policy, articulated on March 12, 1947.

Growing Western concern over the Soviet Union's moves in Eastern Europe and disregard for the Yalta agreements convinced many of both the reality of Soviet expansionism and the threat of communism, which soon became the same thing to many people in the West. Winston Churchill, the venerable British wartime leader, had spoken against communism the year before President Truman's historic policy pronouncement. During a speech at Fulton, Missouri, on March 5, 1946, Churchill had warned that an "iron curtain" had descended on Europe, with Moscow-controlled "police governments" on the other side of it.

American anxiety finally turned to action over communist moves in Greece, Turkey, and Iran. The Soviet Army had occupied some northern provinces in Iran, but pressure from the newly created United Nations and others caused Stalin to withdraw Soviet forces. In Greece, however, communist Greek guerrillas were challenging the established regime, which was supported by the British government. Great Britain had been the traditional power in the Mediterranean, but exhaustion from World War II was forcing the British to pull back. In the belief that Greece would fall to the communists if the government did not receive immediate help, President Truman asked Congress for $400 million ($300 million of which was for Greece alone) to aid both Greece and Turkey.

The long-range significance of the aid request was not America's coming to the aid of a foreign government, it was the philosophy on which the program was based and the doctrine it advanced concerning future American international commitments. The Truman Doctrine recognized (1) the principle of self-determination of peoples, (2) the communist threat to that principle, (3) a concomitant threat to U.S. national security, and (4) a United States obligation to halt the threat. In President Truman's words, contained in his historic Truman Doctrine address to Congress,

To ensure the peaceful development of nations, free from coercion, the United States has taken a leading part in establishing the United Nations. The United Nations is designed to make possible lasting freedom and independence for all its members. We shall not realize our objectives, however, unless we are willing *to help free people to maintain their free institutions and their national integrity* against aggressive movements that seek to impose upon them totalitarian regimes. This is no more than a frank recognition that totalitarian regimes imposed on free peoples, by direct or indirect aggression, *undermine the foundations of international peace and hence the security of the United States.*

The peoples of a number of countries of the world have recently had totalitarian regimes forced upon them against their will. The government of the United States has made frequent protests against coercion and intimidation, in violation of the Yalta agreement, in Poland, Rumania and Bulgaria. I must also state that in a number of other countries there have been similar developments.[8] (Emphasis added)

While Truman was on solid ground in calling attention to Soviet maneuvers, he was not as cautious as he might have been in linking future U.S. policy with Soviet foreign policy (or an American perception of that policy) and in portraying the world in terms of good guys versus bad guys:

At the present moment in world history nearly every nation must choose between alternative ways of life. The choice is too often not a free one.

One way of life is based upon the will of the majority, and is distinguished by free institutions, representative government, free elections, guarantees of individual liberty, freedom of speech and religion and freedom from political oppression.

The second way of life is based upon the will of a minority

8 For complete text, see *Congressional Record*, 80th Cong., 1st Sess., March 12, 1947, pp. 1980–1981.

forcibly imposed upon the majority. It relies upon terror and oppression, a controlled press and radio, fixed elections and the suppression of personal freedom.

Most Americans observing the course of world events during these years, for example in Eastern Europe, would not have challenged President Truman's sincerity or judgment, but the policy direction in which he was leading the United States involved moral abstractions that would later prove awkward. There was no clear way to determine when "free people," "free institutions," or "national integrity" were being threatened, yet the United States drifted into a position of abdicating its foreign policy initiative to those who saw a threat and of supporting the status quo (brushing aside in some cases necessary and valuable change) at virtually any cost if communism could be checked. Soviet political power and communist ideology would be increasingly perceived as identical by many American policy-makers.

Containment

The principle of *containment* was a logical extension of the Truman Doctrine. George F. Kennan, a prominent American diplomat, discussed containment as an American response to Soviet expansionism in a widely read article, "The Sources of Soviet Conduct," appearing under the pseudonym "X" in the journal *Foreign Affairs*.[9] Although his name has become virtually synonymous with the containment philosophy, he has since tried to dissociate himself from the global implications of the Truman Doctrine and the course the containment strategy took. Critics have attacked containment on the grounds that it was too simplistic, dividing the world into good and evil, "us" and "them," freedom and oppression. The United States failed to see distinctions among communist states (Poland and Yugoslavia, for example, were somehow *not* carbon copies of the Soviet Union) or among "friends," for it ended up supporting without discrimination some rather unsavory regimes—hardly more in tune with American democratic ideals than the communists—in the name of anti-communism.

9 X [George F. Kennan], "The Sources of Soviet Conduct," *Foreign Affairs*, 25 (July 1947), 556–583.

Marshall Plan

By 1947 it was apparent that the hoped-for postwar economic recovery of Europe was not materializing. The *Marshall Plan* was a proposal made by Secretary of State George C. Marshall in an address at Harvard University on June 5, 1947, suggesting principles for European recovery. In offering American aid, he (1) called attention to the demoralizing economic plight of Europe and the hope that America might help stabilize war-torn countries, (2) noted that economic recovery was the business of the Europeans, but that the United States would help in drafting a program if the initiative came from Europe, and (3) suggested that any program should be a joint one involving a number of, if not all, European nations.

Under Secretary of State Dean Acheson had earlier expressed American concern that the despair and hardship resulting from the slow pace of recovery without outside aid might encourage extremism of both the political right and left. Indeed, it was not certain that fascism was dead in Europe, and communist agitation and intrigue were hardly disguised. Marshall noted in his address:

Our policy is directed not against any country or doctrine but against hunger, poverty, desperation and chaos. Its purpose should be the revival of a working economy in the world so as to permit the emergence of political and social conditions in which free institutions can exist.[10]

The European response to the American offer was enthusiastic, leading to joint meetings in June and July 1947. The Soviets, however, after meeting with the United States, pulled out of further talks, taking their Eastern European satellites with them. They saw the Marshall Plan as capitalist imperialism. Their pullout had two results. It made the aid program more palatable to an American Congress unimpressed with the prospect of using U.S. dollars to build up communist states, and it also turned one of the more successful postwar American foreign policies into a Cold War weapon, further solidifying the East-versus-West view of world politics. The Marshall Plan was instituted in 1948 when Congress established the European Recovery Program (ERP). The sixteen European countries that participated in the program established, at American urging, the

10 Full text appears in *The New York Times*, July 6, 1947.

Organization for European Economic Cooperation (OEEC) to facilitate regional economic consultation and cooperation.

"Entangling Alliances"

The growing sense of a Soviet and/or communist threat to the Western Hemisphere and Western Europe began to take a politico-military turn in Western capitals as leaders felt that an organized alliance structure pooling military resources was a convincing means of thwarting Soviet designs on Western Europe. Forgetting, or ignoring, George Washington's famous admonition in his Farewell Address against "permanent alliances," the United States entered into *entangling alliances* to contain Soviet power.

Since World War II the United States has entered four collective alliances: (1) the Inter-American Treaty of Reciprocal Assistance (Rio Treaty) of 1947, joining the United States and all Latin American nations in an alliance supporting the Monroe Doctrine; (2) the North Atlantic Treaty Organization (NATO) of 1949, committing twelve (later fifteen) states to the defense of Western Europe; (3) the Security Treaty with Australia and New Zealand (ANZUS) of 1951, to safeguard the security of the Pacific area; and (4) the Southeast Asia Treaty Organization (SEATO) in 1954, to deter aggression in Southeast Asia and the Southwest Pacific area. Although not a formal member, the United States initiated the creation of and continues to support the Central Treaty Organization (CENTO, formerly the Baghdad Pact until Iraq pulled out in 1959), which allied five Middle Eastern countries (now four) against communist aggression. These organizations are discussed in more detail in Chapter 8. In addition to these collective alliances, the United States also concluded bilateral alliances with Japan, the Philippines, South Korea, South Vietnam, and the Republic of China.

Perhaps American goals in creating these alliances initially made sense. The Rio pact was nothing more than an institutionalization of the Monroe Doctrine philosophy, and NATO was the result of very visible Russian actions in Eastern Europe. Subsequent alliances, however, seemed to be trying to seal off the communist countries from the rest of the world and seemed to blur any distinction between communism as an ideology and Soviet aggression. While alliances may be able to stop the concrete threat of Russian army divisions crossing a political frontier, they cannot necessarily contain ideas. Often countries crucial to a sound alliance structure, such as India in the context of SEATO, refused to join because they did not think communism was as much of a threat as the United States did. Other countries (such as Pakistan, which did join SEATO) saw the alliance as a way to obtain military weaponry for their own purposes. Pakistan, for example, tended to perceive India as a bigger threat than either communism or the Soviet Union. The result has been paper organizations that are of little use in fighting communism, but whose continued existence does little to convince the Soviet Union that it is not threatened with hostile capitalist encirclement.

Even the fortunes of the strongest of the American alliance structures, NATO, rise and fall with the credibility of a Soviet attack on Western Europe. The United States would do well to rethink its alliance philosophy. That is not to suggest that the alliances should necessarily be abandoned or that the United States should give up trying to check either Soviet expansionism or the spread of communism. A reappraisal, rather, should gauge the effectiveness of these alliances in terms of modern United States foreign policy goals and, certainly equally important, in terms of a realistic assessment of U.S. capabilities. No doubt the American efforts to exert pressure in Indochina since the French pulled out have led to an overdue reappraisal of American involvements, but unfortunately, precipitous and ill-conceived reactions may result from the desire to close that unhappy chapter in American foreign policy.

Foreign Aid

Foreign aid has been another feature of contemporary American foreign policy. The United States granted foreign aid on a massive scale for the first time to its allies during World War I, followed by the Lend-Lease program of World War II and the postwar reconstruction (e.g., Marshall Plan) efforts.

Since the Second World War, however, both the Soviet Union and the United States have used foreign aid as a weapon in their ideological struggle. Given the military-technological realities discussed in the preceding chapter, Soviet-American maneuverings shifted from primarily military confrontations to the battle for people's minds. The success of the Marshall Plan in stabilizing European economies and ending the social despair that encouraged extremist propaganda led United States policy-makers to think that foreign aid would be a useful diplomatic weapon for combating instability (and hence communism) in Third World countries. American foreign aid to developing countries began with the Point IV program of technical assistance in 1949, and was expanded to include development grants and loans as well as military assistance during the 1950s and 1960s.

Although aid has been effective in some cases, the Marshall Plan approach is not generally transferable to the developing countries. There is a big difference between *rebuilding* a sophisticated industrial society in Western Europe and trying to *create* such a society, virtually from scratch in some cases, simply by introducing dollars and technical advisers—often in the face of explosive indigenous social problems that have been building up and festering perhaps for centuries. Further, the United States has often ended up supporting archaic and oppressive regimes for the sake of stability. Revolutionary communism, on the other hand, often has broad popular appeal because it appears to promise immediate improvement of social conditions through radical social reform.

Intervention

Intervention has come in many forms, ranging from Big Power suppression of unacceptable change in the ideology of close neighbors (e.g., Soviet actions in the Hungarian Revolution of 1956 and the "Prague Spring" of 1968, or the U.S. intervention in the Dominican Republic in 1965) to attempted manipulation of, and/or participation in, another state's internal affairs. Growing American frustration with the continuing inability of recipient states to utilize foreign aid effectively was a significant factor behind American entanglement in Vietnam during the 1960s. America had to intervene to help get the job done, but as the Vietnamese conflict dragged on and became increasingly controversial (as the Korean War had before it), an American pullout became inevitable. The retrenchment was accompanied by a mixed sense of anger, hurt, frustration, and disgust.

Neo-isolationism

The country that had departed in the 1940s from its traditional policy of isolationism to take a major role in world affairs now appeared to be drifting into *neo-isolationism* in the mid-1970s. Although the United States cannot hope to guide the destinies of other countries all over the world, neither will its policies cease to have a worldwide impact. Hopefully this period of apparent neo-isolationism will be used to redefine the American role in international relations. Active American involvement in the search for a Middle East peace in the 1970s has certainly indicated a continuing (although perhaps modified) international role for the United States. As Dean Rusk, secretary of state under President Kennedy, observed, a return to the isolationism of the 1920s and 1930s would be "suicidal." He noted, "it doesn't do much good to reject the mistakes of your fathers, only to embrace the mistakes of your grandfathers." [11]

Like Korea, Vietnam was a place many Americans had never heard of until the United States became involved there. The preceding section has discussed the kinds of foreign policy guidelines that led to American involvement in Indochina. The following case study reviews the story of Vietnam—that unfortunate country in a far corner of the world that has been so instrumental in forcing a major reconsideration of postwar American foreign policy.

VIETNAM

Background

Vietnam is a small, elongated country forming the western flank of the Indochinese peninsula, which juts into the South China Sea. (See Figure 5-1, a sketch map of Indochina.) Much of the country consists of forested mountains and plateaus, although much of the population lives on the coastal plains and the rich river deltas, particularly those of the Red River in the North and the Mekong River in the South. Agriculture (particularly rice) is predominant, although the mineral resources in the North (coal, for example) have supported the development of industry.

All Vietnam comprises 127,556 square miles (North Vietnam: 61,293; South Vietnam: 66,263), making it roughly the size of Norway (125,181 square miles) or the U.S. state of New Mexico (121,666 square miles). South Vietnam is about the size of Washing-

11 *The National Observer,* Apr. 12, 1975, p. 4.

FIGURE 5-1. Indochina

ton state (68,192 square miles). The total population of Vietnam is nearly 40 million, with over 21 million in the North and 16.5 million in the South. As a comparison, the state of California has a population of around 20 million.

The Vietnamese people are believed to have originated in the Yellow River valley of north China. They were slowly driven southward by the Han Chinese, and by the second century B.C. they were inhabiting the area that is now North Vietnam. In 111 B.C. this area was incorporated into China as a southern province and remained tied to China for 1,000 years. By 939 A.D. Vietnam, after many centuries of unsuccessful revolts against the Chinese, finally achieved independence, although there were continuing struggles with Chinese invasions. The early history of the country is primarily the history of the three constituent areas, Tonkin, Annam, and Cochin-China—roughly the northern, middle, and southern thirds, respectively, of a modern, unified Vietnam. The country was named Vietnam at the start of the nineteenth century. The long history of Vietnamese struggle against the Chinese lends some credence to the argument that, left alone, Vietnam would be naturally antipathetic toward China. Intervention by other powers has only driven the Vietnamese toward the Chinese and given the Chinese a role in the Indochinese peninsula that they would not otherwise have had. As the London *Economist* editorialized in 1966, however, it might be misleading to accept Ho Chi Minh, then the North Vietnamese leader, too quickly as the Tito of the East (a comparison with Marshal Josip Tito of Yugoslavia and the independent course he has charted for his country despite Soviet power). The editorial suggested that even if the thesis were valid, Ho Chi Minh was not the amicable Tito of 1966, but the Balkan expansionist of 1948. It noted the past fears of Cambodia and Laos concerning the potential hegemony of a unified and dynamic Vietnam.[12]

The French

The French were in Vietnam as early as the sixteenth century, but the colonial period did not actually start until 1859. During the 1850s and 1860s the French established colonial control over Vietnam, Laos, and Cambodia, all of which they administered as Indochina. Imperial Japan occupied the area from 1940 to 1945, although the French Vichy administration was allowed to continue in power until early 1945, when a regime headed by Bao Dai (a former emperor of Annam) was installed.

A nationalist movement began to develop in Vietnam following World War I, gaining strength during the Japanese occupation in World War II. One of the leading figures in the resistance against the Japanese was Ho Chi Minh (aided by Vo Nguyen Giap, who was subsequently to engineer the defeat of the French at Dien Bien Phu).* Ho Chi Minh had fled Vietnam when he was only nineteen years old to go to France, where he became associated with the

12 *The Economist*, June 4, 1966, pp. 1059–1060.
* Ho Chi Minh (meaning "He Who Enlightens"), who had assumed several different names throughout his life, adopted the name under which he became known to the world at large in 1943 while a resistance leader.

French Communist Party. He spent a couple of years in the Soviet Union during the mid-1920s, subsequently going to China. In 1930 he returned to Vietnam to fight for national independence and founded the Communist Party of Vietnam. He subsequently organized the Viet Minh, or Vietnamese Independence League, which was basically a communist organization presented as a national front movement to attract a wide variety of Vietnamese nationalists.

With the fall of the Japanese in August 1945, Ho Chi Minh was allowed to take over the administration of Hanoi. On September 2, 1945, he read a Vietnamese Declaration of Independence to exuberant crowds in Hanoi. The Bao Dai government quickly collapsed at the end of the war. Two situations developed in Vietnam during 1945–1946 that would make eventual conflict inevitable. The Viet Minh regime, based in Hanoi, resisted French efforts to re-establish themselves in northern Vietnam and began to solidify their own control. This latter effort included conducting elections to a national assembly in order to legitimize their rule. Elections were held both in the North and (secretly) in the South, giving the Viet Minh a majority in the assembly. In spite of the fact that the elections were hardly a valid, formal democratic exercise, Donald Lancaster—a British Legation officer in Saigon from 1950 to 1954—concluded that the election results were nevertheless roughly representative of public opinion at that time.[13] President Eisenhower came to a similar conclusion, noting in his book *Mandate for Change* that it was generally conceded that Ho Chi Minh would have been elected premier had a full election been held.[14]

Concurrently, the French (planters, business people, administrators, and the like) were moving to re-establish their former control in the South. The northern part of Vietnam was occupied by Chinese troops and the southern part by British troops. The 16th parallel was the demarcation line. Both occupying powers tolerated, and in some respects aided, the events transpiring in their zones. As the Viet Minh and the French were each determined to extend their control ultimately to the other zone, the conflict that became the French-Indochina War (1946–1954) was inevitable.

France was at a disadvantage from the start because of a political credibility gap: their claim of fighting for freedom against the

13 See Donald Lancaster, *The Emancipation of French Indochina*, Oxford University Press, London, 1961.
14 Dwight D. Eisenhower, *Mandate for Change*, Doubleday & Company, Inc., Garden City, N.Y., 1963, pp. 337–338, 372.

communist Viet Minh forces seemed to many observers (not the least affected of which were the Vietnamese themselves) to be a fight to re-establish French colonial control. Needless to say, the Viet Minh and their supporters made much of this very issue. The French government itself was ambivalent concerning the "real" French mission in Indochina, and as the war dragged on—draining France of soldiers, matériel, and morale—it became increasingly difficult to justify the war to the French public.

In March of 1949, the French recognized Bao Dai as the Vietnamese head of state and granted his government minimal responsibilities under French control. This arrangement, combined with Bao Dai's reputation as a playboy who preferred to frequent European spas rather than stay home and govern, was hardly convincing evidence that the French supported Vietnamese independence. The average Vietnamese peasant working a rice paddy knew little of communism or Stalin, but did know that the French were foreigners and the Viet Minh were not.

The United States at this time expressed hope that Bao Dai could unite all truly nationalist Vietnamese elements. There was also fear that communist activity in Indochina was part of the Soviet pattern of expansion. If so, American aid could be needed to help contain it. After a meeting with the French in Paris, Secretary of State Dean Acheson issued the following statement in May 1950:

The United States Government, convinced that neither national independence nor democratic evolution exist in any area dominated by Soviet imperialism, considers the situation to be such as to warrant its according economic aid and military equipment to the Associated States of Indochina and to France in order to assist them in restoring stability and permitting these states to pursue their peaceful and democratic development.[15]

In June of 1950, President Truman accelerated military assistance. The intertwining of nationalist independence movements and communism should not be surprising, yet the West during these years was concerned with the belligerent rhetoric of communism. Moscow seemed to many to be directing a worldwide subversion campaign, China had just been taken over by a communist regime (a factor, incidently, which greatly increased the amount of aid crossing the border into Vietnam in support of the Viet Minh), and

15 U.S. Department of State, *Bulletin,* 22 (May 22, 1950), 821.

the Korean War had started—all adding to the image of a general communist offensive.

United States aid to the French during the war was substantial, and there were even plans for joint Franco-American operations, involving according to some rumors the use of atomic weapons. As Viet Minh pressure on Dien Bien Phu increased, United States concern over a possible French defeat intensified. Dien Bien Phu was of minor military significance, but it was believed (correctly, as it turned out) that the fall of the French garrison there would have serious and far-reaching psychological repercussions on the French effort in Indochina. The stand at Dien Bien Phu was part of the Navarre Plan (named after General Henri-Eugene Navarre, who had assumed the French military command in Indochina) to increase the overall size of French forces in Vietnam and to train Vietnamese soldiers.

To counter the disadvantage created by the numerically inferior Viet Minh's reliance on guerrilla warfare, an isolated French garrison was stationed at Dien Bien Phu as bait to draw guerrilla forces out into the open for a more traditional military engagement. Unfortunately, the French underestimated their own resupply capability as well as the Viet Minh's ability to move artillery to the scene of battle.

The United States did not come to the aid of Dien Bien Phu. President Eisenhower, under pressure from the British not to intervene, was reinforced in his belief that only American ground forces could help, and he did not want to get drawn into another Korea.[16]

The French garrison at Dien Bien Phu fell on May 7, 1954. With Great Britain and the Soviet Union cochairing it, the Geneva Conference (May 8, 1954, to July 21, 1954) was called as a vehicle for peace negotiations. Other conference members included France, the United States, mainland China, Cambodia, Laos, Vietnam (to become South Vietnam), and the Viet Minh regime (to become North Vietnam). The Geneva Agreements (or Geneva Accords), signed on July 20 and 21, 1954, set up six primary goals:

1 End the French-Indochina War.

2 Partition Vietnam into North and South at the 17th parallel.

3 Restrict foreign military bases, personnel, and armament increases.

16 Eisenhower, chap. 14.

4 Provide for elections in North and South Vietnam to be held July 20, 1956.

5 Establish an International Control Commission (ICC) to supervise implementation of the agreements, with Canada, Poland, and India to serve on the commission.

6 Call for the neutralization of Cambodia and Laos.

It should be noted that *only* the belligerents (France and the Viet Minh) signed the accords. Of the two countries to become involved subsequently in a second Vietnamese war, South Vietnam and the United States, not only did neither sign the accords, but the former protested them and the latter made a separate unilateral declaration (which had the force of a political statement of intention but was not legally binding). Both the U.S. president and the under secretary of state (Walter Bedell Smith) who was at the conference issued like statements emphasizing the following points: (1) the United States had not been a belligerent in the war, did not sign the accords, and was not bound by them; (2) primary responsibility for ending the war rested with the parties involved; (3) the United States was not pleased with all facets of the Geneva Agreements, but hoped that they would bring peace; (4) the United States continued to support the principles of free elections and national self-determination; (5) the United States would not use force to disturb the settlement; but (6) it would view any renewal of communist aggression with "grave concern" and as "seriously threatening international peace and security." [17]

The Americans

It was only a matter of time before the agreements, which nobody seemed to like very much, were broken in letter as well as spirit. Important events in the interim included the following: Bao Dai, as head of state, appointed Ngo Dinh Diem premier of South Vietnam on July 7, 1954. By August of that year nearly 1,000,000 refugees had fled North Vietnam for the South, while only about 150,000 went North. Although these figures were widely interpreted in the West as "voting for freedom with one's feet," it should be remem-

17 The full text of both statements appears in U.S. Department of State, *Bulletin*, 31 (Aug. 2, 1954), 162–163.

bered that remnants of the native colonial army were among those coming South, while the Viet Minh wanted its sympathizers to remain in the South pending elections. By January 1955, the United States was promising direct aid for the South Vietnamese armed forces, mostly in the form of MAAG (Military Assistance Advisory Group) assistance. In August of 1955, the last French high commissioner left Saigon, effectively absolving the French from any further responsibility, as a signatory of the 1954 Geneva Agreements, for developments in Vietnam. In October 1955, Premier Diem organized a referendum (which gave him a suspicious 98 percent of the vote) to depose Bao Dai, the head of state since 1946. Once victorious, he moved (often by shady means) to consolidate his power, with United States support in return for his promise of stability.

The 1956 elections were never held. The South claimed that it was neither bound by the 1954 Geneva Agreements nor convinced that fair elections could be held as long as there was a "communist dictatorship" in the North. North Vietnam, on the other hand, could now claim that the accords had been broken and that it was now free to disregard them. Between 1956 and 1964, the year of rapid and massive U.S. involvement in Vietnam, the ICC increasingly reported violations of the Geneva Accords. Toward the end of that period, President John Kennedy increased U.S. aid to South Vietnam, although U.S. forces were not yet formally committed.

On August 4, 1964, U.S. President Lyndon Johnson (succeeding to the presidency after Kennedy was assassinated in November 1963) asked for a congressional resolution following North Vietnamese attacks on U.S. ships on August 2 and 4 in international waters within the Gulf of Tonkin—an action that had prompted U.S. air-raid reprisals against North Vietnamese gunboat bases. On August 7, 1964, Congress passed the Southeast Asia Resolution (Tonkin Resolution) by a roll-call vote of 88 to 2 in the Senate and 414 to 0 in the house.[18]

The Tonkin Resolution noted the attacks on the U.S. vessels, attributed them to "part of a deliberate and systematic campaign of aggression that the Communist regime in North Vietnam has been waging against its neighbors," and asserted that the United States

---

18 For congressional apprehensions at the time and later over the long-range meaning of the Tonkin Resolution, see the Congressional Quarterly Service, *National Diplomacy: 1965–1970*, pp. 65–85; and J. William Fulbright, *The Arrogance of Power*, Random House, Inc., New York, 1966, pp. 50–52.

had no ambitions in Southeast Asia, but desired only that the peoples there "be left in peace to work out their own destinies in their own way." The heart of the Resolution resolved:

That the Congress approves and supports the determination of the President, as Commander-in-Chief, to take all necessary measures to repel any armed attack against the forces of the United States and to prevent further aggression.

The United States regards as *vital to its national interest and to world peace* the maintenance of international peace and security in southeast Asia. Consonant with the Constitution of the United States and the Charter of the United Nations and in accordance with its obligations under the Southeast Asia Collective Defense Treaty, the United States is, therefore, prepared, as the President determines, to take all necessary steps, including the use of armed force, to assist any member or protocol state of the Southeast Asia Collective Defense Treaty requesting assistance in defense of its freedom.*

This resolution shall expire when the President shall determine that the peace and security of the area is reasonably assured by international conditions created by action of the United Nations or otherwise, except that it may be terminated earlier by concurrent resolution of the Congress.[19] (Emphasis added)

The American "Vietnam Debate"

After the Tonkin Resolution, American involvement in Vietnam increased. Nevertheless, a succession of South Vietnamese regimes and a massive U.S. military effort could not prevent the worst features of both the French-Indochina War and the Korean War from recurring. As the Vietnam conflict dragged on, a bitter internal debate developed in the United States concerning American foreign policy.

Political and military facets of the debate concerned most basically the question (over which the French had stumbled) of whether there was sufficient native Vietnamese support for the military operation that was being undertaken. More broadly, there was the issue

---

* The protocol states (Cambodia, Laos, and the "free territory under the jurisdiction of the State of Vietnam") were not parties to the SEATO Treaty, but were covered by its provisions in a special protocol.

19 For full text, see *Congressional Quarterly Weekly Report*, 22 (Aug. 7, 1964), 1667. The official justification for American involvement in Vietnam appears in Department of State, *Aggression from the North: The Record of North Vietnam's Campaign to Conquer South Vietnam*, 1965.

of the role of Indochina in United States security (Congress had appeared to speak affirmatively on this point when it passed the Tonkin Resolution in support of the President), the validity of the "domino theory," and the utility of the post-World War II policy of containment. The domino theory, which assumed that if one Southeast Asian state collapsed the others would also fall like a row of dominoes, became a central issue. President Eisenhower, with an eye on French involvement in Indochina, expressed a typical domino position when he wrote:

The loss of all Vietnam, together with Laos on the west and Cambodia in the southwest, would have meant the surrender to Communist enslavement of millions. On the material side, it would have spelled the loss of valuable deposits of tin and prodigious supplies of rubber and rice. It would have meant that Thailand, enjoying buffer territory between itself and Red China, would be exposed on its entire eastern border to infiltration or attack.

And if Indochina fell, not only Thailand but Burma and Malaya would be threatened, with added risks to East Pakistan and South Asia as well as to all Indonesia.[20]

Domino views of events in Asia were by no means an American monopoly, however, for the Russians also worried about Chinese intentions in Asia (no doubt the Chinese had their own fears about Russian and American intentions). A *New York Times* article quoted an excerpt from Moscow's *Literary Gazette* accusing Mao Tse-tung of promoting imperial designs through domino tactics:

Mao proposes to include in his "Reich," apart from China itself, Korea, the Mongolian People's Republic, Vietnam, Cambodia, Laos, Indonesia, Burma and several other countries in that region. In the second stage of the "Storm from the East" it is planned to expand in the direction of the Indian subcontinent, Soviet Central Asia and the Soviet Far East.... We are faced with absolutely clear intentions.[21]

The whole post-World War II direction of U.S. foreign policy came under review as American involvement in Vietnam deepened. President Johnson announced that he would not run for re-election,

20 Eisenhower, p. 333.
21 C. L. Sulzberger, "Foreign Affairs: Russian Dominoes," *The New York Times*, Jan. 10, 1968, p. 42.

and Richard Nixon came into the White House (as had President Eisenhower before him during the Korean War) promising to end the war. The Nixon approach was threefold: (1) "Vietnamization"—increasing South Vietnam's fighting strength and progressively handing control over to them, (2) continuing American aid, and (3) extricating American armed forces in a "peace with honor."

On January 23, 1973, after many months of Paris peace talks, President Nixon announced to the American public that a Vietnam agreement, ending the American phase of the Indochina conflict, had been reached. In addition to a cease-fire, an American withdrawal, and return of Americans held captive in Indochina, the 1973 Vietnam agreement—signed by representatives of the United States, the Republic of Vietnam (South Vietnam), the Democratic Republic of Vietnam (North Vietnam), and the Provisional Revolutionary Government of the Republic of South Vietnam (Viet Cong)—included the following major points concerning the security of South Vietnam.

1 Ban on infiltration of troops and war supplies into South Vietnam.

2 Right of unlimited military replacement aid.

3 Respect for the demilitarized zone (DMZ) separating North and South Vietnam.

4 Reunification only by peaceful means, through negotiation between North and South Vietnam without coercion or annexation (elections were envisaged).

5 Reduction and demobilization of communist and government forces in the South.

6 Ban on use of Laotian or Cambodian base areas to encroach on the sovereignty and security of South Vietnam.

7 Withdrawal of all foreign troops from Laos and Cambodia.

8 Affirmation of the right to self-determination.

9 Reaffirmation of the 1954 and 1962 Geneva Agreements on Cambodia and Laos.

10 U.S. participation in postwar reconstruction efforts throughout Indochina, in accordance with traditional U.S. policy.

11 Creation of new control and supervision machinery.[22]

22 See U.S. Department of State, Bureau of Public Affairs, *News Release*, Jan. 24, 1973.

The agreements seemed to make little difference, and they were soon broken. By mid-1975, the communist Khmer Rouge insurgents had captured Phnom Penh, the capital of Cambodia, and all of South Vietnam had fallen quickly to the Viet Cong. American foreign policy in Indochina seemed a shambles, and recriminations were coming from all sides. All four parties to the peace agreements were accused of breaking them. Both the Saigon and Viet Cong regimes, for example, were receiving substantial outside aid and were trying to increase the areas under their control. The Ho Chi Minh trail, an infiltration route into South Vietnam, had become an all-weather highway. The control machinery was not working (Canada, for example, had pulled out in disgust). There were continuing charges of South Vietnamese governmental corruption and unwillingness to fight. Nguyen Van Thieu, president of South Vietnam, had lost the confidence of most of his supporters—his soldiers were fleeing the battlefield without firing a shot, leaving millions of dollars of U.S.-supplied military equipment behind. Thieu finally had to resign, fleeing into exile abroad. Within the United States there was grim discussion of a secret understanding that the Nixon administration might have made with South Vietnam concerning rescue if Vietnamization failed. The U.S. Congress expressed some uncertainty concerning U.S. commitments and further aid to South Vietnam, but seemed determined to end this particular chapter in America's foreign policy.

While the mood of the United States in the second half of the 1970s was drifting toward neo-isolationism, primarily because of Vietnam (although events elsewhere—Latin America, Southwest Asia, and the Mediterranean, for example—had also affected America's conception of its proper foreign policy role), two general views seemed to characterize the reappraisal that was being undertaken. The first view supported continuing America's foreign policy in the tone set by the Truman Doctrine. When asked during a public appearance in April 1975 whether it was really the Johnson administration or the Kennedy administration that had started the Vietnam War, former Secretary of State Dean Rusk responded: "Neither one of them started the war and neither one of them escalated it. Ho Chi Minh started it, and Ho Chi Minh escalated it. . . . I do not apologize for saying—as Dean Acheson used to say—that the primary object of American foreign policy is to create a situation in the world in which the great experiment in freedom can survive and flourish." [23]

The other view (leaving out a third group, those who would retreat to full isolationism), although it might not necessarily disagree with Rusk's, accepts the idea that the modern world, particularly the Third World, is in a tremendous state of flux, and that neither the United States nor the Soviet Union has guaranteed control over the course of international relations. The United States can no longer automatically back up the ringing promise of President John Kennedy's 1961 Inaugural Address: "Let every nation know that we shall pay any price, bear any burden, meet any hardship, support any friend, oppose any foe to assure the survival and success of liberty."

The realities of American political power vis-à-vis the rest of the world, as tested in Vietnam, suggest that the ideological themes in American foreign policy since World War II will be reappraised carefully by each of the above groups.

THE SOVIET UNION AND INTERNATIONAL COMMUNISM

Без денег везде худенек.
Without money you are a nobody everywhere.

Не всяк пашню пашет, а всяк хлеб есть хочет.
Not everyone plows the field, but everyone wants to eat bread.

The Russian Past

These two proverbs touch in a general way two important themes in Russian history. Throughout much of its history Russia was rather an international nobody, alternately rejecting Western society and embracing those elements which made Western nations "somebody" —technology, court customs and mannerisms, military organization, and the like. Further, as a large and rather backward country, Russia had to struggle to govern and feed its massive peasant population, a creaky and top-heavy bureaucracy, and a self-indulgent aristoc-

23 *The National Observer*, Apr. 12, 1975, p. 4.

racy. The overthrow of Tsar Nicholas II in March 1917* and the attempt to introduce a semblance of democratic government were partly an effort to come to terms with these problems. The Bolshevik Revolution in November 1917, which overthrew the Provisional Government of Alexander Kerensky, promised a radical restructuring of national life and Russia's role in world affairs.

One cannot explain modern Soviet foreign policy solely on the basis of the Bolshevik revolution, however. Although it was a new departure, making communism an important factor in the Soviet Union's international relations, even the Bolshevik's radical vision could not break completely with Russian history, and in that history lie many of the roots of modern policy. Four prominent, interrelated features of the Russian past are geography, national defense, Russian national character, and bureaucratic tyranny mixed with Byzantine traditions.

Geography. As we saw in Chapter 2, *geography* is only one of the variables that define a nation's situation. Certainly Russian geography is impressive: one-sixth of the world's land area, nearly 3,000 miles from north to south and 6,000 miles from east to west, and an abundance of natural resources. Of particular significance has been the interminable Russian plain, stretching across a country that resembles a giant amphitheater facing the Arctic. The limitless plain, combined with a system of natural river highways, allowed a dynamic Russian state to expand outward easily. The backward indigenous people encountered, for example, in Central Asia proved (not unlike the North American Indians for white settlers) to be a minimal barrier to Russian imperialism, as non-Russian nationalities were incorporated into an ever-expanding empire.

National Defense. The geographical situation of Russia was a mixed blessing, however, for when the state was weak, it was a natural prey for outsiders. Consequently, *national defense,* which is a standard governmental problem for any state, has become virtually a national neurosis with the Russians. Historically, the North Polish Plain was an easy invasion route from the West, while Russia served as a buffer for Western Europe by bearing the brunt of attacks

* By the Julian calendar of the Russian Orthodox Church the revolutions were in February and October. The Bolsheviks soon adopted the Western Gregorian calendar.

from the East. Having a history of invasions is bound to affect a country's attitude toward world politics, just as the United States, for example, has been molded by its relatively peaceful development, isolated from outside intruders.

Historically, Russia has also been paranoid concerning outside threats, seeing itself as highly vulnerable because of geographical factors. The country is large and hard to defend. Even though the Russians have often relied on the tactic of retreating across the plains and allowing an advancing enemy to overextend supply lines, the fact remains that distance, combined with insufficient transport capability, makes it potentially difficult for the Russians to supply their own frontiers. Even today, the major land link to the Soviet Far East and Vladivostok is the Trans-Siberian Railroad. While Soviet air transport capability is impressive, the fact remains that this single railroad is crucial (the river systems run south-north and are of no use to east-west traffic) as well as vulnerable. Not only could it easily be interfered with, but it runs for a stretch only a few miles from the border with China—a country with which the Soviet Union has had increasingly sour relations. This is one reason why the Russians decided to start building a new stretch of track further to the north.

Part of the national defense paranoia stems from a fear of being encircled and blockaded by sea. Many historians comment on Russia's continual search for ice-free ports, for although the country has many miles of coastline, most of it is inaccessible much of the year. Further, Russia's main access routes to the open sea are susceptible to blockade. Although the nuclear age has changed ideas about national defense, the Soviet Union's current emphasis on a large naval force and a worldwide network of bases no doubt reflects a continuing concern with being trapped.

Russian National Character. Russian *national character*, like the character of any nation, defies easy definition, and generalization is risky. Certain assessments of Russian character appear with great consistency, however, in the critical scholarly literature. Although the recurrence of commentary is no proof of its validity, these persistent themes offer the beginning student at least a point of departure. For example, the harshness of the Russian winter, the vastness of the terrain, the fight to win a subsistence living from a hostile land, the isolation from the outside world, and the many bloody invasions are said to have permanently affected the Russian mind and soul. For survival Russians turned to the security of the group and submitted to autocratic leadership. Cut off from the liberalizing influences that were sweeping the Western world, the average Russian became backward, superstitious, and intensely xenophobic (distrusting and fearing foreigners).

Russian leaders developed a love/hate relationship with the outside world. Rulers like Peter the Great and Catherine the Great would envy the West and try to import and mimic its technical skills, yet resist the ideas of the Enlightenment. Not unlike many modern developing countries, Russia had both an inferiority complex vis-à-vis the outside world and a sense of innate native superiority that could retreat into itself, not needing (or wanting) Western influences.

Within Russia itself, the norms that were evolved by the dominant nationality group, the Great Russians, and to a lesser extent by the White Russians and Ukrainians, became part of the culture that dominated the country. As the Russian Empire was built, the nationality groups that were added were expected to be "Russified" —much as American Indians and various immigrant minority groups are under subtle, and not-so-subtle, pressure to adhere to white Anglo-Saxon Protestant ethics. Russification has often been associated historically with expansionism, although it is probably fair to say that any dynamic, dominant society is likely to try to spread its cultural values (which it naturally believes to be superior).

Bureaucratic Tyranny and Byzantine Traditions. A fourth feature of the Russian past is *bureaucratic tyranny* mixed with *Byzantine traditions.* Heading both these features was the political autocracy of the tsars, which in fact formed a kind of absolutist theocracy. The tsar was both the undisputed head of the government (and a ponderous bureaucracy) and the spiritual leader of his orthodox faithful. Perhaps it was a result of the need to organize a massive society and protect it from invaders, perhaps it was a legacy of Mongol occupation, or perhaps there was some other cause, but Russia evolved an omnicompetent bureaucracy penetrating every facet of life in the state. Although the chief image of tsarist times is of an unresponsive, corrupt, and even irrelevant bureaucracy exploiting and disregarding the needs of a suffering populace, the image is not without a lighter side. Two delightful short stories capture satirically the foibles of life with bureaucracy: Mikhail Saltykov's *How a Muzhik Fed Two Officials,* and Fyodor Dostoevsky's *The Crocodile* (which inspired the title for the modern Soviet humor magazine *Krokodil*). On the other hand, the weaknesses of the system helped cause its fall in 1917, and it is a common observation that tsarist absolutism was the natural parent of the revolutionary absolutism of Lenin and the state he would build.

The tsars' claim to be heir to the Eastern Roman Empire after the fall of Constantinople not only gave the tsars a claim to spiritual power to complement their temporal power but also bolstered a sense of Russian messianism. The messianic drive has taken different forms throughout Russian history, but generally it involved a belief in Mother Russia as a bastion of the Russian Orthodox Church, with Moscow as a "Third Rome," possessed with a divine mission to emancipate and guide human society. The seeds for two modern situations came from old Russia. Those who saw in Russian messianism just another motivating force for Russian expansionism were suspicious of Moscow's claims to spiritual leadership. On the other hand, Russian alienation and paranoia were further aggravated by a hostile outside world, following the Church of Rome, that challenged Russia's version of spiritual truth. This kind of mutually suspicious relationship has continued into modern times, only assuming different guises, such as Pan-Slavism (writers used to speculate over what kind of insidious, power-seeking ideology this movement represented) or, more recently, communism.

This brief overview of the Russian past hardly explains thoroughly either Russian history or the Soviet Union's present. It can only suggest how a Russian perceives the world and illuminate some continuities that perhaps influence modern policy directions. Both tsarist Russia and Soviet Russia have been accused of imperialism by alarmed observers. One such indictment, entitled *The Russian Menace to Europe,* appeared in 1890. It was written by Friedrich Engels, Marx's collaborator. It would be a mistake to attribute, as some have, the policies of the Soviet Union solely to the threatening rhetoric of Marxist-Leninist ideology. While communist ideology cannot be discounted, it is much more persuasive to view the Soviet Union as a modified product of its past, defining its role in international relations much as any large, dynamic nation-state might.

Dimensions of Soviet Foreign Policy

The Role of Ideology. As the foregoing discussion suggests, it would be a mistake to attempt to explain Soviet foreign policy by references to Marxist-Leninist texts. On the other hand, it would also be a mistake to ignore the role of ideology in the conception and implementation of foreign policy. As Adam B. Ulam, a perceptive student of Soviet affairs, writes: "The practitioners of the world's most totalitarian system must feel the need to believe in the infallibility of their doctrine; that the doctrine itself has become blurred or irrelevant to current situations does not change their tendency to use the magic incantation of Marxism." [24]

In terms of the relevance of Marxism to actual foreign politics, Ulam suggests three main uses of ideology: (1) as a package of implied prescriptions ("implied" because Marx and Engels paid little attention to foreign policy); (2) as a prism for viewing the political world; and (3) as a "symbol and quasi-religion giving its practitioners the sense that they are moving forward with the forces of history and that the success of their state is predicated upon the truth of the doctrine." [25] Because of the importance of ideology and the tortuous weaving of communist truth, it has become customary to examine Soviet policy in terms of particular leaders and the modifications they contributed to communist thought—a practice not unlike examining history in periods linked to the reigns of prominent monarchs. Consequently, the beginning student needs to be familiar with the major periods of rule, by Stalin, Khrushchev, and Brezhnev. The various interregnum periods can be left to the specialists and advanced students.

Stalin. One event not mentioned previously that occurred under Lenin's leadership was the formation of the Comintern, or Communist International, in Moscow (1919). Lenin, whose Bolsheviks had split from the socialist-leaning Mensheviks, feared a resurgence of the Second (Socialist) International under noncommunist leadership. The Comintern was the name given to the Third (Communist) International, which was a communist (largely Russian) effort to preempt leadership of the world socialist movement. Their program

24 Adam B. Ulam, "Soviet Ideology and Soviet Foreign Policy," *World Politics*, 11 (January 1959), 158.
25 *Ibid.*

called for the subordination of communist parties to Moscow's leadership, the uniting of the workers of the world for the coming revolution, and the fomenting of revolution.

When Stalin eventually emerged as the leader of the Soviet Union (following the death of Lenin in 1924), he faced certain practical and theoretical problems. Lenin had converted Marxism into a mechanism for seizing power, but it was Stalin who transformed it into a vehicle for industrializing and modernizing a state. An early battle erupted between Leon Trotsky and Josef Stalin, Lenin's heirs, concerning the nature of the revolution and foreign policy. Trotsky argued for the use of the communist power base in Russia as a springboard for stimulating worldwide revolution. He was outmaneuvered by Stalin, who (using his post as secretary-general of the party) advocated the theory of "socialism in one country," or consolidating power and defending the revolution at home first. This policy also had the effect of linking communism very closely with Russian foreign policy. Trotsky, who was subsequently assassinated in exile in Mexico, attempted to form a Fourth International dedicated to a cosmopolitan version of world communism and revolution. Trotskyism became a synonym for deviationism from communist orthodoxy as interpreted by Moscow.

To build socialism at home, Stalin instituted a series of five-year plans, which were bootstrap efforts to increase heavy industry and collective agriculture—often involving cruel measures. Instead of building the "New Soviet Citizen," the product of a society based on cooperation rather than competition that the communist dream had promised, Stalinism led to a betrayal of the revolution, a new bureaucratic hierarchy, and a degradation of humanity. Prominent indictments on these issues can be found in: Leon Trotsky, *The Revolution Betrayed*; Milovan Djilas (a vice-president of Yugoslavia under Tito who was expelled from the party in 1954 and imprisoned for a number of years), *The New Class*; and the works of the Nobel Prize-winning author Aleksandr Solzhenitsyn, particularly *One Day in the Life of Ivan Denisovich, The First Circle,* and *The Gulag Archipelago*. The last of these blames Lenin for making possible subsequent Stalinist dehumanization of Soviet citizens.

Stalin also refined the Marxist-Leninist theory of the state, which was supposed to wither away, by claiming that such a condition could only prevail when socialism was widely established. As long as the Soviet Union was a socialist island in a hostile capitalist sea, not only could the state not disappear, it had to be strengthened. This explains in part why the communist nations advocate very strongly the concept of national sovereignty in international relations, an advocacy that otherwise would appear to contradict world communist solidarity and the spirit of internationalism.

During the 1930s the Comintern, which had gained in strength during the 1920s, began to modify its militancy and entered into "popular front" arrangements with other political parties in some Western states. The invasion of the Soviet Union by Hitler's Wehrmacht in 1941 forced Stalin into an alliance with the Western powers. As a gesture of wartime cooperation and to calm Western fears of international communism, the Comintern was dissolved in 1943. It was reconstituted in more moderate form as the Cominform (Communist Information Bureau) in 1947. Membership was not obligatory for national communist parties and decisions were not binding, as had been the case under the Comintern. Its goals included the exchange of information among member communist parties (Soviet Union, Bulgaria, Czechoslovakia, France, Hungary, Italy, Poland, Rumania, and Yugoslavia) and a joint propaganda effort.

In 1948, the Yugoslav Communist Party was expelled by the Cominform for the deviationism of Yugoslavia's President Josip Broz Tito. Rejecting the monolithic communism advocated by Stalin, Tito insisted that each communist state must find its "own road to socialism" free from Russian hegemony. Titoism became a synonym for "national communism" and made possible the future development of polycentrism within the communist bloc. Although Stalin tried to crush Tito's independent policy, Khrushchev subsequently made peace with him, and the Cominform was disbanded in 1956 as part of the reconciliation.

International relations with states outside the communist camp (a bloc that had been created in Eastern Europe and the Balkans following World War II) turned into the Cold War as the wartime alliance cooled. The preceding section of this chapter examined the Western perception of threatening Soviet moves, but it should be noted that the Soviet Union was no less aware of Western policies as potential threats. The Soviet Union tended to regard its own solidifying of a sphere of influence in Eastern Europe as a necessary part of building a buffer zone against future Napoleons and Hitlers marching eastward. Events in Western Europe were regarded suspiciously in such terms as German *revanche* politics, bourgeois machinations, or United States hegemony. The Soviet Union proved as ready to divide the world into black and white political spheres as the United States had been. The following excerpts from a speech by Andrei Vishinsky (a Soviet U.N. representative known for the violence of his attacks on the United States) to the United Nations General Assembly on September 18, 1947, illustrate the Soviet interpretation of U.S. postwar policy in Western Europe:

The so-called Truman Doctrine and the Marshall Plan are particularly glaring examples of the manner in which the principles of the United Nations are violated, of the way in which the Organization is ignored.

As the experience of the past few months has shown, the proclamation of this doctrine meant that the United States Government has moved toward a direct renunciation of the principles of international collaboration and concerted action by the great Powers and toward attempts to impose its will on other independent states, while at the same time obviously using the economic resources distributed as relief to individual needy nations as an instrument of political pressure. This is clearly proved by the measures taken by the United States Government with regard to Greece and Turkey which ignore and by-pass the United Nations as well as by the measures proposed under the so-called Marshall Plan in Europe.[26]

Vishinsky then declared the Marshall Plan simply a "variant of the Truman Doctrine adapted to the conditions of postwar Europe" and depicted the whole operation as a naked power play by the United States to control Western Europe. Finally, he noted:

Moreover, this Plan is an attempt to split Europe into two camps and, with the help of the United Kingdom and France, to complete the formation of a bloc of several European countries hostile to the interests of the democratic countries of Eastern Europe and most particularly to the interests of the Soviet Union. . . . The intention is to make use of Western Germany and German heavy industry (the Ruhr) as one of the most important economic bases for American expansion in Europe, in disregard of the national interests of the countries which suffered from German aggression.[27]

26 U.N. General Assembly, *Official Records,* Plenary Meetings, Verbatim Record, Sept. 18, 1947, excerpted from pp. 86–88.
27 *Ibid.*

Under Stalin, the Leninist view of the world as divided into two irreconcilable camps (capitalist and socialist) was reaffirmed and strengthened. The keynote speech at the founding of the Cominform in September 1947 called attention to the nature of these two camps—"the imperialist and the anti-democratic camp having as its chief aim the establishment of world domination of American imperialism and the crushing of democracy, and the anti-imperialist and democratic camp having as its chief aim the undermining of imperialism, the consolidation of democracy, and the liquidation of the remnants of fascism." [28]

Khrushchev. The death of Stalin in 1953 brought some moderation to Soviet foreign policy, suggesting that other Soviet leaders were well aware that Stalin's policies were increasingly out of touch with developments in international relations. This moderation included such things as re-establishing diplomatic relations with Greece and Israel, renouncing Soviet claims to Turkish territory, improving relations with Yugoslavia, withdrawing objections to the appointment of a new U.N. secretary-general, and ending the Korean War.

It is true that the Soviet Union continued to solidify its dominant position in Eastern Europe and to establish a unified military-political alliance structure called the Warsaw Pact. Created in 1955 ostensibly as a response to the formation of NATO, and particularly to the 1954 Paris Accords integrating West Germany into NATO, the Warsaw Pact in fact mostly recognized formally the power structure that already existed in Eastern Europe. As Nikita S. Khrushchev emerged as the dominant figure in the post-Stalin power struggle, he made his own impact on the course of Soviet policy and communist doctrine.

"Khrushchevism" is associated with "de-Stalinization" and the attack on Stalin's "cult of the individual." While de-Stalinization was a move away from the terror and cruelty of Stalin's rule within the Soviet Union, it also set in motion far-reaching changes throughout the communist world. Premier Khrushchev added to communist doctrine the idea that even though classes and the state would eventually wither away, the Communist Party would remain as a social guiding force. Khrushchev also advocated "peaceful coexistence," a reinterpretation of earlier communist doctrine, which stressed the

28 *Pravda*, Oct. 5, 1947.

inevitability of war between the socialist and capitalist states. Peaceful coexistence was a recognition of the Soviet Union's growing confidence in its ability to defend itself, an acknowledgment of the dangers to *both* sides of a nuclear war, and a commitment to the idea that communism could defeat capitalism peacefully by producing a superior social and economic system. Addressing the Twentieth Party Congress in February 1956, Khrushchev commented on foreign policy options in the nuclear age:

Indeed, there are only two ways: either peaceful coexistence or the most destructive war in history. There is no third way.

We believe that countries with differing social systems can do more than exist side by side. It is necessary to proceed further, to improve relations, strengthen confidence among countries and cooperate.[29]

The new doctrine of peaceful coexistence did not end all wars, however, for the Soviet Union retained the right to assist revolutionary movements in "wars of national liberation." The strategy was to avoid Big Power confrontations as an unnecessary risk to the socialist camp, while aiding indigenous groups "struggling" (particularly in the developing countries) against "capitalist imperialism." In spite of this continuing revolutionary emphasis, mainland China was outraged. Khrushchev's doctrinal adjustment was seen as "revisionism" (a very serious crime) of "pure" Marxism/Leninism and as a manifestation of cowardice on the part of Russian leaders, who were afraid to continue the worldwide revolution. Further, the Chinese suspected some kind of conspiracy between the Russians and the West that would be to the disadvantage of China. Thus peaceful coexistence not only became important for East-West relations, but also was a significant element in the Sino-Soviet split.

The Sino-Soviet Split. By the early 1960s the Sino-Soviet split had created a great deal of international stir. It became as difficult, however, to trace the roots of the split as it had been to establish the cause of the Cold War. The quasi-code language of communist rhetoric and invective hampered analysis of the split. Is it, for ex-

29 Text in Leo Gruliow, ed., *Current Soviet Policies II: The Documentary Record of the 20th Communist Party Congress and Its Aftermath,* Frederick A. Praeger, Inc., New York, 1957, pp. 36–38.

ample, a greater insult to be called a revisionist or a deviationist? Or are these pejorative terms equally strong? One thing became certain, though . . . the split was real and would have significant repercussions for the world communist movement, which had always prided itself on unity of purpose and acceptance of a single version of historical truth. It was one thing for Tito to seek a separate road to socialism, but here were communist giants engaging in a bitter dispute over basics.

The initial tendency of observers was to attribute the Sino-Soviet split to a personal dispute between Khrushchev and China's Chairman Mao Tse-tung. Mao was antagonistic to Khrushchev's de-Stalinization speech at the Twentieth Party Congress, which stirred up turmoil within the communist camp. Khrushchev's attack on Stalin's "cult of the individual" could hardly have comforted Mao, who headed a personality cult of his own. Also, the peaceful coexistence policy caused a doctrinal dispute between Moscow and Peking.

Khrushchev's ouster in October 1964, however, failed to alleviate the growing strain between the Soviet Union and China. As this chapter warned earlier, one should be careful not to mistake ideology for reality. Ideology is only a frame of reference that we can use to measure our understanding of concrete events. Ideological dispute is only part of the Sino-Soviet quarrel. It has become enmeshed with the traditional "national interest" issues over which nation-states have always fought—security, hegemony, pride, borders, racial distrust, and the like.

The Soviet Union and China share a 4,500-mile border. The Chinese see the current border as the result of tsarist imperialist stealing of Chinese territory and forcing unequal treaties upon the Chinese. The Russians tend to see their eastern holdings in terms of the pushing back of earlier invaders from the East or as a fair outcome of World War II. There have apparently been numerous border clashes, many of which have not been reported to the outside world. One that became too big to hide was the fight between Soviet and Chinese troops on March 2, 1969, on Damanskii-Chenpao Island in the Ussuri River. Border negotiators appointed by each side to discuss outstanding border claims have made little progress. The feeling on both sides can be shown by the helicopter incident in the spring of 1974. A Soviet helicopter, which Moscow claimed was on a medical mission, became lost in a storm and strayed across the border into China. The Chinese seized the craft, claimed it was on a spying mission, and hinted at a show trial.

There are also Soviet fears of a "yellow peril." They suspect heavily populated China of coveting the wide-open spaces of Siberia. Race also becomes an issue in the status of Outer Mongolia (the Mongolian People's Republic), a Soviet satellite since Bolshevik intervention in 1921 made possible the establishment of a sovereign Mongolian government. Outer Mongolia has been able to maintain Mongolian ethnic and cultural identity, but across the border, Inner Mongolia has been absorbed by China both politically and ethnically. A large influx of Chinese to the area had made the Mongolians a minority in their own land, threatened with the loss of a separate identity. Moscow has exploited the issue by broadcasting Mongolian-language reports of enslavement and racial extermination of Mongolians at the hands of the Chinese.

According to communist doctrine, capitalist states are supposed to fight with one another, and of course open conflict between socialist states and the capitalist states (in spite of peaceful coexistence) is a possibility. The socialist states, however, are supposed to be joined together in peace. Yet, the lessons of the uprisings in East Germany, Hungary, Poland, and Czechoslovakia are surely not lost on Moscow. Communist China, on the other hand, is not a small European country. It is a major power with atomic weapons. The intense efforts of both China and the Soviet Union, aimed at keeping the Ussuri River fighting within bounds, suggest that each understands the implications of an all-out war. Still, Soviet and Chinese troops face each other across their common border. The invective in Soviet newspapers has ranged from accusing Peking of large-scale narcotics trafficking with the outside world through the Portuguese colony of Macao as a way to accumulate foreign capital to invest in a nuclear arsenal to public speculation by Moscow on the virtues of a pre-emptive Soviet military strike against the Chinese nuclear facilities in Sinkiang province.[30]

The elements of the Sino-Soviet dispute discussed above by no means include all the sources of conflict. For example, there were already bitter policy disputes between Mao Tse-tung and Stalin (who initially supported Chiang Kai-shek) in the early days of

30 *The New York Times,* Nov. 18, 1974, p. 15.

China's struggle for nationhood and the war with Japan. The point for observers of international relations is that the Sino-Soviet split is more than an ideological dispute and that the direction it takes will be of significance to the overall course of world politics. If there is a "law of politics" or even a lesson to be found here, it is not that countries of similar ideological persuasion never fight, but rather that nation-states with differing national interests are likely to encounter conflict. There is no intrinsic reason why that conflict cannot be resolved peacefully, however—a feature that is particularly crucial when Big Powers are involved.

Brezhnev. The ouster of Nikita Khrushchev in 1964 was followed by the joint leadership of Leonid I. Brezhnev (head of the Communist Party) and Aleksei N. Kosygin (head of the Council of Ministers, or premier). Largely because of his power base as Communist Party leader, Brezhnev has emerged as the pre-eminent Soviet leader. His style and policies are somewhat of a reaction to those of Khrushchev, whom Brezhnev helped oust.

The reasons for Khrushchev's "retirement" are still not totally clear, although Soviet observers seem to have evolved a general package of possible explanations. Certainly there were domestic difficulties involving consumer discontent over the slow advance of living standards, the failure to meet agricultural objectives, and internal party politics. One facet of party politics that had caused a stir was Khrushchev's widely publicized division of the Party into agricultural and industrial branches. In addition to introducing a certain amount of inefficiency, the party division had the serious consequence of disrupting the pockets of power that old-time party functionaries had built up. This reform was quickly revoked when Khrushchev left.

Internationally Khrushchev received much of the blame for the disintegration of communist unity, particularly for the Sino-Soviet split (although, as this discussion has shown, the roots of the split go much deeper than Khrushchev's policies). There was also the matter of the Cuban missile crisis. While it may not be exactly clear who "won" that confrontation, it was quite clear that the event was precisely what peaceful coexistence was designed to prevent. There was growing uneasiness within the Soviet leadership concerning Khrushchev's personal style of rule and readiness to undertake new adventures. His ebullient personality and peasant earthiness had also caused some embarrassment on occasion—ranging from banging his shoe on a table at the United Nations to charging abstract artists with unnatural sex tendencies to making racial slurs against the Chinese. All this was not in keeping with the collegial, board-of-directors, gray-flannel-suit image of the responsible governance of a major nation.

Since the ascendancy of Leonid Brezhnev, that image has been largely achieved. The reversing or slowing down of Khrushchev's reforms has raised charges of neo-Stalinism in some circles. The major Brezhnev policy vis-à-vis the West has been détente. Building on the idea of peaceful coexistence, détente implied a further relaxing of tensions and a normalization of relations. Détente was to involve agreements in such areas as armament limitation, increased economic and cultural ties, settlement of territorial and other disputes in Europe arising out of World War II, and loosened emigration restrictions on Soviet citizens (e.g., Jews) wishing to leave.

While it would be incorrect to claim that no progress has been made in détente, it would also be inappropriate to claim that any outstanding successes have as yet been achieved. The United States has become disenchanted with Soviet "foot-dragging" and apparent reluctance to adhere to the spirit of détente. A common American assessment is that the Russians want concessions from the West but are afraid to undertake any real liberalization because they believe it will threaten their system. The dissident Russian author Aleksandr Solzhenitsyn has warned that real détente must include specific and basic substantive issues, such as civil liberties, not just the verbiage of grand international politics. The Russians are already having difficulty keeping control over dissident forces, particularly in Eastern Europe. There is some evidence of Moscow's uneasiness over a too-rapid escalation of détente, and the Soviet leaders were visibly (even if only momentarily) shaken by the dramatic Nixon Administration move toward détente with the People's Republic of China— both providing increased flexibility in international relations and making things more complex for Soviet foreign policy-makers. Perhaps the most significant feature of détente between the United States and the Soviet Union is the apparent determination, in spite of setbacks, of both governments to keep détente alive and work for better relations.

One particularly unfortunate incident during the Brezhnev period was the invasion of Czechoslovakia. This incident demonstrated several points: (1) a Soviet retrenchment toward the mood and politics of the Stalin era; (2) the inability of the communist bloc to adapt to "too much change too fast;" (3) a reaffirmation of the traditional expectation of international relations observers that large nation-states will dominate, in one form or another, their smaller neighbors, particularly if security interests are involved; and (4) a suggestion that the Soviet Union, in the face of intense international and domestic reaction to the invasion, might well be considering (as the United States has done following Vietnam) modifying its international profile.

THE INVASION OF CZECHOSLOVAKIA—1968

Proletáři Všech Zemí Spojte Se, Nebo Střelím!!
Proletarians of the World, Unite, or I Will Shoot!!

The above modification of the well-known communist slogan appeared as a caption to a cartoon showing a Russian tank in a publication (since banned) of the Czechoslovak Writers Union.[31] It was part of a dwindling public expression of the new-found literary freedom that had blossomed during the Prague Spring of 1968, before the Soviet Union, with other Warsaw Pact countries, invaded Czechoslovakia to "restore socialist order." The reformers within Czechoslovakia, who claimed to be devout communists, justified their efforts at liberalizing Czechoslovakian social life in terms of giving Marxism a "human face" (a synthesis of democracy and socialism) by backing off from the distortions of Marx introduced by Lenin and Stalin. The cry of "socialism for the people, not the people for socialism," like earlier pleas from this small country for the right to run their own affairs, ultimately fell—as it has on other occasions—before the might of more powerful neighbors.

Background

Czechoslovakia, a small, elongated country in Central Europe (see Figure 5-2, a sketch map of Czechoslovakia), has been described

31 *Literarni listy*, Aug. 28, 1968.

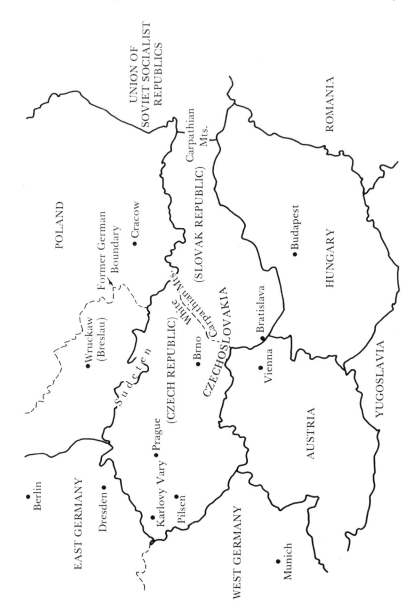

FIGURE 5-2. Czechoslovakia

rather dramatically as a "dagger pointing at the heart of both the Soviet Union and Western Europe." While that statement perhaps calls attention to the strategic importance of Czechoslovakia, it is useful to remember that the country (49,370 square miles) is about the size of the state of New York (49,576 square miles) and has a population (14,497,000) slightly less than that of New York State (18,241,266).

Citizens of Czechoslovakia can point with both egocentric pride and national masochism to the pivotal role their nation has played in so many turbulent major events of world history. The Czech religious reformer John Huss (Jan Hus) inspired the Hussite Movement in the early 1400s, which attacked feudalism and the Roman Catholic Church. The way was paved for both the Protestant Reformation (and the breakup of the ideal of the Universal Church) and the Thirty Years' War (effecting the breakup of the Holy Roman Empire, the rise of modern nationalism, and the launching of the modern nation-state system). The result of all that turmoil was the absorption of Czech territory into the Habsburg Empire and three hundred years of Habsburg rule.

With the collapse of the Austro-Hungarian Empire after World War I, the Czechoslovak Republic was founded in 1918. Since it had ample resources, able governors, and a liberal constitution, the new republic appeared to have a bright future. It was surrounded by dynamic neighbors, however, and beset with internal difficulties. Bohemians, Slovaks, Germans, Magyars, and Ruthenians had all been combined within one country. Hitler, with the participation of Czechoslovakia's other neighbors, exploited these ethnic difficulties and ended up dismembering the country. Munich, the word that became a synonym for appeasement, was the site of the conference between Hitler and English Prime Minister Neville Chamberlain. The Munich Agreement of 1938 effectively yielded Czechoslovakia to Hitler, Czech President Beneš, a target of Hitler's attacks, resigned to be replaced by Emil Hácha, leading to the events described in Chapter 1.

During World War II Eduard Beneš headed a provisional Czech government in London, and Czech units fought with the Allies. Following the war Beneš headed a coalition government in Czechoslovakia. Elections in 1946 made the Communists the strongest single party, with the Communist Klement Gottwald the head of a coalition government. In February 1948, the communists seized power in Czechoslovakia by a coup d'état. Beneš resigned as president and was succeeded by Gottwald. Czechoslovakia was now within Moscow's sphere of influence.

The successor to Gottwald in 1953 was Antonín Novotný, a man who could weather Khrushchev's anti-Stalin campaign and still keep Czechoslovakia on the path of stolid communism. As one respected student of Eastern European affairs, H. Gordon Skilling, observed: "Novotný seemed to have successfully squared the circle, throwing his full support to Moscow in all controversies within the bloc and on all world issues, and yet at the same time avoiding any serious reforms, such as those espoused by Khrushchev." [32] A Czech journalist observed of Novotný that he was the "embodiment of mediocrity, half-educated and without imagination, but through unlimited devotion and obedience he gained support from Big Brother in Moscow." [33]

The Rise of Dubček

Alexander Dubček, the head of the Slovak party, came to power in January 1968 on a wave of anti-Novotný sentiment and Slovak nationalism. In any communist country, change comes from the top down, and the replacement of Novotný by Dubček had widespread repercussions. From the beginning Dubček was faced with the problem of reassuring conservatives within the bureaucracy that liberalization would not threaten them, while at the same time placating impatient liberals regarding the slow pace of democratization. A further complicating feature was public opinion, which quickly outdistanced government action and exuberantly demanded more freedom.

Concern grew in Moscow that Dubček would be unable to control the forces that were being unleashed in Czechoslovakia, and a regime as conservative as Brezhnev's would have no sympathy with the idea that communism in Czechoslovakia would emerge stronger and fresher as the result of the changes. It was no doubt some consolation to the liberal Prague government that the ruling Yugoslav

32 H. Gordon Skilling, "Czechoslovakia," in *The Communist States in Disarray: 1965–1971*, ed. Adam Bromke and Terese Rakowska-Harmstone, University of Minnesota Press, Minneapolis, 1972.
33 Journalist M, *A Year Is Eight Months: Czechoslovakia 1968*, Anchor Books, Doubleday & Company, Inc., New York, 1971, p. 10.

and Rumanian Communist Parties endorsed their actions, as did Communist parties elsewhere in the West.

By March 1968, Soviet and other East European leaders (particularly Walter Ulbricht of East Germany) were beginning to advise the Czechs, at first privately and then publicly, to head off the rising demands for reform. There were even Warsaw Pact military maneuvers on the Czechoslovak border, and in late June on Czechoslovak territory. The withdrawal of the troops following the maneuvers was noticeably unhurried. To make sure the Dubček regime understood, the Soviet Union and other Warsaw Pact allies issued a public "Warsaw letter" formally condemning the events occurring in Czechoslovakia. The letter expressed fear for the safety of socialism and urged tighter control of the mass media and party democracy.

The letter had an unforeseen effect, for it stirred up Czechoslovak nationalism and resentment over the outside interference. The popular aspect of the reform movement took on an anti-Soviet tinge, which no doubt added one more to the Soviet Union's list of reasons for ultimately intervening. Another reason was the famous "Two Thousand Words" proclamation, stemming from a meeting of reform-minded academicians in Prague in June 1968. The intent of the proclamation was to appeal directly to the people for support in the fight for democratization and to warn them of the danger of a conservative, anti-reform comeback. The proclamation received an unanticipated and widespread amount of popular support from both students and workers' groups. But it also became the proof the conservatives needed to show that anarchy had gone too far and had to be put down.

The Tanks Come

Political maneuvering continued into August, but by August 20 the decision had been made. Warsaw Pact forces crossed the Czechoslovak frontier on the evening of August 20, and although the political maneuvering would continue into 1969, the Prague Spring was coming to an end. A West German daily published astonishingly similar pictures of troops from Hitler's Wehrmacht and Ulbricht's East German *Volksarmee* marching into Prague. Soviet behavior was not unlike German behavior toward Dr. Hácha twenty years earlier, although perhaps a bit more dramatic. Czechoslovak government officials were mysteriously kidnapped, official meetings were held under siege by tanks and in some cases conducted under the gaze of armed soldiers, and Dubček was held (with three other leaders) for forty-eight hours handcuffed, isolated, and without food or drink in an underground retreat in the Carpathian mountains before being taken to Moscow for discussions.[34] Only the courage of Ludvik Svoboda, the Czechoslovak president, and strong evidence of popular support kept Dubček from being tried as a traitor.

As it was, the Soviet Union got what it wanted. Dubček and the other leaders of his regime returned to Prague and occupied their former positions, but they did so under "agreements" providing for the "normalization" of national political and social life—the Soviet Union had forced a change of policy and was allowing the erring Czechoslovak leaders to stay on and implement that change.

Even this truce came to an end, however, over the "hockey crisis" in March of 1969. Mass demonstrations by exuberant citizens erupted all over Czechoslovakia after the Czechs defeated the Russian hockey team in Stockholm, and there was some violence against Soviet installations in Czechoslovakia. That was too much for the Russians. Dubček was forced to resign as first secretary of the Czechoslovak Communist Party in April 1969 and was replaced by Gustav Husak, who has turned out to be a neoconservative of the type preferred by Moscow. The memory of 1968 is fading and is apparently being replaced by the sullen, quiet acquiescence upon which conservative regimes thrive. Given its geographical location, Czechoslovakia has little choice for the time being.

Meaning of the Invasion

Although the Soviet Union has attempted to improve the image of the 1968 intervention, the fact remains that it invaded another sovereign state. The move has been justified politically under the "Brezhnev Doctrine," which introduced the idea of limited sovereignty for socialist countries. "Fraternal socialist countries" were required to defend the real sovereignty of Czechoslovakia from those who would undermine it and ultimately threaten the whole socialist camp.

Since the invasion of Czechoslovakia, the Soviet Union has kept a rather low profile regarding involvement in the affairs of other nations, particularly in the "hot spots" of the Middle East, the Medi-

34 *Ibid.*, p. 226.

terranean, and Southeast Asia. No doubt the Soviets are increasingly aware of the same facts the United States has been learning in Vietnam. It is becoming more and more difficult for the Big Powers to control at will events in smaller countries all over the world. Perhaps immediate neighbors are relatively helpless, as the Czechoslovak example shows, but there is no reason to believe that the Soviet Union could control similar events in communist Cuba, for example. But even in Eastern Europe, the Soviet Union—the nearest dominant power—has had difficulty in keeping control. Of the eight communist states there, three have successfully defied the Soviet Union (Yugoslavia in the late 1940s and Albania and Rumania in the 1960s), four have tried and failed (East Germany in 1953, Hungary in 1956, Poland in 1956 and 1970, and Czechoslovakia in 1968), and only one (Bulgaria) has shown no signs of open revolt. The status of the Soviet Union's eastern border with China has already been reviewed. Clearly nationalism emerges as a strong force competing with ideology.

Two factors relating to both ideology and important political forces within a world in conflict have been conspicuously absent from the discussions in this chapter: (1) the People's Republic of China and Mao's brand of communism, and (2) the "neutralism" of the nonaligned countries. Since so much of the Cold War has revolved around the Soviet-American confrontation, this chapter has been devoted to that confrontation. Although they are not unaffected by the Cold War, the nonaligned countries of the Third World (and Communist China, which covets the leadership of that group) are perhaps more appropriately examined within the context of the next chapter.

BIBLIOGRAPHY

Acheson, Dean. *Power and Diplomacy.* Harvard University Press, Cambridge, Mass., 1958.

Almond, Gabriel A. *The Appeals of Communism.* Princeton University Press, Princeton, N.J., 1954.

Alperovitz, Gar. *Atomic Diplomacy: Hiroshima and Potsdam.* Simon & Schuster, Inc., New York, 1965.

Barghoorn, Frederick C. *The Soviet Cultural Offensive.* Princeton University Press, Princeton, N.J., 1960.

Barghoorn, Frederick C. *The Soviet Image of the United States.* Harcourt, Brace, and Company, Inc., New York, 1950.

Bass, Robert H., ed. *The Soviet-Yugoslav Controversy, 1948–1958: A Documentary Record.* Prospect Books, London, 1959.

Brzezinski, Zbigniew K. *The Soviet Bloc: Unity and Conflict,* rev. ed. Harvard University Press, Cambridge, Mass., 1967.

Campbell, John C. *Tito's Separate Road.* Harper & Row, Publishers, Incorporated, New York, 1967.

Clubb, O. Edmund. *China and Russia: The "Great Game."* Columbia University Press, New York, 1971.

Dallin, David J. *Soviet Foreign Policy after Stalin.* J. B. Lippincott Company, Philadelphia, 1961.

Deutscher, Isaac. *The Great Contest: Russia and the West.* Oxford University Press, New York, 1960.

Donnelly, Desmond. *Struggle for the World: The Cold War and Its Causes.* St. Martin's Press, London, 1965.

Djilas, Milovan. *The New Class.* Frederick A. Praeger, Inc., New York, 1957.

Ebenstein, William. *Today's Isms,* 6th ed. Prentice-Hall, Inc., Englewood Cliffs, N.J., 1970.

Feis, Herbert. *Between War and Peace: The Potsdam Conference.* Princeton University Press, Princeton, N.J., 1960.

———. *Churchill, Roosevelt, Stalin: The War They Waged and the Peace They Sought.* Princeton University Press, Princeton, N.J., 1957.

———. *From Trust to Terror: The Onset of the Cold War.* W. W. Norton & Company, Inc., New York, 1970.

Fishel, Wesley R., ed. *Vietnam: Anatomy of a Conflict.* F. E. Peacock Publishers, Inc., Itasca, Ill., 1968.

Fleming, D. F. *The Cold War and Its Origins, 1917–1950.* Doubleday & Company, Inc., Garden City, N.Y., 1961.

Fontaine, Andre. *History of the Cold War: From the Korean War to the Present.* Pantheon Books, New York, 1969.

Graebner, Norman A. *Cold War Diplomacy, 1945–1960.* Princeton University Press, Princeton, N.J., 1962.

Halle, Louis B. *The Cold War as History.* Harper & Row, Publishers, Incorporated, New York, 1967.

Herz, Martin F. *Beginnings of the Cold War.* Indiana University Press, Bloomington, 1966.

Hoffman, Erik P., and Frederic J. Fleron, eds. *The Conduct of Soviet Foreign Policy.* Aldine-Atherton, Inc., Chicago, 1971.

Hoffmann, Stanley. *Gulliver's Troubles, or The Setting of American Foreign Policy.* McGraw-Hill Book Company, New York, 1968.

Horowitz, David. *The Free World Colossus: A Critique of American*

Foreign Policy in the Cold War. Hill and Wang, Inc., New York, 1965.

Jacobson, Harold Karan, ed. *America's Foreign Policy*, rev. ed. Random House, Inc., New York, 1960.

Journalist M. *A Year Is Eight Months: Czechoslovakia 1968*. Anchor Books, Doubleday & Company, Inc., Garden City, N.Y., 1971.

Kennan, George F. *American Diplomacy, 1900–1950*. Mentor Books, New York, 1951.

———. *Memoirs, 1925–1950*. Little, Brown and Company, Boston, 1967.

———. *Memoirs, 1950–1963*. Little, Brown and Company, Boston, 1972.

———. *Soviet Foreign Policy, 1917–1941*. D. Van Nostrand, Inc., Princeton, N.J., 1960.

LaFeber, Walter. *America, Russia, and the Cold War, 1945–1966*. John Wiley & Sons, Inc., New York, 1967.

Lerche, Charles O., Jr. *The Cold War and After*. Prentice-Hall, Inc., Englewood Cliffs, N.J., 1965.

Loewenthal, Richard. *World Communism: The Disintegration of a Secular Faith*. Oxford University Press, New York, 1964.

Luard, Evan, ed. *The Cold War: A Reappraisal*. Frederick A. Praeger, Inc., New York, 1964.

Lukacs, John. *A History of the Cold War*, rev. ed. Doubleday & Company, Inc., Garden City, N.Y., 1962.

Marshall, Charles Burton. *The Cold War: A Concise History*. Franklin Watts, Inc., New York, 1965.

Moore, Barrington, Jr. *Soviet Politics: The Dilemma of Power*. Harvard University Press, Cambridge, Mass., 1950.

Morgenthau, Hans J. *A New Foreign Policy for the United States*. Frederick A. Praeger, Inc., New York, 1969.

———. *In Defense of the National Interest*. Alfred A. Knopf, Inc., New York, 1951.

Mosely, Philip E. *The Kremlin and World Politics*. Vintage Books, New York, 1960.

O'Connor, John F. *The Cold War and Liberation*. Vantage Press, New York, 1961.

Oliva, L. Jay, ed. *Russia and the West from Peter to Khrushchev*. D. C. Heath and Company, Boston, 1965.

Perkins, Dexter. *The Diplomacy of a New Age*. Indiana University Press, Bloomington, 1967.

Rapoport, Anatol. *The Big Two: Soviet-American Perceptions of Foreign Policy*. Pegasus, New York, 1971.

Raskin, Marcus G., and Bernard B. Fall, eds. *The Viet-Nam Reader*, rev. ed. Random House, Inc., New York, 1965.

Readings on Fascism and National Socialism. Alan Swallow, Publisher, Denver, n.d.

Rees, David. *The Age of Containment: The Cold War, 1945–1965.* St. Martin's Press, London, 1967.

Rosser, Richard F. *An Introduction to Soviet Foreign Policy.* Prentice-Hall, Inc., Englewood Cliffs, N.J., 1969.

Rubinstein, Alvin Z., ed. *The Foreign Policy of the Soviet Union,* 2d ed. Random House, Inc., New York, 1960.

Salisbury, Harrison E. *War between Russia and China.* W. W. Norton & Company, Inc., New York, 1969.

Schuman, Frederick L. *The Cold War: Retrospect and Prospect.* Louisiana State University Press, Baton Rouge, 1962.

Seabury, Paul. *The Rise and Decline of the Cold War.* Basic Books, Inc., New York, 1967.

Seton-Watson, Hugh. *From Lenin to Khrushchev: The History of World Communism.* Frederick A. Praeger, Inc., New York, 1960.

———. *The East European Revolution.* Frederick A. Praeger, Inc., New York, 1956.

Shaw, L. Earl, ed. *Modern Competing Ideologies.* D. C. Heath and Company, Lexington, Mass., 1973.

Shulman, Marshall D. *Beyond the Cold War.* Yale University Press, New Haven, Conn., 1966.

Solzhenitsyn, Aleksandr. *The First Circle.* Harper & Row, Publishers, Incorporated, New York, 1968.

Spanier, John W. *American Foreign Policy since World War II.* Frederick A. Praeger, Inc., New York, 1960.

Stoessinger, John G. *Nations in Darkness: China, Russia & America,* 2d ed. Random House, Inc., New York, 1971.

Strausz-Hupé, Robert, et al. *Protracted Conflict.* Harper & Row, Publishers, Incorporated, New York, 1959.

Trotsky, Leon. *The Revolution Betrayed.* Pioneer Publishers, New York, 1945.

Ulam, Adam B. *The Rivals: America and Russia since World War II.* The Viking Press, Inc., New York, 1971.

———. *Titoism and the Cominform.* Harvard University Press, Cambridge, Mass., 1952.

Whetten, Lawrence L. *Germany's Ostpolitik: Relations between the Federal Republic and the Warsaw Pact Countries.* Oxford University Press, New York, 1971.

Wolfe, Thomas W. *Soviet Power and Europe, 1945–1970.* The Johns Hopkins Press, Baltimore, 1970.

———. *Soviet Strategy at the Crossroads.* Harvard University Press, Cambridge, Mass., 1964.

Zimmerman, William. *Soviet Perspectives on International Relations, 1956–1967.* Princeton University Press, Princeton, N.J., 1969.

The Third World

The description of the emerging nations following World War II as *le tiers monde,* or the "Third World," has generally been attributed to the Algerian writer Frantz Fanon. While the term "Third World" has come into general use, there is no solid agreement on precisely what it covers. It conjures up a vague image of new nation-states that have emerged from a colonial past (particularly since World War II). These new states are associated with many contemporary political and economic issues, such as anticolonialism, neonationalism, nonalignment, underdevelopment, overpopulation, hunger, and racial antagonisms.

THE "THIRD WORLD" AS A CONCEPT

The sense that the Third World is an identifiable unit is bolstered by at least two things: the "package" of problems that the whole Third World seems to face and the seeming unity of the Third World bloc within the United Nations General Assembly during votes on certain issues, particularly those having anticolonial overtones. There is no reason why the Third World concept cannot be useful in the study of international relations, particularly since the term is so widely used. One needs only to have some awareness of the complexities subsumed under the term.

The Third World has often been defined in terms of "development." One scholar, Irving Horowitz, has, for example, written a study entitled *Three Worlds of Development.*[1] He describes the First World as primarily Western Europe and the United States. This world is characterized by competitive capitalism, which had begun to erode the feudal system by the sixteenth century. The industrial revolution during the eighteenth and nineteenth centuries produced a technologically advanced world with the capacity to adapt to, and even provoke, dramatic modernization.

Professor Horowitz sees the Second World as the Soviet Union and its bloc. While the problems of development of backward Russia under the tsars resembled those of the contemporary Third World, the Bolshevik Revolution in 1917 forcibly removed Russia from the

1 Irving Louis Horowitz, *Three Worlds of Development,* Oxford University Press, London, 1966.

capitalist path and forced it into a mold of centralized state planning
and development. In the aftermath of World War II, the Soviet
Union's politico-economic model appeared in Eastern Europe and, in
highly modified form, in China. Given their relatively recent and
dramatic emergence as highly developed states, it is not surprising
that the Soviet Union and the People's Republic of China see themselves as ideal models to be emulated by Third World countries
searching for solutions to their own problems of underdevelopment.

The Third World appears as a new entity, recently emerged
from a colonial past, seeking its own path to development. Facing
similar developmental problems, a group of nations in Latin America, Africa, and Asia have evolved a sense of common identity and
unity of purpose. The goal is *development,* a process involving the
borrowing of whatever works from the ideologies, politics, and economics of the First and Second Worlds while remaining nonaligned
in the East-West struggle.

The Third World is more a state of mind than a substantive political unit, in spite of the fact that numerous international meetings
have been held both within the United Nations framework and outside it to draft common approaches. Political diversity and differing
foreign policy stances have combined to frustrate attempts to achieve
unity on issues other than such intense "Third World issues" as anticolonialism or development. Yet even in the area of development,
for example, there is substantial diversity within the Third World.
One observer notes:

Since World War II, the poor or less developed countries of Asia,
Africa, and Latin America have been referred to collectively as the
Third World. Today, however, this term is losing its usefulness.
Asia, Africa, and Latin America are no longer an unrelieved mass of
abject poverty. Many countries have achieved remarkable progress
on both the economic and the social fronts.[2]

Those countries in which progress has been achieved (because development programs have been working or because the export of a
valuable resource such as oil has provided economic and political
leverage) have left behind a group of less-fortunate countries that in
terms of development prospects might be regarded as a Fourth
World. Concentrated on the Indian subcontinent, in sub-Saharan

2 Lester R. Brown, *By Bread Alone,* Frederick A. Praeger, Inc., New York,
1974, p. 246.

Africa, and in parts of Latin America (such as northeastern Brazil), these countries are in a very grim situation indeed. Suffering from overpopulation, hunger, shaky economies, and lack of resources, these Fourth World countries have little chance of catching up even with the rest of the Third World. Some observers even suggest that the mere survival of the Fourth World is virtually hopeless, particularly if the current trend toward energy, fertilizer, and food shortages continues.

Even these categories of Third and Fourth Worlds are useful only for a rather general level of analysis. Certainly the attempt to categorize nations outside the First and Second Worlds on the basis of some standard of development reveals a substantial number of exceptions. Where does one place, for example, such diverse states as Japan, Yugoslavia, Israel, Nationalist China (Taiwan), or even the People's Republic of China (mainland China). When one considers other potential bases for categorization, such as the nature of a country's colonial past or ethnic background, wide diversity hampers tidy labels. There are persuasive reasons, to suggest just one example, for considering Latin America separately from Africa and Asia.

Social scientists are understandably concerned with taxonomy so that meaningful analytical categories can be established for the better ordering of data relating to countries and their problems. But while we can understand the scholarly utility of terms such as Third, Fourth, and other Worlds, we should not forget that there is also a real world. It is surprisingly easy to develop useful, but often impersonal, images of world politics and problems. One must not forget that real human beings live out there in the Third World, subject not only to the factors that affect the human condition everywhere, but also to the particular issues that gave rise to the concept of the Third World.

COLONIALISM AND NATIONALISM

Colonialism

The terms "colonialism" and "imperialism" (as well as "anticolonialism" and "anti-imperialism") are often used virtually interchangeably. Imperialism refers broadly to the extension of political control by one state over another. It may be a deliberate state policy of seeking superiority and control over weaker states, or it may be unplanned, as one dynamic society dominates more passive ones. Imperialism appears in many forms, such as cultural, economic, or technological imperialism. The search for colonies is only one manifestation of imperialism. The overall policy of establishing and maintaining colonies (by definition, territories and peoples held in a dependent and inferior relationship to the parent state) is known as colonialism.

Nationalism

Nationalism is a spirit of cultural awareness and unity evidenced by a national group, or nation (see Chapter 3 for a discussion of "state" and "nation"). A sense of nationalism has clearly been a strong moving force in creating nation-states and in setting the directions of their foreign policies. A strong feeling of nationalism, when combined with the resources and machinery of a powerful state, makes the likelihood of imperialistic foreign policies developing quite great. Nationalism became an important force in medieval Europe, helping to break up the feudal system and develop the nation-state system that forms the basis of modern international relations. Since World War II, nationalism (often called neonationalism) has been associated with the breakup of the colonial empires established by the European powers within the Third World and with the emergence of a host of new states.

The Age of Imperialism

Imperialism is as old as human political organization. In more modern international relations, however, there are two major periods of imperial expansion. As dynamic states began to develop in Europe, as early as the fourteenth and fifteenth centuries, they began to look outward. The emergence of strong, competing governments in England, France, Spain, and Portugal—coinciding with developments in shipbuilding and navigation—stimulated the "age of discovery." Explorers were followed by settlers, who moved to the New World in the Western Hemisphere in increasing numbers in the sixteenth and seventeenth centuries.

Religion, adventure, and avarice were among the factors that

motivated European colonization of the Americas. A particularly
strong force was the politico-economic theory of mercantilism,
which held that national strength and security in a world of competing states were dependent on a favorable balance of trade and the
accumulation of gold in the treasury. One study notes:

Colonies figured prominently in the grand designs of the mercantilist school. The strict control of traffic to and from the colonies,
the creation of commercial companies like the East India Company,
and the restrictions imposed on colonial manufactures were all
responses to this form of political and economic warfare. Under
mercantilist auspices the state took an active interest in overseas ex-
ploration and colonization. However crude and unrealistic in theory
mercantilism influenced the policies of every major power to some
degree.[3]

This first period of imperial expansion came to an end during the
latter half of the eighteenth and first half of the nineteenth centuries.
Distance from the parent countries, growing resistance to economic
exploitation, differing politics, and a new-found national strength
and identity fostered a spirit of independence in the Western Hemisphere colonies that would not be denied. By the late 1800s, however, a second phase of empire-building swept Europe, reaching its
zenith by World War I. Having "lost" the Americas, the European
states now turned their attention toward Africa and Asia. Much of
the impetus came from King Leopold II of Belgium, who took possession of the rich Congo territory in 1876, thus stimulating British
and French interest in Africa. Portugal, Italy, Spain, and Germany
also ended up with colonial holdings there.

European colonial interest in Asia has a long history. As early as
the 1580s, Russia crossed the Urals, and in the 1760s Britain had outmaneuvered the French for control in India (which the British converted into a crown possession in 1858). During the middle to late
1800s the British added Hong Kong (following the Opium War in
1842) and Burma (1885), the French established a protectorate over
Indochina, and the Russians took control of all territory in eastern
Siberia north of the Amur River (1858). They soon founded the
city of Vladivostok, and by 1898 they had pressured the Chinese into
granting them the right to build a railroad through Manchuria to
serve the city. One should not accept too readily, however, the myth

3 George H. Nadel and Perry Curtis, *Imperialism and Colonialism*, The Macmillan Company, New York, 1964, p. 8.

that only white Europeans were imperialists; Japan received Formosa as well as the surrender of Chinese claims to Korea following the Sino-Japanese war in 1894–1895. Of course, by the time of the United States' open door policy in 1899, a whole host of states were maneuvering for influence in China.

The empires created during this second period were severely shaken by World War I, and after World War II the process of breaking apart, which was already under way, proceeded quite rapidly. As the Western European empires disintegrated in the postwar anticolonialism that swept through the Third World, the only countertrend appeared in Eastern Europe. The Soviet Union, already heir to the "internal empire" built by the tsars, unabashedly turned the Eastern European states into satellites.

Imperialism and colonialism are terms with high emotional content, a fact which has hampered careful scholarly analysis. Much of the literature on the subject is intensely polemical. Politically, the terms have been used as slogans and epithets without regard for the facts of the situation. A list of the motives behind imperialism should include at least the following items: simple economic gain; religion; national prestige (during the late 1800s and early 1900s, every European power felt it *had* to have territories somewhere); the White Man's Burden, the social responsibility of civilized Europe to bring civilization to backward colored peoples; surplus population (communist China's policies toward Tibet, Mongolia, and perhaps even Siberia are often analyzed in this light); complex economic dynamics, such as those suggested by the theories of John Hobson and V. I. Lenin (see Chapter 4); adventure, blind chance, and blundering (depending in part on how critical one wished to be of U.S. foreign policy, one could make a rather persuasive case for explaining the U.S. acquisition of the Philippines on this basis); and the nature of people and the nation-state system, linking imperialism with the interpersonal struggle for dominance, survival of the fittest, and power politics.

The Era of Anticolonialism

The collapse, which began with the First World War, of the second phase of colonial expansion became more rapid following the Second World War and the establishment of the United Nations. The era of anticolonialism that developed can be explained by at least five factors: (1) war; (2) world opinion; (3) transplant of Western intellectual precepts; (4) nature of the nation-state system; and (5) neonationalism.

War. At least three aspects of war are relevant to the spirit of anti-colonialism. First, the mature powers had been fighting against one another in world wars. These were the very nations that presumed to offer leadership to the colonies, which were being exploited to help fight wars that were not theirs. Second, the exhaustion from fighting World Wars I and II left the European powers without the strength to control their colonies. Finally, the underdeveloped nations of the Third World, which had been intimidated in the past by superior Western military technology and had virtually come to accept their own inferiority, developed a new sense of confidence after a series of conflicts in which the white, Western nations were beaten by colored, less-developed nations. The defeat of the Russians in the Russo-Japanese war, the roughing up of the French, British, and Dutch by the Japanese in Southeast Asia prior to and during World War II, and the defeat of the French at Dien Bien Phu all had an impressive influence on the Third World's view of itself. The collapse of American policy in Indochina has contributed tremendously to this enhanced self-image and growing confidence.

World Opinion. Modern communications have given the debate on colonialism a worldwide audience. Native leaders have been able to reach their own publics more easily and to define a sense of national consciousness, while the citizens of colonial powers have been able to see instantaneously and first-hand via television the nature of life in colonial areas. The sense of adventure and romance ended when the tales of returning travelers and the reports of colonial administrators and military expeditionary leaders—often captured and enhanced by novelists—were replaced by the unflattering realism of the television camera. Further, the United Nations provided a continuing forum for the often pungent debate on colonialism.

Transplant of Western Intellectual Precepts. The colonial powers rationalized much of their imperial effort in terms of the White Man's Burden and a civilizing mission. Western arts and sciences, naturally regarded as superior, needed to be brought to the backward areas of the world. Although some colonial powers were obviously more sincere than others in their efforts to help native peoples, one has to conclude that the transplanting of Western ideas was a successful—if sometimes painful—process. Native leaders absorbed Western notions of freedom, progress, self-determination, and equality—even if in sometimes unique forms. Not surprisingly, they began to attempt to implement these new ideas.

Because one often tends to associate it with such issues as economic exploitation, cultural hegemony, and racial antagonism, it is easy to regard colonialism in a purely negative light. For the sake of perspective, however, we would do well to heed the view expressed in one important study of imperialism and colonialism:

And yet the record of colonization is scarcely barren. Colonial empires have not been founded on negations—to paraphrase Lord Balfour's reference to the British Empire. However traumatic an experience for those at the receiving end, the expansion of Europe overseas has been a powerful agent of what is fashionably called modernization.[4]

Just as the Renaissance, Reformation, and Industrial Revolution led to years of turmoil in the Western world, the movement of powerful ideas and forces of change to the Third World could hardly be expected to be a quiet, tidy process. Perhaps future generations looking back will see colonialism more as an instrument of change than as a vehicle of oppression, just as current generations remember the wars and crusades in medieval Europe more for the ferment they symbolized than the misery they caused.

Nature of the Nation-State System. The issue of the nature of the nation-state system is worth raising simply because it suggests that anticolonialism may simply be part of the *same* process as colonialism rather than represent a higher morality. If one accepts the idea (as the realist theorists discussed in Chapter 2 certainly do) that the actions of nation-states in international relations are governed by national interest and the struggle for power, then colonialism/anticolonialism or imperialism/anti-imperialism are merely different aspects of the same process. They are different phases of the pushing and shoving that occur in world politics. Strong states will push around their weaker neighbors in one way or another, but as the neighbors become stronger they will push back.

4 *Ibid.,* p. 24.

Neonationalism. Important factors in the so-called neonationalism that has swept the Third World in the last thirty to forty years have been the acceptance of Western ideas by the new leaders and the improved means of communication that have allowed them to develop in their peoples a new sense of identity and nationalism. While Nasser of Egypt could become a rallying point for Arab nationalism, Gandhi and Nehru the symbols of Indian nationalism, or Kwame Nkrumah (Ghana) and Julius Nyerere (Tanzania) speakers for versions of African nationalism, the unity against colonialism that developed from this new nationalism was in many cases illusory.

In many of the new countries, once independence was achieved, problems that had been papered over during the struggle for independence reappeared, particularly as it became apparent that the mere fact of independence did not solve all problems. Many of the new states, particularly in Africa, have inherited political boundary lines that were originally drawn up for the administrative convenience of the colonial powers, with little attention to traditional tribal and ethnic groupings. Consequently it is not uncommon for a new state to include a conglomeration of groups that don't really like one another all that much. Their only unity was often a result of superimposed political boundaries, a shared colonial past, and the fact that they disliked the former colonial power more than each other— hardly an auspicious basis for the launching of a new state. Elsewhere, national antagonisms have developed from the migration of substantial numbers of outsiders into an area. The presence of large numbers of "overseas Chinese" in Southeast Asia provides an example.

The neonationalism that appears to be such a strong force has been in fact heavily influenced by subnational loyalties, traditions, and national hostilities. World attention focuses on prominent native leaders, but easily overlooks the fact that they may be claiming leadership of a backward, illiterate, and largely inert native populace. Such a populace is likely to have confused loyalties—they are not sure if they owe primary allegiance to the family, tribe, ethnic group, or their new nation-state.

The antagonisms of national groups may result in the dismemberment of a state (as happened when East Pakistan—now Bangla Desh—separated from West Pakistan during the civil war of 1970–1971), the near-dismemberment of a state (in 1968, the dissident Ibos tried tragically and unsuccessfully to break away from Nigeria and form the state of Biafra), or the acceptance of an uneasy truce in communal conflict (Malaysia is a good example of "communal pluralism," attempting to include primarily Malays, Chinese, and Indians/ Pakistanis—but also to a lesser degree Eurasians, Kadayans, Melanans, Ibans, and Land Dyaks). Disintegrative national difficulties are hardly a monopoly of the Third World, however, as shown by French-Canadian separatism; ethnic politics by the Dutch-speaking Flemish and French-speaking Walloons in Belgium; and the nationalist movements by the Irish, Scots, and Welsh within the United Kingdom.

The anticolonial mood produced by these five factors became institutionalized in the United Nations' trusteeship function (examined in Chapter 8). Three outstanding examples of the inability of the United Nations, or anybody else, to exercise continuing control over colonialism/neocolonialism are multinational corporations, intervention (e.g., Czechoslovakia, Vietnam), and carry-over colonies (e.g., South West Africa, which is under the control of South Africa).

PROBLEMS OF DEVELOPMENT AND MODERNIZATION

Pressing World Problems

Two United States senators, who had served as members of the U.S. delegation to the twenty-fifth anniversary session of the United Nations, concluded rather glumly that the session "was a reflection of gigantic frustrations, with just enough minor victories scattered here and there to give the impression, if not the illusion, that the U.N. establishment is capable of mustering international cooperation and understanding." [5]

In their report to Congress on the session, they called attention to the world's most pressing problems as identified during U.N. discussions:

As many others have stated and as the Secretary General himself observed . . . , there are two overriding problems confronting the world community: (1) *the tremendous economic imbalance between developed and less-developed countries* and (2) *the build-up in world armaments.*[6] (Emphasis added)

5 U.S. Senate, Committee on Foreign Relations, *The United Nations: The World as a Developing Country*, by Senators Claiborne Pell and Jacob Javits, Committee Print, U.S. Government Printing Office, Washington, D.C., 1971, p. 1.
6 *Ibid.*, p. 2.

They concluded that the United Nations had been able to have only a marginal impact on both these problems and noted a new, emerging dimension of international relations:

International peace and security are, today, threatened less and less by external subversion and aggression and more and more by genuine internal discontent and unrest that arises from the kind of socioeconomic conditions which more than three-quarters of the peoples of the world find themselves in. A fundamental problem is, as Edwin Reischauer observes, "The less developing areas are not pockets of poverty but, rather, seas of poverty surrounding islands of wealth." ... The old balance-of-power way of doing business, accompanied by a proliferation of arms, cannot deal effectively with the situation. Radical new efforts and measures are needed to deal with the underlying reality of world, mass poverty and the political, social and economic convulsions which are products of this reality.[7]

Illustrative of the disparity and imbalance between the rich nations and the poor nations as well as between expenditures for guns and butter are the following statements selected from the senators' report:

One-fifth of the U.N.'s members control more than four-fifths of the total wealth; among the U.N.'s industrialized members individual income is $2,300 a year, or some 20 times greater than $109 a year recorded by its poorest members.

There are similar gaping disparities in education, literacy, population, and life expectancy. For example, among the less-industrialized nations sixty percent of the population is undernourished and 10,000 die daily as a result of prolonged malnutrition.

In the period 1964 to 1969, the United States and the Soviet Union alone expended over one trillion dollars (1,000,000,000,000) for military purposes. Such sum:

... is more than 2 years' income for the world's 93 developing countries, in which over two and one-half billion people live.

And for the period:

... took as much public money as was spent by all governments on all forms of public education and health care.

Drawing on a recent UNESCO study, it was reported last year, "If one silver dollar coin was dropped every second, it would take 126,000 years to exhaust the amount of money that will be spent on world armaments in the next 10 years."

This same report also served to remind us that even at current

7 *Ibid.*

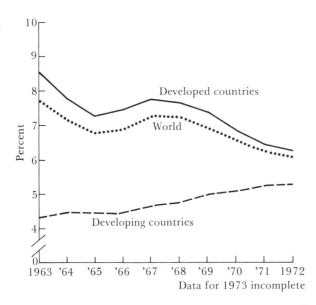

FIGURE 6-1. Trends in Military Expenditures as Percent of GNP, 1963–1972

spending rates, "the average annual expenditure per soldier is $7,800 while the annual average expenditure per child for the estimated one billion children of school age is a mere $100." [8]

All these discouraging observations called attention to the central problem of development (often called modernization) and the proper utilization of resources. One unfortunate development in modern times has been the growing allocation of resources within the developing countries for military expenditures—resources that are often urgently required to meet social needs. As Figure 6-1 shows, the share of the developing countries' GNP devoted to military expenditures is beginning to approach that of developed countries. Even these military expenditure estimates do not reveal the full extent of the military programs within the developing countries because foreign military assistance in the form of outright grants is not included.

It would be a mistake, however, to conclude that all the developing countries are putting a strain on their economies by military spending. Figure 6-2 reveals that Southeast Asia and the Middle

8 *Ibid.*, selected quotes from p. 3.

FIGURE 6-2. Relative Burden of Military Expenditures, 1972

Military Expenditures as % of GNP	GNP Per Capita							
	Less than $100	$100–199	$200–299	$300–499	$500–999	$1,000–1,999	$2,000–2,999	More than $3,000
More than 10%	Cambodia Laos Vietnam, North	Vietnam, South Yemen (Aden)	Egypt Jordan	Iran Iraq Syria	Saudi Arabia		Israel	United Arab Emirates
5–10%	Burma Chad Somalia	China, People's Republic of Nigeria Pakistan Sudan	Equatorial Guinea	China (Taiwan) Korea, North Malaysia Zambia	Albania Cuba Mongolia Portugal	Bulgaria Hungary Poland Qatar Romania Singapore	Czechoslovakia Germany (G.D.R.) Soviet Union United Kingdom	United States
2–4.9%	Ethiopia India Indonesia Mali Rwanda Yemen (San'a)	Bolivia Central African Republic Guinea Mauritania Tanzania	Korea, South Morocco Thailand	Ecuador Turkey	Brazil Lebanon Peru South Africa, Republic of	Greece Spain Yugoslavia	Italy Libya	Australia Belgium Canada Denmark France Germany (F.R.G.)

214

				Uganda, Zaïre	Uruguay			
1–1.9%	Afghanistan, Burundi, Upper Volta	Dahomey, Haiti, Kenya, Malagasy Republic, Niger, Sri Lanka, Togo	Cameroon, Ghana, Honduras, Liberia, Philippines, Senegal	Algeria, Colombia, Congo, Dominican Republic, El Salvador, Guatemala, Guyana, Ivory Coast, Nicaragua, Paraguay, Tunisia	Chile, Gabon, Rhodesia, Southern	Argentina, Cyprus, Ireland, Venezuela	Austria, Finland, New Zealand	Kuwait, Netherlands, Norway, Sweden, Switzerland
Less than 1%	Bangla Desh, Lesotho, Malawi, Nepal	The Gambia, Sierra Leone	Botswana, Swaziland	Mauritius, Oman	Costa Rica, Jamaica, Malta, Mexico, Panama	Trinidad and Tobago	Japan	Iceland, Luxembourg

Source: United States Arms Control and Disarmament Agency, *World Military Expenditures and Arms Trade, 1963–1973*, Government Printing Office, Washington, D.C., 1975, p. 3.

East account for a substantial amount of military expenditure. Nevertheless, Figure 6-2 (which displays the countries in the survey according to two ratios: military expenditures as a proportion of GNP, and per capita GNP) also suggests indirectly that the portion of GNP going for military expenditures could be spent for other societal purposes.

Measuring Development

The General Assembly, in proclaiming the Second United Nations Development Decade beginning January 1, 1971, noted that the First United Nations Development Decade, launched in 1961, had fallen short of its goals. Although not wishing to be pessimistic, the General Assembly frankly noted that

the level of living of countless millions of people in the developing part of the world is still pitifully low. These people are often still undernourished, uneducated, unemployed and wanting in many other basic amenities of life. While a part of the world lives in great comfort and even affluence, much of the larger part suffers from abject poverty, and in fact the disparity is continuing to widen. This lamentable situation has contributed to the aggravation of world tension.[9]

While development may be a central concern in the economic and social realm, it carries with it many of the problems associated with peace in the political realm. It is an intensely normative issue, defying precise measurement. One symptom of this aspect has been sensitivity to the inferiority implied by "underdeveloped," with these countries preferring such terms as "developing" or "less-developed" countries (known academically as LDCs). Another symptom of the normative nature of development is the difficulty of finding a suitable yardstick for measuring degrees of development—a process which in and of itself implies that one end of the yardstick is "good" and the other, if not "bad," is at least "not so good." One prominent student of development, Lucian Pye, has identified no less than ten basic definitions of the term "political development," each carrying with it certain kinds of assumptions about the reality, means, and goals of development.[10]

9 *Ibid.,* p. 87.
10 See Lucian W. Pye, *Aspects of Political Development,* Little, Brown and Company, Boston, 1966, pp. 33–45.

Being a "less-developed country" implies the high likelihood that some combination of the following problems will be present, probably at a debilitating level: low per capita income, low capital formation resulting from the inability to save, low productivity (due to low capital investment, low incentives, inadequate equipment, ignorance of efficient techniques, and incapacitating diseases), a high rate of population growth outstripping a country's ability to care for the population, malnutrition, poor health standards, high illiteracy, minimum impact by the mass media, stifling traditions, and an essentially (often subsistence) agricultural economy.

Measuring these problems within a country as an index of development/underdevelopment is not easy. Measurement may become somewhat arbitary as a means of international comparison. For example, one way of measuring development is to use some economic yardstick, such as GNP (gross national product—the total value of goods and services produced by a nation's economy) or average annual per capita income. Difficulties with this approach include the unreliability of some countries' statistics, differing national inflation rates, distortions caused by variations of currency values, and inaccurate assessments of both economic and population growth factors. Even after adjustments have been made to account for these computational difficulties and a list of countries in rank order has been produced, any dividing line between developed and underdeveloped countries would be arbitrary (hence the value of an open-ended term like "developing"), and one has to watch out for cultural bias in attaching meaning to any particular increment on the scale. For example, the fact that an average worker in country X has an annual income of $50 has to be evaluated in context, not necessarily by the standards of a more affluent culture.

Another measurement of development was mentioned by the U.N.'s proclamation for the Second Development Decade: "the basic amenities of life." This is also susceptible to cultural distortion, for the average citizen of the industrialized West is likely to regard as "basic" a very different list of items from that of an average citizen of a developing country. One concrete way of measuring "basic amenities," however, is by measuring caloric intake. The average human body requires around 2,000 calories per day to supply the energy needed by its cells to sustain life. While the average citizen of the industrialized West receives over 3,000 calories daily, citizens of much of the Third World average less than 2,000 calories per day, which is theoretically less than the minimum required to stay alive. That fact becomes even more significant when one considers the widespread presence of debilitating diseases and hard working conditions (e.g., long hours, hot climate, and minimal machinery).

The level of caloric intake is not sufficient, however, as a measuring device for development. The presence of protein in the human diet is extremely important. One might recall that the widespread starvation in the breakaway region of Biafra during the Nigerian civil war of 1968 was owing as much to the lack of protein in the diet as it was to the lack of food per se. Protein deficiency, prevalent in most developing countries, is particularly critical in young children. Serious protein deficiency (known in its clinical form as kwashiorkor) can result in death. A United Nations study notes that "subclinical protein-calorie malnutrition is so prevalent in some areas that at any one time up to 50 per cent of the children aged from one to five years may be in this condition." [11]

The same United Nations study noted that although experts disagree on the actual figures, they are unanimous concerning the gravity of the protein problem. The study concluded:

Protein deficiency already has serious consequences for the health and working efficiency of the populations of developing countries. If the situation worsens, the physical, economic, social and political development of the populations involved may be completely arrested. Protein-calorie malnutrition not only increases susceptibility to acute and chronic infections, but also causes a compensatory reduction in the capacity for physical activity and promotes apathy. These direct effects on adult populations impede the economic productivity and development of countries which are desperately in need of improving the status and potential of their peoples, quite apart from the human suffering involved.[12]

Even more tragic and significant in the long run is the impact of protein nutritional deficiencies on the children in developing countries, because protein is extremely important during the early growth years. The study revealed the following evidence concerning children's protein deficiency:

In some countries, as many as one third die before reaching school age, and for most of the survivors physical growth and development

11 United Nations Economic and Social Council, *International Action to Avert the Impending Protein Crisis: Report of the Advisory Committee on the Application of Science and Technology to Development,* E/4343/Rev. 1, 1968, p. 52.
12 *Ibid.,* p. 4.

are impaired. Moreover, there is increasing evidence of associated retardation in mental development, learning and behaviour, due in particular to malnutrition in early childhood. Thus, the nutritional deficiencies existing at the present time in many developing countries already are jeopardizing the future for many millions of the world's people.[13]

Foreign Aid

One of the obvious conclusions from any study of the problems of development is that the developing countries could probably use help from the developed countries. For countries with stagnant economies that seem to be drowning in their own problems, foreign aid offers an appealing solution. Pumping in monetary aid and foodstuffs would appear to alleviate (if not solve) the problems. The solution is not that simple, however, for at least three reasons.

The first reason is economic. Because the resources of the developed states are clearly not unlimited, foreign aid is usually granted with the understanding that short-term help will be enough to stimulate a developing economy to become self-maintaining. An example of this progressive development view is that of former U.S. presidential adviser Walt W. Rostow, who felt that a developing society's economic growth could reach a "takeoff point" and then maintain itself without continued outside help.[14] There is, on the other hand, a great deal of discouraging evidence to suggest that even if there is a takeoff point at some stage in economic development, for some Third World countries it may be so far off that aid would be a hopeless economic investment from the standpoint of potential donor countries.

A second reason why foreign aid is not a simple solution for the problems of developing countries is political. While humanitarian motives should be neither disregarded nor discouraged, the fact remains that nations granting foreign aid expect to get some political mileage out of their grants. For that reason they prefer to engage in bilateral aid programs rather than utilize the machinery of an international organization such as the United Nations. Conversely, nations receiving aid prefer an international agency to avoid the political strings that might otherwise be attached to the aid. Donor nations in recent years have become increasingly cool toward foreign

13 *Ibid.*, pp. 4–5.
14 Walt W. Rostow, *The Stages of Economic Growth*, Cambridge University Press, New York, 1960.

aid because they do not perceive the political benefits they expected and because the aid does not necessarily bring either political or economic stability to the recipient state.

Finally, a third factor that undercuts the promise of foreign aid as a solution to Third World problems is rapid population growth, which outstrips the ability of developmental progress to keep pace. A great deal of furor was created following the publication in 1798 of *An Essay on the Principle of Population* by the English economist Thomas Robert Malthus (1766–1834). He predicted that population, which he saw as increasing geometrically (2, 4, 8, 16, 32, ...), would overwhelm the means of subsistence, which he asserted would only increase arithmetically (2, 4, 6, 8, 10,...), ultimately leading to famine and other forms of social disaster.

Overpopulation

After the initial controversy over the Malthusian theory died down, the theory itself was generally disregarded until recent years, when it was revived. The Industrial Revolution, immigration to vast new lands, seemingly unlimited natural resources, and the development of economic systems able to keep food production in step with growing (but still relatively small) populations all seemed to make Malthusian concerns irrelevant. The growing awareness that the world's resources were not unlimited combined with the very obvious evidence of a world population explosion have produced both a re-examination of Malthusian teachings and an outpouring of crisis literature, much of it predicting a very gloomy future indeed for continued human existence on this planet. The population explosion (which is generally referred to in bureaucratic jargon in such guarded phrases as "the accelerated pace of demographic change") is particularly acute in the Third World, where the food supply is inadequate and hungry peasants have been lured to big-city slums by the hope of jobs that never materialized. Commenting on the population problem within the Third World, the United Nations *World Economic Survey* concludes that

[a]t the root of this in the developing countries has been a decline in death rates, at a speed and on a scale without parallel in human history. Accentuating the effects of this reduction in mortality has been an unprecedented increase in human mobility, resulting in the

regrouping and concentration of populations the scope of which has also been without historical parallel.[15]

One particularly disquieting feature of world population growth has been its rapidity. The world's population first reached one billion in the year 1830. Only a hundred years later, in 1930, it passed the two billion mark. And only thirty years later, in 1960, it reached three billion. The United Nations estimates that the world will have

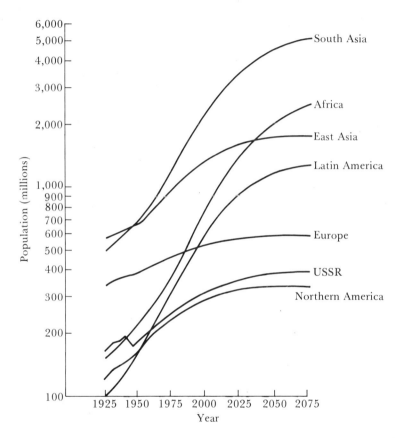

FIGURE 6-3. Population in Major World Areas, 1925–2075, According to "Medium" Variant of Long-range Projections (Charted on a Logarithmic Scale)

15 United Nations Secretariat, Department of Economic and Social Affairs, *World Economic Survey, 1973* (Part 1, Population and Development, E/5486), 1974, p. 1.

about 6.4 billion people by the year 2000 (although other estimates have ranged from 6 to 7.5 billion). The major impact of that growth will occur within the developing countries.

Figure 6-3 portrays graphically the long-range population projections made by the United Nations. Because of the uncertainty in calculating long-range projections, made here for twenty-five-year intervals, only the medium variant is shown, although the actual population trends may be higher or lower. The figure is drawn on a logarithmic scale so that for equal rates of growth the graphs are equally steep. Note that the population of South Asia, which already has a large base, is expected to surpass the present world total around the year 2030. Table 6-1 shows in tabular form the calculations presented in Figure 6-3, and Table 6-2 shows the same population figures as percentages.

TABLE 6-1: Population of the World and Eight Major Areas, at Twenty-five-year Intervals, 1925-2075 (Millions)

Major area	1925	1950	1975	2000	2025	2050	2075
World total	1,960	2,505	3,988	6,406	9,065	11,163	12,210
Northern group	1,203	1,411	1,971	2,530	2,930	3,084	3,107
Northern America	125	166	237	296	332	339	340
Europe	339	392	474	540	580	592	592
USSR	168	180	255	321	368	393	400
East Asia	571	673	1,005	1,373	1,650	1,760	1,775
Southern group	757	1,094	2,017	3,876	6,135	8,079	9,103
Latin America	98	164	326	625	961	1,202	1,297
Africa	153	219	402	834	1,479	2,112	2,522
South Asia	497	698	1,268	2,384	3,651	4,715	5,232
Oceania	9	13	21	33	44	50	52

Source: United Nations Secretariat, Department of Economic and Social Affairs, *Concise Report on the World Population Situation in 1970–1975 and Its Long-Range Implications*, Population Studies, No. 56; ST/ESA/SER.A/56, 1974, p. 59.

TABLE 6-2: Percentage of World Population in Eight Major World Areas, 1925–2075

Major area	1925	1950	1975	2000	2025	2050	2075
World total	100.0	100.0	100.0	100.0	100.0	100.0	100.0
Northern group	61.4	56.3	49.4	39.5	32.3	27.6	25.4
Northern America	6.4	6.6	5.9	4.6	3.7	3.0	2.8
Europe	17.3	15.6	11.9	8.4	6.4	5.3	4.8
USSR	8.6	7.2	6.4	5.0	4.1	3.5	3.3
East Asia	29.1	26.9	25.2	21.4	18.2	15.8	14.5
Southern group	38.6	43.7	50.6	60.5	67.7	72.4	74.6
Latin America	5.0	6.5	8.2	9.8	10.6	10.8	10.6
Africa	7.8	8.7	10.1	13.0	16.3	18.9	20.6
South Asia	25.4	27.9	31.8	37.2	40.3	42.2	42.8
Oceania	0.5	0.5	0.5	0.5	0.5	0.4	0.4

Source: United Nations Secretariat, Department of Economic and Social Affairs, *Concise Report on the World Population Situation in 1970–1975 and Its Long-Range Implications*, Population Studies, No. 56; ST/ESA/SER.A/56, 1974, p. 60.

Food Production

Population growth is of course only part of the equation. Food production is a factor of equal concern. Throughout the developing world during the 1960s, food production outran population growth in only eighteen countries, according to the United Nations:

Argentina
El Salvador
Gabon
Guatemala
Israel
Ivory Coast
Khmer Republic
Lebanon
Malaysia

Mauritius
Mozambique
Nicaragua
Panama
Republic of Korea
Rwanda
Thailand
United Republic of Cameroon
Venezuela[16]

16 *Ibid.*, p. 70.

In thirty-four countries, however, food production lagged seriously behind population growth in the 1960s:

Afghanistan
Algeria
Bangla Desh
Barbados
Burma
Central African Republic
Chad
Colombia
Congo
Dahomey
Democratic Yemen
Egypt
Guinea
Guyana
Indonesia
Iraq
Jamaica

Jordan
Kenya
Lesotho
Libyan Arab Republic
Mali
Mauritania
Nepal
Nigeria
Peru
Republic of Viet-Nam
Senegal
Sierra Leone
Somalia
Southern Rhodesia
Togo
Tunisia
Zambia[17]

In the remaining thirty-six countries listed by the United Nations as developing, food production in the 1960s increased at more or less the same rate as population. That means food production fell just short of (Group A), parallel to (Group B), or just above (Group C) the rate of increase in population:

Group A
Bolivia
Chile
India
Liberia

Philippines
Trinidad and Tobago
Upper Volta
Zaïre

Group B
Angola
Botswana
Brazil
Burundi

Costa Rica
Cuba
Dominican Republic
Ecuador

17 *Ibid.*, p. 72.

Iran	Pakistan
Laos	Paraguay
Mexico	Sudan
Morocco	Syrian Arab Republic

Group C

Ethiopia	Niger
Gambia	Saudi Arabia
Ghana	Sri Lanka
Honduras	United Republic of Tanzania
Madagascar	Uganda
Malawi	Uruguay[18]

Official concern over the overpopulation/food production dilemma has become more acute during the 1970s. The first World Food Conference in history was held under the auspices of the United Nations in Rome, Italy, during November 1974. Earlier that same year, in August, a United Nations World Population Conference had been held in Bucharest, Rumania. While the record of those conferences was mixed, producing both discouraging failures and modest agreement on selected general principles, the result was hardly a determined and unified world commitment to undertaking radical new programs to solve its problems.

The modest results of those conferences may be significant (even fateful) because many observers of the overpopulation/food production problem have expressed the belief that only drastic, immediate, and coordinated action in these areas could stave off widespread famine. The head of the U.S. delegation to the Bucharest World Population Conference, Caspar W. Weinberger (U.S. Secretary of Health, Education, and Welfare), during his address to a plenary meeting, quoted Dr. Norman Borlaug (a Nobel Peace Prize laureate) as warning:

By the green revolution we have only delayed the world food crisis for another 30 years. If the world population continues to increase at the same rate we will destroy the species.[19]

18 *Ibid.*, p. 74.
19 U.S. Department of State, *United Nations World Population Conference,* International Organization and Conference Series 116, Department of State Publication No. 8783 (October 1974), p. 3.

Other observers have asserted that it is already too late to prevent mass deaths through starvation. In a provocative book entitled *Famine—1975!*, which appeared in 1967, William and Paul Paddock argued that there are some countries simply doomed to starve and that the first effects of the awesome food crisis would be making an impression on the world by 1975.[20] In fact, by 1975, the world was painfully aware of diminished food reserves, the energy crisis was upon us, there was serious starvation in some areas (such as the Sahel belt across Africa), and population growth was continuing unabated in spite of the publicity given to the problem by the United Nations and other bodies.

The study by the Paddock brothers was cast in terms of the dilemmas for American foreign policy, which would involve the judicious allocation of foodstuffs to the starving millions clamoring for food. Since there would simply not be enough food to go around, the Paddocks suggested the United States distribute aid according to the concept of "triage," a term used in military medicine.

In battlefield hospitals, where casualties pile up faster than medical personnel can care for them, triage involves sorting casualties into three groups: (1) those who will die no matter what aid is provided, (2) those who will survive (although perhaps painfully) without treatment, and (3) those who can be saved by immediate medical care. Aid should be given to those in category 3 first.

While the concept may appear cruel, it shows the kinds of hard choices that have to be made in pressure situations. In terms of food aid, the Paddocks suggest examples of countries in each category (e.g., Haiti, Egypt, and India are classified as "can't-be-saved") as a guide for U.S. foreign policy.[21] While undue gloom may be premature, the entire world clearly needs to face up to the population/food production issue, because the futures of the developed world and the Third World are interwoven. The following two studies trace the stories of two Third World giants and highlight in a more specific context some of the issues discussed in the preceding sections of this chapter.

20 William Paddock and Paul Paddock, *Famine—1975!*, Little, Brown and Company, Boston, 1967.
21 *Ibid.*, chap. 9.

INDIA: DEMOCRACY IN THE THIRD WORLD

The earliest invasions and conquests of the Indian subcontinent occurred in prehistory. They were part of a pattern of invasion that
would plague India for centuries. The arrival of three particular "outside" groups have had a marked impact on the development of
modern India—the Aryans, the Moslems, and the Europeans (particularly the British).

The Aryans invaded the subcontinent from the northwest about
1500 B.C., bringing with them Hinduism. Over the next 2,000 years
they developed a civilization that unified India's diverse cultures. The
sacred books of Hinduism, the *Vedas* and the *Upanishads,* express a
very tolerant, all-inclusive outlook on life that has allowed diverse
philosophies to be easily integrated into Hindu culture. Two strict
aspects of Hinduism, however, that have been important in modern
India are the concept of caste and the sacred status of cows. The
caste system, based on horizontal divisions of society that originally
related to specific social functions (e.g., warriors, priests), is still a
significant influence on Indian life. The sacred status of cows pro-
hibits Hindus from harming them, eating them, or using products
made from them. The tragic irony is that in India, where chronic
hunger is a way of life (the United Nations estimates average daily
caloric intake at about 1,800), vast numbers of cattle roam free.

Islam came to India about the eighth century. Moslem invaders
ultimately built the great Mogul empire (founded after a significant
battle in the year 1526), which brought nearly all of India under a
very efficient governmental system. After the death of the last
great Mogul ruler in 1707, the empire began to crumble. The introduction of Islam into India split society vertically, for the Moslem
and Hindu communities never really integrated. The eventual result
of this communal separatism based on religion was the partition of
the subcontinent into the separate states of India and Pakistan in 1947.

Vasco da Gama landed in India in 1498, and in 1510 the Portuguese conquered Goa, an enclave on India's west coast. The age of
European interest in the subcontinent followed. The British, French,
Dutch, and Portuguese all competed for influence, but the British
eventually won out. A military victory by Robert Clive in 1757

over a native ruler traditionally marks the beginning of the British Empire in India. Up until 1857, the British ruled India through the British East India Company. In 1857 the Sepoy Mutiny challenged British dominance briefly. The episode was in essence a limited rebellion by sepoys (Indian soldiers) of the British Indian army that began over a minor incident. The rebellion was soon repressed, but as a result of it the British government took over control from the East India Company. The mutiny, which the Indians have regarded as a war of independence, became a landmark in the growth of Indian nationalism.

An early expounder of Indian nationalist sentiment was Rammohun Roy (1772–1833), a religious and educational reformer, often called the father of modern India. An important political organization, the Indian National Congress, was formed in 1885 to seek a greater native voice in British policy-making for India. Two men influential in the Indian independence movement of the Congress were Mohandas Gandhi (1869–1948) and his protégé Jawaharlal Nehru (1889–1964). Gandhi, educated as a lawyer in India and England, gave up his law practice, rejected Western ways, and dedicated his life to Hindu ideals of asceticism. He introduced into India the political tactic of *satyagraha,* or nonviolent civil disobedience, which he had developed while living in South Africa. He was given the title Mahatma ("great-souled"), and his prestige was great enough both to unite his diverse followers and win credibility with the British as a speaker for Indian goals.

Nehru, who like Gandhi devoted his life to Indian independence, participated in the negotiations that led to independence in 1947 and became the prime minister and foreign minister of the new nation. While independence was a victory for Indian pride and nationalism, it not only did not solve India's problems, it created many new ones. One of the lingering "old" problems was poverty, which Nehru described with great feeling in his autobiography *Toward Freedom*:

It is curious how one cannot resist the tendency to give an anthropomorphic form to a country. Such is the force of habit and early associations. India becomes *Bharat Mata*, Mother India, a beautiful lady, very old but ever youthful in appearance, sad-eyed and forlorn, cruelly treated by aliens and outsiders, and calling upon her children to protect her. Some such picture rouses the emotions of hundreds of thousands and drives them to action and sacrifice. And yet India is in the main the peasant and the worker, not beautiful to look at, for poverty is not beautiful.... We seek to cover truth by the creatures of our imaginations and endeavor to escape from reality to a world of dreams.[22]

Another "old" problem was the tremendous national diversity. There are some 350 different languages and dialects spoken in India. Although Hindi is the official national language, less than 40 percent of the population can speak it. National unity is hampered by the existence of strong local linguistic communities, while the real *lingua franca* of the country's political elite is English. The disintegrative effect of India's language diversity is stronger than outsiders often suspect, for it permeates the entire social system. India may never be one true nation.

A "new" problem that was part of the independence process itself was partition. Mahomed Ali Jinnah, head of the Muslim League, led the struggle for an independent Pakistan. Intercommunal riots between Moslems and Hindus made partition inevitable. The mass migrations of millions of refugees, the brutal fighting, and the deaths that created two antagonistic states based on religion were an immense human tragedy for the new states.

Pakistan was a divided state, separated by a thousand miles of Indian territory. East and West Pakistan had nothing in common except religion. Pakistani politics developed along authoritarian lines and were traditionally dominated by West Pakistan, which contained the nation's seat of government. Following a severe storm in 1970 that killed nearly half a million people in East Pakistan, long-simmering, tense relations between the two halves erupted into conflict, sparked by the feeling in the East that the government in the West was callous to its plight. An attempt by West Pakistan (under the leadership of General Yahya Khan) to deal harshly with East Pakistani agitation for autonomy ultimately led to Indian intervention on the side of East Pakistan and to the dismemberment of Pakistan. East Pakistan, under the leadership of Sheik Mujibur Rahman, became the new state of Bangla Desh.

Following partition, India developed along democratic lines. In fact, democracy in India goes back a long way historically to a tradition of village councils. Since independence, in spite of extremist

22 Jawaharlal Nehru, *Toward Freedom*, The John Day Company, Inc., New York, 1941, p. 274.

voices and overwhelming social problems, India has been a sometimes creaky, but nevertheless surprisingly strong, democratic system. Ironically, much of the democratic vigor comes from the pluralist ethnic politics and from caste associations.

In June 1975, however, there was a severe test of India's democratic tradition. A confrontation between the Indian court system and Mrs. Indira Gandhi (Nehru's daughter, elected prime minister in 1966) arose over alleged corrupt campaign practices. An Allahabad high court decision ruled that she should be barred from holding elective office for six years. That court decision so incited her political opposition that she declared a state of emergency and suspended many of India's democratic freedoms to silence her critics while her case was being appealed to the Indian Supreme Court.

Many thousands of dissenters were arrested and detained without a trial while Mrs. Gandhi's ruling Congress Party in Parliament passed retroactively an election-law amendment that changed the law under which Mrs. Gandhi had been found guilty. The formal confrontation was resolved in November 1975, when the Indian Supreme Court upheld the legality of the new law and ruled Mrs. Gandhi innocent. Nevertheless, the emergency decrees and authoritarian politics are an unsettling portent for the future course of Indian democracy.

India's foreign policy stances, while not entirely consistent, have involved certain prominent themes. Nehru favored neutralism, or nonalignment with the Big Powers in the Cold War. However, in 1962 Nehru sought Western military aid against Chinese incursions into India, and Mrs. Indira Gandhi concluded a defense treaty with the Soviet Union in 1971 before sending Indian forces into East Pakistan during their civil war.

India has also been active in promoting the organization of the Afro-Asian world. An early prominent example was the Bandung Conference, held in Bandung, Indonesia, in 1955. This Afro-Asian conference, called by the "Colombo Powers" (a group of over twenty states, including India, that are members of a regional economic aid program established at a Commonwealth Conference at Colombo, Ceylon, in 1950), brought together representatives of twenty-nine states to promote economic and cultural cooperation and to oppose colonialism. The final communiqué of the conference rearticulated Nehru's doctrine of *Panch Shila*, the five principles of peace. Instead of relying on military pacts, nations should accept these principles: mutual respect for territorial integrity and sovereignty, nonaggression, noninterference in internal affairs, equality and mutual benefit, and peaceful coexistence.

With the lessening of Cold War tensions, India's neutralist role has dwindled in significance. India's leaders, however, have remained strong voices for world peace, even while India itself has been caught up in the familiar national "dance of the soldiers." Its relations with Pakistan, although altered somewhat since the 1971 Pakistani civil war, continue to involve confrontation politics. The two have fought several military skirmishes over Kashmir. In 1961, India invaded the tiny Portuguese enclave of Goa and forcibly ejected the Portuguese, who had been there for centuries.

CHINA: GUERRILLA COMMUNISM AND
PEASANT NATIONALISM

Much of the early history of China concerns its isolation from other civilizations. The Chinese, viewing themselves as the "Middle Kingdom" and as the center of world civilization, developed a sense of cultural superiority vis-à-vis other cultures. Although there were invasions back and forth across China's borders, China was insulated by mountains, deserts, and the sea. The Chinese regarded those outsiders with whom they did come in contact as barbarians.

China was jolted rather unceremoniously into the reality of world politics by European intervention, beginning with the Opium War (1839–1842) between China and England, and by the Sino-Japanese War (1894–1895). Western missionaries and merchants had for some time been active in China, although the Chinese persistently tried to curb their influence. The British had developed a thriving opium trade with China. When the Chinese tried to halt the import of the poison (for addiction was becoming a major national health problem), the British provoked the Opium War to reinforce their claim to free trade and extract additional commercial concessions from the Chinese. The Treaty of Nanking (1842), ending the war, was the first of many "unequal treaties" that would give foreigners special rights within Chinese territory. In the Sino-Japanese War China was handily defeated by another Asian power that had adopted Western ways.

By 1898, the Russians, Germans, British, Japanese, and French were all establishing spheres of influence in China. As their resentment grew, the Chinese made one last futile attempt to eject the foreigners, the Boxer Rebellion (1900). Encouraged by the Empress Dowager Tz'u Hsi, the rebellion was an antiforeign, anti-Christian uprising of lower-class Chinese that besieged the foreign legation quarter in Peking. An international relief force took Peking, suppressed the rebellion, and imposed another humiliating peace treaty.

Although the Boxer Rebellion was a landmark in the awakening of national sentiment in China, a great peasant uprising 50 years earlier called the Taiping Rebellion was the first mass Chinese political mobilization. A pseudo-Christian visionary named Hung Hsiuch'üan gathered masses of supporters for his political movement to found a new dynasty, the Taiping ("great peace"). After the rebels captured Nanking (1853), making it their new capital, the Western powers intervened to support and cooperate with the existing Ch'ing (Manchu) dynasty in a move to protect their own trade concessions. The revolt was finally put down, but it lasted from 1848 to 1865. It is hardly surprising that the modern Chinese should be unhappy over the record of outside intervention.

Around the turn of the century, the man who would lead China's nationalist revolution, Dr. Sun Yat-sen (1866–1925), began organizing revolutionary activity against the Ch'ing dynasty and against foreign influence in China with the goal of establishing a Chinese republic. Educated in Honolulu (at an Anglican college) and in Hong Kong, he gave up his medical practice to promote his revolution, often living in exile. His political philosophy revolved around the very basic Three Principles of the People: Nationalism, Democracy, and People's Livelihood. The first principle involved the elimination of foreign imperialism and the building of a unified state. The second provided for democratic participation by the citizenry, but also for a substantial degree of "political tutelage" by the Nationalist leaders. The third principle advocated the redistribution of land and a socialistic pattern of government control (e.g., of heavy industry, communications).

Dr. Sun organized a Revolutionary Alliance (1905) that was transformed in 1912 into the Kuomintang (National People's Party). During his career Sun had sought aid from the West, with mixed success, and had embraced Western principles of democratic thought. He ultimately became disillusioned with the West, however, and moved toward Marxism/Leninism. In 1923 an alliance was concluded between the Soviet government (and the Comintern) and the Kuomintang, the result of which was the sending of Soviet aid, arms, and advisors into China. It also meant, of course, an alliance between the Kuomintang and the Chinese Communist Party. Following Dr. Sun's death in 1925, Chiang Kai-shek (1887–1975), who had emerged as the Kuomintang's leading military figure, tried to crush the Communists.

Chiang's armies had the Communists nearly crushed in 1934, when 100,000 escaped to make the "long march" from Kiangsi Province to Yenan. There the leader of the 20,000 survivors of the march, Mao Tse-tung (1893–1976), plotted his own revolution. The years up until 1949 were characterized by civil war, combined struggle against the Japanese during World War II, and the turmoil of trying to establish a viable national government. Kuomintang rule collapsed in 1949 (from internal corruption and inability to govern effectively or win popular support, the effects of the Japanese invasion, and pressure from the Communists), and Chiang retreated to the island of Formosa (Taiwan) to found the Nationalist Republic of China. Although he did not fulfill his dream of returning to the mainland, he left behind an authoritarian style of government on Taiwan and a country boasting a prosperous living standard (second only to Japan in Asia), both under United States protection.

Mao Tse-tung's rise to power on the mainland is worth examining because his style of "guerrilla communism" has been advanced as a model to be emulated elsewhere. However, the communist revolution in China appears to have been merely the latest in a series of social upheavals during the last century, the period in which China became a modern state. It was the first mass movement to organize the peasants effectively on a continuing basis, although not without human cost.

Maoism, based heavily on collected aphorisms from the "thoughts of chairman Mao," is a modification of Marxism/Leninism to fit the Chinese context. Major elements include the following: (1) the rural peasants, rather than the urban workers, are the sustaining force of revolution in a backward country such as China (Lenin had been skeptical of the peasants' revolutionary dependability); (2) the revolutionary movement must organize and "liberate" rural areas, thereby encircling the urban areas and strangling vestiges of entrenched power; (3) because the revolutionary movement will initially be weak militarily, it must use guerrilla warfare tactics, rely on the active support of the peasantry (and other social classes willing to join a united front), and be prepared for a protracted conflict; (4) this form of insurgency can be used in other developing countries trying to free themselves from colonial or semicolonial control (e.g., Vietnam); (5) on a global scale, the Third World (seen as the "rural" areas of the globe) should carry the revolution to the developed world (the encircled "urban" areas) to stamp out capitalism; and (6) peaceful coexistence, a false doctrine advanced by the "revisionists" in Moscow, must be rejected in favor of continuing with the "permanent revolution."

It must be granted that China has come a long way toward modernization and feeding its millions, although future generations of students will want to ponder carefully the means, costs, alternatives, and significance of Mao's empire. Three internal Chinese political events of some interest are: (1) the brief "hundred flowers" campaign in 1957 to allow open discussion and dissent, which was squelched after the widespread expression of discontent became embarrassing; (2) the "Great Leap Forward" in 1958, which was an ill-fated attempt to push development too fast; and (3) the nearly disastrous Cultural Revolution in 1967, which was an attempt by Mao to rekindle revolutionary spirit by churning up society and pitting societal groups against one another. The country finally had to be stabilized by the military, although Mao's death in September 1976 provides a new basis for tension in China.

Internationally, China has competed with the Soviet Union for leadership of world communism (see the discussion of the Sino-Soviet split in the preceding chapter) and has seen itself as the leader of the developing countries. China (represented by Chou En-lai) was very active, for example, at the Bandung Conference, which was an early effort of the Afro-Asian countries to get organized. The international triangle (United States, Soviet Union, China) has added a new flexibility to international relations that did not exist before the 1970s. While China's rhetoric has been aggressive (for example, China is using the kind of violent language against the Soviet Union in the United Nations that the Soviet Union formerly used against the United States), its specific foreign policy actions have generally been cautious. Certainly China has an identity problem, being at the same time a Great Power, a developing country, a revolutionary regime, and an ancient country trying to put a new face on a traditional society.

MODELS FOR THE FUTURE

Within the Third World, India and China are at least implicit models of alternative political futures. That is not to say that they are either good models or the only models. Both the Soviet Union and the United States, for instance, are examples to emulate, but neither is a Third World member. India and China can each make a credible claim to a common point of departure with other Third World nations.

Both India and China can relate more immediately to most of the past, present, and future issues which confront the Third World: nationalism, newly emerged status in international relations, building of national governmental institutions and traditions, modernization and development, racial identity, hunger, and overpopulation. These two giant nations, substantial powers in their own right, not only are potential natural leaders of the Third World, but can point to their own records of confronting Third World problems when they recommend policy options to others.

India, in spite of Mrs. Gandhi's invocation of emergency powers and suppression of civil freedoms, has hardly become a dictatorship. India remains very much an example of democracy as a form of political organization, although it may well drift in the direction of the "guided democracy" popular in many Third World states. Some of the dramatic social reforms undertaken during Mrs. Gandhi's semi-authoritarian rule, for example, have been both successful and popular.

China, on the other hand, offers the Third World a revolutionary example of the totally organized society and a dynamic vision of world politics. China has actively vied for leadership of the Third World, which it seeks to use as a weapon in the struggle for victory in a world revolution.

Both these models, however, may be overshadowed by the dangers of overpopulation and hunger that constantly threaten the Third World. Food shortages have been particularly severe in the sub-Saharan Sahel countries (Chad, Gambia, Mali, Mauritania, Niger, Senegal, and Upper Volta), Ethiopia, northeastern Brazil, Bangla Desh, and India. Even in China, which is proud of having achieved virtual self-sufficiency in food production, a moderate setback in the harvest could have dire results, especially if there were acute food shortages elsewhere simultaneously.

Food problems have exacerbated the North/South confrontation that has already been prominent in recent years within the United Nations and related forums. Instead of being considered a basic human problem that could elicit common support, the problem of food (much like the problem of environmental degradation considered by the Stockholm Convention, which was discussed in Chapter 1) has only added a strident political tone to the tense relations between the Third World and the developed countries.

At the World Population Conference held in Bucharest, Rumania (August 1974), the pleas by the developed countries for population control to avoid mass starvation were met with political invective from Third World representatives. Some from Latin America claimed that overpopulation was a myth invented by the rich to exploit the poor. A representative from mainland China saw the large Third World population as "an important condition for the fight against imperialism." It was no secret at the Conference that affluence, as well as population, puts tremendous pressure on the world's food supply. The high standard of living in the developed countries generally means that much food is wasted or otherwise injudiciously used—food that could help alleviate Third World hunger.

The continuing and growing combination of issues that separate the Third World from the developed world may outdistance the politics of any individual nation or group of nations. To the extent, however, that national influence may be relevant to the future direction of Third World politics, the policies of the Third World giants—India and China—and what they themselves represent will be significant.

BIBLIOGRAPHY

Almond, Gabriel A., and James S. Coleman. *The Politics of the Developing Areas.* Princeton University Press, Princeton, N.J., 1960.

Akzin, Benjamin. *States and Nations.* Doubleday & Company, Inc., Garden City, N.Y., 1966.

Barnds, William J. *India, Pakistan and the Great Powers.* Frederick A. Praeger, Inc., New York, 1972.

Barnett, A. Doak. *China After Mao.* Princeton University Press, Princeton, N.J., 1967.

——. *Communist China in Perspective.* Frederick A. Praeger, Inc., New York, 1962.

Basham, A. L. *The Wonder that Was India.* Grove Press, Inc., New York, 1954.

Beling, Willard A., and George O. Totten, eds. *Developing Nations: Quest for a Model.* Van Nostrand Reinhold Company, New York, 1970.

Brown, Lester R. *By Bread Alone.* Frederick A. Praeger, Inc., New York, 1974.

Chai, Winberg, ed. *The Foreign Relations of The People's Republic of China.* Capricorn Books, New York, 1972.

——. *The New Politics of Communist China.* Goodyear Publishing Company, Inc., Pacific Palisades, Calif., 1972.

Chawla, Sudershan, et al., eds. *Southeast Asia under the New Balance of Power.* Frederick A. Praeger, Inc., New York, 1974.

Crabb, Cecil V. Jr. *The Elephants and the Grass.* Frederick A. Praeger, Inc., New York, 1965.

Dahl, Robert A., ed. *Regimes and Oppositions.* Yale University Press, New Haven, Conn., 1973.

de Bary, W. Theodore, et al., eds. *Sources of Indian Tradition: Introduction to Oriental Civilizations.* Columbia University Press, New York, 1958.

Deutsch, Karl W., and William J. Foltz. *Nation-Building.* Aldine-Atherton, Inc., Chicago, 1963.

Dodge, Dorothy. *African Politics in Perspective.* D. Van Nostrand Company, Inc., Princeton, N.J., 1966.

Ehrlich, Paul R., and Anne H. Ehrlich. *Population, Resources, Environment: Issues in Human Ecology,* 2d ed. W. H. Freeman and Company, San Francisco, 1972.

Elliott, Charles. *Patterns of Poverty in the Third World: A Study of Social and Economic Stratification.* Frederick A. Praeger, Inc., New York, 1975.

Emerson, Rupert. *From Empire to Nation.* Harvard University Press, Cambridge, Mass., 1960.

Esman, Milton J. *Administration and Development in Malaysia: Institution Building and Reform in a Plural Society.* Cornell Unversity Press, Ithaca, N.Y., 1972.

Gerschenkron, Alexander. *Economic Backwardness in Historical Perspective.* Harvard University Press, Cambridge, Mass., 1962.

Hammond, Thomas T., ed. *The Anatomy of Communist Takeovers.* Yale University Press, New Haven, Conn., 1975.

Hayes, Louis D. *The Impact of U.S. Policy on the Kashmir Conflict.* Institute of Government Research, International Studies No. 2. University of Arizona Press, Tucson, 1971.

Heeger, Gerald A. *The Politics of Underdevelopment.* St. Martin's Press, Inc., New York, 1974.

Heilbroner, Robert L. *The Great Ascent.* Harper & Row, Publishers, Incorporated, New York, 1963.

Hinton, Harold C. *China's Turbulent Quest.* The Macmillan Company, New York, 1970.

Hsiao, Gene T., ed. *Sino-American Detente and Its Policy Implications.* Frederick A. Praeger, Inc., New York, 1974.

Hunter, Robert E., and John E. Rielly, eds. *Development Today: A New Look at U.S. Relations with the Poor Countries.* Frederick A. Praeger, Inc., New York, 1972.

Huntington, Samuel P. *Political Order in Changing Societies.* Yale University Press, New Haven, Conn., 1968.

Johnson, Cecil. *Communist China and Latin America, 1959–1967.* Columbia University Press, New York, 1970.

Johnson, John J., ed. *The Role of the Military in Underdeveloped Countries.* Princeton University Press, Princeton, N.J., 1962.

Kautsky, John H., ed. *Political Change in Underdeveloped Countries.* John Wiley & Sons, Inc., New York, 1962.

Legvold, Robert. *Soviet Policy in West Africa.* Harvard University Press, Cambridge, Mass., 1970.

Lipset, Seymour M. *The First New Nation.* Basic Books, Inc., New York, 1963.

Loh, Pichon P. Y. *The Early Chiang Kai-Shek.* Columbia University Press, New York, 1971.

Lott, Leo B. *Venezuela and Paraguay: Political Modernity and Tradition in Conflict.* Holt, Rinehart and Winston, Inc., New York, 1972.

Martin, Laurence W., ed. *Neutralism and Nonalignment.* Frederick A. Praeger, Inc., New York, 1962.

Maxwell, Neville. *India's China War.* Pantheon Books, New York, 1971.

McCord, William. *The Springtime of Freedom: The Evolution of Developing Societies.* Oxford University Press, New York, 1965.

Millikan, Max F., and Donald L. M. Blackmer, eds. *The Emerging Nations.* Little, Brown and Company, Boston, 1961.

Myrdal, Gunnar. *The Challenge of World Poverty: A World Anti-Poverty Program in Outline.* Pantheon Books, New York, 1970.

Organski, A. F. K. *The Stages of Political Development.* Alfred A. Knopf, Inc., New York, 1965.

Paddock, William, and Paul Paddock. *Famine—1975!* Little, Brown and Company, Boston, 1967.

Palmer, Monte. *The Dilemmas of Political Development: An Introduction to the Politics of the Developing Areas.* F. E. Peacock Publishers, Inc., Itasca, Ill., 1973.

Palmer, Norman D., and Shao Chuan Leng. *Sun Yat-sen and Communism.* Frederick A. Praeger, Inc., New York, 1960.

Pye, Lucian W. *Aspects of Political Development.* Little, Brown and Company, Boston, 1966.

Rostow, W. W. *Stages of Economic Growth.* Cambridge University Press, New York, 1960.

Schram, Stuart. *Mao Tse-tung.* Simon & Schuster, Inc., New York, 1967.

Sharabi, Hisham. *Nationalism and Revolution in the Arab World.* D. Van Nostrand Company, Inc., Princeton, N.J., 1966.

Sigmund, Paul E., ed. *The Ideologies of the Developing Nations,* 2d rev. ed. Frederick A. Praeger, Inc., New York, 1972.

Tachau, Frank, ed. *The Developing Nations: What Path to Modernization?* Dodd, Mead & Company, New York, 1972.

Thompson, Jack H., and Robert D. Reischauer, eds. *Modernization of the Arab World.* D. Van Nostrand Company, Inc., Princeton, N.J., 1966.

Von der Mehden, Fred R. *Politics of the Developing Nations,* 2d ed. Prentice-Hall, Inc., Englewood Cliffs, N.J., 1969.

Ward, Barbara. *Five Ideas That Change the World.* W. W. Norton & Company, Inc., New York, 1959.

————. *The Rich Nations and the Poor Nations.* W. W. Norton & Company, Inc., New York, 1962.

Part III
In Search of Order

International Law

The discussion of major aspects of modern international relations in Part II is apt to leave one overwhelmed by a sense of discouragement and helplessness in the face of all the problems of world politics. There is no doubt that conflict exists in international relations. To accept the inevitability of chaos, however, would be both a capitulation to the prophets of doom and an evasion of our human purpose.

While the nature of international relations (and indeed, of human relations) may be irretrievably linked with the forces of disorder, a basic premise of this book, articulated in Chapter 1, is that people have the ability to seek rational solutions to problems and to rise above their nature. They can at least *attempt* to control the chaos, for to fail even to try would be unworthy of them.

Three important, interrelated, order-building devices in international relations are international law, international organization, and international diplomacy. None of the three offers pat solutions to world problems—in fact, each is itself the subject of intense debate. Each of the three, however, offers useful techniques in the search for world order.

THE ROLE OF LAW IN WORLD POLITICS

Nature of International Law

The roots of international law are quite ancient. Mesopotamian tribes entered into treaties, as did Egyptian pharaohs. The Old Testament relates rules of warfare practiced by the Hebrews. Ancient India produced rules concerning diplomatic privileges and immunities as well as treaties of alliance. The Greeks developed the idea of international arbitration, while the Romans made massive contributions to nearly every area of law.

Modern international law, however, can only be understood within the framework of the nation-state system created by the Peace of Westphalia (1648), which ended the Thirty Years' War.[1]

1 Some of the material appearing in this chapter is taken from Forest Grieves, "American Foreign Policy and International Law," *Montana Business Quarterly*, 11 (Spring 1973), 49–52, and is used by permission.

The state emerged at that time as a legal body possessing certain basic characteristics (population, territory, government, and sovereignty), and it was assumed that some ultimate power within the state could make authoritative decisions that were binding on the entire state.

The classic state was politically viable because these elements provided the state with a coherent basis on which to maintain internal social order. However, states do not exist in a vacuum. The exact number varies depending on how strict one wishes to be in acknowledging the existence of political entities that call themselves states, but there are over 140 states in the world today, each claiming sovereignty, equality, and independence.

The Peace of Westphalia established the legal myth of the sovereign equality of states, although politically, economically, and militarily some states are clearly more equal than others. The nation-state system, then, is an uneasy compromise, as states try to maintain their sovereign independence while at the same time they are being forced to get along with one another. Different national foreign policies are bound to result in conflict; international law is simply one means of trying to control that conflict.

Human law presumes the existence of a social base, of a society. Law represents the legal norms of that society as well as the framework of rules that binds it together and provides order. While we may see in natural or divine law eternal and unchanging principles, it makes sense to suggest simply that human law is not a constant; rather, it is a function of society. Such law is not eternal and unchanging. It develops and changes as the society it represents develops and changes. Human law will not stand on a pedestal separate from society. It will be, rather, the product of competing political forces and will itself have a role in the interplay of those forces. Similarly, international law is not a sterile collection of rules consulted only on special occasions. It is part of the continuing behavior pattern of nation-states.

A highly sophisticated and complex society on the one hand and a very primitive society on the other can be expected to have legal systems corresponding to their respective levels of development. Unlike the modern nation-state, which is highly integrated, the nation-state system is a very loose community, and some critics would deny that it is a community at all. For this reason, international law is often described as a very primitive and weak legal system.

Substance of International Law

If international relations are portrayed as an arena for warring, sovereign nation-states, how can international law properly be regarded as law? International law, as law, only makes sense if it is accepted as law *among* states, rather than law *above* states, for there is, of course, no world sovereign to hand down rules. International law consists of those international rules which "equal" states regard as legally binding upon themselves. Article 38 of the Statute of the International Court of Justice recognizes five major sources of international law.

Treaties. Treaties are contractual obligations between or among states. Generally, treaties are of two types: bilateral (between two states) and multilateral (among three or more states). Bilateral treaties form what is called "particular" international law—rules binding only on the two contracting parties. Most treaties fall into this category. Of much more political interest are multilateral treaties, often called "general" international law. In contradistinction to bilateral treaties, which bind only the signatories, multilateral treaties (particularly those signed by a significant number of important states) can establish rules that can be regarded as binding even on nonsignatories because they set forth a generally accepted norm. One of the more explicit examples is the United Nations Charter. Article 2(6) states: "The Organization shall ensure that states which are not Members of the United Nations act in accordance with these Principles so far as may be necessary for the maintenance of international peace and security."

Custom. Although treaties are an international version of statutory, or written, law, a much older source of international law is custom (an international counterpart of common law). An example of international custom would be the traditional three-mile limit of territorial waters. This custom, which is rapidly being superseded by modern extensions of territorial waters, is allegedly based on the "cannon-shot rule"—the presumed out-of-range distance between old-time ship and shore batteries. As with domestic (or national) law, custom tends to become solidified in written law eventually.

Court Decisions. Both national and international court decisions are a source of international law. National courts handle most cases relevant to international law, but their decisions have no binding force beyond the limits of their particular state. International courts, in particular the Permanent Court of International Justice (PCIJ) of the League of Nations and its successor, the International Court of Justice (ICJ) of the United Nations, are bound even more by the principle of no *stare decisis*, or law of precedent, in rendering decisions. Article 59 of the ICJ Statute, for example, clearly states: "The decision of the Court has no binding force except between the parties and in respect of that particular case."

Court decisions are at best a subsidiary source of international law, as major problems tend to be handled in the political realm (e.g., through diplomatic negotiations). In any case, to the extent that court decisions do play a role in regulating international relations, there is a comforting trend on the part of courts toward trying to maintain some semblance of international unity on principles of law.

General Principles. A very controversial source of international law, "general principles" assumes that some principles are so universally accepted by states (e.g., abhorrence of the slave trade) that they become law. The argument against general principles contends that if indeed there are principles so widely and generally accepted, they are likely to be either so abstract or such truisms as to be of little material importance. Whatever the "real" importance of general principles, they are a vague moral guide for the consciences of states.

Writers and Publicists. There was a time in history when the writings of such people as Hugo Grotius were the only record of actual national practices and the only speculation concerning what states ought to be doing to regulate international politics. The Dutch scholar Grotius is frequently called the "Father of International Law." His classic work *De Jure Belli ac Pacis* (*On the Law of War and Peace,* 1625) is still frequently cited in modern international legal literature. No individual writer, however, can create international law. Writings, at best, can serve as a record of the past, speculation about the future, and advice to national policy-makers—who *do* have an active role in the creation of international law.

In addition to the five major sources of international law listed above, Article 38 of the ICJ Statute does list *ex aequo et bono* (meaning "in equity and good conscience") as one potential additional source. This term means that when no other rule of international law applies, nation-states may by common consent agree to resolve a dispute on the basis of common sense and fairness.

Beyond the text of Article 38, there are other emerging sources of international law. Legal scholars disagree somewhat, but certainly draft conventions, policy decisions by organs of the United Nations, and resolutions of the U.N. General Assembly appear to have varying degrees of legal authoritativeness. They may help establish legal facts, express international agreement on selected principles, or reflect national understanding of customary rules of international law. In this regard, the United Nations serves as an additional forum within which the behavior patterns of states will be reflected and registered over time.

International law at any given time represents the patching together of these various sources into a loose package of rules, sometimes overlapping, sometimes conflicting, and sometimes vague.

Philosophical Schools of International Law

There are three major schools of thought concerning the sources of international law: the naturalist, the positivist, and the eclectic (or Grotian). Although these approaches do not possess the unity the term "school" might suggest, they do represent basic traditions regarding the law. The naturalist approach stems from the medieval period and includes such legal philosophers as Samuel Pufendorf (1632–1694), Emerich de Vattel (1714–1767), and James Lorimer (1818–1890). These scholars, in varying degrees, accepted the basic notion that international obligations are derived from a higher law. The ultimate explanation and validity of human law rests on principles of natural law.

The positivists were generally skeptical about the abstract and vague nature of the higher principles the naturalists claimed existed. The positivists preferred concrete and positive human action as the source of law. They felt that what nations actually *did* provided more relevant norms for the conduct of international relations. People such as Alberico Gentili (1552–1608), Richard Zouche (1590–1660), Cornelius van Bynkershoek (1673–1743), and Johann Jakob Moser (1701–1785) separated law from theological thinking and studied such positive sources of law as treaties and customs. One prominent positivist, John Austin (1790–1859), went so far as to argue that law could be derived only from a sovereign authority. Law had to be "handed down" from a superior, which of course meant that in his view international law was not true law, since there was no world governmental authority.

While the strength of the naturalists lay in their normative interpretation of a "higher law," they were accused of losing touch with reality. On the other hand, while the positivists grounded their law in the solid practice of states, they were susceptible to the charge of accepting the notion that whatever is, is right. Hugo Grotius stressed the eclectic nature of law, arguing that *both* natural law and positive rules were sources of law.

Beyond this debate regarding the sources of international law, a different philosophical issue that also concerns international legal scholars is the relationship of international law to national (often called "municipal") law. Two schools have developed: monism and dualism. The monists see both international and national law as part of one legal system. The dualists regard them as two separate systems of law, although there may be much overlap and integration between them (e.g., a treaty is simultaneously part of a nation's law and part of the body of international law). Much of the debate between monists and dualists concerns the supremacy, equality, or subordination of national to international law. Since most states, in practice, regard international law as part of their national law (that is, as incorporated into their national law, as in the example of treaties), the question of supremacy makes little practical difference.

Weaknesses and Strengths of International Law

Even if it is conceded that international law is real law, critics are quick to point out certain weaknesses that they feel detract from the viability of a true international system of enforceable rules.

There is, for example, no international parliament to "make law" that is binding on nation-states. The United Nations General Assembly clearly does not fulfill this role, as it can only pass resolutions. Likewise, there is no international executive to enforce the law. Although it is true that the U.N. Security Council has certain peace-keeping powers, the successful implementation of these powers hinges on the unanimous agreement of the "Big Five"—a rare occurrence. (See Chapters V and VII of the U.N. Charter. The "Big Five" —or permanent members—on the Security Council are the United States, the United Kingdom, the Soviet Union, France, and China, whose seat currently is being held by the People's Republic of China.) Finally, although the International Court of Justice does provide an adjudicative tribunal for the United Nations (or for any nonmember state that wants to use it), it is attacked as weak because it has no true compulsory jurisdiction. States, by and large, only go before the Court on the basis of common agreement; they cannot be forced into the Court.

These institutional weaknesses merely illustrate the fact that international law, like the nation-state community it represents, is a developing system. In spite of these drawbacks, international law in fact compares favorably not only with rudimentary law of the type found on the frontier, but even with modern national legal systems. Like the murders in domestic law, the wars get the international attention. Both, however, are the tip of the iceberg. Most international rules (e.g., the myriad agreements concerning telecommunications, shipping, extradition, fisheries, and airline traffic), like their domestic counterparts, pose no major problems in either obedience or enforcement.

States support most international law for very basic reasons: (1) logic—many rules (e.g., standardized lights for steamships) simply make sense if there is to be any international order; (2) fear—there is the danger of reprisals from other states if agreed-upon rules are broken; (3) self-interest—states clearly benefit from most rules; and even (4) morals—although this is not a dominant aspect of international relations, appeals to a higher standard of community values do appear in national declarations of foreign policies.

THE "COD WAR"—INTERNATIONAL ADJUDICATION
AND THE MODERN WORLD

Background

Before examining in more detail the legal machinery available to resolve international conflicts, it might be more instructive to examine firsthand the substance of a recent case decided by the International Court of Justice. The case examined here was chosen not because it illustrates either the weaknesses or the strengths of the Court as an institution (although it does both), but because it involves a modern legal and political problem of international relations and offers some exposure to international case law.

Adjudication involves formal legal proceedings before a court of law, with sitting judges, established rules of procedure, and jurisprudence. As such, it is the most formal and institutionalized mechanism available to resolve international conflicts. In arbitration, a slightly less formal legal procedure, disputing parties select arbitrators to hear their dispute and agree in advance to be bound by the arbitral findings. The International Court of Justice (or ICJ), located in The Hague, is one of the six principal organs of the United Nations. Composed of fifteen judges, the Court is responsible for adjudicating disputes between states that choose to use the machinery of the Court (the technical aspects of the Court's jurisdiction will be examined later).

The legal case discussed here involves a tragicomical fishery dispute between Iceland and Great Britain. Issues to note while reading the case are (1) the legal nature of the dispute, (2) the underlying political problems (in particular the worsening modern problem of the earth's dwindling resources), (3) the basis of the Court's jurisdiction (especially since one party, Iceland, refused to take part in the proceedings), and (4) the general way in which the Court approaches a dispute between sovereign states.

As background, it should be noted that Iceland is extremely dependent on its fishing industry. This small island nation in the North Atlantic is surrounded by a continental shelf that extends out into the sea up to seventy miles in some places. Stimulated by the nutrient-rich Gulf Stream, the cold waters off Iceland are an important spawning area for many varieties of fish, including cod, halibut, haddock, and herring.

Concerned over the conservation of fish stocks that were being increasingly exploited by very efficient modern fishing fleets, Iceland progressively extended its claims to territorial waters. While Iceland was still a colonial possession of Denmark, a convention between Denmark and England was signed in 1901 that established the fishery limit and the territorial waters limit at three miles. In 1952 the fishery limit was extended to four miles, to be measured from straight baselines. Traditionally, states measured the outer boundary of territorial waters by following the low-tide mark along the contours of the coast (normal baselines) at whatever distance had been claimed for territorial waters. For states with a highly uneven coast (e.g., offshore rocks, numerous indentations), it is easier and tidier to follow straight baselines connecting outer points along the shore rather than trying to follow the actual coastline. The straight baseline system for measuring territorial waters, which was upheld by the International

Court of Justice in the *Anglo-Norwegian Fisheries Case* (1951), can result in a modest extension of territorial waters—a potentially important issue when access to offshore fish stocks is in question.

Iceland subsequently extended its claim to twelve and then to fifty miles. Of the other countries that fished in these waters, the United Kingdom was particularly disturbed (England and West Germany both ended up with cases before the Court against Iceland). The "Cod War," which was particularly intense between 1958 and 1960, has become a continuing feud between Iceland and England. Iceland has hinted at withdrawal from the North Atlantic Treaty Organization (there is an important NATO base in Iceland that helps control the North Atlantic). British and Icelandic vessels have clashed in numerous incidents ranging from attempted rammings to the firing of blank shells. The British feel they have an historic right to fish these waters, as their ships have fished the area for centuries, and during the past fifty years a significant portion of the British economy has come to depend on this fishing industry.

United Kingdom v. Iceland

The fisheries dispute between the United Kingdom and Iceland was brought before the International Court of Justice in 1972. The following brief reviews the major elements of the case.

FISHERIES JURISDICTION CASE

(United Kingdom v. Iceland)
International Court of Justice, 1974
Decision of July 25, 1974
I.C.J. Reports, 1974, p. 3

Facts

... [I]n 1948 the Althing (the Parliament of Iceland) had passed a law concerning the Scientific Conservation of the Continental Shelf Fisheries which empowered the Government to establish conservation zones wherein all fisheries should be subject to Icelandic rules and control to the extent compatible with agreements with other countries. Subsequently the 1901 Anglo-Danish Convention which had fixed a limit for Iceland's exclusive right of fishery round its coasts was denounced by Iceland as from 1951, new Icelandic Regulations of 1958 proclaimed a 12-mile limit and the Althing declared by a resolution in 1959 'that recognition should be obtained of Iceland's right to the entire continental shelf area in conformity with the policy adopted by the Law of 1948.' Following a number of incidents and a series of negotiations, Iceland and the United Kingdom agreed on an Exchange of Notes which took place on 11 March 1961 and specified *inter alia* that the United Kingdom would no longer object to a 12-mile fishery zone, that Iceland would continue to work for the implementation of the 1959 resolution regarding the extension of fisheries jurisdiction but would give the United Kingdom six months' notice of such extension and that 'in case of a dispute in relation to such extension, the matter shall, at the request of either Party, be referred to the International Court of Justice.'

In 1971, the Icelandic Government announced that the agreement on fisheries jurisdiction with the United Kingdom would be terminated and that the limit of exclusive Icelandic fisheries jurisdiction would be extended to 50 miles. In an aide-mémoire of 24 February 1972 the United Kingdom was formally notified of this intention. In reply the latter emphasized that the Exchange of Notes was not open to unilateral denunciation and that in its view the measure contemplated 'would have no basis in international law.' On 14 July 1972 new Regulations were introduced whereby Iceland's fishery limits would be extended to 50 miles as from 1 September 1972 and all fishing activities by foreign vessels inside those limits be prohibited.[2]

On April 14, 1972, the United Kingdom initiated proceedings against Iceland before the International Court of Justice. Iceland refused to take part in the proceedings. In its Memorial on the merits, the government of the United Kingdom asked that "the Court should adjudge and declare" *inter alia* that Iceland's unilateral extension of an exclusive fisheries zone out to fifty miles "is without foundation in international law and is invalid" and that "to the extent that a need is asserted on conservation grounds, supported by properly attested scientific evidence, for the introduction of restrictions on fishing activities in the said area of the high seas," all interested states should negotiate a mutually acceptable regime for the area.

---

2 United Nations, International Court of Justice, *Yearbook, 1973–1974*, No. 28 (The Hague, 1974), pp. 111–112. The remainder of the case is digested from *I.C.J. Reports*, 1974, pp. 3ff.

Issues

The Court was concerned in this case with the following major issues: (1) the failure of a party to appear, (2) the jurisdiction of the Court, and (3) the right of a coastal state to extend its fisheries jurisdiction unilaterally, in the context of its own preferential rights and the historic rights of other states.

Decision

The Court regretted Iceland's absence, claimed jurisdiction to review the broader aspects of the fishery problem, and voted 10 to 4 to the effect that (1) Iceland is not entitled unilaterally to extend its fishery limits and exclude the United Kingdom; (2) the parties are "under mutual obligations to undertake negotiations in good faith for the equitable solution of their differences"; and (3) the negotiations should take into account selected observations made by the Court concerning fishing rights.

Reasoning

14. Iceland has not taken part in any phase of the present proceedings. . . .

15. The Court is thus confronted with the situation contemplated by Article 53, paragraph 1, of the Statute, that 'Whenever one of the Parties does not appear before the Court, or fails to defend its case, the other party may call upon the Court to decide in favour of its claim.' Paragraph 2 of that Article, however, also provides: 'The Court must, before doing so, satisfy itself, not only that it has jurisdiction in accordance with Articles 36 and 37, but also that the claim is well founded in fact and law.'

.   .   .

49. The Applicant has challenged the Regulations promulgated by the Government of Iceland on 14 July 1972, and since the Court has to pronounce on this challenge, the ascertainment of the law applicable becomes necessary. As the Court stated in the *Fisheries* case:

> '*The delimitation of sea areas has always an international aspect; it cannot be dependent merely upon the will of the coastal State as expressed in its municipal law. Although it is true that the act of delimitation is necessarily a unilateral act, because only the coastal State is competent to undertake it, the validity of the de-*

limitation with regard to other States depends upon international law.' (I.C.J. Reports 1951, p. 132.)

The Court will therefore proceed to the determination of the existing rules of international law relevant to the settlement of the present dispute.

50. The Geneva Convention on the High Seas of 1958, which was adopted 'as generally declaratory of established principles of international law,' defines in Article 1 the term 'high seas' as 'all parts of the sea that are not included in the territorial sea or in the internal waters of a State.' Article 2 then declares that 'The high seas being open to all nations, no State may validly purport to subject any part of them to its sovereignty' and goes on to provide that the freedom of the high seas comprises, *inter alia*, both for coastal and non-coastal States, freedom of navigation and freedom of fishing. The freedoms of the high seas are however made subject to the consideration that they 'shall be exercised by all States with reasonable regard to the interests of other States in their exercise of the freedom of the high seas.'

. . .

67. The provisions of the Icelandic Regulations of 14 July 1972 and the manner of their implementation disregard the fishing rights of the Applicant. Iceland's unilateral action thus constitutes an infringement of the principle enshrined in Article 2 of the 1958 Geneva Convention on the High Seas which requires that all States, including coastal States, in exercising their freedom of fishing, pay reasonable regard to the interests of other States. It also disregards the rights of the Applicant as they result from the Exchange of Notes of 1961. The Applicant is therefore justified in asking the Court to give all necessary protection to its own rights, while at the same time agreeing to recognize Iceland's preferential position. Accordingly, the Court is bound to conclude that the Icelandic Regulations of 14 July 1972 establishing a zone of exclusive fisheries jurisdiction extending to 50 nautical miles from baselines around the coast of Iceland, are not opposable to the United Kingdom, and the latter is under no obligation to accept the unilateral termination by Iceland of United Kingdom fishery rights in the area....

71. ... But the matter does not end there; as the Court has indicated, Iceland is, in view of its special situation, entitled to preferential rights in respect of the fish stocks of the waters adjacent to its coasts. Due recognition must be given to the rights of both Parties, namely the rights of the United Kingdom to fish in the waters in dispute, and the preferential rights of Iceland. Neither right is an absolute one....

75. The obligation to negotiate thus flows from the very nature of the respective rights of the Parties; to direct them to negotiate is

therefore a proper exercise of the judicial function in this case. This also corresponds to the Principles and provisions of the Charter of the United Nations concerning peaceful settlement of disputes. . . .

Developing Law of the Sea

The Court's decision in the *Fisheries Jurisdiction Case* may be irrelevant. While there is an uneasy truce between the United Kingdom and Iceland and while the call to negotiate may be enticing (although Iceland has refused to acknowledge formally the Court's decision), significant areas of traditional sea law are under tremendous strain. Stability will come through political, not legal, solutions. Many states are making various kinds of jurisdictional claims as far as two hundred miles into the sea, primarily because of concern over access to the earth's dwindling resources. Iceland has indicated its interest in the two-hundred-mile zone.

The modern world community has done a great deal to solidify national agreement on important elements of sea law, but much still remains to be done. The First United Nations Conference on the Law of the Sea (Geneva, 1958) produced four basic conventions concerning the Territorial Sea and the Contiguous Zone, the High Seas, Fishing and Conservation of the Living Resources of the High Seas, and the Continental Shelf. Neither that conference nor the Second United Nations Conference on the Law of the Sea (Geneva, 1960) was able to reach agreement on the width of the territorial sea, an issue in the *Fisheries Jurisdiction Case*.

The Third United Nations Conference on the Law of the Sea (meeting for a 1973 organizational session in New York and subsequently for substantive sessions in Caracas, Venezuela, in 1974 and in Geneva during 1975) considered the broad issue of the uses of the oceans and its resources. While a major achievement of the 1975 session was an informal single negotiating text for a further session in 1976, there remained substantive areas of disagreement. One continuing problem was the width of the territorial sea. Maritime states generally fear that extensions of territorial waters will carve up the high seas, close off many straits, and threaten free navigation.

A further problem concerned the concept of a two-hundred-mile economic zone, which received wide support at the 1975 session. States disagree on the amount of control coastal states might exercise in such a zone over freedom of navigation and scientific research, highly migratory fisheries, and protection of the marine environment. Finally, the conference was concerned with the nature of an international regime to exploit deep seabed resources.

This kind of international conference is the most likely vehicle to produce solid world agreement (if there is to be any agreement) on limiting the expanding national claims to the sea and its resources that appeared in the Anglo-Icelandic Cod War. The International Court of Justice is of course hampered in its ability to rule on the law if the world political community is unable to agree on legal norms.

INTERNATIONAL LEGAL MACHINERY

On April 27, 1972, an event took place in the Great Hall of Justice of the Peace Palace in The Hague that probably went unnoticed by most people. The event was nevertheless significant, for it commemorated the fiftieth aniversary of the institution of the international judicial system. Sir Muhammed Zafrulla Khan, president of the Court, in addressing the gathering of government officials representing most states, recalled that the Permanent Court of International Justice of the League of Nations had met for its inaugural sitting on February 15, 1922. He noted:

That event not merely marked the establishment of a particular judicial body, the Permanent Court of International Justice, which after a fruitful career was dissolved some 24 years later; it was a turning point in international relations, and in the development of international law. It was the culmination of a movement towards greater justice and order in international relations, and toward the more effective settlement of international disputes, which, while it had its roots in the distant past, had been particularly observable from the late nineteenth century onwards. It was also an event whose significance and subsequent effects were by no means confined to the career and ultimate fate of the Permanent Court itself.[3]

International Arbitration

The impetus for the development of modern arbitration, part of the "movement towards greater justice and order in international

3 *Ibid.*, p. 128.

relations" referred to by Sir Muhammed Zafrulla Khan, is normally associated with the Jay Treaty of 1794 between the United States and Great Britain. These two parties successfully referred a number of outstanding disputes that had not been resolved by negotiation to arbitral commissions made up of equal numbers of U.S. and British nationals. Following the American Civil War, arbitration was further encouraged by the Washington Treaty of 1871 between the United States and Great Britain. The treaty was the basis for what became known as the *Alabama Claims Arbitration*. A bitter dispute had arisen over the Confederate ship *Alabama*, which had been built in British shipyards and had attacked U.S. shipping in the Atlantic. The arbitral tribunal (composed of a U.S. and a British national, plus three others from Italy, Brazil, and Switzerland) assessed the British government over $15 million in damages, which was subsequently paid.

Arbitration took another step forward at the First Hague Peace Conference (1899), which created the *Permanent Court of Arbitration*. This institutionalization of arbitration is neither a permanent situation nor a court. Previous arbitrations had been ad hoc, and eligible and qualified arbiters had to be sought whenever a dispute arose. The Permanent Court of Arbitration represented an advance in that it provided a preselected panel of arbiters that would be available when needed. Each contracting party could nominate up to four persons as part of a "pool" of 150 to 200 potential arbiters. The pool was permanent, but the service provided was arbitration, not the adjudication of a formal court. The Permanent Court of Arbitration is still in existence, sharing the Hague Peace Palace with the International Court of Justice of the United Nations. In addition to its arbitral function, the Permanent Court of Arbitration nominates judges for the ICJ (who are elected by the U.N. General Assembly and the Security Council in a complicated procedure).

International Adjudication

To date there have been five formal international courts—three of a regional nature (the *Central American Court of Justice*, the *Court of Justice of the European Communities*, and the *European Court of Human Rights*) and two with universal membership (the League's *Permanent Court of International Justice* and its successor, the U.N.'s *International Court of Justice*).

Central American Court of Justice. The Central American Court of Justice (1907–1917) was, in the words of Don Luis Anderson (Costa Rican foreign minister and president of the 1907 Washington Conference that drafted the Court's statute), "the first tribunal of its class in the history of civilization." [4] This Court, compared with subsequent international courts, had extremely broad jurisdiction. This fully independent tribunal, in addition to being the sole international mechanism for regulating Central American disputes, was competent not only to hear nation-states and individuals in contentious cases before it, but to decide certain domestic disputes as well.

Yet in spite of this apparently well-founded claim to recognition, the Central American Court of Justice (located in San José, Costa Rica, after a violent earthquake destroyed its first site in Cartago, Costa Rica) is little remembered and little written about. There appear to be several reasons for this neglect: (1) the Court was a dismal failure, and failures are generally readily forgotten; (2) the difference between the ideas proclaimed by the Court and the reality of its operation discourages objective, serious assessment; (3) the Court kept poor records; and (4) it produced no significant jurisprudence.

This Court deserves some attention, however, for it offers some cautionary lessons concerning attempts to impose international cooperation through legal means when the societal substructure and political agreement are lacking. Historically, the Court represented one of the highest points in international cooperation reached by the five Central American republics of Guatemala, El Salvador, Honduras, Nicaragua, and Costa Rica in their long struggle for unity since independence from Spain in 1820—and if not for unity, at least for peaceful relations. Historian Thomas Karnes very appropriately sums up the nature of Central American politics:

These five nations, whose chief importance to the world is their valued exports and strategic location, have a unique history that reveals much of man's tragic inability to get along with his neighbor. For 135 years these little states have tried to unite, federate, or confederate under numerous forms of government and have failed unconditionally, even though they apparently possess more bonds of

4 Luis Anderson, "The Peace Conference of Central America," *American Journal of International Law*, 2 (January 1908), 145. Some of the material used in the following discussion is taken from Forest Grieves, *Supranationalism and International Adjudication*, University of Illinois Press, Urbana, 1969, chaps. 2–6, and is used with the kind permission of the University of Illinois Press.

similarity than any other small group of nations in the world. Their failure, in fact, should have a sobering effect upon those of us who would expect such great accomplishments from Leagues of Nations, United Nations, or World Federation movements.[5]

The Central American Court consisted of five judges (one from each country) and had jurisdiction over "all controversies or questions which may arise ... of whatsoever nature and no matter what their origin may be...." [6] The Court also had compulsory jurisdiction, which meant that the parties—as in domestic law—*had* to appear before the Court if summoned. In a radical break from the traditional nation-state monopoly of international relations, citizens of one state were allowed to be parties before the Court in cases against any of the other contracting states. During the ten years of its existence the Court heard ten cases, and even though it started off strong, it ended up enmeshed in political disputes among the contracting states. As a result the Court collapsed, a victim of the mistaken belief that a court alone could bring peace to international relations.

Court of Justice of the European Communities. The other two regional courts have had more solid bases of political support. The Court of Justice of the European Communities began as the judicial institution for the European Coal and Steel Community, established by six Western European states (France, West Germany, Italy, and the Benelux countries). It also became the judicial organ for the European Economic Community (EEC) and the European Atomic Energy Community (Euratom), formed by the same states in 1958. The organs created to serve each community were eventually merged, and membership grew to nine with the addition of Ireland, Denmark, and the United Kingdom. Each of the three treaties establishing these communities represents agreement on highly technical areas, with the aim of merging the economies of the member states into a "common market." The Court's jurisdiction includes only the technical areas provided for in these treaties. The Court, within those limits, is strong, vigorous, and busy. Since its creation it has handled several

5 Thomas L. Karnes, *The Failure of Union: Central America, 1824–1960*, University of North Carolina Press, Chapel Hill, 1961, p. 3.
6 Article I of the convention establishing the Central American Court of Justice. The full text appears in *U.S. Foreign Relations*, 2 (1907), 697–701.

hundred cases (many of them quite significant for the development of the European Communities) involving not only member states, but also—in a departure from general international practice—the organs of the Communities, business enterprises, and individual persons.

European Court of Human Rights. The European Court of Human Rights is part of the human rights machinery of the Council of Europe. The Council of Europe joins nearly twenty states in Europe in an intergovernmental consultative organization. Hoping to provide an international organ to which individuals denied their rights could have direct access, the Council of Europe created a Commission and a Court of Human Rights. The Commission (which is a conciliatory body) receives petitions alleging violations of human rights from citizens of contracting states. If the complaint cannot be disposed of there, the case (if complicated jurisdictional preconditions are met) may be referred to the Court (consisting of a number of judges equal to the membership of the Council of Europe). Of the thousands of cases handled by the Commission, only a few have gone to the Court. While the Court's limited jurisprudence has not been without significance, it must be acknowledged that states that are willing to create and participate in international human rights machinery are likely to protect the rights of their citizens anyway.

League of Nations and United Nations Courts. The two universal international courts, the Permanent Court of International Justice (PCIJ) of the League of Nations and the United Nations International Court of Justice (ICJ), are in many respects one court. The ICJ inherited the archives, physical plant, and jurisprudence of its predecessor. Further, the statute constituting the PCIJ, modified and updated, became the statute of the ICJ. The primary change was an organizational one. The PCIJ had existed somewhat in limbo, quasi-affiliated with the League of Nations (largely in the hope that states that did not join the League might at least be parties to the Court). The ICJ, on the other hand, is fully integrated into the United Nations. Article 92 of the United Nations Charter states that the ICJ "shall be the principal judicial organ of the United Nations," and Article 93(1) reads: "All Members of the United Nations are *ipso facto* parties to the Statute of the International Court of Justice." Non-members of the United Nations may be parties to just the statute (currently there are three: San Marino, Liechtenstein, and Switzerland), and nonmembers may use the Court for a particular case if they meet certain minimal conditions.

Only states may be parties in contentious cases before the ICJ (as was true of the PCIJ), although the U.N. Charter allows the Security Council and the General Assembly (and certain other organs and agencies authorized by the General Assembly) to request advisory opinions from the Court. During its existence the Permanent Court rendered judgments in thirty-two contentious cases (all of which were carried out by the parties) and handed down twenty-seven advisory opinions. The International Court of Justice has rendered more than thirty judgments (two of which were ignored by the parties) and fifteen advisory opinions.

The judgments of these two courts have touched a broad range of issues relating to national sovereignty and jurisdiction, and even though many cases have been of marginal significance to the overall flow of world politics, some have had wide implications for the establishment of legal guidelines. Even the advisory opinions, such as the *Bernadotte Case* discussed in Chapter 3, have had a profound influence on international law on occasion.

In examining the modern International Court of Justice, three particular issues deserve close attention: (1) nationality of judges, (2) enforcement, and (3) jurisdiction.

The problem of finding impartial judges for an international court is no less a problem than finding them for national courts, and a judge's nationality is a particularly sensitive issue with international courts. While nations may profess (and indeed believe in) "internationalism," most of them don't really trust foreigners with decisions affecting their national lives.

The statute of the ICJ itself reflects this dilemma. Article 2 states: "The Court shall be composed of a body of independent judges, *elected regardless of their nationality* from among persons of high moral character, who possess the qualifications required in their respective countries for appointment to the highest judicial offices, or are jurisconsults of recognized competence in international law" (italics added). In spite of this stress on individuality rather than nationality, however, the statute elsewhere provides that no two of the fifteen judges shall be of the same nationality (Art. 3), that they should be elected so as to represent "the main forms of civilization" and the "principal legal systems of the world" (Art. 9), and that if the Court does not have a judge of the nationality of a party appearing before it, that party may choose an ad hoc judge to sit for the duration of the case (Art. 31), thus making it possible for there to be as many as seventeen judges hearing any given case. Although the record of the Court is quite good in terms of validating the judges' claim to be impartial individuals, any correlation between a judge's nationality and votes on Court decisions (which indeed comes up from time to time) is bound to aggravate nationalistic suspicions.

The problem of enforcing the Court's decisions is often overstated, for in fact enforcement seldom becomes an issue. One can view enforcement from a purely legal perspective, as did Judge Manley O. Hudson (an American judge on the PCIJ and a prominent legal scholar), who noted: "It is no part of the Court's task to see that its judgments are carried out, and except for the possibility of its interpreting or revising a judgment its competence with reference to a dispute is exhausted when it has delivered a judgment on the merits." [7] Article 94 of the United Nations Charter provides that a party to a case before the Court may have recourse to the Security Council to seek enforcement.

In spite of the concern for enforcement, the real problem is getting states to go to the Court in the first place, not getting them to obey a decision once it has been rendered. States do not exist in isolation; they are concerned about their good names and standings within the community—not to mention the fact that they are vulnerable to countermeasures if they violate the norms of the community. This point was illustrated in the very first case to be heard by the ICJ, the *Corfu Channel Case (United Kingdom v. Albania,* 1949). Albania was assessed damages for mining the Corfu Channel (an international waterway lying between the island of Corfu and the Albanian/Greek coast) and causing damage to two British warships (which were also given part of the blame for the incident). In refusing to pay the damages, Albania overlooked the fact that Albanian gold deposited in Italian banks had been confiscated by the victorious Allies during World War II. Instead of returning the gold to Albania, the Allied authorities passed it on to Great Britain as payment for the *Corfu Channel* judgment.

In the only other judgment by the ICJ involving noncompliance,

7 Manley O. Hudson, *The Permanent Court of International Justice, 1920–1942: A Treatise,* The Macmillan Company, New York, 1943, p. 595.

the *Fisheries Jurisdiction Case* examined earlier in this chapter, it remains to be seen what international forces have been set in motion.* The world community, however, seems to be uncertain regarding the issues (particularly access to dwindling resources) raised in that case.

The problem of jurisdiction is in many respects the most crucial one for an international court because sovereign nation-states cannot be forced into court against their will. Although there are several technical legal options available, the jurisdiction of the International Court of Justice rests primarily on (1) special agreement between states, (2) treaty provisions that provide for resort to the Court in the event of a dispute (in the *Fisheries Jurisdiction Case* the Court ruled that the 1961 Exchange of Notes between Iceland and Great Britain constituted a "treaty in force"), and (3) compulsory jurisdiction.

Compulsory jurisdiction is an option allowing states to make an advance commitment to submit to the Court's jurisdiction in future legal disputes. Acceptance of compulsory jurisdiction (provided for in the "optional clause" of Article 36 of the statute), however, allows a state to be forced into court only by another state that has *also* accepted compulsory jurisdiction. This "principle of reciprocity" protects those states that are willing to commit themselves to internationalism from other states that might wish to exploit that commitment. Of the roughly 140 members of the United Nations, only about 45 have accepted compulsory jurisdiction, and many of those 45 acceptances have important reservations attached. One prominent example is the U.S. Connally Amendment.

During Senate consideration of the U.S. statement accepting compulsory jurisdiction that President Truman was to submit to the secretary-general of the United Nations in August 1946, two reservations (neither of which cause any legal difficulties) were added. The first noted that U.S. acceptance of compulsory jurisdiction would not apply if a commitment had already been made to use another tribunal, and the second excluded disputes regarding "matters which are essentially within the domestic jurisdiction of the

* One other aspect of noncompliance appeared in the *Anglo-Iranian Oil Company Case (United Kingdom v. Iran,* 1952). Iran refused to comply with an interim court order concerning nationalization of foreign oil interests. Great Britain appealed to the U.N. Security Council, but before any official action could be agreed upon, the disputing parties worked out a private settlement.

United States." Senator Tom Connally (D., Tex.), chairman of the Senate Committee on Foreign Relations, added the phrase "as determined by the United States" to the second reservation. The effect of that amendment was to give the United States the appearance of accepting compulsory jurisdiction while actually retaining for its government the final decision about submitting to a court case. The only other Big Power (Great Britain) currently accepting compulsory jurisdiction also has substantial reservations, and a number of other countries have Connally-type reservations. However, a country might wish to consider either accepting or not accepting compulsory jurisdiction, but not try to do both. The Connally Amendment has actually made little difference to the United States in practice.

The International Court of Justice has not been used as much as some observers think it should have, but three points should be noted in that regard. The U.N. Charter encourages peaceful settlement of disputes by many means, only one of which is the Court. Further, the Court doesn't necessarily have to be in constant use to be valuable—it is there if needed, while its existence symbolizes a commitment to the international rule of law. Finally, as the experience of the Central American Court of Justice illustrated, it would be a mistake to try to use an international court to impose a world order that the international political community isn't yet ready to support.

No examination of the major international legal machinery would be complete without mention of the International Law Commission. Established by the U.N. General Assembly in 1947, the Commission is charged with the progressive development and codification of international law. Composed of twenty-five members elected as individuals for five-year terms, the Commission holds annual sessions. It has an impressive record of preparing draft conventions on various topics that have ultimately become international treaty law. One prominent example was the extensive draft material it prepared for the 1958 United Nations Conference on the Law of the Sea. Other Commission work concerns the rights and duties of states, offenses against the peace and security of mankind, problems of statelessness, and diplomatic intercourse and immunities.

International law is more than just the legal machinery examined above. It also serves as an organizing basis for international organizations and as a tool for achieving national foreign-policy goals. The following study of the International Whaling Commission illustrates these points and reviews some of the difficulties in attempting international control of a modern policy problem—conservation of a limited resource.

THE INTERNATIONAL WHALING COMMISSION: LAW AND THE ENVIRONMENT

The 1972 United Nations Conference on the Human Environment in Stockholm focused world attention on the dwindling stocks of whales, but the whale is hardly a new international conservation problem.

The Whales

There are nearly a hundred species of whales, of which about fifty-five are types of dolphins and porpoises.[8] In more basic biological terms, whales (order *Cetacea*) fall into two main suborders: *Mystacoceti* (including all whales having baleen, or whalebone), consisting most prominently as far as commercial use is concerned of right whales, bowhead whales, blue whales, fin whales, sei whales, humpback whales, and gray whales; and *Odontoceti* (whales having true teeth), including sperm whales, porpoises, and dolphins from a commercial standpoint. Whales are air-breathing mammals; they are not fish.

While attention is generally focused primarily on the larger whales, *all* those listed above are of commercial value and either are or have been hunted—even the friendly dolphins and porpoises. Demand was formerly most simply satisfied by taking larger whales, which gave the best yield per unit of hunting effort, but as the herds of larger whales have been decimated, pressure on smaller varieties has grown.

The most impressive cetacean is undoubtedly the blue whale.

8 Remarks of Scott McVay, Chairman, Committee on Whales, Environmental Defense Fund, before U.S. House of Representatives, Committee on Foreign Affairs, *International Moratorium of Ten Years on the Killing of All Species of Whales, Hearings*, before the Subcommittee on International Organizations and Movements, on H. J. Res. 706 and H. Con. Res. 375, 92d Cong., 1st sess., 1971, p. 49. Hereinafter cited as *Moratorium Hearings*. Material for this section has appeared in Forest L. Grieves, "Leviathan, The International Whaling Commission and Conservation as Environmental Aspects of International Law," *Western Political Quarterly*, 25 (December 1972), 711–725. Reprinted by permission of the University of Utah, copyright holder.

This creature is not only the largest mammal but, as far as scientists can determine, the largest animal ever to have existed on earth. The largest known dinosaur (*Brachiosaurus*)—a giant even among dinosaurs—weighed an estimated 50 tons. An adult blue whale can reach one hundred feet or more in length and weigh as much as 160 tons.

The actual numbers of whales remaining are somewhat in dispute, a fact that highlights one feature of the policy process, identifying a public problem and defining its dimensions. Policy-makers are forced to choose among the claims of competing authorities—no small task in the often emotion-laden conservation debates.

Estimates of the number of blue whales range from 10,000 to less than 200 (which is surely less than the genetic pool needed to stave off extinction, especially since they are scattered throughout the oceans), down from approximately 100,000 only fifty years ago. The situations of other species of great whales, although not as desperate as that of the blue whale, reflect similar declines in numbers. Of the great whales, only the finback (second largest of the baleen whales), sei (third largest of the baleen whales), and sperm whales (the only great toothed whales) are still commercially hunted and are without international protection. One of the last official acts of former U.S. Secretary of the Interior Walter Hickel was to put *all* the great whales on the endangered-species list. Although a unilateral act by the United States, this does prohibit importation of products from these whales into the United States (the United States was at that time a market for 25 to 30 percent of the world's whale products) and puts U.S. prestige behind moral and commercial persuasion.

The Whaling Industry

The decimation of some species of whales is partly explained by the fact that whaling is an extremely profitable business, although endangering the species, and hence future business, is not so easily explained. The major products have been oil, baleen (or whalebone), and meat, although virtually every part of the carcass is used. Whale products have become less important with the advent of petroleum and plastics. Nowadays most whale oil is used in margarine and soap, some whale meat is eaten (mostly in Japan, and to a lesser extent in Russia), and the rest is used for domestic animal food and fertilizer.

Human acquaintance with cetaceans is quite old. They are

mentioned in biblical passages. Whales and dolphins were common motifs on vases and coins used by the ancient Greeks. Greeks and Romans did not engage in whaling (at least not with the larger species). Norwegians were apparently the first whale hunters. The trade then spread to Iceland and elsewhere in Northern Europe. The Basques inhabiting the Bay of Biscay are credited with turning whaling into a large-scale industry. Through the voyages of explorers, like the Englishman Jonas Poole seeking the Northeast Passage in 1583, the Arctic area was found to be excellent territory for whalers.

Before 1904, whaling was almost entirely restricted to the Northern Hemisphere. Whaling in the Southern Hemisphere increased after the development of better ocean-going catchers and with the growing scarcity of whales in northern waters. Whaling techniques have become quite sophisticated. Whaling probably began with beach strandings, advanced to hand harpooning, then to the harpoon gun mounted on small steamers (with carcasses towed to shore stations), and finally to fleets of fast catchers serving factory ships. Classic advances in whaling techniques were Svend Foyn's harpoon gun in 1864 and Captain Sørlle's stern slipway in 1925. Post-World War II developments, which have made whaling extremely efficient, include helicopters and sonar devices for spotting whales, more efficient harpoons (e.g., with explosive heads), and modern factory ships that can process a fin whale carcass in half an hour.

In recent years country after country has had to curtail whaling for many reasons (not the least of which is the disappearance of whales from the oceans). Two countries, the Soviet Union and Japan, have engaged in most of the world's recent whaling. All other whaling states combined (Peru, South Africa, Norway, Canada, Australia, Spain, and the United States, which did less than 0.5 percent before it stopped whaling) have accounted for less than 15 percent of the total whaling, not counting some alleged private pirate operations. The decline of the whaling industry suggests that the traditional mechanisms of international relations have not worked properly, particularly since nearly all sides consistently advocated regulation of whale stocks to protect the industry.

Legal Regulation of Whaling

As early as 1910, a Norwegian engineer warned of the risk of exterminating commercially hunted whales. Although some government agencies were formed and the interest of several countries was aroused, nothing significant resulted. The League of Nations expressed concern that the whaling industry needed international regulation in 1924 and in 1927, but no international regulation resulted. The Norwegian government did respond, however, with the Whaling Act of 1929, which created several important national bodies, one of which is the internationally known Bureau of International Whaling Statistics (located in Sandefjord, Norway), which acts as a clearing house of whaling statistics for all nations engaged in pelagic and coastal whaling. The major work of that agency is the annual compilation and publication of the *International Whaling Statistics.*

During the 1930s and 1940s, several international agreements were signed that attempted, with mixed results, to control whaling. Whaling was largely dormant during World War II. Following the war, the military defeat of Japan and Germany increased the hope of regulating the industry, as both countries had been lax in following the prewar agreements. On December 2, 1946, the International Convention for the Regulation of Whaling was signed in Washington, D.C., by fifteen nations. The convention, recognizing the need to conserve and manage whale stocks, created the International Whaling Commission. Article III of the convention provides that the Commission will consist of one member from each contracting government (although that member may be accompanied by one or more experts and advisers), each having one vote. Selection of a chairman, staff, rules of procedure, and meeting place are determined by the Commission.

Article IV gives the Commission a mandate (either independently or in collaboration with various public and private organizations) to:

1 Encourage, recommend, or, if necessary, organize studies and investigations relating to whales and whaling

2 Collect and analyze statistical information concerning the current condition and trend of whale stocks and the effects of whaling activities thereon

3 Study, appraise, and disseminate information concerning methods of maintaining and increasing the populations of whale stocks

The regulatory power of the Commission fits the classic pattern of intergovernmental organizations in that a state cannot be bound without its consent, although strict unanimity on the part of the Commission is not required. Article V provides for a period within which contracting governments may object to Commission amendments. At the close of the delay period, amendments become binding only on those governments that did approve.

Other significant provisions of the Convention concern transmission of whaling statistics by contracting governments to the International Bureau of Whaling Statistics at Sandefjord, Norway (Article VII) and special permission for contracting governments to grant permits to their nationals for the taking of whales for scientific research (Article VIII).

Finally, each contracting government promises to "... take appropriate measures to ensure the application of the provisions of this Convention and the punishment of infractions against said provisions in operations carried out by persons or by vessels under its jurisdiction" (Article IX). Appropriate measures, according to Article IX of the convention, consist of withholding any "bonus or other remuneration" calculated on the basis of the results of work performed by gunners and crews of whale catchers vis-à-vis forbidden whales. Contracting governments further promise to provide full details of infractions and actions taken to the Commission.

The Record of the International Whaling Commission

A fair and value-free assessment of the International Whaling Commission is very difficult to make. On the one hand is the allegation that the whales are disappearing (or verging on extinction in the case of some species). The Commission has not prevented this, as its mandate suggests it should have, and it has therefore failed. On the other hand the Whaling Commission can be viewed as a typical intergovernmental agency doing the best that could be expected under the strictures that this status implies.

Perhaps the most basic question involves a value judgment: "Why save the whale?" The conservationist answers were well presented in the U.S. congressional hearings (1971) on an international moratorium on the killing of whales. The texts of the resolutions under consideration mentioned the following reasons for protecting whales: the threat of extinction, the dramatic comeback of the gray whale after years of protection, the fact that "whales are mammals with large brains and a complex social life and produce fascinating sounds which have inspired serious musical works," the scientific potential in the study of whale behavior, and the whales' great potential as a food resource for a hungry world.[9] Immediate action (such as a moratorium on whale killing) is generally advocated by conservationists.

Against this, one finds not necessarily a counter position, but rather an assumption that conservation is not the single most important issue. The most moderate position seems to overlap somewhat with a conservationist view, but maintains that solid scientific research is needed before restrictions are placed on the taking of whales. This view is exemplified by Professor G. Carlton Ray's statement before the House Subcommittee on International Organizations and Movements during the moratorium hearings:

We need to build up the animals. What I think we need to do is to build them up while maintaining a small fishing effort. I don't find it very relevant to hear that whales produce music. Cock-a-doodle-doo produces music, too. Whales are smarter than chickens, but it is not relevant to the purpose of this bill. Neither is it relevant to say that whales have a complex social life. So do all the animals, including cows that we eat. The point is to talk good international research and management sense.[10]

Whatever the relative merits of these varying views on the conservation of whales, two observations may be made at this point. First, there is something eerie and eternal about the potential extinction of a species that cannot help but move human emotions. For this reason nearly everyone is at least verbally committed to some kind of preservation of whales. Second, while conservation of a species may have aesthetic and metaphysical implications, for the social scientist it is also a policy problem. Given the legal and political commitment in the International Convention for the Regulation of Whaling, 1946, to the preservation of whales, how does this mandate compare with the record?

The International Whaling Commission has several handicaps, many of which are common to similar international agencies. Most obviously, it must operate within the framework of an intergovernmental

9 Texts of H. J. Res. 706, 92d Cong., 1st sess. and H. Con. Res. 375, 92d Cong., 1st sess. are reprinted in *Moratorium Hearings*, pp. 1 and 2. This subject is treated at length throughout the hearings.
10 *Moratorium Hearings*, p. 35.

organization, which, although the Commission does not require unanimity, puts a severe limitation on the Commission's powers to regulate its members. Further, its enforcement power is dependent on the good will and honesty of the contracting parties and the whaling companies. Although observers have been placed on whaling vessels, reports of negligence on the part of observers and whaling crews in observing whaling regulations (e.g., taking of protected species or lactating females and inspectors ignoring it) appear frequently enough to create doubt concerning the Commission's efficacy. In fact, one of the main problems of the Commission has been the difficulty of implementing an *international* observer scheme, in which inspectors would serve on ships of other nationalities, which would presumably ensure greater honesty.

The commissioners themselves are generally civil servants, representatives of the whaling industry, or academicians. The fact that the whaling industries are represented seems to some like having the wolf guard the flock. Because of the need for people familiar with a technical area, this is not an uncommon problem. The same situation exists in many U.S. regulatory agencies.

Much of the Commission's work is conducted behind closed doors, so that there is not as much public scrutiny of its work as there should be. This is particularly serious since the mere existence of the Commission gives the public the impression that the whales are being looked after. This situation is not entirely the fault of the Commission, however. Both national publics and national governments have an obligation to perceive public problems and act on them. Unfortunately, whales are a sufficiently exotic topic—in an era of massive retaliation, graduated response, and deterrence strategy—that they have not captured public attention and concern.

Another problem is that several whaling nations (and likewise some "pirate" whaling companies) are not parties to the 1946 convention. This does not necessarily mean that these countries follow less rigid whaling standards, but it does detract from the Commission's "international" mandate to put forth whaling guidelines.

Finally, the Commission has apparently had some difficulty in obtaining scientific data on whale populations that it considers adequate to justify very restrictive whaling quotas. This seems to have been a controversial point, as the Commission has allegedly sought solid data as a basis for decision-making, while critics charge that the Commission continually pleads for more "facts" as the whales are dying.

Whatever the problems and record of the Commission, the fact seems to be that the great whales are in peril. As a policy problem, the declining whale stocks present a tremendous challenge to policy-makers and legal advisers. U. Alexis Johnson, U.S. undersecretary of state for political affairs, speaking at the 23d Annual Meeting of the International Whaling Commission in Washington, D.C. (June 21 to 25, 1971), set the tone for this challenge:

The importance of this annual meeting of the Whaling Commission cannot be overemphasized. In many respects it is the most critical meeting ever held by the Commission. The results of your scientific investigations have been challenged in this country and elsewhere in the world. Past actions of the Commission are being criticized by world conservationists and in the conservation press. *But of even greater concern is that there is on trial at this meeting the whole concept of the multilateral international commission as an effective means of dealing with the conservation of major living marine resources.*[11] (Emphasis added.)

Observations

Several species of whales appear to be in a critical situation. Given the commitment to protect them that the International Convention for the Regulation of Whaling, 1946, supposedly represents, the international mechanism established in the International Whaling Commission has not been adequate. Or put another way, if the mechanism has been adequate, then member states have not properly supported it.

Several basic observations can be made here. First, the attempt to regulate whaling involves a classic problem of international law—*res nullius* versus *res communis*. If whales are *res nullius*, they are the property of no one and are there for the taking. If, on the other hand, whales are *res communis*, then they are the common property of the world community and cannot be exploited without some sort of international mandate. Until the community of nations can take a clear stand on such resources as whales, the whales are at the mercy of individual states.

Second, an ultimate assessment of the International Whaling Commission as an international agency must involve the adage, "People get the government they deserve." Any judgment of the Com-

11 U. A. Johnson, "International Whaling Commission Meets at Washington," *Department of State Bulletin*, 65 (July 26, 1971), 116.

mission must take into account what was demanded of it. If it failed, public leaders in fact failed because they did not adequately articulate expected norms and insist that they be upheld. An encouraging note, however, is that growing international concern for conservation seems to have brought some changes in attitudes among the states on the Commission since 1965. A proper assessment of these changes will of course depend on a continuing evaluation of results.

Finally, whatever the ultimate fate of the whales, there is a lesson for us all in the history of the international attempt to regulate whaling. While whales are perhaps exotic enough to escape major public attention, the policy procedures involved are basic. If the whales become extinct, it will be tragic for reasons independent of law and politics, but it will also represent a far-reaching failure of international procedure. Tomorrow states will be facing the problem of conserving deep-sea petroleum and valuable mineral resources, ocean fishery stocks, and perhaps space resources from the moon and elsewhere. The fact that whale oil and whalebone corset stays are not vital to national defense or other nationally important needs makes the lessons of our handling of the whales no less valuable.

THE ROLE OF INTERNATIONAL LAW
IN THE MODERN WORLD

A system of international law, if its limitations are understood and if it is properly used, can be of great benefit to states. No doubt most states have more to gain than to lose from the kind of stability law can bring.

If international law did not exist, it would have to be created simply because any community needs a frame of reference and a sense of order, no matter how fragile. The mechanisms of international law can serve as a face-saving alternative for disputing states. International law can also serve as a standard of diplomatic communication among states which they can use to define their foreign policy goals in legal terms and challenge the goals of others. Finally, law serves as a symbol of the world as a political community, which is itself strengthened by the sense of unity fostered by common support for the rule of law. International law should not occupy a false pedestal, but a realistic recognition of the kinds of roles it can play is a necessary part of national foreign policies.

BIBLIOGRAPHY

Bozeman, Adda B. *The Future of Law in a Multicultural World*. Princeton University Press, Princeton, N.J., 1971.

Brierly, J. L. *The Law of Nations*, 6th ed. Oxford University Press, New York, 1963.

Carlston, Kenneth S. *Law and Organization in World Society*. University of Illinois Press, Urbana, 1962.

Clark, Grenville, and Louis B. Sohn. *World Peace through World Law*, 3d ed. rev. Harvard University Press, Cambridge, Mass., 1966.

Coplin, William D. *The Function of International Law: An Introduction to the Role of International Law in the Contemporary World*. Rand McNally & Company, Chicago, 1966.

Corbett, Percy E. *Law and Society in the Relations of States*. Harcourt, Brace and Company, Inc., New York, 1951.

———. *The Growth of World Law*. Princeton University Press, Princeton, N.J., 1971.

Deutsch, Karl W., and Stanley Hoffmann, eds. *The Relevance of International Law*. Schenkman Publishing Co., Inc., Cambridge, Mass., 1968.

DeVisscher, Charles. *Theory and Reality in Public International Law*. Princeton University Press, Princeton, N.J., 1968.

Falk, Richard A. *Legal Order in a Violent World*. Princeton University Press, Princeton, N.J., 1968.

———. *The Status of Law in International Society*. Princeton University Press, Princeton, N.J., 1970.

Grieves, Forest L. *International Law, Organization, and the Environment: A Bibliography and Research Guide*. Institute of Government Research, International Studies No. 4. University of Arizona Press, Tucson, 1974.

———. *Supranationalism and International Adjudication*. University of Illinois Press, Urbana, 1969.

Henkin, Louis. *How Nations Behave: Law and Foreign Policy*. Frederick A. Praeger, Inc., New York, 1968.

Jenks, C. Wilfred. *The Prospects of International Adjudication*. Stevens & Sons, Ltd., London, 1964.

Jessup, Philip C. *The Price of International Justice*. Columbia University Press, New York, 1971.

Katz, Milton. *The Relevance of International Adjudication*. Harvard University Press, Cambridge, Mass., 1968.

Rosenne, Shabtai. *The International Court of Justice: An Essay in Political and Legal Theory*. A. W. Sijthoff's Uitgeversmaatschappij N.V., Leyden, Holland, 1957.

Rosenne, Shabtai. *The World Court, What It Is, How It Works*. Oceana Publications, Dobbs Ferry, N.Y., 1974.

Schwarzenberger, Georg. *International Law and Order*. Frederick A. Praeger, Inc., New York, 1971.

Simpson, J. L., and Hazel Fox. *International Arbitration*. Frederick A. Praeger, Inc., New York, 1959.

White, Irvin L. *Decision-making for Space: Law and Politics in Air, Sea, and Outer Space*. Purdue University Studies, Lafayette, Ind., 1970.

White, Irvin L., Clifton E. Wilson, and John A. Vosburgh. *Law and Politics in Outer Space: A Bibliography*. University of Arizona Press, Tucson, 1972.

Wright, Quincy. *Contemporary International Law: A Balance Sheet*. Doubleday & Company, Inc., New York, 1955.

International Organization

The study of international organization is the study of the institutional structures that may be set up for the purpose of (or in the hope of) organizing and regulating international relations.

There are several potential solutions to the problem of achieving world order. One approach, of course, is to assume that there is no solution—that the nation-state system renders order impossible. Another approach is balance-of-power schemes or a *Pax Romana* situation, in which one nation becomes strong enough to impose its vision of order on the rest of the world. Still another possibility is the institutional approach, involving some form of international organization.

The institutional approach will probably assume one of three basic structural models: unitary, federal, or confederal. The unitary model would involve an all-powerful central world government. The nation-states would either be abolished or become some kind of administrative subunit for the new central government. Under a world federal system, the present sovereign nation-states would share power with a central government. A federal structure would require that both levels of government have independent spheres of power, the limits of which would probably be spelled out in a written constitution and subject to change only with the consent of both levels. The example of thirteen sovereign states merging to form the United States of America as a federal union (combining both unity and diversity) is often offered as a model for world federalism.

Many individuals and groups have advocated, often eloquently, that the world be organized on a unitary or federal basis; however, such plans invariably come up against national sovereignty. The American example was in many respects unique, joining together units that already possessed great cultural unity. Yet, as the impressive post–World War II efforts of Western Europe to unite reveal, even though nations may have much in common, national forces do not give up power easily—nor should they necessarily.

Nation-states exist because they are perceived as the primary protectors of national values. There is no reason to expect support for international integration without simultaneous guarantees of those values. Consequently, confederal organization (often called intergovernmental organization) tends to be the most popular form of institutional commitment among nation-states. A confederation allows states to retain ultimate control over their destinies while extending minimum powers to the organizational framework that binds them together. This unity without risk produces a weak central authority based on the lowest common denominator of agreement among the constituent states. Common features of confederations, in addition to the weak central organization, include the freedom to pull out of the organization, requiring unanimity of member states on important decisions, and giving each member an equal voice in organizational decisions.

Both the United Nations and the North Atlantic Treaty Organization (NATO), for example, are structured along confederal, or intergovernmental, lines. The United Nations is a *universal* international organization, while NATO is one of the many *regional* international organizations. The former is worldwide; the latter, based primarily (but not exclusively) on geographical proximity, has a limited membership.

There has been a rather shallow debate between the advocates of universalism as an approach to world order on the one hand and the advocates of regionalism on the other. Some universalists have tended to claim that since the *real* problems in the world either were universal (e.g., disarmament) or required universal resources to solve (e.g., hunger, development), only a universal organization would do. With some suspicion, they have often regarded regional organizations as obstructionist and detracting from world order by seeking to build parochial power blocs.

Some regionalists, for their part, have seen universalism as an unrealistic attempt to do too much too quickly. The world as a whole seems to be deeply divided on many issues; therefore organizational effort should be directed toward those countries (apt to be located in the same region) that have enough in common to allow meaningful cooperation. Rather than hampering efforts to organize the world, the regionalists see their approach as a method of preparing a solid substructure for ultimate universal organization. There is, however, no reason why the universalist and regionalist positions must be mutually exclusive. In fact, the United Nations Charter itself is an example of universal and regional accommodation (see Chapter VIII of the charter). The goal of both is to reduce conflict between nation-states so as to organize more effectively the machinery that will treat human problems.

Background

The United Nations Conference on International Organization, which met in San Francisco from April 25 to June 26, 1945, to draft the charter, may have seemed to many to be a radical new departure in the history of international relations. The United Nations, which officially came into existence on October 24, 1945 (now universally recognized as United Nations Day), reflected both the grimness of the past two world wars and the promise of a new future.

The Preamble expressed the determination of "the peoples of the United Nations . . . to save succeeding generations from the scourge of war, which twice in our lifetime has brought untold sorrow to mankind." It therefore set forth such goals as the practice of toleration in human relations, the maintenance of "international peace and security," and the employment of "international machinery for the promotion of the economic and social advancement of all peoples."

While the founding of the United Nations justly deserves recognition as an important event in the history of international relations, it must be seen in historical perspective for at least two reasons. First, the United Nations is not the dramatic break with the past that it might at first seem. Rather, it is simply an evolutionary product of organizational forces that have been at work in international relations for some time. Second, one should not assume that the United Nations somehow automatically supersedes or replaces previous mechanisms of international cooperation. Actually, although the United Nations has replaced some antecedents, it is primarily an addition to other forms of international machinery and a centralized clearing house that can facilitate and coordinate traditional kinds of international intercourse.

The United Nations is in effect a standing international conference. Its modern roots can be traced from the Conferences at Münster and Osnabrück that produced the Peace of Westphalia (1648) and launched the nation-state system. Subsequent important conferences included the Congress of Vienna (1815), which brought over two hundred delegations together to consider problems of post-Napoleonic Europe, and the Concert of Europe (1815–1914), which was a series of ad hoc conferences convoked over a hundred-year period by the great powers of Europe to resolve their disputes and guide their relations "in concert." The eventual breakdown of that system was a significant factor in bringing about World War I.

Two very important conferences that were held toward the close of the Concert period were The Hague Peace Conferences (1899 and 1907). Initially called at the urging of Tsar Nicholas II of Russia, those conferences produced qualified agreement on arbitration and rules of warfare, but failed in their primary objective of disarmament. A Russian delegate to the second conference proposed that they meet again in eight years (which would have been 1915) to face the problem of disarmament once again, but World War I intervened.

Following the war, the League of Nations was created in response to the last of President Wilson's famous "Fourteen Points," which proclaimed: "A general association of nations must be formed under specific covenants for the purpose of affording mutual guarantees of political independence and territorial integrity to great and small states alike." Although intended as a universal organization, the League suffered from the refusal of the United States to join (the U.S. Senate would not support President Wilson) and from the fact that other major powers were in and out of the League.

Although the League had some modest successes, its most glaring failure was its inability to prevent World War II. That failure was due in part to internal structural and theoretical problems (in particular, the theory of collective security, discussed below as a problem for the United Nations). In fairness, however, it should be remembered that the world, quite apart from the League, was in a state of economic and political deterioration. There was stress in Europe over the Versailles Settlement that followed the war, several nations were undergoing economic depression, and the United States was intensely isolationist. And on top of everything, Mussolini, Hitler, Stalin, and Tojo were all in power at the same time.

Even before the end of World War II efforts were under way to organize the postwar world. Following a series of Allied meetings and declarations that began with the Inter-Allied Declaration of June 12, 1941, at St. James' Palace in London—in which the Allies united against the Axis promised to cooperate both during the war and in the peace that would presumably follow—the first concrete step toward creating the United Nations took place at the mansion in Washington, D.C., known as Dumbarton Oaks. The Dumbarton

Oaks Conference met from August 21 to September 28, 1944, and brought together the United States, the United Kingdom, and the Soviet Union. During a second phase of conversations lasting from September 29 to October 7, 1944, the Soviet delegates dropped out and were replaced by the Chinese—a move intended to avoid jeopardizing Soviet neutrality in the war against Japan. The basic framework and goals of the United Nations were hammered out at these meetings. A few major unresolved questions (such as the issue of a Big Power veto) were decided a few months later by Franklin Roosevelt, Winston Churchill, and Joseph Stalin at the famous Big Three conference in Yalta (February 1945). The results of the Dumbarton Oaks and Yalta conferences provided the basis for the work of the San Francisco Conference, which actually drafted the U.N. Charter.

The forces of World War II were not the only ones impelling the creation of an international organization such as the United Nations. Nations were becoming more interdependent, and human relations—because of the impact of science and technology—were becoming more complex. The United Nations is also the result of pressures to centralize such traditional diplomatic functions as negotiations, treaty-making, conferences, peaceful settlement of disputes, and various kinds of international administrative activity.

Organization

The core of the United Nations structure consists of six principal organs: the *General Assembly*, the *Security Council*, the *Economic and Social Council*, the *Trusteeship Council*, the *Secretariat*, and the *International Court of Justice* (the Court was discussed in the preceding chapter).

General Assembly. The General Assembly, in which all member states are represented and have one vote, is the center of the United Nations system (see Figure 8-1). It is a standing diplomatic conference that holds an annual session beginning in September of each year. There are provisions for calling special sessions and, since the passage of the 1950 Uniting for Peace resolution, for calling emergency special sessions within twenty-four hours. In fact, however, most nations have representatives on hand at the United Nations all year for continuing diplomatic consultations.

The heart of the General Assembly's role is provided by Article 10 of the charter, which gives the General Assembly authority to "discuss any questions or any matters within the scope of the present Charter or relating to the powers and functions of any organs provided for in the present Charter, and . . . may make recommendations to the Members of the United Nations or to the Security Council or to both on any such questions or matter." The only exception (provided for in Article 12) is that the General Assembly should not make recommendations concerning a dispute that the Security Council is considering under its own authority.

Although the General Assembly resembles a parliament, that resemblance extends only to the debate and the parliamentary forms of procedure. The body, of course, has no power to make law binding nation-states. Its authority extends only to binding decisions on matters internal to the operation of the organization and to recommendations to the members, which can be passed by majority vote (or in the case of "important questions," by a two-thirds majority vote). As the foregoing chapter suggested, however, these recommendations take on political and legal importance to the extent that they have true world support.

In addition to the discuss-and-recommend function, which has emerged as a political instrument within the United Nations, the General Assembly also has a supervisory role in overseeing and coordinating the many U.N. activities. The General Assembly is responsible for the finances of the United Nations, it elects (either on its own or in conjunction with the Security Council) the members of other U.N. organs, and it approves amendments to the charter.

The president of the General Assembly (usually a very prestigious and influential person within the United Nations) and seventeen vice presidents are elected for each session. The major work of the General Assembly is accomplished by seven Main Committees (each U.N. member has a seat on each committee), which study, debate, and prepare recommendations for approval by plenary meetings of the General Assembly. The Main Committees are:

First Committee—Political and Security Committee

Special Political Committee—shares work of First Committee (was an ad hoc committee until it was made a permanent committee in 1956)

Second Committee—Economic and Financial Committee

THE UNITED NATIONS

The Specialized Agencies
and IAEA

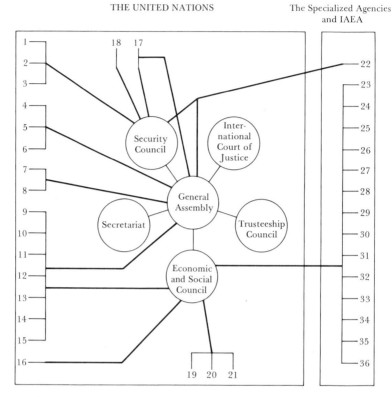

The United Nations

1 United Nations Truce Supervision Organization in Palestine (UNTSO)
2 United Nations Military Observer Group in India and Pakistan (UNMOGIP)
3 United Nations Peace-keeping Force in Cyprus (UNFICYP)
4 Main Committees
5 Standing and Procedural Committees
6 Other Subsidiary Organs of General Assembly
7 United Nations Relief and Works Agency for Palestine Refugees in the
   Near East (UNRWA)
8 United Nations Conference on Trade and Development (UNCTAD)
9 Trade and Development Board
10 United Nations Development Programme (UNDP)
11 United Nations Capital Development Fund
12 United Nations Industrial Development Organization (UNIDO)
13 United Nations Institute for Training and Research (UNITAR)
14 United Nations Children's Fund (UNICEF)
15 United Nations High Commissioner for Refugees (UNHCR)
16 Joint United Nations—FAO World Food Programme
17 Disarmament Commission
18 Military Staff Committee
19 Regional Economic Commission
20 Functional Commissions
21 Sessional, Standing and *Ad Hoc* Committees

FIGURE 8-1. The United Nations System

Third Committee—Social, Humanitarian and Cultural Committee

Fourth Committee—Trusteeship Committee

Fifth Committee—Administrative and Budgetary Committee

Sixth Committee—Legal Committee

The General Assembly also has a number of standing and ad hoc committees that handle specialized matters. In addition, it has the authority to create subsidiary organs to assist in particular areas.

Security Council. The Security Council is a specialized organ that bears "primary responsibility for the maintenance of international peace and security," while other members of the United Nations "agree that in carrying out its duties under this responsibility the Security Council acts on their behalf" (Article 24 of the Charter). This responsibility includes the authority to call upon disputing states to settle their differences peacefully, to investigate potential threats to peace, and ultimately to order enforcement measures (ranging from diplomatic pressure to the use of military force) to halt threats to peace. Members of the United Nations (Article 25) "agree to accept and carry out the decisions of the Security Council in accordance with the present Charter."

The Security Council is a continuation of the Concert of Europe in which the large, strong (and presumably responsible) powers assume a special responsibility for preserving international peace. Because of this special responsibility, there are five permanent mem-

FIGURE 8-1 (continued)

The specialized agencies and IAEA

22	IAEA	International Atomic Energy Agency
23	ILO	International Labour Organisation
24	FAO	Food and Agriculture Organization of the United Nations
25	UNESCO	United Nations Educational, Scientific and Cultural Organization
26	WHO	World Health Organization
27	IMF	International Monetary Fund
28	IDA	International Development Association
29	IBRD	International Bank for Reconstruction and Development
30	IFC	International Finance Corporation
31	ICAO	International Civil Aviation Organization
32	UPU	Universal Postal Union
33	ITU	International Telecommunication Union
34	WMO	World Meteorological Organization
35	IMCO	Inter-Governmental Maritime Consultative Organization
36	GATT	General Agreement on Tariffs and Trade

bers (the Big Five of World War II: United States, United Kingdom, France, Soviet Union, and China) of the Security Council. The ten (six until the Charter was amended in 1965 to provide greater representation for the newer states) nonpermanent members are elected by the General Assembly for staggered two-year terms. A majority of nine votes (formerly seven) decides "procedural" matters within the Security Council, but on "important" matters the nine votes must include the votes of the permanent members.

The Security Council is organized to function continuously. Perhaps because it is so often involved during times of international crisis, many people tend to regard the Security Council as the central organ of the United Nations. In fact it is a specialized council limited to peace and security questions.

Economic and Social Council. The Economic and Social Council (ECOSOC) is composed of fifty-four (formerly eighteen and then twenty-seven before respective charter revisions in 1965 and 1973) members, eighteen of whom are elected each year by the General Assembly for three-year terms. Although it is formally a principal organ of the United Nations, the Economic and Social Council operates under the authority of the General Assembly (Article 60). While peace and security problems often monopolize public attention, other United Nations activities—the services many think "just happen"—are concerned with the mandate to promote higher standards of living; to seek solutions to economic, social, health, and related problems; to cooperate in educational and cultural matters; and to respect human rights and fundamental freedoms.

Recognizing that world peace cannot be assured solely by enforcement or other institutional means, the Charter calls attention to the importance of the root causes of social conflict. In economic and social affairs, the United Nations is charged with "the creation of conditions of stability and well-being which are necessary for peaceful and friendly relations among nations based on respect for the principle of equal rights and self-determination of peoples. . . ." (Article 55).

ECOSOC oversees many subsidiary bodies with quite complex organizations and missions. The most important of those bodies are six functional commissions (Statistical, Social Development, Human Rights, Population, Status of Women, and Narcotic Drugs) and four regional economic commissions (Economic Commissions for Europe, ECE; Latin America, ECLA; Asia and the Far East, ECAFE; and Africa, ECA) that study, coordinate, and make recommendations concerning regional economic policies. Perhaps the best-known of the other related bodies is the United Nations Children's Fund (UNICEF).

The Economic and Social Council also serves as the primary agency through which autonomous organizations (many of which existed long before the United Nations was ever thought of) may be associated with the United Nations by special arrangement. Among these specialized agencies are such intergovernmental organizations as the Universal Postal Union (UPU), the World Health Organization (WHO), the Food and Agricultural Organization (FAO), the United Nations Educational, Scientific and Cultural Organization (UNESCO), the International Labor Organization (ILO), and many others. There is also a group of nongovernmental or private organizations (NGOs) that are affiliated with the United Nations because their areas of activity are of particular relevance to U.N. efforts.

Trusteeship Council. The Trusteeship Council, like ECOSOC, operates under the authority of the General Assembly (Article 85). When the charter was drafted, colonialism was considered a major international problem (about one-fourth of the world's population lived in dependent territories at that time). Three whole chapters of the charter (XI, XII, and XIII) were devoted to non-self-governing territories and the trusteeship system.

The United Nations trusteeship system is basically an expanded version of the mandate system that had worked so well under the League. The mandate structure, according to Article 22 of the League's covenant, was directed "to those colonies and territories which as a consequence of the late war have ceased to be under the sovereignty of the States which formerly governed them and which are inhabited by peoples not yet able to stand by themselves under the strenuous conditions of the modern world. . . ." The development of those peoples was recognized by the covenant as a "sacred trust of civilization." The covenant further proclaimed (Article 22) that "the tutelage of such peoples should be entrusted to advanced nations who by reason of their resources, their experience or their geographical position can best undertake this responsibility, and who are willing to accept it. ..." This tutelage was to be exercised on behalf of the League.

The League mandate spirit was carried over into the United Nations. Three categories of territories were made part of the U.N. trusteeship system: (1) territories held under League mandate, (2) territories detached from Axis states as a result of World War II, and (3) territories voluntarily placed under the system.

Membership on the Trusteeship Council is variable, including those permanent members of the Security Council not administering trust territories, the states administering trust territories, and a "balancing" number of states elected for three-year terms by the General Assembly to ensure that there is an equal number of administering and nonadministering states on the Council. Each member gets one vote; decisions are by a majority of those present and voting. The Trusteeship Council's main forms of operation include receiving annual reports from the administering states, periodically visiting the trust territories, and receiving petitions from the territories.

Secretariat. The Secretariat includes the secretary-general, who serves as the chief administrative officer of the United Nations, and a staff that functions as an international civil service. The creation of a permanent Secretariat under the League of Nations was a great advance over previous international conferences. The establishment of a full-time bureaucracy not only made the technical machinery available to serve the member states more effectively, but more significantly, it gave a sense of identity and continuity to the League. Similarly, the U.N. Secretariat is the administrative core of the organization.

The secretary-general is appointed by the General Assembly upon the recommendation of the Security Council. In addition to being responsible for the administrative services of the United Nations, the secretary-general derives some political initiative from the office. He may bring to the attention of the Security Council matters that he feels threaten international peace and security. He also makes an annual report to the organization, which gives him an opportunity not only to summarize the work of the organization but also to emphasize important issues, express opinions, and make recommendations. Further, he is able to propose items for inclusion in the agenda.

Although the secretary-general's real policy-making authority is limited by the effects of national sovereignty, which are reflected in the charter, he nonetheless has some discretion and influence concerning the policy process. The secretary-general's influence, of course, also derives from his personal prestige and from the pre-eminence of his office, which alone represents the United Nations as a whole.

Like any organization, the United Nations has become slightly more than the sum of its parts. Even though it is an intergovernmental organization in a world of sovereign nation-states, internal dynamics tend to give the United Nations a limited life of its own. The U.N. Charter helps define the legal life of the organization. Article 104 provides that the organization will have within its members' territories "such legal capacity as may be necessary for the exercise of its functions and the fulfillment of its purposes," while Article 105 provides for the "privileges and immunities" necessary if the United Nations and its officials are to conduct its business.

The United Nations may hold property, display a flag, make contracts, and otherwise conduct itself as a legal person. An important test of the United Nations' status as a legal person occurred in 1948 after the assassination of Count Folke Bernadotte, a president of the Swedish Red Cross who had been chosen to serve as a U.N. mediator in Palestine. The International Court of Justice decided unanimously in an advisory opinion that the United Nations could bring a claim against a state (Israel) for reparations based on injury to one of its agents.

Major Problems and Dilemmas

The functioning of the United Nations has not been without problems, some of which are inherent in the nature of the organization and others of which have developed from the United Nations' encounter with international political reality.

Myth of Sovereign Equality and Membership Problems. A basic principle of the United Nations is the sovereign equality of its members, which is nothing more than institutional recognition of the international formula produced by the Peace of Westphalia (1648). While nations may have formal, legal equality within the United Nations, the disparity in their relative strengths and weaknesses in the world outside the U.N. structure makes United Nations resolutions based on the voting of "equals" appear somewhat unreal.

U.N. membership includes military superpowers, states inhabited by millions, two nonstates (the Ukraine and Byelorussia—Soviet republics—were admitted as original members of the United Nations under the political agreement at Yalta to compensate the Soviet Union for what it perceived as voting inferiority vis-à-vis the West), very rich and miserably poor states, and microstates. Secretary-General U Thant finally warned of the increasing problem of admitting microstates—barely viable small states, in some cases with only several thousand inhabitants. Earlier chapters have reviewed the military disparity among the world's states, but the economic disparity is no less real. It is instructive to note that the annual sales of a surprising number of private multinational corporations are greater than the GNP of most member states in the United Nations.[1] The General Motors Corporation, for example, ranks in the top 25 when compared with U.N. members.

Weaker countries strongly support equality of membership in the United Nations, while stronger states tolerate it as long as they do not feel unduly threatened. The Big Five, of course, have the protection of the veto in the Security Council (which can order an international peace-keeping action), since the majority voting in the General Assembly can produce only recommendations. Nevertheless, the United States for one has become increasingly disenchanted in recent years with what it perceives as antagonistic majorities in the General Assembly that produce resolutions out of keeping with the real world power structure. It should be remembered in this regard that the United States was largely able to produce favorable voting majorities during the earlier years of the United Nations, which disenchanted, among others, the Soviet Union and its allies. Whether the artificiality of General Assembly voting will drive the stronger states away from the United Nations remains to be seen; however, past suggestions for weighted voting (based on military

1 U.S. Senate, Committee on Finance, Subcommittee on International Trade, *Hearings, Multinational Corporations,* 93rd Cong., 1st sess. (1973), pp. 475–476.

strength, GNP, population, or other factors) have not received wide support.

Although the United Nations aspires to be a universal international organization, with membership open to everyone, its membership policy has been neither coherently developed nor free of politics. The original fifty-one members of the United Nations, consisting primarily of states allied against the Axis Powers in World War II, were charter members. Subsequent members must be recommended for membership by the Security Council (an action subject to a Big Five veto) and then admitted by a vote in the General Assembly. The formal qualifications for membership are spelled out in Article 4 of the charter, which requires that applicants (1) be "peace-loving states," (2) "accept the obligations contained in the present Charter," and (3) be states that "in the judgment of the Organization, are able and willing to carry out these obligations." It does not require much thought to compile a long list of U.N. members that for one reason or another probably do not truly meet the membership requirements —not that it necessarily matters.

In the early years of the United Nations both the United States and the Soviet Union practiced a policy of competitive exclusion, refusing to support the admission of any state that might support the other side in Cold War politics. In 1955, however, a compromise was reached between the two that admitted en masse a group of applicant states on each side. Since 1955 membership has been available to virtually any applicant—one of the factors that led to the problem of the microstates. The growth in U.N. membership since the mid-1950s has primarily coincided with the emergence of new states out of the crumbling colonial empires.

The only independent political entities in recent years that have been prominent nonmembers of the U.N. are: (1) Switzerland, which is not a member by choice on the theory that membership would jeopardize traditional Swiss neutrality (although the Swiss are very active in peripheral U.N. agencies); (2) the quasi-states, such as Andorra, San Marino, Monaco, and Liechtenstein (although they too participate in U.N.-related activities); (3) the divided states—the two Koreas, the Vietnams (currently reunified forcibly by North Vietnam), and the Germanies (both East and West Germany are now members); and (4) mainland China (which was seated in 1971, replacing Nationalist China, which is now an outsider). During 1975 it looked as though the Big Powers might be returning to a partial policy of competitive exclusion over the issue of membership for the Vietnams and the Koreas.

The seating of the People's Republic of China was an issue before the United Nations for some twenty-two years, and presents an interesting example of one facet of U.N. politics. China, led by Chiang Kai-shek, had been one of the founding members of the United Nations, but in 1949 domestic turmoil resulted in the communist regime of Mao Tse-tung ruling the mainland as the People's Republic of China, while Chiang's forces retreated to the island of Formosa to establish the Republic of China (Nationalist China). The problem for the United Nations became primarily a credentials issue of determining which was the "real" China. The issue was highly political from the beginning, as a group of states, led by the United States, supported the continuing presence in the United Nations of Nationalist China.

The popular press often referred to the "admission" or the "recognition" of mainland China. "Admission," however, was not really the question, as China was already a U.N. member; the difficulty was determining whose credentials to accept. "Recognition" was also not the problem, since it relates to the private willingness of one state to engage in normal diplomatic business with another and does not necessarily hinge on what other states or an international organization might choose as their own policy. "Representation" (that is, credentials) was the crux of the problem.

The arguments supporting the representation of mainland China focused on such points as the United Nations' goal of universal membership, the Peking regime's de facto control over the mainland, the fact that only mainland China had the resources to be a Big Power on the Security Council, the claim that the internal political struggle within China was not the business of the international community, and the suggestion that seating the mainland Chinese might make them feel a part of the world community and soften their belligerent rhetoric.

Those opposed to mainland Chinese representation called attention to such issues as communist China's disregard for human rights (e.g., allegations of mass executions), the belligerent attitude toward the world community (e.g., invasions of Korea, Tibet, and India; export of revolutionary ideology to the Afro-Asian world; and the Sino-Soviet split, which showed that mainland China could not even coexist peacefully with another communist state), the claim that seat-ing mainland China would not only legitimize the regime's past ac-tions but encourage further aggression, as the Munich meeting had done for Hitler, and the belief that no state had an automatic right to U.N. membership—mainland China should not be able to muscle its way in just because it was strong.

From 1951 through 1960 the United Nations General Assembly voted in support of a United States proposal to keep the question of Chinese representation off the agenda. Then the question was put on the agenda, but a parliamentary tactic was employed at each session of the General Assembly that required two votes. The first vote (simple majority) was to decide whether or not the issue of Chinese representation was an "important question" (under Article 18 of the charter) requiring a two-thirds majority on a second vote. Although support for mainland China fluctuated over the years, depending on its international reputation as a trustworthy state, world opinion seemed to be shifting slowly in favor of bringing it into the world community as a full member. The visit to Peking by U.S. Secretary of State Henry Kissinger and the support given by President Nixon to normalizing U.S. relations with the People's Republic of China (including not starting a major fight over the U.N. representation issue) finally resulted in a General Assembly vote to seat the main-land Chinese delegation and expel the Nationalist Chinese.

Other proposals to resolve the Chinese question had been put forth over the years, such as the various "two Chinas" formulas, which would have permitted both Chinas to be seated (an approach generally favored by other states, but opposed by the two Chinas, each of whom claimed to be the sole representative of all China), but none of them seemed to be able to gain definitive support. That is unfortunate, for while mainland China is a political reality that should be represented in the United Nations, Formosa appears to be no less of a reality and should also have a U.N. voice.

Parliamentary Diplomacy, Bloc Voting, and the Veto. The principle of open debate in the General Assembly is a continuation of the Wil-sonian reaction to the secret dealings and treaties that were widely blamed for causing World War I. The opening phrase of the first of President Wilson's Fourteen Points called for "open covenants of peace, openly arrived at. . . ." This widely misunderstood phrase ush-ered in a new form of diplomatic practice known as "open" or "parliamentary" diplomacy, which was institutionalized in the League Assembly and the United Nations General Assembly. The diplomatic techniques of parliamentary diplomacy will be evaluated in the following chapter; however, this new diplomatic method uses public debate, following parliamentary rules of procedure. Debate is terminated by formal conclusions (resolutions) based on voting.

The importance of voting has spawned voting blocs. Blocs have developed in support of policy positions, and they are a means of increasing leverage in the selection process by which the General Assembly fills the seats on other bodies (e.g., nonpermanent members of the Security Council and ECOSOC) or elects its own officers. Voting coalitions have been transferred into the United Nations from political alignments outside (e.g., Latin American states, Arab states, Commonwealth states) and developed inside as a natural consequence of parliamentary dynamics. Voting alignments vary in cohesiveness from the tightly knit Soviet bloc to the loose, informal groups that consult on issues but vote as they choose.[2]

There is a temptation to view the voting blocs as incipient political parties in an international parliament. While cooperation on international policy issues is encouraging, it must not be forgotten that the U.N. envoys represent sovereign states and do not have the kind of flexibility that make national political parties viable instruments of governance. In fact, voting alignments have brought to General Assembly politics an element of rigidity that does not enhance the spirit of compromise so necessary in international diplomacy.

During the early years of the United Nations, the overall voting alignment in the General Assembly was heavily influenced by East-West world politics. As the Third World emerged—concerned with issues of colonialism, racial discrimination, and development—a North-South alignment began to appear. Third World voting majorities on economic issues are a prominent example of the new alignment within the General Assembly. The Sixth Special Session of the General Assembly, which met in early 1974, reflected this alignment with its adoption of a Declaration on the Establishment of a New International Economic Order.

Among the principles of a new international economic order included in the declaration are sovereign equality of states, cooperation

2 A landmark study of U.N. voting patterns is Thomas Hovet, Jr., *Bloc Politics in the United Nations*, Harvard University Press, Cambridge, Mass., 1960.

to end the disparities between rich and poor countries, the need to stimulate progress in the developing countries, the right of each country to its own economic and social system, and full sovereignty over natural resources (including the right of nationalization). The declaration also noted that all countries have the right to full compensation for colonialist exploitation, called for the transfer of financial resources and technology to the developing countries, and urged a more active United Nations role in creating a new world economic order.

A number of developed countries, including the United States, have voiced reservations and objections to the declaration. It remains to be seen to what extent North-South cooperation to implement the declaration's goals will materialize.

A somewhat different voting issue occurs within the Security Council—the famous veto. The term "veto" is not actually used in the charter. The veto is a consequence of the requirement (Article 27) that Security Council votes on other than procedural matters need the affirmative votes of nine members "including the concurring votes of the permanent members." In practice, the absence or abstention of one of the permanent members from a vote has not been considered to constitute a veto. There is also a "double veto," which stems from a Big Power agreement at the San Francisco Conference that the issue of whether a question is procedural or substantive is itself subject to a veto, although this has only been used three times, all during the early years of the United Nations.

Over a hundred vetoes have been cast in the Security Council, most of them by the Soviet Union. Some observers have maintained that the Soviet Union has abused the veto, and no doubt it has in some cases. Yet it would be wrong to argue that the veto should somehow be abolished, for it ensures that the United Nations cannot undertake a major peace-keeping action without Big Power support. An attempt to force policies upon an unwilling Big Power could easily lead to military confrontation, and even a world war. Besides, a thorough evaluation of the veto cannot be achieved by simply tabulating votes; rather, one must examine individual vetoes within the political context in which they were cast. For example, the Soviet vetoes generally reflect the fact that for many years the West controlled an automatic majority on the Security Council, which made the veto the Soviet Union's only defense. For example, about half the Soviet vetoes were cast on membership questions during the period of Cold War "competitive exclusion" referred to in the preceding section. The United States achieved the same goal by controlling a friendly voting majority on the Security Council.

The veto is, needless to say, a defense for the other Big Powers as well. The United States, which was as anxious as the Soviet Union to have the veto included in the charter when the United Nations was being created, has begun to use the veto in recent years now that it cannot count on automatic voting majorities in the Security Council. Further, as Sydney Bailey concludes in a solid study of Security Council voting,

I have no wish to deny that the veto has been used effectively for such purposes as to prevent the admission of states to the United Nations or the establishment of procedures for observation or investigation. But the fact is that the United Nations has been hamstrung by the veto neither as frequently nor as decisively as has sometimes been suggested.[3]

Finances. The regular budget of the United Nations is financed by assessments made each year by the General Assembly, based primarily on each member state's ability to pay (although upper and lower limits are also set). United Nations members undertake an obligation to pay their assessments, but since the organization does not have the power to tax, the payments are actually akin to contributions. The rapidity with which the Soviet Union and France brought the United Nations to its knees during the "financial crisis" made it clear where the money power lies. The regular budget has not been a source of problems, however. The financial crisis of the 1960s stemmed from a dispute over assessments for special peace-keeping budgets for the 1956 Middle East and the 1960 Congo crises.

In spite of inflation and the expanding load of United Nations activities, the regular budget of the organization is rather modest. It has increased from an annual appropriation of $19.4 million in 1946 to around $270 million by the mid-1970s, yet in terms of the costs of other kinds of governmental activities it involves very little money indeed.

In addition to the regular budget, there are assessed budgets for the specialized agencies of roughly $300 million a year. Also, special voluntary programs such as the Children's Fund (which subsist on

3 Sydney D. Bailey, *Voting in the Security Council,* Indiana University Press, Bloomington, 1970, p. 62.

government and private contributions) account for another $900 million. Finally, there are special peace-keeping expenses, which, with the exception of the extraordinary burden ($120 million a year) of the Congo operation that produced the financial crisis discussed below, average about $20 million a year.

The total expenditure for the entire United Nations system is roughly a billion and a half dollars a year. By way of comparison, world military expenditures alone were over $240 billion a year in the early 1970s. When the United Nations found itself with a deficit of some $122 million at the beginning of 1964 (largely because of the arrears of the Soviet bloc in meeting the assessments of the special peace-keeping budget, although France also became delinquent), a major financial crisis developed that threatened the very foundations of the United Nations.

The United States provoked a confrontation over the issue of arrears, claiming that Article 19 of the charter required that states two or more years in arrears automatically lost their vote in the General Assembly. Bolstering the case against the delinquents was the secretary-general's view that Article 17 of the charter gave the General Assembly budgetary authority, while Article 22 allowed it to establish subsidiary organs (such as the peace-keeping forces). Further, the International Court of Justice had rendered an advisory opinion (at the request of the General Assembly) in 1962 supporting the claim that the General Assembly had the legal authority to assess members to support the special peace-keeping expenditures— an opinion that the Assembly voted overwhelmingly to accept.

The Soviet position, on the other hand, was that the peace-keeping operations in the Middle East and the Congo, both of which have been organized by the General Assembly following a Security Council veto, were attempts to circumvent the charter. Only the Security Council has authority to order a peace-keeping operation, but if the claim is advanced that the General Assembly is only *co-ordinating* the peace-keeping efforts through its discuss-and-recommend authority, then it can also only *recommend* that states pay— which the Soviet Union refused to do. Also, the Soviet Union insisted that the deprivation of voting rights in the General Assembly was not automatic because Article 18 required a two-thirds vote on budgetary questions.

The nineteenth General Assembly met for only a few weeks in 1964, trying by common agreement to avoid taking any formal votes in order to postpone a showdown, but the Albanian delegation insisted on calling for a vote. Although it had been able to conduct some business through the device of acclamation, the session finally gave up and adjourned. By the twentieth session in 1965, the United States, faced with a Soviet threat to pull out of the United Nations and a lack of member support for further confrontation, backed down. However, U.S. Ambassador to the United Nations Arthur Goldberg announced that the United States would henceforth reserve for itself the right not to pay for U.N. undertakings it did not like (a power it had anyway as a practical matter).

The United Nations is looking for new sources of revenue both to keep itself currently solvent and to avoid future financial crises. In addition to the voluntary contributions it receives, it sells bonds (although there is likely to be some political controversy when the interest on those bonds falls due) and engages in some minor money-making activity (e.g., selling stamps). There have been many suggestions for ways to put the United Nations on an independent financial footing (e.g., taxing satellites, exploiting the seas and other "international" areas, getting a percentage of customs duties), but the fact is that many nation-states don't want the United Nations to be independent. They are jealous of the financial leverage they exercise and are fearful that an independent international organization might challenge their own power.

International Civil Service. The Secretariat has three special problems: (1) administrative isolation, (2) internationality, and (3) the political role of the secretary-general. First, the Secretariat has administrative responsibility for the United Nations, yet it is cut loose from both the stabilizing traditions of a national environment and the political guidance a civil service would normally receive from such authoritative policy-makers as a prime minister and a cabinet.

Second, internationality leads to the obvious conflict between the neutrality of an international civil service and the national origins of the individuals who seek careers within the U.N. administration. Sir Eric Drummond, the first secretary-general of the League of Nations, instituted the modern U.N. Secretariat practice of having an integrated bureaucracy rather than national groups. The pattern was solidified under Trygve Lie, the first secretary-general of the United Nations. In response to difficulties some member states raised over the national loyalty of their citizens serving with the United Nations, it became policy that such citizens owed ultimate allegiance to their states, but were to be free from day-to-day policy directives from them.

A related problem involves Article 101(3) of the charter, which presents a dilemma not unknown to the administrations of multinational companies. The article notes: "The paramount consideration in the employment of the staff and in the determination of the conditions of service shall be the necessity of securing the highest standards of efficiency, competence, and integrity." Yet after certifying the importance of professionalism, the same article goes on to state a potentially conflicting consideration that some critics feel has become too dominant: "Due regard shall be paid to the importance of recruiting the staff on as wide a geographical basis as possible." Quota hiring is never likely to be a happy solution. In the U.N. context it has been exacerbated by allegations that some states use their quota for nepotism and as an international spoils system. On the other hand, all nations have a right to feel they have a fair share in the operation of the common organization. One can only hope that this particular problem will eventually adjust itself.

The third special problem of the Secretariat concerns the political role of the secretary-general. Since he is the primary elected official of the United Nations and its major individual representative, the secretary-general's actions naturally become political—a role for which there is in fact adequate charter authority. The secretary-general must walk a fine line, however, between aggravating states (especially the Big Powers) by political activism and dooming the international voice to impotency. States can easily see the secretary-general as a great international spirit and leader for peace when they happen to agree, but condemn him quickly as a meddling fool when they do not agree.

Trygve Lie, who had been an active politician and had served as Norwegian foreign minister, brought political activism and controversy to the office. During his term (1946–1953), which was complicated by the fledgling nature of the United Nations and the intensity of Cold War politics, he did not hesitate to take political positions—he supported, for example, both the U.N. action in Korea and the seating of mainland China, which earned him the antagonism of both sides. When the Soviet Union vetoed his re-election in 1951, the General Assembly simply extended his term three years (although he resigned in 1953). The charter does not specify the term of office, although the General Assembly has agreed on five years (which can be modified if circumstances call for it).

Dag Hammarskjöld of Sweden (1953–1961), the second secretary-general, brought quiet diplomacy and technical professionalism to the office. He had served as a professional diplomat. Unfortunately he became embroiled in the Congo crisis, which prompted the Soviet Union at one point to advocate a "troika," or three-headed Secretariat (the two Cold War sides and a neutral)—providing in effect a veto over Secretariat activities. It was during a night flight in the Congo, trying to bring peace to the area, that Hammarskjöld was killed in a plane crash. U Thant of Burma (1961–1971) and Kurt Waldheim of Austria (1971–   ) have tried to use the secretary-generalship to reduce Cold War hostilities and bring disputants into discussions. Both have tried to be innovative within the limits of the office and focus world attention on problems that need attention.

Economic, Social, and Trusteeship Efforts. In line with the United Nations' duty to promote economic and social development, several important agencies and programs have been established. Important ones include (1) the United Nations Conference on Trade and Development (UNCTAD), established as a permanent organ of the General Assembly in 1964 to promote international trade with the goal of accelerating economic development; (2) the United Nations Development Program (UNDP), which is the main channel for multilateral technical and preinvestment assistance to low-income nations; (3) the United Nations Industrial Development Organization (UNIDO), established in 1967 by the General Assembly to stimulate the industrialization of developing countries; (4) the United Nations Institute for Training and Research (UNITAR), which helps developing countries train national officials; and (5) the World Food Program, a joint U.N./Food and Agriculture Organization (FAO) operation that seeks to stimulate economic and social development via food aid.

United Nations efforts in these areas have had encouraging success, although not nearly as much success as many would like, considering what remains to be done in the world. There are problems as well, however. The overwhelming nature of the world's economic and social problems, as reviewed in Chapter 6, make even the best U.N. efforts seem insignificant. Further, there have been difficulties coordinating programs, controlling duplication and bureaucratic empire-building, and keeping politics out of the aid programs. Donor nations tend to prefer bilateral aid (given directly to a recipient country), which they can more easily relate to their own foreign policy goals, rather than multilateral aid given through the machinery of the United Nations. Recipient countries, on the other hand, prefer U.N. aid on the theory that it will come without political strings attached. International aid, which is nowhere near as generous as it might be, also often gets tangled up in such administrative issues as "give aid *only* when it is a *good investment*" and "watch out for local corruption, poor planning, and waste." Whether aid is given under tight controls or given blindly, however, the truly needy often barely benefit.

In addition to the general administrative responsibility of the General Assembly and ECOSOC concerning the above kinds of programs, thirteen separate, autonomous "specialized agencies" are integrated into the U.N. system through the machinery of ECOSOC. Including such agencies as the World Health Organization (WHO), the Food and Agriculture Organization (FAO), the International Labor Organization (ILO), the International Bank for Reconstruction and Development (IBRD, or World Bank), and others (see Figure 8-1), the specialized agencies bear a large part of the United Nations' economic and social burden. They share the successes and difficulties discussed above, as well as posing some dilemmas of their own. For example, WHO has been able to save many lives throughout the world through improved health care, yet FAO has not been able simultaneously to feed all those extra people who normally might have died. Policy problems of distributing aid then are combined with agonizing moral questions. Saving x number of lives by better health care may only postpone death from ultimate starvation and in the process cause the death of y others because of the extra demand for limited food supplies. What then is the "good" policy?

In the area of trusteeship, much of the problem would appear to have been solved. The colonial empires that existed at the time of World War II have disappeared. By the mid-1970s, even the Portuguese colonies in Africa, which were the last of the imperial holdings and which only months before the Portuguese government had said would never be given up, were achieving independence. Of the eleven trust territories originally placed under the Trusteeship Council, only one remains: the Pacific Islands (Marianas, Carolines, and Marshalls) administered by the United States as a strategic trust (that is, under the ultimate supervision of the Security Council rather than the General Assembly). The prospects for the full independence of this remaining trust area depend in part on whom one listens to, but it would seem that there is at least some movement toward a termination of the Trusteeship Agreement. The Marianas expressed in a plebiscite in June 1975 a desire for political union with the United States, but political divisions in the remainder of the islands leave their status unclear.

The only major problem area left seems to be South West Africa (Namibia), although there are other non-self-governing territories in which the United Nations takes an interest. South West Africa (a former German colony) was administered by the Union (now Republic) of South Africa under the League of Nations mandate system, but following the demise of the League, South Africa refused to place the territory under the U.N.'s Trusteeship System.

Because of South Africa's practice of apartheid (racial segregation), its control of South West Africa has been a particularly sensitive issue with the growing number of black African states in the United Nations (although to be fair, it should be noted that several of South Africa's accusers hardly have clean hands regarding the equal treatment of racial and ethnic groups within their own countries). Liberia and Ethiopia took the question of South West Africa's status to the ICJ, but in July 1966 the Court declined to rule on the merits of the case on the grounds that the two plaintiffs had not established any legal right in the subject of their claims.

In October 1966, the General Assembly voted overwhelmingly to terminate South Africa's mandate over the territory and administer the area through an eleven-member U.N. council. On January 30, 1970, the Security Council adopted a resolution declaring the continued presence of South African authorities in Namibia illegal, and in July 1970, the Security Council asked the International Court of Justice for an advisory opinion on the legal consequences of South Africa's continued presence in Namibia. The Court's opinion, delivered on June 21, 1971, was that South Africa should withdraw from Namibia and that U.N. members "are under obligation to recognize the illegality of South Africa's presence in Namibia and the invalidity of its acts on behalf of or concerning Namibia."

In spite of continuing U.N. declarations concerning South West Africa, however, the Republic of South Africa continues to control the area. While U.N. members may be willing to take positive and often strident verbal positions in U.N. resolutions, few seem to be prepared to move deliberately against another sovereign state.

Collective Security and Peace-keeping. Every scholar who studies the United Nations must ponder the idea of "collective security," for not only is keeping world peace the major function of the United Nations, but one has to examine whether or not the peace-keeping structure of the United Nations is based on sound premises.

Collective security exists because of the realization that states cannot (or will not) always settle their disputes peacefully. When trouble does appear, collective security means that the world community will police itself by uniting against the troublemaker(s). Any potential law-breaking state, knowing in advance that the other states would line up against it, should ideally be dissuaded from threatening world peace in the first place. The international instrument for coordinating the collective security effort is the United Nations Security Council.

The scholarly literature discussing collective security generally emphasizes the world's present inability to meet the preconditions implicit in a viable theory of collective security and stresses certain basic themes.[4] The idea of collective security involves the same kind of dilemma as does the Bible. If human beings really would conduct themselves as the Bible advises, the Bible would not be needed. Collective security assumes that states are both foolish enough to get into trouble and wise enough to get out of it. The logical question then becomes, "If they are so smart, why do they get into trouble to begin with?"

The strongest aspect of collective security is the legal mandate to keep the peace given to the Security Council by the U.N. Charter. That mandate is backed up by an organizational structure that, in addition to the Security Council, includes the Military Staff Committee (Article 47). The Military Staff Committee is composed of the chiefs of staff of the five permanent members of the Security Council (or their representatives) and is charged with advising and assisting the Council on military matters, with the strategic direction of

4 See, for example, the discussions in Inis Claude, Jr., *Swords into Plowshares*, 3d ed. rev., Random House, Inc., New York, 1971, chap. 12; Hans J. Morgenthau, *Politics among Nations*, 5th ed., Alfred A. Knopf, Inc., New York, 1973, chap. 24; and A. F. K. Organski, *World Politics*, 2d ed., Alfred A. Knopf, Inc., New York, 1968, chap. 16.

armed forces placed at its disposal, and with the regulation of armaments and possible disarmament. This strength has remained only a potential, however, because Big Power disagreements have tended to deadlock the Security Council and have made the Military Staff Committee dormant.

Much of the problem (and a consistent theme in the literature on collective security) relates to the difficulty, discussed in earlier chapters, of defining peace and of identifying a status quo or "condition x" that everyone agrees is desirable and worthy of worldwide support. It is unreasonable to expect solid community support for the maintenance of a common peace, considering the political, ideological, and power diversity of the world. This diversity is reflected in political and military alliance systems. National suspicions are reflected in the notable failure of U.N. disarmament efforts, in the guarded support for arms regulation (such as the Nuclear Non-Proliferation Treaty and the SALT Agreements), and in the unwillingness to hamper future foreign policy flexibility.

While the foregoing factors explain why collective security is not working (and cannot be expected to work under current world conditions) as the charter intended, the United Nations is not necessarily left without a valid peace-keeping role. In fact, the United Nations peace-keeping efforts over the years reflect its continuing attempts to define that role.

The United Nations has been rather successful in sending observer groups to supervise truce areas and ceasefires. Since the earliest days of the United Nations, groups have been sent to such areas as the Balkans, Indonesia, Palestine, Kashmir, and the Middle East. The real controversy between the Security Council and General Assembly over peace-keeping responsibility has occurred when major U.N. peace forces have been fielded.

The Korean operation in 1950 began under the direction of the Security Council (due to the chance absence of the Soviet delegate in protest over the Chinese representation question), but it became a General Assembly responsibility under the Uniting for Peace resolution after the Soviet delegate returned in August 1950 and cast a veto. The resolution (adopted in November 1950) had the following major provisions: (1) if it is not already in session, the General Assembly can meet in emergency special session within twenty-four hours upon a request of either a majority of its own members or any nine (seven until it was changed by the 1965 charter amendment to

Art. 27) members of the Security Council; (2) the General Assembly, if the Security Council fails to exercise its primary responsibility for the maintenance of peace, may consider threats or breaches of the peace and acts of aggression and may make *recommendations* (remember that *only* the Security Council has a legal mandate to *order* action under Chapters V and VII of the charter) to members concerning collective measures to restore international peace and security; (3) a Peace Observation Commission of fourteen members (including the five permanent members of the Security Council) is to observe and report on tension areas; and (4) a Collective Measures Committee of fourteen members is to report on collective methods that might help maintain peace.

Since the Korean conflict, the Uniting for Peace resolution has been invoked four times: during the 1956 Middle East crisis, following an Anglo-French veto, at the time of the Hungarian Revolution, during the 1958 Middle East tension, and during the 1960 Congo crisis—the last three following a Soviet veto. The Hungarian situation was over quickly after Russian tanks moved to re-establish "socialist order," but there was probably little the United Nations could have done anyway given the serious Big Power (that is, Soviet) interest in the area.

The 1958 Middle East affair was also resolved fairly quickly. Lebanon had complained to the Security Council in May 1958 that the United Arab Republic (U.A.R.) was interfering in its internal affairs (the accusations included arms-smuggling, infiltration of armed bands, and acts of terrorism). A United Nations Observer Group (UNOGIL) was sent to Lebanon in June. At the request of the Lebanese government, the United States sent marines to Lebanon in July. At about that time Jordan also complained to the Security Council about U.A.R. activities and requested troops from the U.S. and the United Kingdom, to which the latter responded. The Arab states then moved to resolve the problem on their own by agreeing to honor the provisions of the pact establishing the Arab League, by which member states had promised not to interfere in one another's internal affairs. United States and British troops were pulled out in late October/early November, and by December 1958 UNOGIL ceased operations.

The 1956 Middle East UNEF (United Nations Emergency Force) and the 1960 ONUC (Opération des Nations Unies au Congo), however, raised significant questions concerning the U.N.'s peace-keeping function (the financial crisis they caused was discussed earlier in this chapter).

After Egypt nationalized the Suez Canal on July 26, 1956, and while talks were still in progress concerning compensation, Israeli forces invaded Egypt (October 1956) in response to alleged commando raids from Egyptian territory. The British and French governments announced the landing of Anglo-French paratroopers because they said Israeli and Egyptian forces had not responded to their demand to withdraw from the canal area. The United Nations General Assembly called for a cease-fire, following a Security Council deadlock, and Lester Pearson of Canada proposed UNEF, establishing a U.N. presence between opposing forces to pacify the area until political solutions could be reached. Twenty-four U.N. member states offered to participate in UNEF, but troops were accepted from only ten states: Brazil, Canada, Colombia, Denmark, Finland, India, Indonesia, Norway, Sweden, and Yugoslavia. The Arab-Israeli confrontation will be examined further in the next chapter.

ONUC was a response to the chaos created by Belgium's precipitous withdrawal from the Congo, leaving behind a new country ill-prepared for independence. Within a week after independence on June 30, 1960, the Congolese army mutinied. In an effort to protect Belgian citizens still within the Congo, the Belgian army re-entered the country. Civil chaos spread as the Congolese government asked the United States for aid. U.S. President Dwight Eisenhower wisely responded that the United Nations should be asked for help, not just one country.

In July of 1960 the Security Council urged Belgium to withdraw its troops (which was accomplished by September 1960) and authorized the secretary-general to take the necessary measures, in cooperation with the Congolese government, to restore domestic order in the Congo. ONUC began as a Security Council undertaking because both the United States and the Soviet Union saw a chance to advance their own foreign policy interests by supporting ONUC and also deny the other an excuse to become personally involved.

ONUC quickly ran into trouble, however. United Nations action, as peace-keeping has developed, depends absolutely upon a request for help from a host government, yet ONUC faced both a breakdown of basic civil law and order and a constitutional crisis. The Congolese government fell apart amid secessionist movements and competing claims to governmental authority. When the General

Assembly, in November 1960, resolved a credentials question in favor of the West-leaning Congo government of Joseph Kasavubu (the Republic of the Congo—now called Zaïre—had been admitted to the United Nations in September 1960), the Soviet Union became increasingly disenchanted with ONUC and with Dag Hammarskjöld, whom they began to criticize bitterly. The Soviet-leaning man in the Congo, Patrice Lumumba, was killed under mysterious circumstances in February 1961. After a Soviet veto of a Security Council resolution that would have endorsed the policies and actions of the secretary-general concerning the Congo, direction of the operation shifted to the General Assembly.

ONUC was in an impossible situation. Depending on voluntary troops from twenty-nine nations, some contingents of which were not well disciplined, ONUC found that its actions—or lack of actions—ended up favoring one of the disputing factions. The action dragged on, not only involving the United Nations in the domestic affairs of a sovereign state but running up debts to continue supporting the undertaking. ONUC was finally able to withdraw by mid-1964, its most successful accomplishment, perhaps often overlooked, being providing technical assistance to train the Congolese to fill the positions suddenly vacated by the Belgians.

ONUC probably was a high point for General Assembly involvement in peace-keeping. To avoid future unending entanglements, there seems to be a consensus that peace-keeping forces, if there are to be any at all, should be under the auspices of the Security Council. The U.N. Force in Cyprus (UNFICYP), agreed on by the Security Council in March 1964, seems to represent the new pattern of U.N. peace-keeping. Following intercommunal violence between Greek and Turkish Cypriots in late 1963, the Security Council, continuing the practice of soliciting voluntary troops, ultimately sent in UNFICYP with the approval and cooperation of the host government. In addition, the mandate for the force was to expire automatically after a limited time (three months) unless it was explicitly extended and received prior financing.

Clearly the United Nations cannot act in areas where the Big Powers have important and immediate foreign-policy interests, as the Hungarian example shows. Further, it can act in other areas only dissolve, as happened in the Congo, U.N. peace-keeping efforts will so long as it has at least tacit Big Power support. Should this support encounter difficulty. Dag Hammarskjöld offered the concept of "preventive diplomacy" in his Annual Report to the General Assembly in 1960 to describe the United Nations' actual peace-keeping role.[5]

He conceded that the United Nations could not be effective in areas within the spheres of influence of the parties involved in the Cold War, but only in the peripheral areas where the Big Powers would find it in their mutual interest to curb the intrusion of Cold War politics. Figure 8-2 suggests a more modern view of preventive diplomacy, showing a triangular structure for Big Power spheres of influence. The areas where two spheres overlap are outstanding points of contact and conflict between Big Powers. In the shaded area where all three spheres overlap, the primary level of dispute among the three is probably more ideological than specific (the figure itself is intended only to be suggestive, not comprehensive). The United Nations can do little within those spheres, but with Big Power support (and with the support of the lesser powers, who must resist trying to play the Big Powers off against one another), it can establish a U.N. diplomatic presence in other areas and work to stabilize tense situations while preventing active Big Power involvement. So while collective security is not working as the charter intended, the United Nations has not given up on its peace-keeping role.

REGIONAL EFFORTS AT ORDER

Attempts to organize and regulate international relations on a regional basis have old historical roots. Article 21 of the League of Nations Covenant recognized the role of pre-existing regional arrangements:

Nothing in this Covenant shall be deemed to affect the validity of international engagements, such as treaties of arbitration or regional understandings like the Monroe Doctrine, for securing the maintenance of peace.

By the time of the San Francisco Conference several groups, such as pan-European groups, the Latin American group, the Arab

5 U.N. General Assembly, *Official Records,* Fifteenth Session, 1960, Suppl. No. 1 A (A/4390/add. 1).

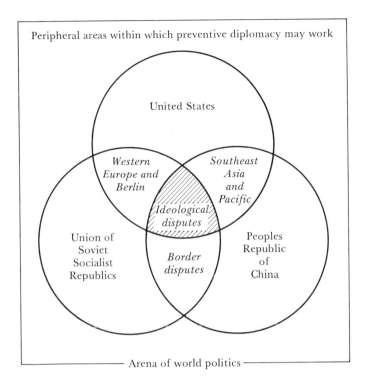

Peripheral areas within which preventive diplomacy may work

United States

Western Europe and Berlin

Southeast Asia and Pacific

Ideological disputes

Union of Soviet Socialist Republics

Border disputes

Peoples Republic of China

Arena of world politics

FIGURE 8-2. World Spheres of Influence of the Major Powers and Area for Preventive Diplomacy

group, and the Soviet bloc, were expressing interest in regionalism. The U.N. Charter seems to provide for regional arrangements in a rather negative fashion through the text of Article 52 (1):

Nothing in the present Charter precludes the existence of regional arrangements or agencies for dealing with such matters relating to the maintenance of international peace and security as are appropriate for regional action, provided that such arrangements or agencies and their activities are consistent with the Purposes and Principles of the United Nations.

The remainder of Article 52, however, encourages the use of regional arrangements "to achieve pacific settlement of local disputes ... before referring them to the Security Council." Elsewhere the United Nations has supported the idea of regionalism by creating the four regional economic commissions (ECE, ECAFE, ECLA,

ECA) under ECOSOC, and has made it clear that regionalism is concerned not only with peace and security matters, but also with economic and social issues.

Nowhere in the Charter is regionalism defined; however, international practice indicates that general geographical proximity is the dominant factor linking members of regional organizations. Also important is political attitude—the willingness (and/or determination) of a nation-state to consider itself part of a regional group, whether or not it is geographically close. Classifying regional organizations is not easy, in spite of the fact that there appear to be several easily identifiable types. Some observers suggest categorizing them as political, economic, and military, which is somewhat arbitrary, as regional organizations generally serve more than one specific purpose. Other scholars prefer geographical classification, e.g. into European, Asian, or African organizations, but that approach overlooks the fact that organizations in different parts of the world may be much more comparable than neighboring regional organizations. Rather than attempting to be comprehensive, the following section examines primarily three organizations (NATO, the European Communities, and the Organization of American States) simply because they are interesting examples of regional organizations.

NATO

The North Atlantic Treaty Organization (NATO) was formed in 1949 as a defensive alliance to protect the North Atlantic countries from the growing Soviet power in Eastern Europe. Because Chapter VIII (Articles 52, 53, and 54) of the charter appears to place regional arrangements under the ultimate authority of the Security Council, it would have been politically difficult, once the Cold War had started, for the West to create a defensive organization against the Soviets, since the Soviets might have been able to use their Security Council position to disrupt it. Consequently, NATO (setting a pattern for the regional defensive organizations) is based on the text of Article 51 (Chapter VII) of the charter, which recognizes "the inherent right of individual or collective self-defense." The only obligation to the Security Council is to report immediately any "measures taken."

The NATO alliance united twelve countries (Belgium, Canada, Denmark, France, Iceland, Italy, Luxembourg, the Netherlands, Norway, Portugal, the United Kingdom, and the United States) in

1949. Greece and Turkey joined in 1952, and West Germany became a member in 1955 (an event which the Soviet bloc claimed provoked their formation of the Warsaw Pact to counter NATO and a rearmed Germany).

The major organ of the alliance is the North Atlantic Council, which is in permanent session, often meeting several times a week, and attended by ambassadors (called permanent representatives) from the fifteen member countries. Two or three times a year the Council convenes at the ministerial level, with foreign, defense, or finance ministers present. Decisions of the Council are reached by unanimous consent. The Council is chaired by a secretary-general, who also directs an international secretariat. NATO's military structure is under a Military Committee, which is subordinate to the Defense Planning Committee (composed of permanent representatives and chaired by the secretary-general). The Council has also created a series of committees, reporting to it, dealing with such areas as information, economic affairs, nuclear defense affairs, political affairs, armament, and emergency planning. Since 1955, an "unofficial" Parliamentary Conference (made up of parliamentarians from the member countries) has evolved. Now meeting annually, this Conference makes recommendations to the NATO Council.

The crucial paragraph of the NATO Treaty is Article 5, which is often misunderstood by the public. The member states have no automatic commitment to go to war; rather, the actual commitment is *to cooperate* and *to consider* appropriate assistance to one another. Article 5 of the NATO Treaty reads:

The Parties agree that an armed attack against one or more of them in Europe or North America shall be considered an attack against them all, and consequently they agree that, if such an armed attack occurs, each of them, in exercise of the right of individual or collective self-defense recognized by Article 51 of the Charter of the United Nations, will assist the Party or Parties so attacked by taking forthwith, individually and in concert with the other Parties, such action *as it deems necessary*, including the use of armed force, to restore and maintain the security of the North Atlantic area. (Emphasis added)

Any such armed attack and all measures taken as a result thereof shall immediately be reported to the Security Council. Such measures shall be terminated when the Security Council has taken the measures necessary to restore and maintain international peace and security.

Although NATO is primarily a defense organization, the NATO Treaty also directs the member countries to cooperate on political and economic matters. At the military level, NATO has fostered an unprecedented degree of coordination. In other areas NATO has served as a vehicle for Western discussions on a broad range of topics and has sponsored programs dealing with such areas as scientific research, exchange of scholars, and environmental studies.

The NATO alliance has had at least three major problems. First, because it was created in response to a perceived Soviet threat to Western Europe, NATO's cohesiveness has tended to fluctuate with the bellicosity of Soviet foreign policy. Second, in spite of their promise to consult with one another, the member governments of NATO have tended to work out important policy matters on their own and then inform their partners. A politically embarrassing example of this occurred in 1956, when the British and French failed to consult with the Americans before their intervention in Egypt over the Suez Canal. In any case, NATO members have often followed individualistic foreign policy courses, as illustrated rather prominently by France's decision in 1966 to withdraw French forces from NATO's integrated command (which resulted in the transfer of NATO headquarters from Paris to Brussels).

A third problem has been caused by the domestic politics of NATO's member states and their political squabbles with one another. Examples include Portugal's fight with India over Goa; difficulties caused by the existence of Portugal's African colonies, the collapse of that empire, and the emergence of strong leftist parties in Portugal; the presence of large Communist parties in France and Italy; conflict between Greece and Turkey over Cyprus; U.S. involvement in Vietnam; and Iceland's tense relations with the United Kingdom over fishing rights. While NATO was not primarily intended to handle these kinds of problems, it has weathered them remarkably well. Its cohesion has been good in times of military crisis, and it remains the West's major defensive alliance.

The European Communities

Dreams of European Unity and the Council of Europe. The dream of European unification is as old as Europe itself. From before the Holy Roman Empire to modern times, political and military efforts to integrate Europe have been attempted, without success. Following World War II the attraction of European integration was as great as ever, and it was bolstered by the cruel realities of two world wars.

Many prominent European leaders have been associated with the postwar unification effort, as have several national and international organizations. Organizational efforts had some success in 1947, when the four main organizations working for European union united to form the International Committee of the Movements for European Unity, which set about organizing a massive European conference. The resultant conference, the Congress of Europe, met in May 1948 at The Hague with Winston Churchill as honorary president. The resolutions agreed upon concerned the problems of national sovereignty, the need to merge some sovereign rights for the common good, the need for a European Parliament, the desirability of a court and a charter of human rights, and the goal of a united Europe.

The desire for a European parliament was realized with the signing of the Statute of the Council of Europe in London on May 5, 1949. Linking most of the Western European states, the Council's Statute proclaims in Article 1:

The aim of the Council of Europe is to achieve a greater unity between its members for the purpose of safeguarding and realizing the ideals and principles which are their common heritage and to facilitate their economic and social progress. This aim shall be pursued through the organs of the Council by discussion of questions of common concern and by agreements and common action in economic, social, cultural, scientific, legal and administrative matters, and in the maintenance and further realization of human rights and fundamental freedoms. . . .

The main organs of the Council of Europe are a Committee of Ministers (made up of the foreign ministers of the member states) and a Consultative Assembly (consisting of members drawn from the parliaments of the member states). Given a general mandate and created as a weak intergovernmental organization, the Council has not lived up to its founders' hopes. It has remained largely a political sounding board. Its prominent accomplishments, however, include the articulation of European issues, the formation of transnational political party groups, and the creation of the human rights machinery discussed in the preceding chapter.

The Communities. The European integrative effort that has captured the attention of scholars has been the three European Communities: the European Coal and Steel Community (ECSC), the European Economic Community (EEC), and the European Atomic Energy Community (Euratom). Founded in the same spirit that fostered the Council of Europe, the European Communities were intended to merge the economies, and ultimately the politics, of the member countries through a series of deliberate, concrete steps.

The first step came on May 9, 1950, when French Foreign Minister Robert Schuman proposed the pooling of French and German coal and steel production under a common authority in an organization open to all the countries of Europe. This revolutionary Schuman Plan resulted in the establishment of the ECSC (the ECSC Treaty went into effect in 1952), joining France, Germany, Italy, and the Benelux countries in a common European authority able to make decisions independent of the various member governments. Explaining his plan before the Assembly of the Council of Europe, Robert Schuman said: "The Authority would thus be the first example of a supra-national institution, in the interests of which the participating countries would have to agree to a partial abandonment of sovereignty." [6]

In the same spirit, the six members of ECSC signed two additional treaties, establishing the EEC and Euratom, in 1957. The three treaties are complex instruments for integrating and managing areas of the members' economies, but at least three general themes emerge from the technical complexity. First is the establishment of a customs union, providing for a common external tariff and the free movement of labor, capital, and services among the member states. Second is the goal of ultimate economic union based on fair competition (e.g., restrictive market practices are banned) and common policies in the economic, social, and technical areas. A third theme concerns the pattern of supranational power the member states have vested in specific organs of the Communities.

Since the merging of the organs of the three Communities in 1967, there have been four basic Community institutions (whose authority varies somewhat according to which of the three treaties they are implementing in a specific case): a Council of Ministers

6 "Summary of the Debates in the Consultative Assembly of the Council of Europe," *European Assembly*, 1 (August 7–11, 1950), 49. (Published by authority of the Council of Europe by the Hansard Society.)

(the only institution whose members directly represent the member governments), which makes major policy decisions; a Commission, which initiates and implements policy based on majority vote (although the Council of Ministers is part of the policy process); a European Parliament (currently elected from and by the parliaments of the member states, although the treaties envision eventual direct election), which is consulted and has a modest parliamentary role in Community affairs; and a Court of Justice (discussed in the previous chapter), which rules on judicial matters arising under the treaties. Community institutions should not be confused with those of other European organizations such as the Council of Europe, which have similar labels.

In several impressive respects the Community organs have important and independent (that is, supranational) decision-making powers never before yielded to an international organization by sovereign nation-states. The European Communities are an interesting test of functionalist theory (as are likewise the specialized agencies of the United Nations). Functionalism assumes that the path to international unity lies not in a head-on confrontation with national sovereignty, but rather in the quiet transnational organization of social functions.

Ideally, transnational organization would first involve technical and noncontroversial (that is, not *politically* sensitive) areas. It would then spread (picking up a momentum of its own) to other sectors that are politically more important, but without provoking national fears of a threat to sovereignty because the approach is piecemeal, building gradually on past concrete agreements. For example, the transnational agreement to standardize railroad gauges could expand step by step to include common load limits, tariffs, railway employment practices, wages, and retirement benefits, ultimately directing transnational attention toward social and economic policies.

While the European Communities follow somewhat the functionalist scenario, experience has shown that integration quickly leaves the noncontroversial and touches sensitive national nerves. Many Europeans may dream of realizing Winston Churchill's famous call during a 1946 speech in Zurich for a "United States of Europe," but many others are more impressed with Charles de Gaulle's call for "*l'Europe des États*"—a Europe that cooperates within the more traditional intergovernmental framework and favors national sovereignty over supranational institutions. The expansion of the Communities in 1973 (to include the United Kingdom, Denmark, and Ireland), the potential future growth through expansion and association with other states, and the obvious political and economic issues that will have to be faced by the member states make the future direction of the European experiment no foregone conclusion. Nevertheless, the fate of the experiment will have important implications for the concept of international regional organizations.

Organization of American States and Other Regional Organizations

Organization of American States. While NATO is primarily military and the European Communities are economic and political, the Organization of American States (OAS) is concerned with all three areas. Historically, the OAS can be traced organizationally to the formation in 1890 of the International Union of American Republics, which was not really an organization at all, but rather a series of conferences designed to promote trade and peaceful settlement of disputes. This "organization" was assisted by a bureau that came to be known as the Pan-American Union.

Intrahemispheric cooperation was hampered by U.S. hegemony, rationalized by the Monroe Doctrine and its Roosevelt Corollary (see the discussion of U.S. foreign policy in Chapter 5), but President Franklin Roosevelt's formal articulation of the Good Neighbor Policy in 1933 made possible increased hemispheric cooperation based on national sovereign equality.

Following World War II, at the 1945 Mexico City Conference, the Act of Chapultepec reaffirmed the concept of the security of the hemisphere against outside intervention and the principle that an attack against one was an attack against all. This declaration of principles appeared formally in the 1947 Inter-American Treaty of Reciprocal Assistance (Rio Treaty), which, among other features, provided for a mutual security system against aggression in the Western Hemisphere and in this respect became the model for subsequent defense organizations such as NATO and SEATO. The following year (1948), the Ninth International Conference of American States, meeting in Bogotá, established the OAS. Twenty-one American states agreed to the OAS Charter, although Cuban participation (that of Fidel Castro's government) was suspended in 1962.

The major organs of the OAS include (1) an Inter-American Conference, the "supreme organ" of the OAS, which meets every five years to consider a wide range of American matters; (2) the Meeting of Consultation of Ministers of Foreign Affairs, which is responsible for security matters under the Rio Treaty and other urgent problems; (3) the Council, an ambassadorial-level body (subordinate to the previous two organs) that serves as a coordinating agency for the OAS; (4) the Pan-American Union, which serves as a secretariat for the OAS; (5) Specialized Conferences, called to develop cooperation in technical areas; and (6) Specialized Organizations, which are similar in function to the specialized agencies that are part of the U.N. system.

At the San Francisco Conference, the American states pressed actively for regional dispute settlement procedures, which eventually appeared in Article 51 and Chapter VIII of the U.N. Charter. In fact the OAS has been active in dealing with regional problems and crises, including Castro's revolution, the 1965 Dominican Republic crisis (which resulted in the intervention of an OAS Peace Force), and revolutionary guerrilla activity. The OAS's peace-keeping record has not reflected, however, the kind of cooperation with the U.N. Security Council that the charter calls for. Further, the OAS has tended to be dominated by the United States, which is not surprising since it is the major partner in the organization. Questions of hemispheric social progress, economic development, and political stability are continuing challenges for the region. The fate of the Alliance for Progress, a plan for development aid to Latin America suggested by President John Kennedy in 1961, has perhaps been symptomatic of the hemisphere's organizational difficulties. This ambitious plan was unsuccessful as a result of the overwhelming nature of the problem, lack of solid support, and mutual recriminations.

A thorough understanding of the world's regional organizational efforts depends on a careful review of the national politics of the countries in a region and a study of the organizational dynamics that have developed within the framework of a given organization. The foregoing examination of three regional efforts has been intended to provide a minimum acquaintance with the kinds of things regionalism represents.

Other Regional Organizations. There are several other regional organizations of note. The *Arab League,* founded in 1945, joins Islamic states in the Middle East and North Africa in a loose political and economic cooperative union. Although unity has been a problem in the past, the organization has served as an agent of Arab nationalism, of anti-Israel sentiment, of caucus politics in the United Nations, and even of modest regional peace-keeping. The other major organization in the area is the *Organization of African Unity* (OAU), created in 1963. Comprising nearly all the states on the continent (South Africa and Rhodesia are notable exceptions), this loose association of states has been concerned with ending colonialism, promoting political unity (pan-Africanism has, for example, been a fleeting vision) and economic development, and providing security for African states. The OAU has also served as a caucusing group in the United Nations on questions of mutual interest.

Two significant Asian regional economic efforts are the *Colombo Plan* and the *Association of Southeast Asian Nations* (ASEAN). Started as a Commonwealth development program in 1950, the Colombo Plan provides multilateral consultative machinery for coordinating assistance programs among its more than twenty members, primarily from the Southeast Asian area. The United States (a major aid donor), the United Kingdom, and Canada are also members. ASEAN was established in 1967 to promote regional economic and social progress among its members (Indonesia, Malaysia, Philippines, Singapore, and Thailand).

BIBLIOGRAPHY

Alker, Hayward R., and B. N. Russet. *World Politics in the General Assembly*, rev. ed. Yale University Press, New Haven, Conn., 1965.

Bailey, Sydney D. *Voting in the Security Council.* Indiana University Press, Bloomington, 1970.

Ball, Margaret M. *The OAS in Transition.* The Duke University Press, Durham, N.C., 1969.

Beer, Francis A. *Integration and Disintegration in NATO.* Ohio State University Press, Columbus, 1969.

Beloff, Max. *Europe and the Europeans.* Chatto & Windus, Ltd., London, 1957.

Bowett, D. W. *The Law of International Institutions.* Frederick A. Praeger, Inc., New York, 1963.

Boyd, James M. *United Nations Peace-Keeping Operations: A Military and Political Appraisal.* Frederick A. Praeger, Inc., New York, 1971.

Buchan, Alastair, *NATO in the 1960's.* Frederick A. Praeger, Inc., New York, 1960.

Burns, Arthur Lee, and Nina Heathcote. *Peace-Keeping by UN Forces: From Suez to the Congo.* Frederick A. Praeger, Inc., New York, 1963.

Claude, Inis L., Jr. *Swords into Plowshares,* 3d ed. Random House, Inc., New York, 1971.

———. *The Changing United Nations.* Random House, Inc., New York, 1967.

Collective Defense in South East Asia. A Report by a Chatham House Study Group. Oxford University Press, London, 1958.

Dallin, Alexander. *The Soviet Union at the United Nations.* Frederick A. Praeger, Inc., New York, 1962.

El-Ayouty, Yassin. *The United Nations and Decolonization.* Nijhoff, The Hague, 1971.

Fedder, Edwin H. *NATO: The Dynamics of Alliance in the Postwar World.* Dodd, Mead & Company, Inc., New York, 1973.

Gardner, Richard N. *In Pursuit of World Order.* Frederick A. Praeger, Inc., New York, 1964.

Gordenker, Leon, ed. *The United Nations in International Politics.* Princeton University Press, Princeton, N.J., 1971.

Haas, Ernst B. *Beyond the Nation State: Functionalism and International Organization.* Stanford University Press, Stanford, Calif., 1964.

Hovet, Thomas, Jr. *Bloc Politics in the United Nations.* Harvard University Press, Cambridge, Mass., 1960.

Jacob, Philip E., Alexine L. Atherton, and Arthur Wallenstein. *The Dynamics of International Organization,* rev. ed. The Dorsey Press, Homewood, Ill., 1972.

Kay, David A. *The New Nations in the United Nations, 1960–1967.* Columbia University Press, New York, 1970.

Lacqueur, Walter. *The Rebirth of Europe.* Holt, Rinehart and Winston, Inc., New York, 1970.

Lefever, Ernst W. *Crisis in the Congo.* The Brookings Institution, Washington, D.C., 1965.

Mayne, Richard. *The Community of Europe: Past, Present and Future.* W. W. Norton & Company, Inc., New York, 1963.

McDonald, Robert W. *The League of Arab States.* Princeton University Press, Princeton, N.J., 1965.

Mitrany, David. *A Working Peace System.* Quadrangle Books, Inc., Chicago, 1966.

Mydral, Gunnar. *Realities and Illusions in Regard to Inter-Governmental Organizations.* Oxford University Press, New York, 1955.

Nye, Joseph S., ed. *International Regionalism: Readings.* Little, Brown and Company, Boston, 1968.

Nye, Joseph S. *Peace in Parts: Integration and Conflict in Regional Organization.* Little, Brown and Company, Boston, 1971.

Robertson, A. H. *The Council of Europe—Its Structure, Functions and Achievements.* Frederick A. Praeger, Inc., New York, 1956.

Rubinstein, Alvin Z., and George Ginsburgs, eds. *Soviet and American Policies in the United Nations: A Twenty-five Year Perspective.* New York University Press, New York, 1971.

Russell, Ruth B. *The United Nations and United States Security Policy.* The Brookings Institution, Washington, D.C., 1968.

Sewell, James Patrick. *Functionalism in World Politics.* Princeton University Press, Princeton, N.J., 1966.

Solomon, Slonim. *South West Africa and the United Nations: An International Mandate in Dispute.* The Johns Hopkins Press, Baltimore, 1973.

Stoessinger, John G. *The United Nations and the Superpowers,* rev. ed. Random House, Inc., New York, 1970.

Wainhouse, David W., et al. *International Peacekeeping at the Crossroads.* The Johns Hopkins Press, Baltimore, 1973.

International Diplomacy

International law and organization provide a framework for international relations, but it is international diplomacy that makes the process work. Diplomacy is the vehicle through which nation-states "talk" to each other.

The prominent British diplomat-scholar Sir Harold Nicolson called attention to the careless and varied use of the term "diplomacy" and identified five different meanings. "Diplomacy," he wrote, could be used from one moment to the next to mean such varied things as (1) a synonym for foreign policy, (2) another term for "negotiation," (3) the "processes and machinery" for conducting negotiations, (4) a specific branch of the Foreign Service, or (5) an abstract personal "quality or gift." [1] With a little careful thought, one could probably add several further meanings.

Sir Harold Nicolson suggests that "diplomacy is the management of international relations by negotiation." [2] Perhaps the only basic definitional distinction that needs to be made here is between "foreign policy" and "diplomacy." Foreign policy concerns the political direction and goals of a nation-state in international relations. Diplomacy provides the tools for achieving foreign policy goals.

Yet even the distinction between politician and diplomat, and their respective professions, is often blurred. Particularly in modern times with rapid means of communication, political leaders of one country are tempted to try to deal directly with their political counterparts in other countries, bypassing (and sometimes ignoring entirely) traditional diplomatic channels. While a direct diplomatic role for political leaders is occasionally very useful, such a practice should be used wisely and sparingly. Diplomats and politicians bring different skills to a task, and each is professionally responsible to a different constituency. Diplomacy conducted by political leaders is likely to be most effective when there has been careful advance diplomatic preparation and when the publicity that naturally accompanies national figures will be of special value to the particular foreign policy goal being sought. On the other hand, traditional diplomatic channels allow continuing, quiet negotiations without publicity and the resulting danger of prematurely or inadvertently raising public hopes and expectations regarding outcomes.

1 Harold Nicolson, *Diplomacy*, 3d ed., Oxford University Press, London, 1963, pp. 13–14.
2 *Ibid.*, p. 15.

One further distinction: the consular service should not be confused with the diplomatic service. The diplomatic service is responsible for formal intergovernmental negotiations, whereas the consular service looks after commercial and industrial interests and offers protection and other services (e.g., passports and visas) to citizens traveling abroad. Many states have combined the two services. The United States, for example, combined the two as the Foreign Service by the Rogers Act of 1924.

CLASSICAL AND MODERN DIPLOMACY

The evolution of diplomatic methods is interesting because it reveals a great deal about the progressive refinement of this basic element of international relations and about the increasing sophistication and professionalism of governmental attitudes toward other nation-states.

It has become common practice to divide the history of diplomacy into two general periods, classical and modern, or old and new diplomacy. The accepted dividing line is the close of World War I, when Wilson attacked the practices of classical diplomacy and advocated new diplomatic methods.

The Evolution of Classical Diplomacy

Diplomacy can be traced back to antiquity. There are records of the exchange of envoys, the negotiation of treaties, and other basic diplomatic practices in ancient China, India, and Egypt. By the time of ancient Greece, diplomatic practices had begun to assume some established forms. Although there were as yet no permanent embassies or permanent class of professional diplomats, the Greeks conducted interstate relations through ambassadors and missions; they also developed rules concerning diplomatic privileges and immunities. The right to send ambassadors was regarded as inherent in the sovereign powers of a state, and the right to send envoys implied an obligation to receive them from other states. Prominent citizens of a city-state were well informed on the political issues of the day and were called upon to perform ambassadorial duties. It was not unusual for poets, musicians, military officers, or actors to be sent on occasion as envoys. The Romans, for the most part, accepted the diplomatic practices of the Greeks and built upon them.

One scholar concludes the following from the Greek and Roman period:

Even a brief consideration of the development of the rights of envoys among the Greeks and Romans indicates that many of the fundamental principles as they exist today had already been well established more than two thousand years ago in this early cradle of European culture. The fundamental difference was that the embassies at that time were temporary rather than permanent. Permanent legations did not exist because they did not fit the needs of the time.[3]

The growth of political and mercantile contact during the Middle Ages, however, made more formal diplomatic intercourse necessary. Toward the end of the Middle Ages, diplomacy evolved into an established profession.

The Italian city-states were active in laying the groundwork for the classical diplomatic system that developed in Europe. Venice was apparently the first power to maintain permanent residents in foreign capitals. Although the prestige of ambassadors was enhanced by the creation of permanent, professional diplomatic missions, receiving states still regarded diplomats with a great deal of suspicion. This suspicion was not ill-founded, for diplomats as a matter of course engaged in many forms of skulduggery, including espionage, antigovernmental plots, and trickery.

The diplomatic practices established by the Italians in the fifteenth and sixteenth centuries became popular in the rest of Europe. During the next two centuries, however, it was the French who refined those practices and developed the classical style of diplomacy that would last formally until the end of World War I.

Sir Harold Nicolson, in his study *The Evolution of Diplomatic Method*, credits Cardinal Richelieu with establishing several basic principles of classical diplomacy. He notes that "Richelieu was the first to establish that the art of negotiation must be a permanent activity and not merely a hurried endeavour." [4] He also helped

3 Graham H. Stuart, *American Diplomatic and Consular Practice*, 2d ed., Appleton-Century-Crofts, Inc., New York, 1952, p. 118.
4 Harold Nicolson, *The Evolution of Diplomatic Method*, Constable & Co., Ltd., London, 1954, pp. 50–51.

solidify the idea, which would become a central element of European balance-of-power politics, of the primacy of national interest over sentiment. Recall the view of Britain's Lord Palmerston concerning no permanent friends and no permanent enemies—just permanent interests (Chapter 3). Nicolson further notes that "in an age of undisputed autocracy, Richelieu was original also in contending that no policy could succeed unless it had national opinion behind it." [5] So even though diplomacy continued to be a secretive process removed from democratic influence, Richelieu believed diplomatic goals should be supported by a domestic propaganda effort. Other lessons advanced by the Cardinal included caution in signing treaties, serious attention to the exact wording of treaties, and the vesting of control over diplomacy in a single ministry. [6]

Under Louis XIV the French diplomatic service was organized very efficiently, and French replaced Latin as the language of international intercourse (and French has been replaced as a diplomatic language by English in the twentieth century). As the French pattern of diplomacy spread throughout Europe, one of the problems that developed was confusion over titles and precedence among the diplomatic ranks. The Congress of Vienna (1815) established a classification scheme (which was later revised) for diplomats based upon the rank of the agents rather than upon the (often disputed) relative importance of the states they represented.

Classical diplomacy was marked by elaborate ritual, responsible in large measure for the less than flattering modern connotations of powdered wigs and striped pants. The history of the period is filled with examples of international "incidents" and near incidents developing out of diplomatic slights and breaches of etiquette. One such occurrence, although not serious in itself, shows how seriously diplomats regarded their status. The carriages of the French and Spanish ambassadors met on a narrow street in The Hague in 1659, and each refused to yield to the other. After some three hours of stalemate it was decided to tear down a fence to allow the carriages to pass, thus avoiding a diplomatic slight to either ambassador. [7]

The inviolability of diplomatic representatives, a principle that had been evolving for centuries, also became solidly entrenched during this period. As one modern scholar, Clifton Wilson, notes:

5 *Ibid.*, p. 51.
6 *Ibid.*, pp. 52–53.
7 Reported by Stuart, p. 125.

"[t]he international rules of diplomatic privileges and immunities, which are among the oldest examples of international law, are firmly entrenched in practice, treaties and municipal legislation." [8] While special diplomatic rights are occasionally violated, particularly during periods of international tension, the principle is nevertheless a sound one, for it is necessary in order to facilitate international intercourse.

Many theories have been advanced to explain the existence of diplomatic privileges and immunities, but Professor Wilson sees three basic ones—the theories of *personal representation, exterritoriality*, and *functional necessity*.[9] The theory of *personal representation* assumes that the diplomat personally represents the sovereign, and any harm or insult to the diplomat is a personal affront to the sovereign. This was generally more relevant to the classical monachies than it is to modern republican governments.

The theory of *exterritoriality* linked diplomatic immunities with the idea that embassy grounds were foreign territory, not subject to local jurisdiction. Diplomatic personnel were treated as though they were not officially living within the host country. This theory, however, also becomes legally and philosophically hard to rationalize under modern interpretations of the nation-state and government.

The most persuasive explanation of diplomatic privileges and immunities is the theory of *functional necessity*. This theory is based on a dynamic interpretation of the need of sovereign and equal nation-states to conduct daily business with one another in an interdependent world. Diplomatic personnel must be free to conduct their nation's affairs in a foreign state, just as the host state not only needs to do business with foreign diplomats but needs to have reciprocal freedom for its own envoys abroad.

The Launching of Modern Diplomacy

Although classical diplomacy was sound in many respects, its more objectionable aspects became associated with the events leading to World War I. Coinciding largely with the period of classical European balance-of-power politics (1815–1914) discussed in Chapter 3, the "old" diplomacy received part of the blame for the war.

8 Clifton E. Wilson, *Diplomatic Privileges and Immunities*, University of Arizona Press, Tucson, 1967, p. vii.
9 These theories are discussed in *ibid.*, chap. 1.

Classical diplomacy appeared to be dominated by aristocrats, a pompous international elite that conducted a personal foreign policy, garnished with frivolous ritual and insulated from the growing democratic domestic political pressures. "Secret diplomacy" became an expression of opprobrium that summed up for many the secret agreements and understandings that pulled one nation after another into World War I.

President Woodrow Wilson, for one, felt that public knowledge of diplomatic undertakings and agreements would help avoid such disasters. He called for as much in the first of his Fourteen Points:

Open covenants of peace, openly arrived at, after which there shall be no private international understanding of any kind but diplomacy shall proceed always frankly and in the public view.

The founding of the League of Nations represented, formally at least, a break with the old diplomacy and the launching of modern, open diplomacy. The commitment to open diplomacy can be seen most clearly in the parliamentary diplomacy of the League's Assembly and the U.N. General Assembly. There is also institutional support for open agreements in the requirement (Article 102 of the U.N. Charter) that members of the United Nations register "every treaty and every international agreement . . . as soon as possible" with the Secretariat for publication. A sanction is provided by Article 102 in that "[n]o party to any such treaty or international agreement which has not been registered . . . may invoke that treaty or agreement before any organ of the United Nations." The League of Nations Covenant had a similar requirement (Article 18) except that it provided that "[n]o such treaty or international engagement shall be binding until so registered."

Although states have generally supported the principle of registering treaties, there is really no international control (and sometimes even no national control) over private understandings and other kinds of secretive agreements entered into by governments. Two examples are the secret Yalta agreement of February 1945, which was entered into by Roosevelt, Churchill, and Stalin (without the participation of either the U.S. State Department or the British Foreign Office), and the private assurances President Nixon apparently gave to the South Vietnamese government concerning American aid in the event of a major attack from North Vietnam.

The terms of the Yalta agreement were made known to the American Congress after the fact (the full text was released by the State Department in March 1947), much as the American public learned of alleged Nixon administration promises to South Vietnam only after military collapse was imminent.

PARLIAMENTARY AND OTHER FORMS OF
MODERN DIPLOMACY

The "New" Diplomatic Techniques

In the post-Wilsonian era of "new," "modern," "open" diplomacy, many new terms have become popular: parliamentary diplomacy, conference diplomacy, summit diplomacy, and a number of specialized forms of diplomacy (e.g., cultural, technical, economic).

Before these "new" diplomatic techniques are examined, however, two qualifiers should be interjected. First, much of the new diplomacy is nothing more than traditional diplomacy in a new guise. In fact, one of the failings of parliamentary diplomacy has been the tendency of some to assume that all previous negotiation techniques have been superseded by the League of Nations Assembly or the United Nations General Assembly.

Second, although President Wilson advocated change in international relations, helped effect it, and became a symbol for it, to ignore other forces of change would be a mistake. The turmoil of World War I, the revolution in technology and communications (which both undercut the role of the ambassador as an international go-between, since political leaders could now communicate more directly, and enhanced that role by allowing more efficient travel and exchange of information with the home government), increasing popular influence on government policy and more democratic access to foreign service careers, and the growing number of new states that were not familiar with the traditions of European classical diplomacy all helped foster new ground rules for diplomatic intercourse.

Parliamentary Diplomacy

The mechanics of parliamentary diplomacy in the United Nations General Assembly were discussed in the preceding chapter. The

General Assembly (like the League's Assembly before it) is the realization of the hope for a world forum that could discuss problems of international relations publicly. There is value, of course, in that kind of forum. Every nation-state has an opportunity to articulate its problems and its dreams before a world audience. Open debate can serve an educational function by identifying problems, explaining national positions, and proposing solutions. Nation-states may be forced to defend and re-examine their policies in the light of world opinion. International standards may emerge.

On the other hand, excitement over the potential of a world assembly should not cause one to forget the realities of the nation-state system. While the policy majorities that are evident in the General Assembly are a natural result of a parliamentary-style situation, there are limits beyond which sovereign states will not be pushed by voting groups of foreign states. Unfortunately, compromise, which is so necessary to good diplomacy, is often hindered because states have taken public positions in the General Assembly from which they cannot retreat without losing face. Public debate, which can be extremely useful and constructive, can also degenerate into grandstanding, propagandizing, mutual vilifying, and a mindless repeating of national policy lines. The experience of working together in the General Assembly can foster international cooperation, but parliamentary diplomacy can also become a shallow public exercise.

The solution to avoiding a misuse of parliamentary diplomacy lies in understanding (and respecting) the strengths and limitations of public diplomacy. Lester B. Pearson of Canada, founder of the United Nations Emergency Force (UNEF) and recipient of the 1957 Nobel Peace Prize, supported the idea that *all* negotiations should be conducted confidentially, with two reservations.

First, the policies which govern and guide negotiations should be publicly decided and publicly explained. There should be no secret commitments, specific or implied. The people who are asked to make the sacrifices, to man the barricades or die in the trenches when the breakdown of negotiation leads to war, have the right to know, and to approve or disapprove through their elected representatives, every commitment, every major policy that is proposed, and, indeed, every minor one that involves any kind of national obligation. There should be no secret diplomacy of that kind. In other words, the covenants should be open, as well as the policies on which they are based. But the detailed negotiations leading up to them need not be so.

The second reservation covers certain international situations concerning which negotiation can usefully be preceded by open conferences, conducted even with a maximum of publicity, so that international opinion, the international conscience, if you will, can be mobilized and brought to bear on a particular development with maximum impact.[10]

Conference Diplomacy and Summitry

Another form of open diplomacy is conference diplomacy, which results from multilateral international meetings. Parliamentary diplomacy, properly regarded, is in fact an offshoot of the international conference. The United Nations, for example, is a standing diplomatic conference. Although conference diplomacy is not all that new as a diplomatic technique (international conferences in the nation-state era go back to the Peace of Westphalia in 1648), there have been several modern modifications. For one thing, modern means of news reporting and information dissemination make such conferences more open and public access more of a reality. Also, better means of travel allow both more frequent meetings and a greater number of participants. Finally, the growing emphasis on technology and the increasingly interdependent world have increased the need for international consultation and cooperation in a broad range of technical areas.

Conferences may meet regularly at the regional or universal level, like NATO or the International Monetary Fund, or they may meet on an ad hoc basis, like the 1955 Bandung Conference of Afro-Asian states or the 1975 Conference on Security and Cooperation in Europe (CSCE) held in Helsinki, Finland. The CSCE was an interesting combination of conference and summit diplomacy. Summit diplomacy developed under the old monarchical system in Europe when monarchs would meet and personally decide the course of international relations. In modern times, beginning with Woodrow Wilson, a number of U.S. presidents have participated in summit diplomacy. Wilson went to Paris in 1919. Franklin Roosevelt went to a series of famous meetings in such places as Quebec, Casablanca, Cairo, Teheran, and Yalta. President Harry Truman met with Stalin at Potsdam. As Cold War tensions between the United States and

10 Lester B. Pearson, *Diplomacy in the Nuclear Age,* Harvard University Press, Cambridge, Mass., 1959, p. 36.

the Soviet Union increased, people began to view the summit conference as a means of somehow cutting through bureaucratic red tape, brushing aside hindrances, and resolving differences quickly at the highest level. President Dwight Eisenhower went to Geneva in 1955 to meet with the Soviets, which they used primarily for propaganda purposes, and to an ill-fated meeting with Soviet Premier Khrushchev in Paris during 1960 following the U-2 spy plane incident. President Kennedy met with Khrushchev in Vienna in 1961, and President Lyndon Johnson met with Soviet Premier Aleksei Kosygin at Glassboro, New Jersey, in 1967. President Nixon and President Ford have likewise gone to summit meetings.

1975 Conference on Security and Cooperation in Europe (CSCE)

President Gerald Ford's appearance at the Helsinki Conference in 1975 was an example of the type of summit diplomacy that has evolved since the Kennedy administration. Without careful and detailed advance preparation, summit meetings are an inefficient and even potentially dangerous form of diplomacy. The high drama of chiefs gathering may raise public hopes that cannot be fulfilled, and there is no particular reason why heads of state acting in public should be able to solve problems more easily than ministries of foreign affairs working quietly on a problem full time. Former U.S. Secretary of State Dean Rusk commented: "The direct confrontation of the chiefs of government of the great powers involves an extra tension because the court of last resort is in session." [11] Summitry is likely to work best if the heads of state gather to formalize (and publicize) agreements that have already been worked out in detail by professional staffs.

The Helsinki Conference on Security and Cooperation in Europe had been in preparation for many years. Since 1954, the Soviet Union and its Warsaw Pact allies had pushed for such a conference, initially limited to European states. It was agreed in 1970 that the United States and Canada, as NATO members with important interests in Europe, would also participate. As part of the preparatory work, NATO insisted that some progress be made on the status

11 Dean Rusk, "The President," *Foreign Affairs*, 38 (April 1960), 365.

of Berlin, which was accomplished in June 1972 with the Quadripartite Protocol on Berlin.

In November 1972, the Multilateral Preparatory Talks to explore the bases for a possible conference began. In July 1973, the Conference on Security and Cooperation in Europe opened formally at the foreign-minister level. Work on the substantive areas of CSCE concern lasted from September 1973 to July 1975 in Geneva, when it was announced that a final document would be signed at a summit meeting (July 30–August 1, 1975) in Helsinki. The leaders of thirty-five states showed up for a largely ceremonial conference, signed agreements that had already been hammered out by negotiators, and conducted a little quiet bilateral diplomacy on the side before returning home.

While that kind of stage-managed diplomacy can capitalize on the strengths of both conference and summit diplomacy, the specific document agreed upon at the Helsinki meeting has been the subject of considerable controversy. Supporters have seen it as a first step in preventing World War III, while detractors have called it another Kellogg-Briand Pact—that ill-fated 1928 agreement that was to outlaw war. Supporters from both West and East believe that important concessions have been extracted from the other side, and critics sense a sellout to the other side. The document is not an international treaty, but simply a political statement of intent; it is presumed to have great moral and political weight.

The document has four main sections. The Russians vigorously supported the first, while the West seemed more interested in the implications of the third section. *Section one* concerns *European security* and supports ten principles of interstate relations:

 1 Respect for sovereignty
 2 Nonuse of force
 3 Inviolability of frontiers
 4 Territorial integrity
 5 Peaceful settlement of disputes
 6 Nonintervention
 7 Respect for human rights and fundamental freedoms
 8 Equal rights and self-determination of peoples
 9 Cooperation among states
 10 Fulfillment of international obligations

Western critics have claimed that this section gave the Soviet Union exactly what it wanted, namely, the legitimization of its hegemony in Eastern Europe. On the other hand, Western supporters believe that the ten principles were a realistic recognition of the postwar status quo (in fact the intent of the Conference was not to freeze the status quo, but to improve it) and an official reversal of the "Brezhnev Doctrine" of limited sovereignty, which was used to justify the 1968 Soviet invasion of Czechoslovakia. Further, at Western insistence, a statement was included to note that borders might be changed by peaceful means—a statement directed toward the possible reunification of Germany.

Section two treats *economic, scientific, technical, and environmental cooperation;* it provides for commercial exchanges, increased cooperation, and the promotion of tourism. *Section three* concerns *cooperation in humanitarian and other fields* and provides for such things as freer movement of people, increased exchange and distribution of information (including printed and broadcast media), family reunions, and increased educational and cultural exchange. *Section four* provides for *followup action to the CSCE,* including a 1977 meeting in Belgrade to review results and decide on further courses of action. The Conference on Security and Cooperation was a glowing manifestation of the spirit of East-West détente, but it remains to be seen what concrete results develop out of it.

Specialized Forms of Diplomacy

Several specialized forms of diplomacy (*cultural, technical, economic*) mentioned at the start of this subsection of the present chapter deserve further discussion. *Cultural diplomacy,* which also is not a new idea, is based on the assumption that national foreign policies can be furthered through cultural means—e.g., educational, scientific, or art exchanges; tourism; or propaganda efforts. Cultural diplomacy is presented as a "people-to-people" effort directed toward greater human understanding. If citizens of one state could simply realize that foreigners were basically no different—that they shared the same human hopes and dreams—the task of governments would be made easier. In fact, however, governments often use cultural diplomacy not to promote human understanding but rather as a subtle (and sometimes not so subtle) way to "convert the foreigners," or at least to build foreign support for foreign policy objectives.

Most governments participate in at least modest forms of cultural diplomacy or support private cultural efforts. Two well-known and respected cultural undertakings are the *Alliance française*, founded in 1883 to extend France's influence abroad through the propagation of French language and culture, and the *Goethe Institut*, offering libraries and German-language studies abroad. Many governments also use short-wave radio broadcasts, such as West Germany's *Deutsche Welle*, to present cultural, informational, and political events.

The two governments, however, that have exploited cultural diplomacy most fully, using all the sophisticated communications technology of the twentieth century, are the Soviet Union and the United States. Communist ideology generates an intense urge to proselytize, and the Soviet Union has spared little effort in spreading its version of Truth. There are regular worldwide broadcasts by Radio Moscow, and the world communist press generally supports Soviet policy. The Soviet Union supports massive youth festivals, engages in trade and educational exchanges, supports communist movements abroad, distributes tons of communist literature, and participates in a wide variety of related activities calculated to further the communist movement and/or Soviet foreign policy.

The United States became involved in propaganda on a major scale following World War II and the advent of the Cold War. The chief government agency charged with disseminating the U.S. version of Truth is the United States Information Agency (USIA), which was created in 1953 and operates under the policy control of the U.S. Department of State. One of the USIA's better-known activities is the Voice of America (VOA) broadcast service, but it also engages in motion picture, television, press, and other informational activities. The USIA supports many libraries abroad that feature a sampling of American literature, current periodicals, and cultural lecture series. In several countries USIA facilities have been a target of mob violence in protest against U.S. foreign policy.

Other significant United States cultural efforts include the Fulbright Act of 1946, which uses foreign currencies and credits to finance exchanges of scholars, and the 1948 Smith-Mundt Act, which provides for the exchange of artists, scientists, business executives, and representatives of other prominent cultural areas. The Peace Corps, initiated under the Kennedy administration in 1961, was an effort to send skilled workers as foreign aid. Although the Peace Corps has had its problems, it is an interesting experiment in the export of people-to-people assistance.

Another well-known Western information agency is the strongly anticommunist **Radio Free Europe (RFE)**. Although it is supported by private funds, some observers allege that RFE secretly receives U.S. government money, probably from the Central Intelligence Agency (CIA). Staffed primarily by Eastern European refugees, Radio Free Europe broadcasts to the Eastern European area. Not always in tune with U.S. foreign policy, Radio Free Europe was widely blamed for fostering the false impression among the Hungarians that the United States would come to their aid during the 1956 Hungarian uprising.

The **United Nations** is also involved in cultural diplomacy, primarily through its specialized agency the **United Nations Educational, Scientific and Cultural Organization (UNESCO)**. Headquartered in Paris, UNESCO's purpose is to contribute to peace and security by promoting international collaboration, through recommendations to its member governments and through its own programs, in a broad spectrum of educational, scientific, and cultural areas. Although UNESCO has engaged in some impressive undertakings, it has been the most controversial of the specialized agencies. In the cultural area, for example, some Western states have accused UNESCO of propagating atheistic, procommunist values and advocating world government, while the East has complained of the spread of bourgeois values and Western cultural imperialism. UNESCO's experience surely demonstrates that nation-states regard cultural diplomacy with suspicion if it is not in approximate harmony with national foreign policy objectives.

Another specialized form of foreign policy is *technical diplomacy*. It involves the sending of technical experts and advisers, sophisticated machinery, and scientific technology abroad. Depending upon one's perspective, technical aid may appear to be a means by which the advanced industrial states can help the less developed countries, a means by which the developed states can make the less developed states technologically dependent (which might be translated into foreign policy support), or some combination of both.

Economic diplomacy is similarly used to attain foreign policy objectives. The granting or withholding of foreign aid has traditionally been used as an instrument of foreign policy, as have such economic techniques as the embargo (a government order prohibiting or restricting commerce with foreign states), the boycott (government or privately sponsored cooperative effort to abstain from certain kinds of commercial intercourse with selected target states), and the blockade (a military action to seal off a target state from receiving goods, normally considered an act of war, although traditional international law provides for "pacific blockades" as reprisals for legal wrongs). Bribes are not unknown as an element of economic persuasion in international relations.

For years many Western countries have participated, with mixed success, in an embargo on various categories of exports (particularly "strategic goods") to communist states. The United States has for many years withheld "most-favored-nation" status from the Soviet Union and Eastern Europe, although this policy seems to be changing slowly as a result of détente. Most-favored-nation status means that there will be no trade discrimination, that a trade agreement between one nation and another with most-favored-nation status will be on the same basis as the most favorable agreement already worked out between the first nation and others. Subsequent favorable agreements concluded will automatically apply to all states granted most-favored-nation status.

In other areas of economic diplomacy, African states have urged a boycott of South African goods, Arab states have engaged in a boycott of firms doing business with Israel, and the Soviet Union has sponsored boycotts against Yugoslavia and Albania. Blockades, a very serious undertaking, were used effectively by the North against the South in the American Civil War and by the British against the Germans in World Wars I and II. The Russian attempt in 1948–1949 to strangle the city of Berlin by blockading Western land access routes across East Germany was checked by the famous Berlin Airlift. The U.S. "quarantine" of Cuba in 1962 (discussed in Chapter 1) seemed very much like a blockade, although great care was taken to define it as a selective measure taken against the import of offensive missiles. During the Vietnamese conflict, the possibility of a blockade of the North Vietnamese port of Haiphong was discussed by the United States. Although Haiphong harbor was mined, no formal blockade was undertaken.

At the international level, the League of Nations tried to implement economic sanctions against Italy for its Ethiopian activities. There have been several United Nations resolutions regarding economic sanctions, involving such states as North Korea and communist China, Portugal, South Africa, and Rhodesia. In none of those cases, however, have the sanctions had the desired result. The reasons for this include the lack of unanimity among nations in support of internationally organized economic sanctions and the technical difficulty of enforcing sanctions, given the tremendous complexity of modern world-trading patterns. The most dramatic modern example of economic diplomacy certainly has been the Arab oil embargo.

The United States, Western Europe, and Japan were stunned in 1973 when, after the Fourth Arab-Israeli War, the Arab states initiated an oil embargo to put political pressure on those states that were friendly toward Israel. The Arab states, which had failed in their past attempts to pursue common international goals, surprised both themselves and the world in two significant respects. After three humiliating defeats the 1973 October War revealed that the Arab forces could hold their own in coordinated military action against the Israelis. Also, the effectiveness of the Arab oil embargo revealed both the political utility of an international commodity cartel (a cartel is an international combine, or similar arrangement, formed to regulate prices and production in some business area) and the vulnerability of the industrialized nations to interference with the market for important resources.

There are two basic themes involved in Arab petroleum diplomacy: (1) the relationship between the oil companies and the oil-producing countries and (2) the history of Arab-Israeli relations. Other internationally important factors involved include the overwhelming importance of petroleum in the modern world, the strategic significance of the Middle East, Soviet and American maneuvering for influence in the Arab world, politics among the Arab states and more broadly among the petroleum-exporting states, politics among the petroleum-consuming nations, and the potential new relationships between industrialized states and developing states that have a commodity they feel they can exploit.

The Oil Companies and the Oil-producing Countries

The relationship between the oil companies and the oil-producing countries had been developing in such a way that petroleum diplomacy was rapidly becoming a factor anyway. The 1973 October

War appears to have been merely the catalyst. From the earliest days of the international petroleum industry there never really has been a free market. In fact, from the beginning a few large international companies have attempted, with progressively less success, to restrict competition and control prices. At first the United States was the dominant producer and exporter of petroleum, accounting for over 80 percent of world production during the 1860s and 1870s. The British (particularly in Iran and Iraq) and the Dutch (in Indonesia) soon also became major participants in the market.

Oil companies from these three countries explored for oil in the Middle East under a system of concessions. These concessions provided for the long-term lease of large areas of land, upon which the oil companies would prospect for oil. In the event of an oil discovery, the host country and the company would share the profits according to a formula that had already been worked out. Although the system was efficient, it not surprisingly came under increasing pressure as Arab nationalism increased and the Arabs demanded either new contracts that were more favorable to the host states or outright nationalization.

Seven "international majors" controlled most Middle East oil until the 1970s. These seven major oil companies were Exxon (formerly Standard Oil of New Jersey), Mobil Oil, Standard Oil of California, Gulf Oil, Texaco, the Royal Dutch/Shell Oil Company, and British Petroleum (formerly the Anglo-Iranian Oil Company). Whatever judgments one may wish to pass on their control of oil production and pricing, it was the crumbling of that control that pushed the oil-producing countries into assuming control themselves. There are several explanations for the price instability that had developed by 1960, namely, the entrance of independent oil companies into the Middle East market, overproduction, pressure from oil-consuming nations to keep prices low, and an influx of Soviet oil into Europe.

At a meeting in Baghdad in 1960, oil-producing states gathered to discuss the stabilization of the market and their common interests. With the encouragement of the Venezuelan delegate, five states (Iran, Iraq, Kuwait, Saudi Arabia, and Venezuela) formed the Organization of Petroleum Exporting Countries (OPEC). Membership has since increased to thirteen, including, in addition to the original five, Algeria, Ecuador, Gabon, Indonesia, Libya, Nigeria, Qatar, and the United Arab Emirates.

Although OPEC is widely associated in the public mind with the 1973 oil embargo, the organization was formed primarily to achieve economic goals. Political activism has been encouraged by a smaller organization with membership restricted to Arab countries. This organization, known as OAPEC (Organization of Arab Petroleum Exporting Countries), grew out of discussions held in Baghdad in August 1967 on the Arab-Israeli Six-Day War, which had occurred in June of that year. Arab recognition of the political leverage of oil was not new. The Arab League had established a committee of oil experts in the early 1950s to discuss petroleum diplomacy. A formal Petroleum Bureau was created in 1954 (renamed the Department of Oil Affairs in 1959) by the League, and it has sponsored periodic Arab Oil Congresses to discuss oil and politics. Following the 1967 Baghdad meeting, OAPEC was formally established at a 1968 meeting in Beirut by Kuwait, Libya, and Saudi Arabia. Although none of the founding countries had fought in the Six-Day War, the Arabs' humiliation in that war made them more receptive to OAPEC's message that Arab oil could be a political weapon. Since then, other members of OAPEC have included Abu Dhabi, Algeria, Dubai (withdrew in 1972), Egypt, Iraq, Qatar, and Syria, and various other Arab states (e.g., Oman and Tunisia) have applied for membership.

Active oil diplomacy seems to have begun after the 1969 coup in Libya that overthrew the government of King Idris and brought to power a group of activist, young military officers led by Colonel Muammar Qaddafi. Libya led the movement among OPEC members to gain control over the oil companies that had previously dominated international oil policy. The growing unity and strength of OPEC happened to coincide with the 1973 Arab-Israeli war, provoking an immediate test of petroleum diplomacy.

Arab-Israeli Conflict

The 1973 war was the latest dramatic event in the long and painful history of Arab-Israeli relations—the second main factor behind Arab petroleum diplomacy. One might say that the whole Arab-Israeli conflict grew out of the founding of the Zionist movement in 1897 by an Austrian journalist, Dr. Theodor Herzl. The movement supported the re-creation of a Jewish homeland in Palestine, a land occupied by the Arabs for a thousand years. By the start of World War I, thousands of Jews had emigrated to the Promised Land and purchased land for Jewish settlements. On November 2, 1917, British Foreign Minister Lord Balfour issued the **Balfour Declaration** (submitted to and approved by the Cabinet), which stated:

His Majesty's Government view with favour the establishment in Palestine of a National Home for the Jewish people, and will use their best endeavours to facilitate the achievement of this object, it being clearly understood that nothing shall be done which may prejudice the civil and religious rights of existing non-Jewish communities in Palestine, or the rights and political status enjoyed by Jews in any other country.

Britain was given a League of Nations mandate over Palestine in 1922, and Jewish immigrants continued to flow into the area, their numbers increasing as Nazi power grew in Europe. In the meantime the Arab population of Palestine became increasingly concerned over the influx of immigrants and pointed out that the Balfour Declaration was promising something that was not Britain's to give. By the close of World War II Jewish nationalism in Palestine began to clash with awakening Arab nationalism. By 1947, the British decided to give up the Palestine mandate and place the fate of this increasingly troubled area before the United Nations. The United Nations supported the partition of Palestine into Arab and Jewish sectors. The proclamation of the state of Israel on May 14, 1948, by David Ben-Gurion, began the continuing, desperate struggle for land both Arabs and Jews regard as theirs. This first Arab-Israeli war in 1948 resulted in nearly a million Arab refugees from Palestine coming into the Gaza Strip and neighboring states. This situation has spawned the Fedayeen and Palestine liberation movements.

The second Arab-Israeli war was fought in the context of the 1956 Suez crisis. The third war was the 1967 Six-Day War, which resulted in a quick Israeli victory following lightning strikes against Egypt, Jordan, and Syria. The resupply of Arab war matériel by the Soviet Union and Arab determination to be revenged for their defeats in the three previous conflicts (combined with Israeli overconfidence in their own military power) paved the way for the fourth war, the 1973 October War (also called the Yom Kippur War because Egypt and Syria launched their coordinated attack on Yom Kippur, the Jewish Day of Atonement). The 1973 war ended after seventeen days of heavy fighting, as the Israelis turned back the Arab attack at great cost. It was a Pyrrhic victory for Israel and a psychological victory for the Arabs. Beyond the obvious importance of an ultimate peace settlement for the Middle East, the implications of petroleum diplomacy for international relations are already profound.

The Response of the Industrialized West to Petroleum Diplomacy

The United States, Western Europe, and other industrialized countries have clearly been forced to reassess their Middle East policies and their national energy policies. The Arab oil embargo was conducted within the framework, and with the support, of OPEC. Although there were "leaks" in the embargo, its political message was clear. The industrialized countries, which for years had been disdainful of the Arab countries' inability to work together, found themselves in the embarrassing position of being unable to produce a common policy. The Western Alliance that could unite in the face of a Soviet threat could not agree in the face of an energy threat. In some respects, that disunity was probably good. In spite of the OPEC countries' claim that they had every right to manipulate the oil market (as the international oil companies had done previously) and ultimately to demand higher oil prices (based on the true value of the commodity, the fact that oil was a nonrenewable resource, and the fact that OPEC oil resources had been exploited for years by outsiders), the mood in some industrialized countries was becoming ugly; they charged "economic blackmail" and spoke of a retaliatory embargo (for example, of foodstuffs or other crucial items).

A primary forum for the economic cooperation of the industrialized West has been the twenty-three-member Organization for Economic Cooperation and Development (OECD), headquartered in Paris. In 1961 the OECD replaced the Organization for European Economic Cooperation (OEEC), which had been established in 1948 to help organize Marshall Plan recipient countries. Although OECD has been active for some time in reviewing common energy problems (it even has had several committees studying oil and other energy issues), its unanimity rule and lack of agreement among prominent members prevented a coordinated response to the 1973–1974 oil embargo.

A new agency called the International Energy Agency (IEA), which attempted to link the oil-consuming nations, was created in Brussels in 1974. By 1975 there were seventeen members: Austria,

Belgium, Canada, Denmark, Eire, Federal Republic of Germany, Italy, Japan, Luxembourg, Netherlands, New Zealand, Sweden, Switzerland, Spain, Turkey, United Kingdom, and United States. Norway had observer status, and France was the only major nonmember in Western Europe.

Although the OPEC states called it the anti-OPEC, the IEA has nevertheless been committed not only to reaction, but also to a positive program of action to find a solution to international energy problems. The International Energy Agency has four primary responsibilities of an International Energy Program (IEP):

1 Development of joint crisis machinery

2 Introduction of an oil market information system and consultations with the oil companies

3 Long-term cooperation in developing alternative sources of energy and rationalizing energy consumption

4 Preparation of a dialogue with the petroleum-exporting countries and other consumers

IEA has not been a great success. Its critics might even argue that it has been a total failure and waste of effort, but there is a great deal of difference between confrontation and dialogue. A bitter world-trade war would appear to serve no country's interests. The OPEC countries have already learned some of the limits to petroleum diplomacy from the ill will generated, the massive disruption of the world economy, and the problem of investing the extra money that resulted from the oil price rise. One would hope that other countries currently interested in the commodity cartel as a promising diplomatic lever would proceed with prudent and rational caution. Radical economic diplomacy is a multisided game with few prospective winners and many potential losers.

THE ROLE OF THE DIPLOMAT

This survey of the broad dimensions of international diplomacy should not obscure the fact that diplomacy is conducted by individuals. The role of the individual diplomat deserves a closer look.

Critics have often charged that "a diplomat is an honest man sent abroad to lie for his country." Even though diplomats are formally charged with supporting the official foreign policy of their country, they are not freed from moral choices. Virtually every treatise on the art of diplomacy refers to the agony of decision-making. Also, almost every portrayal of the ideal diplomat will include among the desired virtues such qualities as decency, honesty, and dependability.

Perhaps the more basic agonizing decisions must be made by those who must formulate a nation's policy, although they clearly interact with the diplomats. Two basic dilemmas of national policy formation and execution are the realities of international power politics versus the obligations of morality, and an individual's personal moral standard versus a national government's moral obligations to an entire nation-state.

U.S. Secretary of State Henry Kissinger observed in the conclusion to his study of the nineteenth century diplomacy of Metternich and Castlereagh, *A World Restored*:

It cannot be denied, of course, that policy does not occur in a void, that the statesman is confronted with material he must treat as given. Not only geography and the availability of resources trace the limits of statesmanship, but also the character of the people and the nature of its historical experience. . . .

The test of a statesman, then, is his ability to recognize the real relationship of forces and to make this knowledge serve his ends. . . .

But it is not sufficient to judge the statesman by his conceptions alone, for unlike the philosopher he must implement his vision. And the statesman is inevitably confronted by the inertia of his material, by the fact that other powers are not factors to be manipulated but forces to be reconciled; that the requirements of security differ with the geographic location and the domestic structure of the powers. His instrument is diplomacy, the art of relating states to each other by agreement rather than by the exercise of force, by the representation of a ground of action which reconciles particular aspirations with a general consensus.[12]

Kissinger further notes that "the acid test of a policy . . . is its ability to obtain domestic support."[13] Certainly the necessity for domestic support is one of the best long-range guarantees of morally sound policies.

12 Henry A. Kissinger, *A World Restored: Metternich, Castlereagh and the Problems of Peace, 1812–1822*, Houghton Mifflin Company, Boston, 1973, pp. 324, 325, and 326.
13 *Ibid.*, p. 326.

The diplomat has three primary roles in foreign policy: negotiation, observation, and representation. The diplomat is the primary point of contact between countries, and diplomatic negotiation is the most wide-ranging and flexible policy option available in international relations. Article 33 of the U.N. Charter, which calls upon members to settle their disputes peacefully, gives negotiation as the first of many options listed in ascending order of formality (e.g., negotiation, enquiry, mediation, conciliation, arbitration, judicial settlement). A nation-state's flexibility becomes more limited as the mechanism of conflict resolution becomes more formal; hence, nation-states prefer negotiations, making the diplomat's role even more vital. There will be hope for the peaceful conduct of international relations as long as governments are at least willing to talk to each other, to negotiate their differences.

Observation is part of the diplomat's role, for being in the field makes the diplomat an important part of the "eyes and ears" of the state. In spite of the undercover activities of such intelligence agencies as the CIA (Central Intelligence Agency) and the KGB (Russian acronym for State Security Committee), clandestine intelligence gathering is a small (although vital) part of the overall intelligence function. Much of the work of intelligence is carried out by very obvious, simple, and normal kinds of embassy duties: attendance at important functions, discussions with local officials, subcriptions to host-country periodicals, meeting with the local populace in everyday life, and the like. Diplomatic observations may have an important impact on policy formation back in the home country.

Finally, the diplomat serves as the country's official representative and becomes in part a symbol for it. Although host countries will have their own diplomatic corps abroad, diplomats are still very important as interpreters of their countries to the host governments, which will turn to them as official representatives.

In the foreseeable future, diplomacy will surely continue to be what it has been in the past, a primary vehicle of international intercourse.

BIBLIOGRAPHY

Bailey, Thomas A. *A Diplomatic History of the American People*, 6th ed. Appleton-Century-Crofts, Inc., New York, 1958
———. *The Art of Diplomacy: The American Experience*. Appleton-Century-Crofts, Inc., New York, 1968.

Barghoorn, Frederick C. *The Soviet Cultural Offensive*. Princeton University Press, Princeton, N.J., 1960.

Bill, James A., and Robert W. Stookey. *Politics and Petroleum*. King's Court Communications, Inc., Brunswick, Ohio, 1975.

Bowles, Chester. *Ambassador's Report*. Harper & Row, Publishers, Incorporated, New York, 1954.

Corbett, Percy E. *Law in Diplomacy*. Princeton University Press, Princeton, N.J., 1959.

Craig, Gordon A., and Felix Gilbert. *The Diplomats: 1919–1939*. Princeton University Press, Princeton, N.J., 1953.

Dennett, Raymond, and Joseph E. Johnson, eds. *Negotiation with the Russians*. World Peace Foundation, Boston, 1951.

Doxey, Margaret P. *Economic Sanctions and International Enforcement*. Oxford University Press, London, 1971.

Esterline, John H., and Robert B. Black. *Inside Foreign Policy*. Mayfield Publishing Company, Palo Alto, Calif., 1975.

Foster, J. W. *The Practice of Diplomacy*. Houghton Mifflin Company, Boston, 1906.

Graebner, Norman A. *Cold War Diplomacy, 1945–1960*. D. Van Nostrand Company, Inc., Princeton, N.J., 1962.

Hankey, Maurice P. *Diplomacy by Conference*. G. P. Putnam's Sons, New York, 1946.

Iklé, Fred. *How Nations Negotiate*. Frederick A. Praeger, Inc., New York, 1964.

Johnson, E. A. J., ed. *The Dimensions of Diplomacy*. The Johns Hopkins Press, Baltimore, 1964.

Kennan, George F. *American Diplomacy, 1900–1950*. The University of Chicago Press, Chicago, 1951.

Kissinger, Henry A. *A World Restored: Metternich, Castlereagh, and the Problems of Peace, 1812–1822*. Sentry Edition. Houghton Mifflin Company, Boston, 1973.

Krueger, Robert B. *The United States and International Oil.* Frederick A. Praeger, Inc., New York, 1975.

Lall, Arthur. *Modern International Negotiations.* Columbia University Press, New York, 1966.

Landau, David. *Kissinger: The Uses of Power.* Houghton Mifflin Company, Boston, 1972.

Mattingly, Garrett. *Renaissance Diplomacy.* Jonathan Cape, Ltd., London, 1954.

McCamy, James L. *Conduct of the New Diplomacy.* Harper & Row, Publishers, Incorporated, New York, 1964.

Nicolson, Harold. *Diplomacy,* 3d ed. Oxford University Press, London, 1963.

————. *The Evolution of Diplomatic Method.* Constable & Co., Ltd., London, 1954.

Pearson, Lester B. *Diplomacy in the Nuclear Age.* Harvard University Press, Cambridge, Mass., 1959.

Smith, Daniel M. *The American Diplomatic Experience.* Houghton Mifflin Company, Boston, 1972.

Spender, Sir Percy. *Exercises in Diplomacy.* New York University Press, New York, 1970.

Stuart, Graham H. *American Diplomatic and Consular Practice,* 2d ed. Appleton-Century-Crofts, Inc., New York, 1952.

Szyliowicz, Joseph S., and Bard E. O'Neill, eds. *The Energy Crisis and U.S. Foreign Policy.* Frederick A. Praeger, Inc., New York, 1975.

Thayer, Charles W. *Diplomat.* Harper & Row, Publishers, Incorporated, New York, 1959.

Wilson, Clifton E. *Cold War Diplomacy: The Impact of International Conflicts on Diplomatic Communications and Travel.* Institute of Government Research, International Studies No. 1. University of Arizona Press, Tucson, 1966.

————. *Diplomatic Privileges and Immunities.* University of Arizona Press, Tucson, 1967.

Part IV
The Future of
International Relations

Perspective

Former United States Ambassador to the United Nations John Scali, speaking before the U.S. Senate Foreign Relations Committee in 1975, called attention to the continuing crisis within the United Nations and speculated on its dual nature. He noted:

The Chinese word for "crisis" combines the characters for danger and opportunity. This is a good description of the current state of the United Nations—an organization in crisis, poised between imminent opportunity and eventual disaster.[1]

Scali might well have expanded these remarks to cover international relations in general. In fact, a description of international relations comes strikingly close to the assessment of the business executive who, when asked how business was going, responded that "between crises everything appears to be normal."

EVOLVING PATTERNS

There is constant turmoil in modern international relations, although viewed in the relevant context of historical time and place, the international tension level has probably always been rather high. Modern international relations are different, and certainly more intense, than international relations a hundred—or even fifty—years ago. Changes in international relations, however, reflect more than quantitative changes—the increased pace of modern life and the increased number of participating nation-states. Although both those increases are indeed factors, the most startling developments have been the qualitative changes in such areas as general technology, thermonuclear weapons, strategic military planning, ideology, environmental threat, overpopulation, and dwindling food supplies.

The rapid, complex, and interwoven international changes have perhaps left us all somewhat overwhelmed, trying to understand a world we must somehow manage. One of the primary dilemmas of international relations is posed by the existence on the one hand of the nation-state system, impelling the world toward apparent perpetual chaos, and the destructive potential, on the other hand, of

---

1 U.S. Department of State, Bureau of Public Affairs, Office of Media Services, *News Release* (May 22, 1975), p. 1.

thermonuclear weapons and other such creations of the human mind. The continuing impetus toward political conflict is met by the technological capability of immediate and total destruction should conflict, by accident or design, get "out of hand." We have to try to avoid disaster by organizing and managing a world that seems to defy all such efforts.

Professional observers of international relations are of course not just standing by and waiting for world events. Chapter 2 reviewed the major kinds of organizing theories that these observers have advanced, thus giving beginning students of international relations some familiarity with scholarly work being done and lines of thought being pursued. This book has not endorsed any single theory, although parts of several of them have been used when they seemed helpful in explaining some particular substantive problem. Although some individual theories are most persuasive, and indeed have a large number of distinguished adherents, none can actually be considered "the answer." Students who wish to pursue more advanced topics in international relations should investigate the operating propositions of selected international relations theories more thoroughly, measure them against their own personal frames of reference, and reach their own conclusions as to the most meaningful explanation of world events.

Two general premises have been accepted in the earlier chapters. The first is the assumption that conflict is a fact of social life, whether it be at the level of interpersonal contact or of international relations among sovereign states. This text has not tried to advance a comprehensive theory of social conflict, but has simply acknowledged that wherever social situations develop (whether among a group of individuals or a community of states), there are likely to be divergent interpretations of both social goals and the means to achieve them. While social conflict may be inevitable, however, there is no reason why it must automatically escalate into violent conflict. In fact, there is much to suggest that a resort to violence is an increasingly risky and less appealing policy option in modern international relations.

The second general premise of the foregoing chapters is a belief in human rationality, a belief that human beings are able to sort out their experiences and attach meaning to them. This book has not been intended as a definitive explanation of international relations, but rather has stressed the human ability to confront complex problems and has tried to encourage readers to search further for their own individual conclusions. We can (and we must if we are to survive) find reasonable ways of managing conflict in international relations. Readers must decide for *themselves,* in terms of their own frames of reference, what *they* think the future world should look like—for example, whether some kind of world government or some version of the present nation-state system is the best way of organizing the world. This study does not propose any ultimate vision of international relations, but rather stresses the presence of conflict and the importance of a commitment to seek peaceful, rational resolutions of that conflict.

By accepting the nation-state and the nation-state system as current political givens, and gaining some conception of the historical dimensions and limitations of those givens, a beginning student of international relations can develop a basic understanding of world politics through two general themes: the impetus toward world conflict and the search for world order. Significant aspects of international tension and conflict were surveyed in Part II under the very general headings of the Bomb, ideology and political power, and the Third World. Obviously, however, more advanced students of international relations would need to break down these broadly defined problem areas and make a more detailed study of specific issues.

Part III reviewed the structure, the record, and the promise of three major instruments concerned with the international search for order: international law, international organization, and international diplomacy. None of these instruments guarantees world peace, and none of them predetermines the direction of world politics. They are in fact instruments (not goals) that have been developed and supported over the years by nation-states because government leaders saw them as promising instruments for the peaceful management of international relations. As mentioned earlier, world peace will require international agreement on and support for a "Condition X," a status quo that is substantially in accord with everyone's political ideal. No less important, however, is an international commitment to seek that ideal by peaceful means. Certainly law, organization, and diplomacy do not include everything that could be said about the international search for order. They are, nevertheless, three major, historically tested means of resolving international differences and building international consensus—two essential ingredients of a viable world community.

That great scholar of international law Hugo Grotius reminds us that law offers both a stabilizing influence and a rational procedure for managing international relations:

Law is not founded on expediency alone, there is no state so powerful that it may not some time need the help of others outside itself, either for purposes of trade, or even to ward off the forces of many foreign nations united against it. In consequence we see that even the most powerful peoples and sovereigns seek alliances, which are quite devoid of significance according to the point of view of those who confine law within the boundaries of states. Most true is the saying, that all things are uncertain the moment men depart from law.[2]

International law cannot organize the world and make it peaceful. The organization for peace must be linked to political consensus. Law, however, can crystallize that consensus, while legal mechanisms can aid in its orderly extension.

International organization provides a convenient forum, at both the universal and regional levels, in which to address the issue of political consensus formally, although there is no guarantee of success. The most prominent political confrontation within the United Nations was initially the Cold War maneuvering of the Big Powers. Big Power disagreement continues to be important in United Nations politics, but the rapid influx into the United Nations of newly independent, less-developed states has shifted the emphasis from an East-West confrontation to a developing North-South confrontation. United States concern over the increasing number of "unpalatable and arbitrary" decisions pushed through the United Nations by "one-sided" majorities provided the context for Ambassador Scali's remarks to the Senate Foreign Relations Committee referred to at the beginning of this chapter. He called attention to the issues that concerned most U.N. members:

It is not hard to pinpoint the present sources of tension at the United Nations. There are three—the Arab-Israeli dispute, the battle for racial justice in southern Africa, and the growing gap in living standards between developed and developing nations. These three

2 Hugo Grotius, *De Jure Belli ac Pacis Libri Tres, Prolegomena*, Vol. II, trans. of the 1646 edition by Francis W. Kelsey et al., Carnegie Endowment Series, The Classics of International Law, ed. James Brown Scott, Clarendon Press, Oxford, 1925, p. 17.

issues dominate all U.N. deliberations for a good reason: These are the problems that most of the world's people feel most keenly. For most member nations a United Nations which cannot promote progress on these issues is not worth having.[3]

The Big Powers, and for that matter also many lesser powers, do not necessarily perceive the world's problems, the solutions to them, or even the role of the United Nations the same way as do current voting majorities. It would be unfortunate, however, if careless confrontation and lack of political determination on all sides to seek out mutually acceptable solutions to current problems were to drive nations away from the United Nations. As Mr. Scali remarked further:

If, because of choice or neglect, the world community fails to make the United Nations work, the alternative is not cooperation elsewhere in some other more promising forum, but inevitably a fundamental breakdown of the main path to international cooperation. The dream of an open and cooperative world order to which mankind committed itself 30 years ago will wither and die. In its place there certainly will arise a world divided into exclusive, selfish, and rival camps, where each nation's gain is another's loss.[4]

Petroleum diplomacy, which was examined in the previous chapter, shows what could happen if the world should drift in the direction Mr. Scali was warning about. It takes little imagination to foresee a world in which each nation is trying to gain international leverage, not with military weapons, but by exploiting the products of nature and human technology (e.g., food, petroleum, machinery, fertilizer, medicine, and the like). It takes no additional imagination to see that world politics of this kind is sure to lead to armed conflict.

Diplomacy is also an instrument, and it can be used to build consensus and resolve disputes as well as to provoke foreign policy confrontations. The necessary ingredients are the courage and commitment to seek mutually acceptable solutions to our problems, and to continue to search for peace, no matter how discouraging the prospects and how tempting it is to resort to arms. As Canada's Lester Pearson advised in his Nobel Peace Prize Lecture (Oslo, Norway, December 11, 1957) concerning diplomacy,

3 U.S. Department of State, *News Release* (May 22, 1975), p. 1.
4 *Ibid.*, p. 2.

What is needed is a new and vigorous determination to use every technique of discussion and negotiation that is available, or more important, that can be made available, for the solution of the tangled, frightening problems that divide today, in fear and hostility, the two power-blocs and thereby endanger peace. We must keep on trying to solve problems, one by one, stage by stage, if not on the basis of confidence and cooperation, at least on that of mutual toleration and self-interest.[5]

His remarks were delivered in an era of Cold War confrontation, but that makes them no less meaningful for the present and the future.

NEW DIMENSIONS OF INTERNATIONAL RELATIONS

For over 300 years the nation-state and the nation-state system have been the primary participants in and the basic framework for international relations. There is no pressing reason to believe that there will be any immediate and dramatic change in that basic pattern. On the contrary, there is much to suggest that the Westphalian structure will continue indefinitely. Nevertheless, there are several interesting developments that deserve continuing and close scrutiny, for they involve new dimensions of traditional international relations.

First, the nation-state itself appears to be moving in two directions. On the one hand there is a great deal of excitement over the prospects of regional integration and the creation of organizations with supranational powers. There is even the possibility that states will join in federal union and produce, for example, a United States of Europe. The prospect of the European Communities evolving into a viable and lasting economic and political force could provoke a competitive response elsewhere, causing African, Asian, or Latin American states to seek integration. Although the European Communities have been a promising example of integration, it still remains to be seen to what extent the sovereign functions of the member states might ultimately be supplanted by a new political unit.

The remainder of the world has clearly come nowhere near the level of cooperation reached in Western Europe. In addition to the

5 Lester B. Pearson, *Diplomacy in the Nuclear Age,* Harvard University Press, Cambridge, Mass., 1959, pp. 106–107.

integrative forces at work in the modern world, there is a substantial level of disintegrative pressure threatening to break apart states that already exist, or at least to restructure fundamentally the internal shape of national power. Subnational disintegrative forces are even at work within member states of the European Communities, most notably Belgium (where the Flemish compete with French-speaking Walloons) and the United Kingdom (where Welsh, Scottish, and Irish groups are developing a new and stronger sense of ethnic identity and ethnic politics).

Many states in the world contain the potential for disintegration, and in fact a number of states were created as uneasy coalitions of subnational forces. Observers of international relations have generally focused with varying degrees of expectation on the prospects for regional and universal unity, and it would be surprising if it were discovered that the future would lead to the breakup of nation-states. It is true that some states have always been regarded as unstable, and their continued existence has been somewhat of a surprise, but the disintegration of a state has always seemed an invitation to disaster, making the dissident subnational groups easy prey for outsiders. The nation-state made sense because it was the minimum viable unit that could compete politically, economically, and militarily with other similar units that emerged at the end of the Middle Ages. For this reason, supranational integration has seemed likely, as states would move toward integration in order to be able to compete with the superpowers. Yet since World War II, many small states that hardly seemed viable have emerged and continued to exist. No one, of course, can predict with certainty which course states will take—integration, disintegration, or neither. This is an area, however, that will warrant continued observation.

A *second* new dimension of international relations, which was discussed in previous chapters and deserves the careful attention of serious students, is the appearance of new international actors other than nation-states. These include international organizations (public and private), business corporations, and even single individuals. International organizations, with the primary exception of the supranational organizations in Western Europe, have generally existed at the intergovernmental, or confederal, level. Emphasis has been on cooperation and recommended common policies, rather than on the serious surrendering of national sovereign prerogatives. As we saw, however, international organizations tend to become something more than the mere sum of their parts.

Largely within the context of international organizations, individuals have attained an enhanced international status. This has occurred particularly through emphasizing human rights increasingly and, within such European organizations as the European Communities and the Council of Europe, granting individuals formal legal standing before an international court.

Multinational business corporations have also emerged as important new participants in international relations, and they deserve a great deal of careful attention and study in the years to come for at least three reasons. First, the big multinational corporations have more economic power than many nation-states. Second, these multinationals are in many respects beyond the control of either nation-states or international organizations. The brief discussion of the major international oil companies in Chapter 9 indicated the power of these companies, and the oil companies are just some of the multinational corporations. Their power lies in their size, their sophisticated ability to move goods and services worldwide, and the generally poor public (and governmental) knowledge of their structure and operation. A third reason why a careful study of the multinational corporations is needed is that they have been highly successful in their transnational organization. Their international control of goods, services, capital, labor, management, resources, and the like—on an extremely efficient basis—must hold some lessons from which governments (among others) could benefit. Also, it would not be unexpected if labor unions became more important in international relations. Airline pilots, for example, have already given some indication of the pressure an international association can exert.

A *third* dimension of modern international relations that demands attention is the new international significance of terrorism, insurrections, guerrilla warfare, civil war, and similar violent activities that were once primarily of domestic concern and responsibility. There are three points to note here: (1) because of modern communications, dissident national groups can easily solicit worldwide support; (2) it is easy for foreign governments to aid surreptitiously dissidents (or in fact even provoke and lead them); and (3) because of modern mobility and the vulnerability of modern industrial states, terrorist groups can have considerable international effect. No future understanding of international relations will be complete without some careful study of the internationalization of domestic conflict.

A *fourth* dimension of international relations that should be mentioned here involves the evidence of a developing world culture. It may seem surprising to speak of a world culture after the foregoing chapters emphasized the diversity of national cultures and the difficulty of achieving worldwide agreement on international standards. While it is possible to speak philosophically of the Family of Man, it would be premature to assert that a world culture has truly crystallized. Yet there are nonetheless significant forces at work that require closer study. Modern communications and the growing internationalization of human experiences are bound to force us to refocus our conceptions of ourselves and others. The implications of a world culture, should that in fact be the direction in which we are heading, are uncertain. It surely brings no clear guarantee of peace, and perhaps portends the opposite. Social conflict will continue simply because people are in contact, and history shows that peoples with a great deal in common can fight with a determination hardly equaled by fights among strangers. We should hope that as the world "gets smaller," our common problems will provoke a common determination to solve them.

THE STUDY OF INTERNATIONAL RELATIONS

The distinguished scholar Quincy Wright some years ago addressed the question of the development of a discipline of international relations in the following manner:

International relations, as a discipline contributing to the understanding, prediction, evaluation, and control of the relations among states and of the conditions of the world community, is at the same time a history, a science, a philosophy, and an art. . . .

An effort to synthesize the studies important for international relations, therefore, appears to approach the ambitious task of synthesizing all the disciplines—humanistic, social, and natural.

The effort to unify the study of international relations resembles the effort to unify all knowledge.[6]

6 Quincy Wright, *The Study of International Relations*, Appleton-Century-Crofts, Inc., New York, 1955, p. 481.

While we cannot expect to understand all knowledge, Professor Wright makes an extremely important point in calling attention to the eclectic nature of international relations. Although the formal study of international relations, as we find it appearing in university and college catalogs, may provide one with theoretical tools and an intellectual perspective for better understanding the ebb and flow of world politics, it would be a grave mistake to neglect the substantive and theoretical contributions of the many disciplines that relate to international affairs.

Students interested in pursuing their study of international relations, whether for pure intellectual satisfaction or as further training in preparation for one of the many varied careers relating to international relations, would be well advised to include in their work some study of a foreign language. In an age that frankly admits the importance of human communication, one of the basic tools of communication—language—is often neglected. More than a tool, however, language is also a key to culture. If we are to understand others better, we might begin by talking with them.

Students continuing with a study of international relations should possess intellectual curiosity and a healthy sense of skepticism. We *can* gain an understanding of complex world events, but as disciplined observers, we should subject popular prophets and easy answers to the kind of thorough scrutiny that must be applied to all new ideas. That, after all, is what the coherent study of international relations is all about.

Appendix A

Charter of the United Nations

Preamble

We the Peoples of the United Nations Determined to save succeeding generations from the scourge of war, which twice in our lifetime has brought untold sorrow to mankind, and

to reaffirm faith in fundamental human rights, in the dignity and worth of the human person, in the equal rights of men and women and of nations large and small, and

to establish conditions under which justice and respect for the obligations arising from treaties and other sources of international law can be maintained, and

to promote social progress and better standards of life in larger freedom,

And for these Ends to practice tolerance and live together in peace with one another as good neighbors, and

to unite our strength to maintain international peace and security, and

to ensure, by the acceptance of principles and the institution of methods, that armed force shall not be used, save in the common interest, and

to employ international machinery for the promotion of the economic and social advancement of all peoples,

Have Resolved to Combine Our Efforts to Accomplish These Aims. Accordingly, our respective Governments, through representatives assembled in the city of San Francisco, who have exhibited their full powers found to be in good and due form, have agreed to the present Charter of the United Nations and do hereby establish an international organization to be known as the United Nations.

The Charter of the United Nations was adopted at San Francisco on June 25, 1945, and was signed the following day. It came into force on October 24, 1945, when a majority of the signatories had ratified it.

Amendments to Articles 23, 27, and 61 of the Charter were approved by the United Nations General Assembly on December 17, 1963, at the Assembly's eighteenth session, and came into force on August 31, 1965.

Source: United Nations, Office of Public Information, *Everyman's United Nations*, 8th ed., United Nations, New York, 1968, pp. 553-574.

CHAPTER I
PURPOSES AND PRINCIPLES

Article One   The Purposes of the United Nations are:

1. To maintain international peace and security, and to that end: to take effective collective measures for the prevention and removal of threats to the peace, and for the suppression of acts of aggression or other breaches of the peace, and to bring about by peaceful means, and in conformity with the principles of justice and international law, adjustment or settlement of international disputes or situations which might lead to a breach of the peace;

2. To develop friendly relations among nations based on respect for the principle of equal rights and self-determination of peoples, and to take other appropriate measures to strengthen universal peace;

3. To achieve international cooperation in solving international problems of an economic, social, cultural, or humanitarian character, and in promoting and encouraging respect for human rights and for fundamental freedoms for all without distinction as to race, sex, language, or religion; and

4. To be a center for harmonizing the actions of nations in the attainment of these common ends.

Article Two   The Organization and its Members, in pursuit of the Purposes stated in Article 1, shall act in accordance with the following Principles.

1. The Organization is based on the principle of the sovereign equality of all its Members.

2. All Members, in order to ensure to all of them the rights and benefits resulting from membership, shall fulfill in good faith the obligations assumed by them in accordance with the present Charter.

3. All Members shall settle their international disputes by peaceful means in such a manner that international peace and security, and justice, are not endangered.

4. All Members shall refrain in their international relations from the threat or use of force against the territorial integrity or political independence of any state, or in any other manner inconsistent with the Purposes of the United Nations.

5. All Members shall give the United Nations every assistance in any action it takes in accordance with the present Charter, and shall refrain from giving assistance to any state against which the United Nations is taking preventive or enforcement action.

6. The Organization shall ensure that states which are not Members of the United Nations act in accordance with these Principles so far as may be necessary for the maintenance of international peace and security.

7. Nothing contained in the present Charter shall authorize the United Nations to intervene in matters which are essentially within the domestic jurisdiction of any state or shall require the Members to submit such matters to settlement under the present Charter; but this principle shall not prejudice the application of enforcement measures under Chapter VII.

CHAPTER II

MEMBERSHIP

Article Three   The original Members of the United Nations shall be the states which, having participated in the United Nations Conference on International Organization at San Francisco, or having previously signed the Declaration by United Nations of January 1, 1942, sign the present Charter and ratify it in accordance with Article 110.

Article Four   1. Membership in the United Nations is open to all other peace-loving states which accept the obligations contained in the present Charter and, in the judgment of the Organization, are able and willing to carry out these obligations.

2. The admission of any such state to membership in the United Nations will be effected by a decision of the General Assembly upon the recommendation of the Security Council.

Article Five   A Member of the United Nations against which preventive or enforcement action has been taken by the Security Council may be suspended from the exercise of the rights and privileges of membership by the General Assembly upon the recommendation of the Security Council. The exercise of these rights and privileges may be restored by the Security Council.

Article Six   A Member of the United Nations which has persistently violated the Principles contained in the present Charter may be expelled from the Organization by the General Assembly upon the recommendation of the Security Council.

CHAPTER III

ORGANS

Article Seven 1. There are established as the principal organs of the United Nations: a General Assembly, a Security Council, an Economic and Social Council, a Trusteeship Council, an International Court of Justice, and a Secretariat.

2. Such subsidiary organs as may be found necessary may be established in accordance with the present Charter.

Article Eight The United Nations shall place no restrictions on the eligibility of men and women to participate in any capacity and under conditions of equality in its principal and subsidiary organs.

CHAPTER IV

THE GENERAL ASSEMBLY

Composition

Article Nine 1. The General Assembly shall consist of all the Members of the United Nations.

2. Each member shall have not more than five representatives in the General Assembly.

Functions and Powers

Article Ten The General Assembly may discuss any questions or any matters within the scope of the present Charter or relating to the powers and functions of any organs provided for in the present Charter, and, except as provided in Article 12, may make recommendations to the Members of the United Nations or to the Security Council or to both on any such questions or matters.

Article Eleven 1. The General Assembly may consider the general principles of cooperation in the maintenance of international peace and security, including the principles governing disarmament and the regulation of armaments, and may make recommendations with regard to such principles to the Members or to the Security Council or to both.

2. The General Assembly may discuss any questions relating to the maintenance of international peace and security brought before it by any

Member of the United Nations, or by the Security Council, or by a state which is not a Member of the United Nations in accordance with Article 35, paragraph 2, and, except as provided in Article 12, may make recommendations with regard to any such questions to the state or states concerned or to the Security Council or to both. Any such question on which action is necessary shall be referred to the Security Council by the General Assembly either before or after discussion.

3. The General Assembly may call the attention of the Security Council to situations which are likely to endanger international peace and security.

4. The powers of the General Assembly set forth in this Article shall not limit the general scope of Article 10.

Article Twelve 1. While the Security Council is exercising in respect of any dispute or situation the functions assigned to it in the present Charter, the General Assembly shall not make any recommendation with regard to that dispute or situation unless the Security Council so requests.

2. The Secretary-General, with the consent of the Security Council, shall notify the General Assembly at each session of any matters relative to the maintenance of international peace and security which are being dealt with by the Security Council and shall similarly notify the General Assembly, or the Members of the United Nations if the General Assembly is not in session, immediately the Security Council ceases to deal with such matters.

Article Thirteen 1. The General Assembly shall initiate studies and make recommendations for the purpose of:
a. promoting international cooperation in the political field and encouraging the progressive development of international law and its codification;
b. promoting international cooperation in the economic, social, cultural, educational, and health fields, and assisting in the realization of human rights and fundamental freedoms for all without distinction as to race, sex, language, or religion.

2. The further responsibilities, functions and powers of the General Assembly with respect to matters mentioned in paragraph 1(b) above are set forth in Chapters IX and X.

Article Fourteen Subject to the provisions of Article 12, the General Assembly may recommend measures for the peaceful adjustment of any situation, regardless of origin, which it deems likely to impair the general welfare or friendly relations among nations, including situations resulting from a violation of the provisions of the present Charter setting forth the Purposes and Principles of the United Nations.

Article Fifteen 1. The General Assembly shall receive and consider annual and special reports from the Security Council; these reports shall include an account of the measures that the Security Council has decided upon or taken to maintain international peace and security.

2. The General Assembly shall receive and consider reports from the other organs of the United Nations.

Article Sixteen The General Assembly shall perform such functions with respect to the international trusteeship system as are assigned to it under Chapters XII and XIII, including the approval of the trusteeship agreements for areas not designated as strategic.

Article Seventeen 1. The General Assembly shall consider and approve the budget of the Organization.

2. The expenses of the Organization shall be borne by the Members as apportioned by the General Assembly.

3. The General Assembly shall consider and approve any financial and budgetary arrangements with specialized agencies referred to in Article 57 and shall examine the administrative budgets of such specialized agencies with a view to making recommendations to the agencies concerned.

Voting

Article Eighteen 1. Each member of the General Assembly shall have one vote.

2. Decisions of the General Assembly on important questions shall be made by a two-thirds majority of the members present and voting. These questions shall include: recommendations with respect to the maintenance of international peace and security, the election of the nonpermanent members of the Security Council, the election of the members of the Economic and Social Council, the election of members of the Trusteeship Council in accordance with paragraph 1(c) of Article 86, the admission of new Members to the United Nations, the suspension of the rights and privileges of membership, the expulsion of Members, questions relating to the operation of the trusteeship system, and budgetary questions.

3. Decisions on other questions, including the determination of additional categories of questions to be decided by a two-thirds majority, shall be made by a majority of the members present and voting.

Article Nineteen A Member of the United Nations which is in arrears in the payment of its financial contributions to the Organization shall have no vote in the General Assembly if the amount of its arrears equals or exceeds the amount of the contributions due from it for the preceding two full years. The General Assembly may, nevertheless, permit such a Member to vote if it is satisfied that the failure to pay is due to conditions beyond the control of the Member.

Procedure

Article Twenty The General Assembly shall meet in regular annual sessions and in such special sessions as occasion may require. Special sessions shall be convoked by the Secretary-General at the request of the Security Council or of a majority of the Members of the United Nations.

Article Twenty-one The General Assembly shall adopt its own rules of procedure. It shall elect its President for each session.

Article Twenty-two The General Assembly may establish such subsidiary organs as it deems necessary for the performance of its functions.

CHAPTER V

THE SECURITY COUNCIL

Composition

*Article Twenty-three** 1. The Security Council shall consist of fifteen

*As amended. The original text of Article 23 reads as follows:
1. The Security Council shall consist of eleven Members of the United Nations. The Republic of China, France, the Union of Soviet Socialist Republics, the United Kingdom of Great Britain and Northern Ireland, and the United States of America shall be permanent members of the Security Council. The General Assembly shall elect six other Members of the United Nations to be non-permanent members of the Security Council, due regard being specially paid, in the first instance to the contribution of Members of the United Nations to the maintenance of international peace and security and to the other purposes of the Organization, and also to equitable geographical distribution.
2. The non-permanent members of the Security Council shall be elected for a term of two years. In the first election of the non-permanent members, however, three shall be chosen for a term of one year. A retiring member shall not be eligible for immediate re-election.
3. Each member of the Security Council shall have one representative.

Members of the United Nations. The Republic of China, France, the Union of Soviet Socialist Republics, the United Kingdom of Great Britain and Northern Ireland, and the United States of America shall be permanent members of the Security Council. The General Assembly shall elect ten other Members of the United Nations to be non-permanent members of the Security Council, due regard being specially paid, in the first instance to the contribution of Members of the United Nations to the maintenance of international peace and security and to the other purposes of the Organization, and also to equitable geographical distribution.

2. The non-permanent members of the Security Council shall be elected for a term of two years. In the first election of the non-permanent members after the increase of the membership of the Security Council from eleven to fifteen, two of the four additional members shall be chosen for a term of one year. A retiring member shall not be eligible for immediate re-election.

3. Each member of the Security Council shall have one representative.

Functions and Powers

Article Twenty-four 1. In order to ensure prompt and effective action by the United Nations, its Members confer on the Security Council primary responsibility for the maintenance of international peace and security, and agree that in carrying out its duties under this responsibility the Security Council acts on their behalf.

2. In discharging these duties the Security Council shall act in accordance with the Purposes and Principles of the United Nations. The specific powers granted to the Security Council for the discharge of these duties are laid down in Chapters VI, VII, VIII, and XII.

3. The Security Council shall submit annual and, when necessary, special reports to the General Assembly for its consideration.

Article Twenty-five The Members of the United Nations agree to accept and carry out the decisions of the Security Council in accordance with the present Charter.

Article Twenty-six In order to promote the establishment and maintenance of international peace and security with the least diversion for armaments of the world's human and economic resources, the Security Council shall be responsible for formulating, with the assistance of the Military Staff Committee referred to in Article 47, plans to be submitted to the Members of the United Nations for the establishment of a system for the regulation of armaments.

Voting

*Article Twenty-seven** 1. Each member of the Security Council shall have one vote.

2. Decisions of the Security Council on procedural matters shall be made by an affirmative vote of nine members.

3. Decisions of the Security Council on all other matters shall be made by an affirmative vote of nine members including the concurring votes of the permanent members; provided that, in decisions under Chapter VI, and under paragraph 3 of Article 52, a party to a dispute shall abstain from voting.

Procedure

Article Twenty-eight 1. The Security Council shall be so organized as to be able to function continuously. Each member of the Security Council shall for this purpose be represented at all times at the seat of the Organization.

2. The Security Council shall hold periodic meetings at which each of its members may, if it so desires, be represented by a member of the government or by some other specially designated representative.

3. The Security Council may hold meetings at such places other than the seat of the Organization as in its judgment will best facilitate its work.

Article Twenty-nine The Security Council may establish such subsidiary organs as it deems necessary for the performance of its functions.

Article Thirty The Security Council shall adopt its own rules of procedure, including the method of selecting its President.

Article Thirty-one Any Member of the United Nations which is not a member of the Security Council may participate, without vote, in the discussion of any question brought before the Security Council whenever the latter considers that the interests of that Member are specially affected.

*As amended. The original text of Article 27 reads as follows:
1. Each member of the Security Council shall have one vote.
2. Decisions of the Security Council on procedural matters shall be made by an affirmative vote of seven members.
3. Decisions of the Security Council on all other matters shall be made by an affirmative vote of seven members including the concurring votes of the permanent members; provided that, in decisions under Chapter VI, and under paragraph 3 of Article 52, a party to a dispute shall abstain from voting.

Article Thirty-two Any Member of the United Nations which is not a member of the Security Council or any state which is not a Member of the United Nations, if it is a party to a dispute under consideration by the Security Council, shall be invited to participate, without vote, in the discussion relating to the dispute. The Security Council shall lay down such conditions as it deems just for the participation of a state which is not a Member of the United Nations.

CHAPTER VI

PACIFIC SETTLEMENT OF DISPUTES

Article Thirty-three 1. The parties to any dispute, the continuance of which is likely to endanger the maintenance of international peace and security, shall, first of all, seek a solution by negotiation, enquiry, mediation, conciliation, arbitration, judicial settlement, resort to regional agencies or arrangements, or other peaceful means of their own choice.

2. The Security Council shall, when it deems necessary, call upon the parties to settle their dispute by such means.

Article Thirty-four The Security Council may investigate any dispute, or any situation which might lead to international friction or give rise to a dispute, in order to determine whether the continuance of the dispute or situation is likely to endanger the maintenance of international peace and security.

Article Thirty-five 1. Any Member of the United Nations may bring any dispute, or any situation of the nature referred to in Article 34, to the attention of the Security Council or of the General Assembly.

2. A state which is not a Member of the United Nations may bring to the attention of the Security Council or of the General Assembly any dispute to which it is a party if it accepts in advance, for the purposes of the dispute, the obligations of pacific settlement provided in the present Charter.

3. The proceedings of the General Assembly in respect of matters brought to its attention under this Article will be subject to the provisions of Articles 11 and 12.

Article Thirty-six 1. The Security Council may, at any stage of a dispute of the nature referred to in Article 33 or of a situation of like nature, recommend appropriate procedures or methods of adjustment.

2. The Security Council should take into consideration any proce-

dures for the settlement of the dispute which have already been adopted by the parties.

3. In making recommendations under this Article the Security Council should also take into consideration that legal disputes should as a general rule be referred by the parties to the International Court of Justice in accordance with the provisions of the Statute of the Court.

Article Thirty-seven 1. Should the parties to a dispute of the nature referred to in Article 33 fail to settle it by the means indicated in that Article, they shall refer it to the Security Council.

2. If the Security Council deems that the continuance of the dispute is in fact likely to endanger the maintenance of international peace and security, it shall decide whether to take action under Article 36 or to recommend such terms of settlement as it may consider appropriate.

Article Thirty-eight Without prejudice to the provisions of Articles 33 to 37, the Security Council may, if all the parties to any dispute so request, make recommendations to the parties with a view to a pacific settlement of the dispute.

CHAPTER VII

ACTION WITH RESPECT TO THREATS TO THE PEACE,
BREACHES OF THE PEACE, AND ACTS OF AGGRESSION

Article Thirty-nine The Security Council shall determine the existence of any threat to the peace, breach of the peace, or act of aggression and shall make recommendations, or decide what measures shall be taken in accordance with Articles 41 and 42, to maintain or restore international peace and security.

Article Forty In order to prevent an aggravation of the situation, the Security Council may, before making the recommendations or deciding upon the measures provided for in Article 39, call upon the parties concerned to comply with such provisional measures as it deems necessary or desirable. Such provisional measures shall be without prejudice to the rights, claims, or position of the parties concerned. The Security Council shall duly take account of failure to comply with such provisional measures.

Article Forty-one The Security Council may decide what measures not involving the use of armed force are to be employed to give effect to its decisions, and it may call upon the Members of the United Nations to apply such measures. These may include complete or partial interruption of economic relations and of rail, sea, air, postal, telegraphic, radio, and other means of communication, and the severance of diplomatic relations.

Article Forty-two Should the Security Council consider that measures provided for in Article 41 would be inadequate or have proved to be inadequate, it may take such action by air, sea, or land forces as may be necessary to maintain or restore international peace and security. Such action may include demonstrations, blockade, and other operations by air, sea, or land forces of Members of the United Nations.

Article Forty-three 1. All Members of the United Nations, in order to contribute to the maintenance of international peace and security, undertake to make available to the Security Council, on its call and in accordance with a special agreement or agreements, armed forces, assistance, and facilities, including rights of passage, necessary for the purpose of maintaining international peace and security.

2. Such agreement or agreements shall govern the numbers and types of forces, their degree of readiness and general location, and the nature of the facilities and assistance to be provided.

3. The agreement or agreements shall be negotiated as soon as possible on the initiative of the Security Council. They shall be concluded between the Security Council and Members or between the Security Council and groups of Members and shall be subject to ratification by the signatory states in accordance with their respective constitutional processes.

Article Forty-four When the Security Council has decided to use force it shall, before calling upon a Member not represented on it to provide armed forces in fulfillment of the obligations assumed under Article 43, invite that Member, if the Member so desires, to participate in the decisions of the Security Council concerning the employment of contingents of that Member's armed forces.

Article Forty-five In order to enable the United Nations to take urgent military measures, Members shall hold immediately available national air-force contingents for combined international enforcement action. The strength and degree of readiness of these contingents and plans for their combined action shall be determined, within the limits laid down in the special agreement or agreements referred to in Article 43, by the Security Council with the assistance of the Military Staff Committee.

Article Forty-six Plans for the application of armed force shall be made by the Security Council with the assistance of the Military Staff Committee.

Article Forty-seven 1. There shall be established a Military Staff Committee to advise and assist the Security Council on all questions relating to the Security Council's military requirements for the maintenance of international peace and security, the employment and command of forces placed at its disposal, the regulation of armaments, and possible disarmament.

2. The Military Staff Committee shall consist of the Chiefs of Staff of the permanent members of the Security Council or their representatives. Any Member of the United Nations not permanently represented on the Committee shall be invited by the Committee to be associated with it when the efficient discharge of the Committee's responsibilities requires the participation of that Member in its work.

3. The Military Staff Committee shall be responsible under the Security Council for the strategic direction of any armed forces placed at the disposal of the Security Council. Questions relating to the command of such forces shall be worked out subsequently.

4. The Military Staff Committee, with the authorization of the Security Council and after consultation with appropriate regional agencies, may establish regional subcommittees.

Article Forty-eight 1. The action required to carry out the decisions of the Security Council for the maintenance of international peace and security shall be taken by all the Members of the United Nations or by some of them, as the Security Council may determine.

2. Such decisions shall be carried out by the Members of the United Nations directly and through their action in the appropriate international agencies of which they are members.

Article Forty-nine The Members of the United Nations shall join in affording mutual assistance in carrying out the measures decided upon by the Security Council.

Article Fifty If preventive or enforcement measures against any state are taken by the Security Council, any other state, whether a Member of the United Nations or not, which finds itself confronted with special economic problems arising from the carrying out of those measures shall have the right to consult the Security Council with regard to a solution of those problems.

Article Fifty-one Nothing in the present Charter shall impair the inherent right of individual or collective self-defense if an armed attack occurs against a Member of the United Nations, until the Security Council has taken measures necessary to maintain international peace and security. Measures taken by Members in the exercise of this right of self-defense shall be immediately reported to the Security Council and shall not in any way affect the authority and responsibility of the Security Council under the present Charter to take at any time such action as it deems necessary in order to maintain or restore international peace and security.

CHAPTER VIII
REGIONAL ARRANGEMENTS

Article Fifty-two 1. Nothing in the present Charter precludes the existence of regional arrangements or agencies for dealing with such matters relating to the maintenance of international peace and security as are appropriate for regional action, provided that such arrangements or agencies and their activities are consistent with the Purposes and Principles of the United Nations.

2. The Members of the United Nations entering into such arrangements or constituting such agencies shall make every effort to achieve pacific settlement of local disputes through such regional arrangements or by such regional agencies before referring them to the Security Council.

3. The Security Council shall encourage the development of pacific settlement of local disputes through such regional arrangements or by such regional agencies either on the initiative of the states concerned or by reference from the Security Council.

4. This Article in no way impairs the application of Articles 34 and 35.

Article Fifty-three 1. The Security Council shall where appropriate, utilize such regional arrangements or agencies for enforcement action under its authority. But no enforcement action shall be taken under regional arrangements or by regional agencies without the authorization of the Security Council, with the exception of measures against any enemy state, as defined in paragraph 2 of this Article, provided for pursuant to Article 107 or in regional arrangements directed against renewal of aggressive policy on the part of any such state, until such time as the Organization may, on request of the Governments concerned, be charged with the responsibility for preventing further aggression by such a state.

2. The term enemy state as used in paragraph 1 of this Article applies to any state which during the Second World War has been an enemy of any signatory of the present Charter.

Article Fifty-four The Security Council shall at all times be kept fully informed of activities undertaken or in contemplation under regional arrangements or by regional agencies for the maintenance of international peace and security.

CHAPTER IX
INTERNATIONAL ECONOMIC AND SOCIAL COOPERATION

Article Fifty-five With a view to the creation of conditions of stability and well-being which are necessary for peaceful and friendly relations among nations based on respect for the principle of equal rights and self-determination of peoples, the United Nations shall promote:
a. higher standards of living, full employment, and conditions of economic and social progress and development;
b. solutions of international economic, social, health, and related problems; and international cultural and educational cooperation; and
c. universal respect for, and observance of, human rights and fundamental freedoms for all without distinction as to race, sex, language, or religion.

Article Fifty-six All Members pledge themselves to take joint and separate action in cooperation with the Organization for the achievement of the purposes set forth in Article 55.

Article Fifty-seven 1. The various specialized agencies, established by intergovernmental agreement and having wide international responsibilities, as defined in their basic instruments, in economic, social, cultural, educational, health, and related fields, shall be brought into relationship with the United Nations in accordance with the provisions of Article 63.

2. Such agencies thus brought into relationship with the United Nations are hereinafter referred to as specialized agencies.

Article Fifty-eight The Organization shall make recommendations for the coordination of the policies and activities of the specialized agencies.

Article Fifty-nine The Organization shall, where appropriate, initiate negotiations among the states concerned for the creation of any new specialized agencies required for the accomplishment of the purposes set forth in Article 55.

Article Sixty Responsibility for the discharge of the functions of the Organization set forth in this Chapter shall be vested in the General Assembly and, under the authority of the General Assembly, in the Economic and Social Council, which shall have for this purpose the powers set forth in Chapter X.

CHAPTER X
THE ECONOMIC AND SOCIAL COUNCIL

Composition

*Article Sixty-one** 1. The Economic and Social Council shall consist of twenty-seven Members of the United Nations elected by the General Assembly.

2. Subject to the Provisions of paragraph 3, nine members of the Economic and Social Council shall be elected each year for a term of three years. A retiring member shall be eligible for immediate re-election.

3. At the first election after the increase in the membership of the Economic and Social Council from eighteen to twenty-seven members, in addition to the members elected in place of the six members whose term of office expires at the end of that year, nine additional members shall be elected. Of these nine additional members, the term of office of three members so elected shall expire at the end of one year, and of three other members at the end of two years, in accordance with arrangements made by the General Assembly.

4. Each member of the Economic and Social Council shall have one representative.

*As amended. The original text of Article 61 reads as follows:
1. The Economic and Social Council shall consist of eighteen Members of the United Nations elected by the General Assembly.
2. Subject to the provisions of paragraph 3, six members of the Economic and Social Council shall be elected each year for a term of three years. A retiring member shall be eligible for immediate re-election.
3. At the first election, eighteen members of the Economic and Social Council shall be chosen. The term of office of six members so chosen shall expire at the end of one year, and of six other members at the end of two years, in accordance with arrangements made by the General Assembly.
4. Each member of the Economic and Social Council shall have one representative.

Functions and Powers

Article Sixty-two 1. The Economic and Social Council may make or initiate studies and reports with respect to international economic, social, cultural, educational, health, and related matters and may make recommendations with respect to any such matters to the General Assembly, to the Members of the United Nations, and to the specialized agencies concerned.

2. It may make recommendations for the purpose of promoting respect for, and observance of, human rights and fundamental freedoms for all.

3. It may prepare draft conventions for submission to the General Assembly, with respect to matters falling within its competence.

4. It may call, in accordance with the rules prescribed by the United Nations, international conferences on matters falling within its competence.

Article Sixty-three 1. The Economic and Social Council may enter into agreements with any of the agencies referred to in Article 57, defining the terms on which the agency concerned shall be brought into relationship with the United Nations. Such agreements shall be subject to approval by the General Assembly.

2. It may coordinate the activities of the specialized agencies through consultation with and recommendations to such agencies and through recommendations to the General Assembly and to the Members of the United Nations.

Article Sixty-four 1. The Economic and Social Council may take appropriate steps to obtain regular reports from the specialized agencies. It may make arrangements with the Members of the United Nations and with the specialized agencies to obtain reports on the steps taken to give effect to its own recommendations and to recommendations on matters falling within its competence made by the General Assembly.

2. It may communicate its observations on these reports to the General Assembly.

Article Sixty-five The Economic and Social Council may furnish information to the Security Council and shall assist the Security Council upon its request.

Article Sixty-six 1. The Economic and Social Council shall perform such functions as fall within its competence in connection with the carrying out of the recommendations of the General Assembly.

2. It may, with the approval of the General Assembly, perform services at the request of Members of the United Nations and at the request of specialized agencies.

3. It shall perform such other functions as are specified elsewhere in the present Charter or as may be assigned to it by the General Assembly.

Voting

Article Sixty-seven 1. Each member of the Economic and Social Council shall have one vote.

2. Decisions of the Economic and Social Council shall be made by a majority of the members present and voting.

Procedure

Article Sixty-eight The Economic and Social Council shall set up commissions in economic and social fields and for the promotion of human rights, and such other commissions as may be required for the performance of its functions.

Article Sixty-nine The Economic and Social Council shall invite any Member of the United Nations to participate, without vote, in its deliberations on any matter of particular concern to that Member.

Article Seventy The Economic and Social Council may make arrangements for representatives of the specialized agencies to participate, without vote, in its deliberations and in those of the commissions established by it, and for its representatives to participate in the deliberations of the specialized agencies.

Article Seventy-one The Economic and Social Council may make suitable arrangements for consultation with non-governmental organizations which are concerned with matters within its competence. Such arrangements may be made with international organizations and, where appropriate, with national organizations after consultation with the Member of the United Nations concerned.

Article Seventy-two 1. The Economic and Social Council shall adopt its own rules of procedure, including the method of selecting its President.

2. The Economic and Social Council shall meet as required in accordance with its rules, which shall include provision for the convening of meetings on the request of a majority of its members.

CHAPTER XI

DECLARATION REGARDING NON-SELF-GOVERNING TERRITORIES

Article Seventy-three Members of the United Nations which have or assume responsibilities for the administration of territories whose peoples have not yet attained a full measure of self-government recognize the principle that the interests of the inhabitants of these territories are paramount, and accept as a sacred trust the obligation to promote to the utmost, within the system of international peace and security established by the present Charter, the well-being of the inhabitants of these territories, and, to this end:

a. to ensure, with due respect for the culture of the peoples concerned, their political, economic, social, and educational advancement, their just treatment, and their protection against abuses;

b. to develop self-government, to take due account of the political aspirations of the peoples, and to assist them in the progressive development of their free political institutions, according to the particular circumstances of each territory and its peoples and their varying stages of advancement;

c. to further international peace and security;

d. to promote constructive measures of development, to encourage research, and to cooperate with one another and, when and where appropriate, with specialized international bodies with a view to the practical achievement of the social, economic, and scientific purposes set forth in this Article; and

e. to transmit regularly to the Secretary-General for information purposes, subject to such limitation as security and constitutional considerations may require, statistical and other information of a technical nature relating to economic, social, and educational conditions in the territories for which they are respectively responsible other than those territories to which Chapters XII and XIII apply.

Article Seventy-four Members of the United Nations also agree that their policy in respect of the territories to which this Chapter applies, no less than in respect of their metropolitan areas, must be based on the general principle of good-neighborliness, due account being taken of the interests and well-being of the rest of the world, in social, economic, and commercial matters.

CHAPTER XII

INTERNATIONAL TRUSTEESHIP SYSTEM

Article Seventy-five The United Nations shall establish under its authority an international trusteeship system for the administration and supervision of such territories as may be placed thereunder by subsequent individual agreements. These territories are hereinafter referred to as trust territories.

Article Seventy-six The basic objectives of the trusteeship system, in accordance with the Purposes of the United Nations laid down in Article 1 of the present Charter, shall be:

a. to further international peace and security;

b. to promote the political, economic, social, and educational advancement of the inhabitants of the trust territories, and their progressive development towards self-government or independence as may be appropriate to the particular circumstances of each territory and its peoples and the freely expressed wishes of the peoples concerned, and as may be provided by the terms of each trusteeship agreement;

c. to encourage respect for human rights and for fundamental freedoms for all without distinction as to race, sex, language, or religion, and to encourage recognition of the interdependence of the peoples of the world; and

d. to ensure equal treatment in social, economic, and commercial matters for all Members of the United Nations and their nationals, and also equal treatment for the latter in the administration of justice, without prejudice to the attainment of the foregoing objectives and subject to the provisions of Article 80.

Article Seventy-seven 1. The trusteeship system shall apply to such territories in the following categories as may be placed thereunder by means of trusteeship agreements:

a. territories now held under mandate;

b. territories which may be detached from enemy states as a result of the Second World War; and

c. territories voluntarily placed under the system by states responsible for their administration.

2. It will be a matter for subsequent agreement as to which territories in the foregoing categories will be brought under the trusteeship system and upon what terms.

Article Seventy-eight The trusteeship system shall not apply to territories which have become Members of the United Nations, relationship among which shall be based on respect for the principle of sovereign equality.

Article Seventy-nine The terms of trusteeship for each territory to be placed under the trusteeship system, including any alteration or amendment, shall be agreed upon by the states directly concerned, including the mandatory power in the case of territories held under mandate by a Member of the United Nations, and shall be approved as provided for in Articles 83 and 85.

Article Eighty 1. Except as may be agreed upon in individual trusteeship agreements, made under Articles 77, 79, and 81, placing each territory under the trusteeship system, and until such agreements have been concluded, nothing in this Chapter shall be construed in or of itself to alter in any manner whatsoever the rights of any states or any peoples or the terms of existing international instruments to which Members of the United Nations may respectively be parties.

2. Paragraph 1 of this Article shall not be interpreted as giving grounds for delay or postponement of the negotiation and conclusion of agreements for placing mandated and other territories under the trusteeship system as provided for in Article 77.

Article Eighty-one The trusteeship agreement shall in each case include the terms under which the trust territory will be administered and designate the authority which will exercise the administration of the trust territory. Such authority, hereinafter called the administering authority, may be one or more states or the Organization itself.

Article Eighty-two There may be designated, in any trusteeship agreement, a strategic area or areas which may include part or all of the trust territory to which the agreement applies, without prejudice to any special agreement or agreements made under Article 43.

Article Eighty-three 1. All functions of the United Nations relating to strategic areas, including the approval of the terms of the trusteeship agreements and of their alteration or amendment, shall be exercised by the Security Council.

2. The basic objectives set forth in Article 76 shall be applicable to the people of each strategic area.

3. The Security Council shall, subject to the provisions of the trusteeship agreements and without prejudice to security considerations, avail itself of the assistance of the Trusteeship Council to perform those func-

tions of the United Nations under the trusteeship system relating to political, economic, social, and educational matters in the strategic areas.

Article Eighty-four It shall be the duty of the administering authority to ensure that the trust territory shall play its part in the maintenance of international peace and security. To this end the administering authority may make use of volunteer forces, facilities, and assistance from the trust territory in carrying out the obligations towards the Security Council undertaken in this regard by the administering authority, as well as for local defense and the maintenance of law and order within the trust territory.

Article Eighty-five 1. The functions of the United Nations with regard to trusteeship agreements for all areas not designated as strategic, including the approval of the terms of the trusteeship agreements and of their alteration or amendment, shall be exercised by the General Assembly.

2. The Trusteeship Council, operating under the authority of the General Assembly, shall assist the General Assembly in carrying out these functions.

CHAPTER XIII

THE TRUSTEESHIP COUNCIL

Composition

Article Eighty-six 1. The Trusteeship Council shall consist of the following Members of the United Nations:

a. those Members administering trust territories;

b. such of those Members mentioned by name in Article 23 as are not administering trust territories; and

c. as many other Members elected for three-year terms by the General Assembly as may be necessary to ensure that the total number of members of the Trusteeship Council is equally divided between those Members of the United Nations which administer trust territories and those which do not.

2. Each member of the Trusteeship Council shall designate one specially qualified person to represent it therein.

Functions and Powers

Article Eighty-seven The General Assembly and, under its authority, the Trusteeship Council, in carrying out their functions, may:

a. consider reports submitted by the administering authority;

b. accept petitions and examine them in consultation with the administering authority;

c. provide for periodic visits to the respective trust territories at times agreed upon with the administering authority; and

d. take these and other actions in conformity with the terms of the trusteeship agreements.

Article Eighty-eight The Trusteeship Council shall formulate a questionnaire on the political, economic, social, and educational advancement of the inhabitants of each trust territory, and the administering authority for each trust territory within the competence of the General Assembly shall make an annual report to the General Assembly upon the basis of such questionnaire.

Voting

Article Eighty-nine 1. Each member of the Trusteeship Council shall have one vote.

2. Decisions of the Trusteeship Council shall be made by a majority of the members present and voting.

Procedure

Article Ninety 1. The Trusteeship Council shall adopt its own rules of procedure, including the method of selecting its President.

2. The Trusteeship Council shall meet as required in accordance with its rules, which shall include provision for the convening of meetings on the request of a majority of its members.

Article Ninety-one The Trusteeship Council shall, when appropriate, avail itself of the assistance of the Economic and Social Council and of the specialized agencies in regard to matters with which they are respectively concerned.

CHAPTER XIV

THE INTERNATIONAL COURT OF JUSTICE

Article Ninety-two The International Court of Justice shall be the principal judicial organ of the United Nations. It shall function in accordance with the annexed Statute, which is based upon the Statute of the

Permanent Court of International Justice and forms an integral part of the present Charter.

Article Ninety-three 1. All Members of the United Nations are *ipso facto* parties to the Statute of the International Court of Justice.

2. A state which is not a Member of the United Nations may become a party to the Statute of the International Court of Justice on conditions to be determined in each case by the General Assembly upon the recommendation of the Security Council.

Article Ninety-four 1. Each Member of the United Nations undertakes to comply with the decision of the International Court of Justice in any case to which it is a party.

2. If any party to a case fails to perform the obligations incumbent upon it under a judgment rendered by the Court, the other party may have recourse to the Security Council, which may, if it deems necessary, make recommendations or decide upon measures to be taken to give effect to the judgment.

Article Ninety-five Nothing in the present Charter shall prevent Members of the United Nations from entrusting the solution of their differences to other tribunals by virtue of agreements already in existence or which may be concluded in the future.

Article Ninety-six 1. The General Assembly or the Security Council may request the International Court of Justice to give an advisory opinion on any legal question.

2. Other organs of the United Nations and specialized agencies, which may at any time be so authorized by the General Assembly, may also request advisory opinions of the Court on legal questions arising within the scope of their activities.

CHAPTER XV

THE SECRETARIAT

Article Ninety-seven The Secretariat shall comprise a Secretary-General and such staff as the Organization may require. The Secretary-General shall be appointed by the General Assembly upon the recommendation of the Security Council. He shall be the chief administrative officer of the Organization.

Article Ninety-eight The Secretary-General shall act in that capacity in all meetings of the General Assembly, of the Security Council, of the Economic and Social Council, and of the Trusteeship Council, and shall perform such other functions as are entrusted to him by these organs. The Secretary-General shall make an annual report to the General Assembly on the work of the Organization.

Article Ninety-nine The Secretary-General may bring to the attention of the Security Council any matter which in his opinion may threaten the maintenance of international peace and security.

Article One hundred 1. In the performance of their duties the Secretary-General and the staff shall not seek or receive instructions from any government or from any other authority external to the Organization. They shall refrain from any action which might reflect on their position as international officials responsible only to the Organization.

2. Each Member of the United Nations undertakes to respect the exclusively international character of the responsibilities of the Secretary-General and the staff and not to seek to influence them in the discharge of their responsibilities.

Article One hundred one 1. The staff shall be appointed by the Secretary-General under regulations established by the General Assembly.

2. Appropriate staffs shall be permanently assigned to the Economic and Social Council, the Trusteeship Council, and, as required, to other organs of the United Nations. These staffs shall form a part of the Secretariat.

3. The paramount consideration in the employment of the staff and in the determination of the conditions of service shall be the necessity of securing the highest standards of efficiency, competence, and integrity. Due regard shall be paid to the importance of recruiting the staff on as wide a geographical basis as possible.

CHAPTER XVI
MISCELLANEOUS PROVISIONS

Article One hundred two 1. Every treaty and every international agreement entered into by any Member of the United Nations after the present Charter comes into force shall as soon as possible be registered with the Secretariat and published by it.

2. No party to any such treaty or international agreement which has not been registered in accordance with the provisions of paragraph 1 of this Article may invoke that treaty or agreement before any organ of the United Nations.

Article One hundred three In the event of a conflict between the obligations of the Members of the United Nations under the present Charter and their obligations under any other international agreement, their obligations under the present Charter shall prevail.

Article One hundred four The Organization shall enjoy in the territory of each of its Members such legal capacity as may be necessary for the exercise of its functions and the fulfillment of its purposes.

Article One hundred five 1. The Organization shall enjoy in the territory of each of its Members such privileges and immunities as are necessary for the fulfillment of its purposes.

2. Representatives of the Members of the United Nations and officials of the Organization shall similarly enjoy such privileges and immunities as are necessary for the independent exercise of their functions in connection with the Organization.

3. The General Assembly may make recommendations with a view to determining the details of the application of paragraphs 1 and 2 of this Article or may propose conventions to the Members of the United Nations for this purpose.

CHAPTER XVII
TRANSITIONAL SECURITY ARRANGEMENTS

Article One hundred six Pending the coming into force of such special agreements referred to in Article 43 as in the opinion of the Security Council enable it to begin the exercise of its responsibilities under Article 42, the parties to the Four-Nation Declaration, signed at Moscow, October 30, 1943, and France, shall, in accordance with the provisions of paragraph 5 of that Declaration, consult with one another and as occasion requires with other Members of the United Nations with a view to such joint action on behalf of the Organization as may be necessary for the purpose of maintaining international peace and security.

Article One hundred seven Nothing in the present Charter shall invalidate or preclude action, in relation to any state which during the Second World War has been an enemy of any signatory to the present

Charter, taken or authorized as a result of that war by the Governments having responsibility for such action.

CHAPTER XVIII

AMENDMENTS

Article One hundred eight Amendments to the present Charter shall come into force for all Members of the United Nations when they have been adopted by a vote of two thirds of the members of the General Assembly and ratified in accordance with their respective constitutional processes by two thirds of the Members of the United Nations, including all the permanent members of the Security Council.

Article One hundred nine 1. A General Conference of the Members of the United Nations for the purpose of reviewing the present Charter may be held at a date and place to be fixed by a two-thirds vote of the members of the General Assembly and by a vote of any seven members of the Security Council. Each Member of the United Nations shall have one vote in the conference.

2. Any alteration of the present Charter recommended by a two-thirds vote of the conference shall take effect when ratified in accordance with their respective constitutional processes by two thirds of the Members of the United Nations including all the permanent members of the Security Council.

3. If such a conference has not been held before the tenth annual session of the General Assembly following the coming into force of the present Charter, the proposal to call such a conference shall be placed on the agenda of that session of the General Assembly, and the conference shall be held if so decided by a majority vote of the members of the General Assembly and by a vote of any seven members of the Security Council.

CHAPTER XIX

RATIFICATION AND SIGNATURE

Article One hundred ten 1. The present Charter shall be ratified by the signatory states in accordance with their respective constitutional processes.

2. The ratifications shall be deposited with the Government of the United States of America, which shall notify all the signatory states of

each deposit as well as the Secretary-General of the Organization when he has been appointed.

3. The present Charter shall come into force upon the deposit of ratifications by the Republic of China, France, the Union of Soviet Socialist Republics, the United Kingdom of Great Britain and Northern Ireland, and the United States of America, and by a majority of the other signatory states. A protocol of the ratifications deposited shall thereupon be drawn up by the Government of the United States of America which shall communicate copies thereof to all the signatory states.

4. The states signatory to the present Charter which ratify it after it has come into force will become original Members of the United Nations on the date of the deposit of their respective ratifications.

Article One hundred eleven The present Charter, of which the Chinese, French, Russian, English, and Spanish texts are equally authentic, shall remain deposited in the archives of the Government of the United States of America. Duly certified copies thereof shall be transmitted by that Government to the Governments of the other signatory states.

IN FAITH WHEREOF the representatives of the Governments of the United Nations have signed the present Charter.

DONE at the city of San Francisco the twenty-sixth day of June, one thousand nine hundred and forty-five.

Appendix B

Selected Articles from the Statute of the International Court of Justice

Article Thirty-six 1. The jurisdiction of the Court comprises all cases which the parties refer to it and all matters specially provided for in the Charter of the United Nations or in treaties and conventions in force.

2. The states parties to the present Statute may at any time declare that they recognize as compulsory *ipso facto* and without special agreement, in relation to any other state accepting the same obligation, the jurisdiction of the Court in all legal disputes concerning:
a. the interpretation of a treaty;
b. any question of international law;
c. the existence of any fact which, if established, would constitute a breach of an international obligation;
d. the nature or extent of the reparation to be made for the breach of an international obligation.

3. The declarations referred to above may be made unconditionally or on condition of reciprocity on the part of several or certain states, or for a certain time.

4. Such declarations shall be deposited with the Secretary-General of the United Nations, who shall transmit copies thereof to the parties to the Statute and to the Registrar of the Court.

5. Declarations made under Article 36 of the Statute of the Permanent Court of International Justice and which are still in force shall be deemed, as between the parties to the present Statute, to be acceptances of the compulsory jurisdiction of the International Court of Justice for the period which they still have to run and in accordance with their terms.

6. In the event of a dispute as to whether the Court has jurisdiction, the matter shall be settled by the decision of the Court.

Article Thirty-eight 1. The Court, whose function is to decide in accordance with international law such disputes as are submitted to it, shall apply:
a. international conventions, whether general or particular, establishing rules expressly recognized by the contesting states;

Source: United Nations, Office of Public Information, *Everyman's United Nations*, 8th ed., United Nations, New York, 1968, pp. 580–581.

b. international custom, as evidence of a general practice accepted as law;

c. the general principles of law recognized by civilized nations;

d. subject to the provisions of Article 59, judicial decisions and the teachings of the most highly qualified publicists of the various nations, as subsidiary means for the determination of rules of law.

2. This provision shall not prejudice the power of the Court to decide a case *ex aequo et bono*, if the parties agree thereto.

Appendix C

Member States of the United Nations

(144 as of January 1976)

Member	Date of admission
Afghanistan	19 November 1946
Albania	14 December 1955
Algeria	8 October 1962
*Argentina	24 October 1945
*Australia	1 November 1945
Austria	14 December 1955
Bahamas	18 September 1973
Bahrain	21 September 1971
Bangla Desh	17 September 1974
Barbados	9 December 1966
*Belgium	27 December 1945
Bhutan	21 September 1971
*Bolivia	14 November 1945
Botswana	17 October 1966
*Brazil	24 October 1945
Bulgaria	14 December 1955
Burma	19 April 1948
Burundi	18 September 1962
*Byelorussian Soviet Socialist Republic	24 October 1945
Cameroon	20 September 1960
*Canada	9 November 1945
Cape Verde	16 September 1975
Central African Republic	20 September 1960
Chad	20 September 1960
*Chile	24 October 1945
*China[1]	24 October 1945

Source: United Nations, Office of Public Information, *Member States of the United Nations*, rev. ed., United Nations, New York, January 1975 (with additions through January 1976).

*Original Member

1 By resolution 2758 (XXVI) of 25 October 1971, the General Assembly decided "to restore all its rights to the People's Republic of China and to recognize the representatives of its Government as the only legitimate representatives of China to the United Nations, and to expel forthwith the representatives of Chiang Kai-shek from the place which they unlawfully occupy at the United Nations and in all the organizations related to it."

*Colombia	5 November 1945
Comoros	12 November 1975
Congo	20 September 1960
*Costa Rica	2 November 1945
*Cuba	24 October 1945
Cyprus	20 September 1960
*Czechoslovakia	24 October 1945
Dahomey	20 September 1960
Democratic Yemen	14 December 1967
*Denmark	24 October 1945
*Dominican Republic	24 October 1945
*Ecuador	21 December 1945
*Egypt[2]	24 October 1945
*El Salvador	24 October 1945
Equatorial Guinea	12 November 1968
*Ethiopia	13 November 1945
Fiji	13 October 1970
Finland	14 December 1955
*France	24 October 1945
Gabon	20 September 1960
Gambia	21 September 1965
German Democratic Republic	18 September 1973
Germany, Federal Republic of	18 September 1973
Ghana	8 March 1957
*Greece	25 October 1945
Grenada	17 September 1974
*Guatemala	21 November 1945
Guinea	12 December 1958
Guinea-Bissau	17 September 1974
Guyana	20 September 1966
*Haiti	24 October 1945
*Honduras	17 December 1945
Hungary	14 December 1955
Iceland	19 November 1946
*India	30 October 1945
Indonesia[3]	28 September 1950

2 Egypt and Syria were original Members of the United Nations from 24 October 1945. Following a plebiscite on 21 February 1958, the United Arab Republic was established by a union of Egypt and Syria and continued as a single Member. On 13 October 1961, Syria resumed its status as an independent State and simultaneously its United Nations membership. On 2 September 1971, the United Arab Republic changed its name to Arab Republic of Egypt.

3 By letter of 20 January 1965, Indonesia announced its decision to withdraw from the United Nations "at this stage and under the present circumstances." By telegram of 19 September 1966, it announced its decision "to resume full co-operation with the United Nations and to resume participation in its activities." On 28 September 1966, the General Assembly took note of this de-

*Iran	24 October 1945
*Iraq	21 December 1945
Ireland	14 December 1955
Israel	11 May 1949
Italy	14 December 1955
Ivory Coast	20 September 1960
Jamaica	18 September 1962
Japan	18 December 1956
Jordan	14 December 1955
Kenya	16 December 1963
Khmer Republic	14 December 1955
Kuwait	14 May 1963
Laos	14 December 1955
*Lebanon	24 October 1945
Lesotho	17 October 1966
*Liberia	2 November 1945
Libyan Arab Republic	14 December 1955
*Luxembourg	24 October 1945
Madagascar	20 September 1960
Malawi	1 December 1964
Malaysia[4]	17 September 1957
Maldives	21 September 1965
Mali	28 September 1960
Malta	1 December 1964
Mauritania	27 October 1961
Mauritius	24 April 1968
*Mexico	7 November 1945
Mongolia	27 October 1961
Morocco	12 November 1956
Mozambique	16 September 1975
Nepal	14 December 1955
*Netherlands	10 December 1945
*New Zealand	24 October 1945
*Nicaragua	24 October 1945
Niger	20 September 1960
Nigeria	7 October 1960
*Norway	27 November 1945
Oman	7 October 1971
Pakistan	30 September 1947
*Panama	13 November 1945

cision and the President invited the representatives of Indonesia to take seats in the Assembly.

4 The Federation of Malaya joined the United Nations on 17 September 1957. On 16 September 1963, its name changed to Malaysia, following the admission to the new federation of Singapore, Sabah (North Borneo) and Sarawak. Singapore became an independent State on 9 August 1965 and a United Nations Member on 21 September 1965.

Papua New Guinea	10 October 1975
*Paraguay	24 October 1945
*Peru	31 October 1945
*Philippines	24 October 1945
*Poland	24 October 1945
Portugal	14 December 1955
Qatar	21 September 1971
Romania	14 December 1955
Rwanda	18 September 1962
São Tomé and Príncipe	16 September 1975
*Saudi Arabia	24 October 1945
Senegal	28 September 1960
Sierra Leone	27 September 1961
Singapore	21 September 1965
Somalia	20 September 1960
*South Africa	7 November 1945
Spain	14 December 1955
Sri Lanka	14 December 1955
Sudan	12 November 1956
Surinam	4 December 1975
Swaziland	24 September 1968
Sweden	19 November 1946
*Syrian Arab Republic[2]	24 October 1945
Thailand	16 December 1946
Togo	20 September 1960
Trinidad and Tobago	18 September 1962
Tunisia	12 November 1956
*Turkey	24 October 1945
Uganda	25 October 1962
*Ukrainian Soviet Socialist Republic	24 October 1945
*Union of Soviet Socialist Republics	24 October 1945
United Arab Emirates	9 December 1971
*United Kingdom of Great Britain and Northern Ireland	24 October 1945
United Republic of Tanzania[5]	14 December 1961
*United States of America	24 October 1945
Upper Volta	20 September 1960
*Uruguay	18 December 1945
*Venezuela	15 November 1945

5 Tanganyika was a United Nations Member from 14 December 1961; Zanzibar was a Member from 16 December 1963. Following the ratification on 26 April 1964 of Articles of Union between Tanganyika and Zanzibar, the United Republic of Tanganyika and Zanzibar continued as a single Member, changing its name to United Republic of Tanzania on 1 November 1964.

Yemen	30 September 1947
*Yugoslavia	24 October 1945
Zaïre	20 September 1960
Zambia	1 December 1964

Index